KU-099-619

A Practitioner's Guide to Money Laundering Compliance

Tim Bennett
LLB, LLM, TEP, Solicitor
Chief Executive, Belgrave SA

U.W.E.L.
LEARNING RESOURCES

ACC. No. 2327252   CLASS 321

CONTROL   341.

0406971471   751

DATE 12. JUL. 2004   CITE BEN

LPC

LexisNexis™ UK

Members of the LexisNexis Group worldwide

United Kingdom	LexisNexis UK, a Division of Reed Elsevier (UK) Ltd, Halsbury House, 35 Chancery Lane, LONDON, WC2A 1EL, and 4 Hill Street, EDINBURGH EH2 3JZ
Argentina	LexisNexis Argentina, BUENOS AIRES
Australia	LexisNexis Butterworths, CHATSWOOD, New South Wales
Austria	LexisNexis Verlag ARD Orac GmbH & Co KG, VIENNA
Canada	LexisNexis Butterworths, MARKHAM, Ontario
Chile	LexisNexis Chile Ltda, SANTIAGO DE CHILE
Czech Republic	Nakladatelství Orac sro, PRAGUE
France	Editions du Juris-Classeur SA, PARIS
Germany	LexisNexis Deutschland GmbH, FRANKFURT and MUNSTER
Hong Kong	LexisNexis Butterworths, HONG KONG
Hungary	HVG-Orac, BUDAPEST
India	LexisNexis Butterworths, NEW DELHI
Ireland	LexisNexis, DUBLIN
Italy	Giuffrè Editore, MILAN
Malaysia	Malayan Law Journal Sdn Bhd, KUALA LUMPUR
New Zealand	LexisNexis Butterworths, WELLINGTON
Poland	Wydawnictwo Prawnicze LexisNexis, WARSAW
Singapore	LexisNexis Butterworths, SINGAPORE
South Africa	LexisNexis Butterworths, Durban
Switzerland	Stämpfli Verlag AG, BERNE
USA	LexisNexis, DAYTON, Ohio

© Reed Elsevier (UK) Ltd 2004

All rights reserved. No part of this publication may be reproduced in any material form (including photocopying or storing it in any medium by electronic means and whether or not transiently or incidentally to some other use of this publication) without the written permission of the copyright owner except in accordance with the provisions of the Copyright, Designs and Patents Act 1988 or under the terms of a licence issued by the Copyright Licensing Agency Ltd, 90 Tottenham Court Road, London, England W1T 4LP. Applications for the copyright owner's written permission to reproduce any part of this publication should be addressed to the publisher.

Warning: The doing of an unauthorised act in relation to a copyright work may result in both a civil claim for damages and criminal prosecution.

Crown copyright material is reproduced with the permission of the Controller of HMSO and the Queen's Printer for Scotland. Parliamentary copyright material is reproduced with the permission of the Controller of Her Majesty's Stationery Office on behalf of Parliament. Any European material in this work which has been reproduced from EUR-lex, the official European Communities legislation website, is European Communities copyright.

A CIP Catalogue record for this book is available from the British Library.

ISBN 0 4069 71471

Typeset by Kerrypress Ltd, Luton, Beds
Printed and bound in Great Britain by The Cromwell Press Limited, Trowbridge, Wiltshire
Visit LexisNexis UK at www.lexisnexis.co.uk

A Practitioner's Guide to Money Laundering Compliance

WITHDRAWN

While every care has been taken to ensure the accuracy of this work, no responsibility for loss or damage occasioned to any person acting or refraining from action as a result of any statement in it can be accepted by the authors, editors or publishers.

Other titles in this series
A Practitioner's Guide to Advising Charities
A Practitioner's Guide to Beneficiaries' Actions
A Practitioner's Guide to Charity Fundraising
A Practitioner's Guide to Contentious Trusts and Estates
A Practitioner's Guide to the Court of Protection
A Practitioner's Guide to Drafting Trusts
A Practitioner's Guide to Executorship and Administration
A Practitioner's Guide to Inheritance Claims
A Practitioner's Guide to Legacies
A Practitioner's Guide to Powers and Duties of Trustees
A Practitioner's Guide to Powers of Attorney
A Practitioner's Guide to Probate
A Practitioner's Guide to Trustee Investment
A Practitioner's Guide to Trusts

Preface

This book is not intended to be an AML textbook as there are already a number of comprehensive works on the subject.

As one of the *Practitioner's Guide* series, this book will serve as a reference to practical and procedural aspects of the AML environment.

AML rules are not new, they have been around for twenty years or more. The cataclysmic events of 11 September 2001 and the loss of over 3,000 lives gave AML a turbo-boost. The attacks left a vivid imprint, and the consequential *War on Terrorism* has become the drive for the rapid evolution of AML laws and regulations. Recent AML initiatives have been designed to combat international terrorism by striking at the flow of funds to (and from) terrorists. Policy-makers and legislators believe this will lead to the end of terror organisations and rogue nations. It remains to be seen whether this partial-privatisation of law enforcement will be effective. One thing is clear, that during the last two years AML procedures have had an increasing impact on business and private life for many people.

They are also having a direct effect on the financial well-being of many of the offshore 'tax evasion' havens. There is a parallel in terms of extinctions between the dark clouds stirred up some 65 million years ago in New Mexico, and the billowing clouds of dark smoke emanating from the twin towers (the German composer Karl-Heinz Stockhausen described the 11 September 2001 attacks as 'Lucifer's greatest work of art' – the imagery is tragically compelling). While the former caused the extinction of the dinosaurs when the meteor hit, the latter it seems is leading to the extinction of many of the havens, and the imposition in most financial centres of full transparency requirements coupled with the AML criminalisation of the proceeds of foreign tax offences.

The author welcomes the STEP co-branding, and believes that STEP members are an important practitioner group world-wide.

Finally, the author invites reader's feedback and comments by email address to tim@belgrave.ch. All comments (positive or negative) are most welcome, as is feedback on errors/omissions, points of clarification, and ideas or suggestions for areas of development for future editions. Your support is appreciated!

Tim Bennett

LLB, LLM, TEP, Solicitor

Chief Executive, Belgrave SA

Contents

Table of Cases

Table of Statutes

References in the right-hand column are to paragraph number. Paragraph references printed in **bold** type indicate where the Act is set out in part or in full.

Table of Statutory Instruments

References in the right-hand column are to paragraph number. Paragraph references printed in **bold** type indicate where the Statutory Instrument is set out in part or in full.

Table of Foreign Legislation

References in the right-hand column are to paragraph. Paragraph references printed in **bold** type indicate where the legislation is set out in part or in full.

Table of European Legislation

Primary legislation

Treaties and Conventions

Secondary legislation

Directives

Chapter 1

Introduction

1.1 A simple definition of money laundering is to describe it as the concealment of the identity of illegally obtained money, so that it appears to have come from a legitimate source. This is a definition that requires regard to be had to the source of funds.

The definition has been made more complex by the addition of 'assisting terrorist financing' that requires regard to be had to the destination of funds. The new challenges for financial services and related businesses as regards both *source* and *destination* of funds have added hugely to the operational burden of running the business.

With the addition of the proceeds of tax evasion (see CHAPTER 7: THE UK AML FRAMEWORK – FISCAL OFFENCES AND FOREIGN TAX ENFORCEMENT) anti-money laundering law ('AML') and regulation has become all-embracing, and has become of particular concern to professionals and practitioners both onshore and offshore the UK following the *P v P [2003] EWHC 2260 (Fam)*, (see 11.4).

The study of AML law and regulation in this handbook will commence with a close look at the UK. With the entering into force of Proceeds of Crime Act 2002 ('PoCA') (see CHAPTER 3 – CHAPTER 5) UK professionals have become the soft target for enforcement.

The text will also look at AML in an international context (both 'onshore' and 'offshore'), as many overseas jurisdictions (especially the 'offshore' ones) have derived their AML framework from the UK. Where references to statutes etc appear, these will refer to the United Kingdom unless otherwise stated.

It is appropriate that this handbook should focus primarily on the UK, since the UK, as the second biggest money centre after the USA, is thus the second biggest money laundering centre in the world. However, as a result of the Author's extensive experience dealing in international transactions, including lengthy spells resident in offshore jurisdictions, it is appropriate for the guide also to makes extensive references to the AML laws and practices of various other islands and jurisdictions.

All the more reason for the focus on the UK derives from the UK's historical position as one of the biggest centres of expertise in the planning of international structures, using the laws of present and many former colonies, near and far. Many of these structures are nowadays concealing money laundering as currently defined. The execution of the planning behind these structures may appear to be undertaken far from the UK, but many of the strings lead back to the UK. Thus, the UK 'string-pullers' need to have to hand an informative guide as to just what they can and cannot do, and what they must and must not do, in order to prevent them from becoming inadvertent money launderers, tippers-off, etc.

This handbook seeks to set out in some detail what must and what must not be done, and hopefully, what can still be done safely.

Chapter 2

The UK AML Framework – Background

Legislative history

2.1   There is nothing new about the notion of criminal offences similar to the anti-money laundering ('AML') offences that are currently causing such a stir. Section 22(1) of the Theft Act 1968 (also see the Theft Act 1978 and the Theft (Amendment) Act 1996) was the first 'money laundering' style offence created under English law, involving the receipt of goods derived from an underlying crime of theft, prior to a dishonest involvement in their retention, removal, disposal or realisation on behalf of another person. Although the provision is confined to 'goods' and the underlying offences of theft and robbery, it has a wide-ranging effect covering a multitude of 'laundering' activities (that is, retention, removal, disposal or realisation) and it is significant that, by virtue of s 34 Theft Act 1968, 'goods' includes money. The offence has consistently been applied to those laundering money and facilitating the realisation of unlawfully obtained property. In addition, the inchoate offences of *aiding and abetting, counselling or procuring* have long been part of the English legal system, thereby rendering criminal those who somehow participate in the crime of another.

Measures against drug trafficking

2.2   With the enactment of the Misuse of Drugs Act 1971 it became possible under s 27(1) for the courts to order the forfeiture of property – whether it be money, drugs, weapons or vehicles – of a person convicted of a drugs-related offence classified as an 'offence under this Act'. However, the House of Lords severely curtailed the application of s 27(1) in *R v Cuthbertson [1981] AC 470, [1980] 2 All ER 401*. As a result of *Cuthbertson*, the Hodgson Committee Report of 1984 recommended the introduction of specific offences to deal with persons laundering the proceeds of drug trafficking. This in turn prompted a 1985 report by the Home Affairs Committee, resulting in the enactment of the Drug Trafficking Offences Act 1986 ('DTOA') which created the forerunner to s 50 Drug Trafficking Act 1994 ('DTA') by establishing the offence of 'assisting another to retain the benefits of drug trafficking'.

The enactment of specific money laundering legislation in relation to drug trafficking prompted Parliament in 1989 to introduce an offence modelled on s 24 DTOA 1986 in relation to terrorism. Given the increasing concern that terrorist organisations were involved in organised crime and were effectively laundering the resulting proceeds, s 11 Prevention of Terrorism (Temporary Provisions) Act 1989 ('PT(TP)A 1989') created *inter alia* the offence of 'assisting in the retention or control of terrorist funds'.

On 5 April 1990, the Criminal Justice (International Co-operation) Act 1990 received its Royal Assent, thereby enabling the UK government to ratify both the *European Convention on Mutual Assistance 1957* and the money laundering legislative obligations imposed by the *Vienna Convention against Illicit Traffic in Narcotic Drugs and Psychotropic Substances 1988* which created a new offence in s 14 of concealing or transferring proceeds of drug trafficking. This offence has since been consolidated into s 51 DTA 1994. The enactment of the 1990 Act took place within the background of a review of drug trafficking and money laundering laws by the House of Commons Home Affairs Committee, whose report in November 1989 resulted in the extension of money laundering laws in s 14.

CJA 1988 and 1993: extension to 'other serious crimes'

2.3   The Criminal Justice Act 1993 ('CJA') extended the scope of the AML offences in the 1988 Act from specific defined crimes (drugs, terrorism, etc) to the non-specific category of 'other serious crimes', pursuant to the First and Second EU AML Directives. The principal money laundering offences created by CJA 1993 were as follows:

(a)   Assisting the retention or control of the proceeds of criminal conduct by another, *knowing or suspecting* that other to be involved in money laundering (s 93A CJA 1988).

(b)   Acquisition, possession or use of proceeds of criminal conduct, *knowing* the property concerned to be tainted (s 93B CJA 1988).

(c)   Concealing or transferring property, *knowing or having reasonable grounds to suspect* that property is the proceeds of criminal conduct (s 93C CJA 1988). This includes transferring or removing property from the jurisdiction.

The Proceeds of Crime Act 2002

2.4   The sections of CJA 1988 and CJA 1993 noted at 2.3 above were replaced in 2002 by PoCA. The impact of this important piece of legislation is reviewed in detail in CHAPTER 3: THE UK AML FRAMEWORK – PRINCIPAL OFFENCES to CHAPTER 5: THE UK AML FRAMEWORK – ASSET RECOVERY AND FORFEITURE.

The Proceeds of Crime Act 2002 can be found on the HMSO website at www.hmso.gov.uk

Chapter 3

The UK AML Framework – the Principal UK Money Laundering Offences

Introduction

3.1   The Proceeds of Crime Act 2002 ('PoCA 2002') (Royal Assent 24 July 2003, see A1.1 for new sections 327–330) replaces the AML provisions of Criminal Justice Act 1988 and the Criminal Justice Act 1993, and the Drug Trafficking Act 1994.

The PoCA 2002 introduces a requirement for mandatory reporting on an 'all crimes' basis. The PoCA 2002 restates the money laundering offences, replacing the parallel drug and non-drug crime money laundering offences with single offences that do not distinguish between the proceeds of drug trafficking and other crime.

The principal offences

3.2   There are three principal new offences. These are as follows:

(a)   concealing etc (s 327 PoCA 2002);

(b)   assisting with arrangements etc (s 328 PoCA 2002); and

(c)   acquisition, use or possession etc (s 329 PoCA 2002).

— *Concealing etc*

The offence is committed where a person conceals, disguises, converts, transfers or removes 'criminal property' from the jurisdiction (s 327 PoCA 2002).

— *Assisting with arrangements etc*

The offence is committed where a person enters into or becomes concerned in an arrangement which facilitates another person to acquire, retain, use or control 'criminal property' and that the person concerned also 'knows' or 'suspects' that the property constitutes or represents benefit from 'criminal conduc*t*' (s 328 PoCA 2002).

— *Acquisition, use or possession etc*

The offence is committed where a person 'knows' or 'suspects' that the property which he acquires, uses or has possession of constitutes or represents his own or another's benefit from 'criminal conduct' (s 329 PoCA 2002)

Elements

3.3   There are four elements of the main money laundering offences:

(i)   criminal ('unlawful') conduct; leading to

(ii) criminal property; with

(iii) some act in relation to the 'criminal property'; and coupled with

(iv) knowledge or suspicion.

There must be *criminal conduct* (known as the 'predicate offence') which results in 'criminal property' (defined as property which the alleged offender 'knows' or 'suspects' constitutes or represents benefit from such 'criminal conduct'). See CHAPTER 8: THE UK AML FRAMEWORK – OTHER TECHNICAL ISSUES on the technical issues relating to the concept of 'knowledge' or 'suspicion'.

There must also be some act in relation to the 'criminal property' (the *actus reus*) such as concealing, assisting with arrangements, or acquisition/possession (see 3.2 above). Knowledge or suspicion is also required (the *mens rea*) (see 8.5). Also refer to the principles stated by Lord Scarman in *Gammon (Hong Kong) Ltd v A-G of Hong Kong [1984] 2 All ER 503* on the presumption of *mens rea* and strict liability.

Penalties

3.4   The maximum penalty for each of the above offences is 14 years' imprisonment and an unlimited fine for conviction on indictment. Summary conviction carries the lesser penalties of six months' imprisonment and a fine not exceeding the statutory maximum.

Defences

3.5   It is a defence to each of these PoCA offences for the person in question to have reported his/her knowledge or suspicion to a constable or if the law enforcement agency has given permission ('a consent') for the transaction to proceed (see CHAPTER 10: UK AML REPORTING PROCEDURES).

In fact, suspicious activity reports ('SAR') (previously known as suspicious transaction reports or 'STR') are made to National Criminal Intelligence

Service ('NCIS') or to the money laundering reporting officer ('MLRO') of the firm or business in which the person works. The SAR must, of course, have been made at the person's own volition, and either before any criminal conduct occurred, or as soon as it was reasonable for him/her to make it.

Filing an SAR does not, however, provide a defence to the person filing it in respect of common law offences such as fraud, false accounting or cheating the revenue, or inchoate offences such as conspiring or inciting, or the related offences of aiding and abetting, counselling or procuring. There is a conundrum here, in that filing an SAR may appear to be an act of exoneration or expiation: however, it may in some circumstances be evidence of guilt, and could even be used in evidence against the reporter (see CHAPTER 10: UK AML REPORTING PROCEDURES).

Chapter 4

The UK AML Framework – Failure to Disclose and Tipping-Off

Failure to disclose (regulated sector)

4.1   Section 330 Proceeds of Crime Act 2002 ('PoCA') widens the scope of the former 'drug money' reporting offence to the proceeds of *any criminal conduct*. There is a negligence test for liability under the new offence of 'failure to disclose' or negligently failing to report a money laundering offence.

The provisions apply to those working in the UK 'regulated financial sector', thus including accountants, lawyers, trustees, tax advisers and many other categories (see 6.1). The new negligence threshold replaces the requirement for 'suspicion' of an offence with an objective standard, namely whether it was reasonable for a professional in that position to have had a suspicion. The maximum penalty for the offence is five years' imprisonment and/or an unlimited fine.

The offence is committed if the following three conditions are satisfied:

(a)   a person knew or suspected, or has reasonable (ie, objective) grounds for knowing or suspecting, that another person is engaged in money laundering, even if they did not actually know or suspect;

(b)   the information or other matter on which the knowledge or suspicion is based, or which gives reasonable grounds for such knowledge or suspicion, came to the person in the course of a business in the 'regulated sector'; and

(c)   the person failed to report the information or suspicion of money laundering by means of an suspicious activity report ('SAR') to the authorities as soon as is practicable after it came to that person.

The duty to disclose (by filing an SAR) is restricted to persons receiving information in the course of a business in the regulated sector (as defined in PoCA 2002, Schedule 9). This reflects the fact that persons who are carrying out activities in the regulated sector should be expected to exercise a higher level of diligence in handling transactions than those employed in other businesses.

An article by Ryan Myint, *Solicitors Beware: Money Laundering after R v Duff* (JICTCP Vol 10 No 2 of 2003), notes the difficulties inherent in concept of suspicion in the new statutory offence (see 8.5).

There is a defence for a person who has a reasonable excuse for not disclosing the information, and also for lawyers where the information came to them in privileged circumstances. Once a disclosure is made, the National Criminal Intelligence Service (UK) ('NCIS') has seven days to respond.

There is also a defence for staff who have not had adequate training (see CHAPTER 6: THE UK AML FRAMEWORK – THE MONEY LAUNDERING REGULATIONS AND GUIDANCE NOTES) concerning the identification of transactions which may be indicative of money laundering. However, in order to use this defence successfully, the defendant would have to show that he did not actually know or suspect that another person was engaged in money laundering, and that, in his case, his employer had not complied with requirements to provide employees with the training specified by relevant Ministerial Order (such an Order referring to the training which all employers are required to provide to employees under the Money Laundering Regulations).

Tipping-off

4.2   One of the keystones of the anti-money laundering ('AML') legislation is the concept of gaining immunity from future prosecution for an offence under PoCA by filing a SAR with the proper authorities (see 3.5 above).

In order to address the possible temptation a professional or practitioner may have to warn their client (perhaps out of loyalty, or for some other reason), the legislation also includes the offence of 'tipping-off' in relation to criminal conduct (s 333 PoCA 2002). This applies when a suspicion of money laundering has been disclosed to the authorities by means of a SAR, and when a money laundering investigation is being, or is about to be conducted.

The 'tipping-off' offence is in making a disclosure likely to prejudice the money laundering investigation.

The penalties for 'tipping-off' are five years' imprisonment and an unlimited fine for conviction on indictment. Summary conviction again carries a lesser penalty of six months' imprisonment, and a fine not exceeding the statutory maximum.

Conflict issues, involving tipping-off and constructive trust arguments, arose in *Bank of Scotland v A Ltd [2001] EWCA Civ 52.*

This case illustrates the tensions between criminal law provisions relating to tipping-off and the potential civil liability that may arise if an institution deals with the proceeds of a serious crime. In this case, the Bank applied to the court for directions as to what it should do, and the court made an order freezing the accounts.

The customer whose account had been frozen (and who had not been notified of the reason) brought proceedings for the release of the funds. At first instance,

Laddie J laid down guidelines as to what an institution should do in the future, either if it wants to make payments from the account, or if it does not.

The Court of Appeal did not endorse the guidelines, but confirmed the likelihood of a constructive trust arising in circumstances of suspicion of its customer's dishonesty. But the Court suggested that the Serious Fraud Office should have been made a party to the directions application.

The bankers' concern in this case was that their failure to implement their customer's instructions would in and of itself serve to tip him off.

In a subsequent English case the judge distinguished the Bank of Scotland decision, He found that 'tipping-off' was not an issue in the case, and ruled that in such circumstances a bank or other financial institution which *suspects* that it holds funds that are the proceeds of crime should not seek declaratory relief from the court but must make a commercial decision whether or not to contest proceedings if they are brought by the account holder. The judge alluded to some other tipping-off cases heard in private, where a refusal to comply with a customer's instruction might tip off a customer that there was an investigation. In those cases, Commercial Court judges in the UK had made 'show cause' orders against the police, and this no doubt influenced the way this case was resolved (*Amalgamated Metal Trading Ltd v City of London Police Financial Investigation Unit [2003] EWHC 703 (Comm)*).

Section 330(8) PoCA 2002 has elevated the Joint Money Laundering Steering Group (UK) ('JMLSG') *Guidance Notes* (see CHAPTER 6: THE UK AML FRAMEWORK – THE MONEY LAUNDERING REGULATIONS AND GUIDANCE NOTES) to a formal status as the court is required to consider such *Guidance Notes* in deciding whether a person has committed this AML offence.

Reporting

4.3   The procedure relating to reporting to an MLRO and the filing of a SAR is covered in detail in CHAPTER 10: UK AML REPORTING PROCEDURES.

Chapter 5

The UK AML Framework – Asset Recovery and Forfeiture

Assets Recovery Agency

5.1   Part 1 of the Proceeds of Crime Act 2002 ('PoCA') establishes the Assets Recovery Agency ('ARA') while Parts 2–5 of the Act provide for confiscation, civil recovery and recovery of cash.

These Parts of the Act have two purposes:

(a)   to enable the ARA to bring civil proceedings in the High Court to recover property that is or represents property obtained through *unlawful conduct* (civil recovery). This is an entirely new right of action, and is reserved to the enforcement authority; and

(b)   to enable cash which is, or represents, property obtained through *unlawful conduct*, or is intended to be used in such conduct, to be forfeited in civil proceedings before a magistrates' court.

For further information see the article by Jonathan Fisher 'A review of the new investigation powers under PoCA 2002' [2003] JIBL 15, issue 1.

Confiscation

5.2   Parts 2–4 of PoCA provide for confiscation orders following a conviction in the Criminal Courts.

Civil recovery and 'recovery order'

5.3   Part 5 of PoCA 2002 provides for the civil recovery of the proceeds etc of 'unlawful conduct' and allows for forfeiture of assets even following a criminal acquittal if a civil court determines that the accused had a 'criminal lifestyle' (see 5.1 above), ie, has demonstrably benefited from criminal activity with reference to a specified number of convictions within a specified, time period (see 5.5).

'Unlawful conduct' is defined in s 241 PoCA broadly so as to cover conduct that is, or would be, unlawful under the criminal law, wherever it occurred.

Recovery of cash

5.4   Part 5 of PoCA 2002 also provides for the recovery of cash in summary proceedings.

Criminal lifestyle

5.5   'Criminal lifestyle' is defined in s 75 PoCA according in particular to whether the defendant has committed any one of the 'lifestyle offences' set out in PoCA Schedule 2. These are set out in A1.1, and include drug trafficking, directing terrorism, people trafficking, arms trafficking, counterfeiting, intellectual property offences, sexual offences relating to pimps and brothels, and blackmail.

In addition, the 'lifestyle offences' also include not only the anti-money laundering ('AML') offences under s 327 or s 328 PoCA but also the *inchoate* offences of attempting, conspiring or inciting the commission of a 'lifestyle offence', and of aiding, abetting, counselling or procuring the commission of any such offence.

There must also be a 'course of criminal activity', which is defined as three or more convictions in the instant proceedings, or two convictions in the last six years. The defendant must also be shown to have benefited for the conduct.

There is no general examination into whether an accused may be living beyond his/her means relative to his/her declared sources of income and gains, although this may be taken into account, judged on a balance of probabilities (ie, to the civil court standard of proof) *and not* beyond all reasonable doubt (the criminal court standard of proof).

Comments

5.6   Note that the recovery provisions of PoCA 2002 do not extend to seizing the financial receipts from, for example, writing a book or newspaper article about a crime that has taken place and for which a conviction was obtained (for example, at the time of publication of this title, the government and press complaints commission are investigating the media deal signed by Tony Martin, who was jailed for killing a burglar on his property).

On the other hand, not all crimes lead to AML charges. For example, it remains to be seen whether AML charges will be brought against the Scotland Yard detectives who laundered over £15 million in drug money as part of a ten-year undercover sting operation in Gibraltar known as 'Operation Cotton' and who may have undoubtedly enjoyed elements of a 'criminal lifestyle' funded by laundered money, albeit as undercover agents.

Tracing

5.7   'Tracing' is a remedy available to a defrauded party in conjunction with constructive trust arguments: it literally concerns following the money, or its proceeds or fruits, as it is moved around and invested. The remedy exists in parallel with a finding that a constructive trust exists – see 12.5 and the cases referred to therein.

It is quite different from asset forfeiture, which is a right or remedy available to the State. Recent English cases include *Foskett v McKeown [2001] 1 AC 102, Shalson v Russo [2003] WTLR 1169.*

Nevertheless, s 305 PoCA (see A1.1) contains provisions on tracing, which provide for virtually unlimited tracing in respect of the 'recoverable property' (defined as 'property obtained through unlawful conduct'). Such tracing is limited by s 308(1) PoCA if the property is disposed of to a person who 'obtains it in good faith, for value and without notice that it was recoverable property' (the 'equitable superhero' and possibly now also 'the money launderer's darling'). Note that there is no requirement for the disposal to be for money or money's worth, but in practice it is unlikely that a gift could fall within this exception, as 'without notice' must be taken to include constructive notice: in any event, it might be caught by the 'tainted gifts' provisions of s 77 PoCA.

Chapter 6

The UK AML Framework – the Money Laundering Regulations and Guidance Notes

The Money Laundering Regulations

6.1 Money Laundering Regulations were first published by the UK Treasury in 1993 (SI 1993 No 1933). They form an essential part of the UK's anti-money laundering ('AML') defences. The regulations require financial institutions to put in place systems to deter money laundering and to assist the authorities to detect money laundering activities.

The revised Money Laundering Regulations 2003 (SI 2003 No 3075), replacing the 1993 Regulations and the 2001 Regulations (SI 2001 No 3641). Regulations 3–8 (set out at APPENDIX 1) were laid by HM Treasury on 28 November 2003. They are generally in force as of 1 March 2004 (although certain activities come into force on later dates). The new Regulations apply to every 'relevant business', which is defined in Regulation 2(2). This section replaces and extends the definition of 'relevant financial business' in the 1993 Regulations. The types of activity covered by the 1993 Regulations are listed in sub-paragraphs (a) to (e), and new sub-paragraphs (f) to (n) are added as follows:

'(f)   estate agency work;

(g)   operating a casino by way of business;

(h)   the activities of an insolvency practitioner;

(i)   providing tax advice;

(j)   providing accountancy services;

(k)   providing audit services by a person eligible for appointment as a company auditor;

(l)   providing legal services which involve participation in a financial or real property transaction (whether by assisting in the planning or execution of any such transaction or otherwise by acting for, or on behalf of, a client in any such transaction);

(m)   providing services in relation to the formation of a company or the formation, operation or management of a trust; and

(n)   the activity of dealing in goods of any description whenever a transaction involves accepting a total cash payment of €15,000 or more.'

The Regulations define money laundering widely, as 'an act which falls within s 340(11) of the Proceeds of Crime Act 2002 ('PoCA') or an offence under s 18 of the Terrorism Act 2000', which is a wider definition than PoCA.

The Regulations back up the criminal provisions in the PoCA 2002 and Part II (Regulations 3 to 8) further develop standards in the following main areas:

— systems and training for employees who are involved in the recognition and handling of transactions which may be money laundering (Reg 3) (see 6.4);

— identification procedures (customer verification or know-your-customer ('KYC') (Reg 4) (see CHAPTER 9: UK AML PROCEDURES – KYC, DUE DILIGENCE AND COMPLIANCE);

— record-keeping procedures relating to identification and transactions (Reg 6);

— internal reporting procedures of 'suspicious transactions' (Reg 7) including the role of the money laundering reporting officer (see CHAPTER 10: UK AML REPORTING PROCEDURES).

And there are penalties for those who fail to ensure adequate systems are in place and maintained.

Regulation 3 provides that everyone who is carrying out relevant business in the UK must:

(a)   comply with the requirements of Regulation 4 (identification procedures), Regulation 6 (record keeping procedures) and Regulation 7 (internal reporting procedures);

(b)   establish such other procedures of internal control and communication as may be appropriate for the purposes of forestalling and preventing money laundering; and

(c)   take appropriate measures so that relevant employees are:

(i)   made aware of the relevant legal provisions (Money Laundering Regulations 2003, Part 7 PoCA and s 18 Terrorism Act); and

(ii)   given training in how to recognise and deal with transactions which may be related to money laundering.

Failing to do any of these things is punishable by two years' imprisonment.

Although there is relatively little detail in the Regulations about identification procedures, record keeping procedures and internal reporting procedures with which a person undertaking relevant business must comply, guidance issued by a supervisory authority or appropriate body will be important in determining whether or not there has been adequate compliance.

Regulation 4 deals with identification procedures (customer verification or know-your-customer ('KYC')) (and see CHAPTER 9: UK AML FRAMEWORK – KYC, DUE DILIGENCE, AND COMPLIANCE). 'Satisfactory evidence of identity' is defined as 'evidence which is reasonably capable of establishing (and does in fact establish to the satisfaction of the person who obtains it) that the applicant for business is the person he claims to be' (Reg 2(5)). There is no specific legal requirement to obtain particular types of evidence for everyone it is necessary to identify. However, guidance issued by 'supervisory authorities' and others can be relevant in determining whether or not there has been effective compliance with the Regulations.

It is worth noting that under Regulation 2(7), 'supervisory authorities' includes:

—   the Bank of England;

—   the Financial Services Authority;

—   the Council of Lloyd's;

—   the Office of Fair Trading;

—   the Occupational Pensions Regulatory Authority;

—   bodies which are designated professional bodies for the purposes of Part 20 of the Finances and Services Markets Act 2000 ('FSMA'); and

—   the Gaming Board for Great Britain.

It should be noted that the Society of Trust and Estate Practitioners ('STEP') is not a 'supervisory authority', although the Institute of Chartered Accountants of England and Wales (ICAEW) and the Law Society (and others) are.

Regulation 6 deals with record-keeping procedures relating to identification and transactions and requires those who are carrying out relevant business in the UK to maintain procedures which require records to be retained for at least five years from the date on which the relationship ends.

Regulation 7 deals with internal reporting procedures of 'suspicious transactions' including the role of the money laundering reporting officer ('MLRO') (see CHAPTER 10: UK AML REPORTING PROCEDURES), and requires that anyone carrying on relevant business in the UK must maintain internal reporting procedures which require that:

(a)   someone in the organisation is nominated as MLRO;

(b)   anyone within the organisation who is handling relevant business who *knows or suspects* that a person is engaged in money laundering must report the matter to the MLRO;

(c)   the MLRO *must consider* the report in the light of any relevant information which is available to the person carrying on relevant business and determine whether it gives rise to knowledge or suspicion of money laundering; and

(d)   that where the MLRO determines that there is knowledge or suspicion the matter must be reported to 'a constable' which, in practice means National Criminal Intelligence Service (UK) ('NCIS').

FSMA and FSA

6.2   The Financial Services and Markets Act ('FSMA') 2000 has been in force in the UK since 30 November 2001, since which date the Financial Services Authority ('FSA') (see www.fsa.gov.uk) became the sole regulator of all financial services in the UK, with power to make and enforce regulatory rules on money laundering, prosecute criminal breaches of AML regulations, and publicise the outcome of disciplinary proceedings. The FSA also has the responsibility of reducing financial crime, by a combination of supervision and training. The FSA *Money Laundering Sourcebook* (coupled with the Joint Money Laundering Steering Group (UK) (JMLSG) *Guidance Notes*) are the reference points for the UK financial services sector. The AML standards are common.

Current FSA priorities include tracking the JMLSG *Guidance Notes* 2004 project (see 6.3 below) and commencing response work on the proposed *Third EU Money Laundering Directive*.

The Joint Money Laundering Steering Group

6.3   The JMLSG of the British Bankers Association has for a number of years published guidance notes for the UK financial sector (available at www-.jmlsg.org.uk), in association with the Building Societies Association and the law enforcement authorities. Similar guidance notes have also been produced for the insurance and investment business sectors.

JMLSG Guidance Notes for the UK financial sector

6.4   The original JMLSG *Guidance Notes* were first published in June 1997, and have been regularly updated since. The *Guidance Notes* 2003 were published in February 2004, following the publication of the revised Money Laundering Regulations which were published in November 2003 (see 6.1 above).

The *Guidance Notes* 2003 recognise the 'risk-based' approach to money laundering prevention (1.6 to 1.12 of the *Notes*).

They also contain guidance on constructive trust issues (2.20 to 2.27 of the *Notes* – and see CHAPTER 11: ISSUES FACING PROFESSIONAL AND PRACTITION-ERS) following recent UK case law.

They also contain detailed guidance on the procedures for reporting, and discuss what is meant by *knowledge* and *suspicion* (see 8.5). The JMLSG advises that cases of 'genuine doubt' should be reported. The confusion caused by inconsistent terminology is unfortunate, as the *Guidance Notes'* threshold of 'genuine doubt' seems synonymous with a standard amounting to 'belief' (as only a 'belief' can amount to a 'genuine doubt'). If so, this may be inconsistent with the case law cited (see 8.5) where it has been expressly stated that 'the creation of suspicion requires a lesser factual basis than the creation of a belief'.

When published, the revised JMLSG *Guidance Notes* will have been approved by HM Treasury, which gives them a limited force of law, in that, in considering a charge under s 330 PoCA (see 4.1), a UK court is required to consider whether an individual has complied with them.

The Law Society has issued their own separate AML guidance which can found on its website at www.lawsoc.org.uk, this does not have the force of law. Chapter 6 of the guidance (entitled 'Practical Help') attempts to deal with the question of 'suspicion' and 'cause for concern'.

The ICAEW (in conjunction with the other members of the Consultative Committee of Accountancy Bodies) has issued interim guidance (see www.icaew.co.uk), to assist its members in fulfilling anti-money laundering requirements. Further formal guidance was issued on 16 February 2004, which deals with a number of practical issues to do with SARs.

Training

6.5   As is noted at 6.1 training is one of the six main areas covered by the Regulations.

CHAPTER 4: UK AML REPORTING PROCEDURES notes that s 330 PoCA 2002 creates the new offence of negligently failing to report a money laundering offence, which is applicable only to those working in the 'regulated financial sector', thus including UK accountants, lawyers and trustees. Note also the defence for staff who have not had adequate training concerning the identification of transactions which may be indicative of money laundering.

However, in order to use this defence successfully, the defendant would have to show that he did not actually know or suspect that another person was engaged in money laundering, and that, in his case, his employer had not complied with requirements to provide employees with such training specified by the Secretary of State by order (such an order will reference to training which all employers are required to provide to employees under Regulation 5(1)(b) and (c) of the 1993 Money Laundering Regulations).

As a result there are now a host of training initiatives, both in the UK and internationally.

For example, the British Bankers Association launched an online training initiative in October 2001 at www.bbae-learning.com/_corpsite/default.asp

The FSA also undertakes industry training in AML through courses and workshops – see www.fsa.gov.uk/industry-training/ml_workshop.html

Internationally, the International Compliance Association and the University of Manchester Business School, with the approval of STEP and the International Trust Companies Association have created two new international diplomas, 'International Diploma in Anti-Money Laundering' and 'International Diploma in Compliance' – see www.step.org

Other AML training and publications include:

— *International Enforcement Law Reporter* edited by Bruce Zagari Washington DC;

— Money Laundering Bulletin, by *Informa*;

— SWAT's Money Laundering *The New Law and Your Obligations* training CD.

Chapter 7

Fiscal Offences and Foreign Tax Enforcement

Historical background

7.1 The following quote, taken from John Rhodes article 'The United Kingdom's Pursuit of Fiscal Crime' (Chase Journal, Vol II, Issue 3, 1998) summarises the traditional approach English courts have taken to enforcement of foreign tax laws within the UK:

'Historically the stance of the English court has been to subscribe to the generally accepted principle of international law that, in the absence of specific treaty provisions to the contrary, no government will enforce the revenue claims of another.

This has a long history in English law, which was comprehensively reviewed by the House of Lords in the 1955 case of *Government of India v Taylor [1955] AC 491, HL*. In this case the Indian government attempted to recover an Indian tax liability through the English courts from the liquidator of an Indian company. The company had made a large profit on selling assets in India to the Indian government, which was then embarrassed to find the proceeds of sale had been swiftly removed from India without payment of tax. So, proceedings were started in England against the liquidator because he was resident here. The action was pursued through to the UK final court of appeal, but never got off the ground. Viscount Simonds gave the leading judgment in the House of Lords, in which he relied on four main points:

1   Case law going back over 200 years, including a series of eighteenth century cases in which Lord Mansfield had clearly repeated the dictum "for no country ever takes notice of the revenue laws of another";

2   The fact that the Foreign Judgments (Reciprocal Enforcement) Act 1933 excluded "a sum payable in respect of taxes or other charges of a like nature or in respect of a fine or other penalty";

3   Evidence produced that other countries, such as Eire, France and the United States, would not allow the collection of foreign taxes through their courts;

4   The rule as stated in Dicey's authoritative treatise The Conflict of Laws that "the English courts have no jurisdiction to entertain an action for the enforcement, either directly or indirectly, of a penal, revenue, or other public law of a foreign state".

The philosophical basis of the rule was debated in the case. Lord Keith concluded that enforcement of such claims is an extension of the sovereign power which imposed the taxes and that "an assertion of sovereign authority by one state within the territory of another … is (treaty or convention apart) contrary to all concepts of independent sovereignties".

Also, it was just generally thought inappropriate for one country to become involved in what might turn out to be the penal or confiscatory actions of another.

It was argued that the English courts might consider collecting taxes which they could classify as non-penal, in other words "the sort of tax which is recognised in this country", but Viscount Simonds stated that he was not "disposed to introduce so nice a refinement into a rule which has hitherto been stated in terms that are so easy to understand and apply".

In taking this line the English courts have in effect left it to government to determine which tax regimes, if any, should be assisted by introducing specific enforcement provisions in tax treaties. So far as I am aware, however, there are as yet no UK treaties which comprehensively do this'.

The traditional position was reaffirmed by the Court of Appeal in 1997 in *Camdex International Ltd v Bank of Zambia (No 2) (1997), Times, 28 January*, which held that the English courts had no power to entertain an action for enforcement in the UK of a public law of a foreign state (in the event, a garnishee order, sought by the Bank of Zambia, to remit funds to Zambia pursuant to their exchange control legislation). Interestingly, the same divergence of approach is reflected in two Jersey Cases, *Le Marquand and Backhurst v Chiltmead Limited (by its Liquidator) 1987–88 JLR 86*, and *In the Matter of Tucker 1987–88 JLR 473*.

The collection of foreign taxes is not the only factor to be considered, as demonstrated by the different approach taken by the Court of Appeal in the *Nuland* case in 1988 (*R v Chief Metropolitan Stipendiary Magistrate, ex p Secretary of State for the Home Department [1988] 1 WLR 1204*). The case concerned an extradition application by the Norwegian government against a Norwegian tax offender who had been convicted in Norway of eleven offences (including five offences relating to evasion of Norwegian tax) and had fled to London. The Court of Appeal (Divisional Court) confirmed that, even though the offences related to foreign tax evasion, extradition could still be ordered. Stuart Smith LJ suggested that the principle enunciated in *Government of India v Taylor* 'plainly relates to civil proceedings'. In other words, recovery of tax would not be enforced, but return of a criminal fugitive would.

Fiscal offences

7.2   Given this background, few professionals in the mid-1990s considered that the new anti-money laundering ('AML') laws extended to tax offences, let alone non-UK tax offences, committed outside the UK by non-UK citizens (see 8.2).

However, as soon as practitioners started to realise the potential implications of a broader interpretation, a debate began in earnest. Two schools of thought emerged. Constitutional purists argued for the narrower, more restrictive interpretation based on the historical position and the principle of construing criminal statutes narrowly (see *DPP v Ottewell [1970] AC 642, HL at 649*), and concluded that the new AML legislation could not criminalise UK practitioners and financial institutions who were simply involved with the proceeds of a foreign client's domestic tax evasion, but recognised that assistance in evasionary acts (fraud, conspiring to cheat, false accounting etc) would render the UK person liable. The debate was primarily as to whether there are 'proceeds' of a tax crime (see 8.3).The question of tracing and identifying such 'proceeds' was apparently resolved following *Foskett v McKeown [2000] 3 All ER 97, HL* (see CHAPTER 12: ISSUES FACING TRUSTEES AND EXECUTORS).

Other practitioners advanced a more extensive purposive interpretation, echoing the Joint Money Laundering Steering Group ('JMLSG')(UK) guidelines that 'tax-related offences are not in a special category', and concluded that the broader application was not only appropriate and inevitable, but was also fully in accordance with the UK's international obligations (see *Butterworths Money Laundering Law*).

Despite the initial ambiguity in its legislative history, the UK government position is now quite clear, in extending the concept of '… other serious crime …' to include tax evasion (domestic or foreign). The Criminal Justice Acts and now the Proceeds of Crime Act ('PoCA') 2002, have indeed brought within the scope of the UK AML offences any dealings by UK professionals or financial institutions with the proceeds of tax evasion.

'The prudent course is to assume that tax evasion is a predicate offence' (*Butterworths International Guide to Money Laundering Law and Practice* (2nd edn, 2002), as it is likely that it would be accompanied by other tax-related offences such as fraud, cheating the public revenue (cases where the concept of cheating are considered include *R v Mavji [1986] STC 508 and R v Loss (1993) The Times, 30 March*), false accounting, and the inchoate offences such as conspiracy to cheat etc – offences which would in any event render the UK person liable. Assistance in evasionary acts such as fraud, conspiracy to cheat, false accounting, etc will give rise to criminal liability in most jurisdictions.

Interestingly, Article 26 of the US-Swiss Income Tax Treaty provides for exchange of information ('EoI') where necessary 'for the prevention of tax fraud and the like …'. On 26 January 2003, the interpretation of the Article 26 was broadened by agreement on the scope of the words 'and the like'. On 21 May 2003 the Swiss Federal Department of Finance issued a press release, confirming amongst other matters that the words did not extend to cover mere tax evasion, but that fraud would, for example, include the preparation of false documents. The Treaty is up for renegotiation by the end of 2005.

Also, the Second EU Money Laundering Directive does not contain any clear definition of the concept of 'serious crime'. 'Criminal activity' is defined in

Article 1 of the 1991 Directive. The Second EU AML Directive extends the definition to a range of serious crimes, but requires Member States before 15 December 2004 to amend the definition so as to base it on set threshold periods of imprisonment or detention (see EU Joint action of 3 December 1998, OJ L 333, 9.12.98).

As noted in more detail in CHAPTER 11: ISSUES FACING PROFESSIONALS AND PRACTITIONERS, in the UK High Court (Family Division) the President of the Family Division Dame Justice Butler-Sloss handed down her judgment on 8 October 2003 in the case of *P v P [2003] EWHC 2260 (Fam), [2003] 4 All ER 843*. This decision, requiring careful reading, contains valuable guidance on a number of vexed questions, including:

— the extent to which a solicitor handling a divorce case for a client might come within the ambit of s 328 PoCA (arrangements etc) in relation to a proposed financial settlement where part of the funds had not been declared for tax;

— whether the facts should be disclosed to National Criminal Service ('NCIS')(UK) in the form of a suspicious activity report ('SAR');

— the seeking of a consent order under s 335 PoCA;

— that there is no professional privilege exemption under ss 327, 328 or 329 PoCA; and

— that ss 33 and 342 PoCA provide an exemption from the offence of 'tipping-off' where the mere fact of the SAR would suffice to tip off the client.

The only glimmer of light at the end of this particularly dark tunnel arises out of the recently updated FATF *Forty Recommendations*, which for the first time contains in the glossary a definition of 'designated category of offences' – this is set out in APPENDIX 3. Hardly surprisingly 'fraud' is included, but notable by its omission is 'tax evasion' which is specifically omitted. However, it is likely to be a monumental task to reverse the UK interpretation, even though other jurisdictions may seize on the FATF categories with some relief.

It remains to be seen if the 'two-tier' reporting system announced at the end of January 2004 (see 10.4) may enable NCIS treat SARs relating to tax evasion as crimes of 'lesser intelligence value', and allow for abbreviated SAR reporting.

Fraudulent evasion of income tax

7.3   In the UK, the Taxes Acts did not contain any criminal offence of 'tax evasion' prior to the Finance Act ('FA') 2000. This introduced a new clause which was first tabled and reported on 27 June 2000 in an inland revenue press release. It was then debated and passed by Parliament on 29 June 2000. This created some controversy as it left practically no time for external comment or reaction. The clause is effective as regards involvement in fraudulent evasion of income tax after 1 January 2001. It can be found in s 144 FA 2000, and introduces a statutory offence of fraudulent evasion of income tax:

'A person commits an offence if he is knowingly concerned in the fraudulent evasion of income tax by him or any other person'.

Within the EU, cross-border assistance procedures for recovery of tax debts (including income tax, corporation tax and capital gains tax) are being established as between member states by widening existing procedures applying only to indirect taxes (implemented in the UK by s 134 and Schedule 39 FA 2002).

The UK Inland Revenue have stated that s 144 does not criminalise conduct which is already an offence under current law, and that its ambit should be regarded as similar to the offence of 'cheating the public revenue' (see 7.2 above).

It is likely that an offence will only be committed if the taxpayer (or his adviser):

— has actual knowledge of the fraud, or at least wilful blindness to it (so constructive knowledge – that is, what the defendant ought to have known – is not enough); and

— has acted in some way dishonestly (see Andrew Watters and Jonathan Levy 'Avoiding evasion – disclosure concealment and fraud' The Tax Journal (2003) 29 September).

Foreign tax evasion

7.4   As is explained in more detail at 8.2, the AML panoply of the proceeds of tax offences does not differentiate where the offence took place. A foreign act of tax evasion, provided it results from conduct the equivalent of which in the UK is an offence, can by itself amount to criminal conduct under PoCA. This view (see *Butterworths Money Laundering Law*) relies on the fact that tax evasion in the UK can be an offence by virtue of ss 17 and 32 Theft Act 1968 and s 2 Theft Act 1978. The IR brings criminal prosecutions against tax evaders under these sections, albeit infrequently, for:

— false accounting (s 17 Theft Act 1968);

— the old common law offence of cheating the public revenue (s 32 Theft Act 1968); and

— evading liability by deception (s 2 Theft Act 1978).

Since an act (as opposed to an omission) of foreign tax evasion usually results from a deception of some kind, it is the deception which, if committed in the UK, would constitute the criminal conduct required under PoCA. In this regard, the *dictum* in *Hawkins Pleas of the Crown* that 'all frauds affecting the Crown and public at large are indictable as cheats at common law', cited favourably in

R v Mulligan [1990] Crim LR 427 (a case on the offence of cheating), would nowadays probably not be taken to exclude 'cheating a foreign revenue'.

In other words, an offence under PoCA can occur where the serious crime is tax evasion, and the UK courts should not differentiate whether the taxes that were evaded were domestic or foreign. All that is required is that some element of the activities of the underlying crime occur within the territorial borders of the jurisdiction, such as either the evasionary act itself occurring in the UK, or (if it occurred elsewhere) then at least having the criminal proceeds of the tax evasion enter the UK.

As regards *suspicion* in relation to foreign tax offences, the JMLSG *Guidance Notes* 2003 concede that there is no requirement for institutions to have knowledge of the tax (or other) laws in the countries in which criminal conduct may have occurred (*Guidance Notes*, Appendix C at p 206). This may be of considerable assistance to an 'average' practitioner: but it aggravates the position for large international businesses and professional organisations with offices in different countries round the world, as these may have the 'in house' facility of checking the position on overseas tax evasion with their sister offices in such overseas jurisdiction.

On the other hand, they do need to be absolutely clear on whether the conduct abroad would constitute an offence if committed in the UK. In the UK there is no policy ambiguity on this point: the UK courts only need to answer one question, namely would the facts have constituted criminal activity had they occurred in the UK?

In other jurisdictions, the position on this crucial point is less clear, and CHAPTER 14: APPLICATION OF AML PRINCIPLES OUTSIDE THE UK: THE GENERAL APPROACH IN OTHER SELECTED JURISDICTIONS reviews selected jurisdictions.

Practical difficulties

7.5   John Rhodes has summed up the difficulties in the new UK position thus:

> 'I am not condoning or encouraging tax evasion: to do so is quite simply untenable. Life is less complicated when people pay their taxes. If everyone willingly did so, no doubt tax rates everywhere could fall.
>
> I therefore agree in principle with the overall objective of stamping out tax evasion, but I still question the route the UK government has taken. Anecdotal evidence suggests that there is far more tax evasion (as opposed to tax planning/avoidance) outside the US and the United Kingdom; yet the UK government has gone out on a limb on this issue. In doing so it has apparently:
>
> • made no attempt to distinguish between OECD-type taxes and those imposed by regimes it abhors (Iraq, Libya, Serbia etc);

- paid no attention to the fact that a large proportion of funds in question were originally "hidden" in time of war, or by families who had suffered religious or political persecution;

- not offered the present generation of such families any sensible way in which to reintroduce funds into the open without threat of criminal prosecution;

- ignored the fact that almost all the funds were invested one way or another back in the Western economies via New York, London, or Zurich;

- ignored the proportion they may represent of such markets;

- ignored the difficulty this rapid change of agenda causes some of the world's largest financial institutions, most of which are major players and employers in the City of London and elsewhere'. (See the *United Kingdoms Pursuit of Fiscal Crime*, p 58.)

In the same article, John Rhodes refers to the dilemma of two 'awful alternatives':

'If situations involving suspicion of foreign tax evasion alone are within the CJA, UK bankers, accountants and lawyers are already faced with two awful alternatives, particularly in relation to families for whom they were acting prior to 15 February 1995, when these new provisions took effect:

[either:] They report the clients (without telling them) to NCIS, knowing this may now result in the immediate transfer of information to the clients' home revenue authority.

[or:] They don't report and risk prosecution'.

The UK approach to foreign fiscal offences also ignores the politics of foreign countries and administrations. For example, some countries have a procedure in their fiscal code whereby a minister or tax official can deliver a 'certificate' that a certain transaction is approved: the law also allows for such certifications to be obtained after the event. An arbitrary refusal of such a certificate to a political 'enemy' or member of a former regime would thus trigger UK AML sanctions.

Countries that include fiscal crime in money laundering

7.6   Along with the UK, a number of countries now include fiscal crime in money laundering: these include Belgium, Finland, France, Ireland, Italy, Netherlands, New Zealand, Norway, Spain and Sweden. On the other hand, Australia, Brazil, Canada, Denmark, Japan, Luxembourg, Portugal, Singapore, Switzerland and the United States do not. For more specific information see CHAPTER 14: APPLICATION OF AML PRINCIPLES OUTSIDE OF THE UK: THE SPECIFIC APPROACH TO FISCAL OFFENCES IN SELECTED JURISDICTIONS.

Other legal and technical issues relating to fiscal offences being AML offences

7.7   If an offshore trust is found to have been established in its entirety with the proceeds of a domestic fraud or a foreign tax crime, then there is a possibility that there are no assets capable of disposal by the purported settlor for the trust to bite on. In such circumstances, the trust on the documents would simply be non-existent (neither 'void' nor even 'voidable'), and the trustee would be no more than a custodian of the property for whomever could establish title, for example via tracing (see para 12.4 on constructive trust issues). Further difficulties will ensue for the 'trustee' in respect of any distributions made to 'beneficiaries' in the interim.

In the context of a foreign fiscal offence s 340(2) PoCA 2002 seems to make it necessary to deem that the offence was committed in the UK and that the 'deemed victim' was (presumably) the UK Inland Revenue (see para 8.2). Thus, there is a high element of extra territoriality. The JMLSG *Guidance Notes* suggest that a SAR should still be made (this may be prudent, albeit technically incorrect), even though the concerned UK professional need not have an encyclopaedic knowledge of world tax systems.

Is it sufficient simply to judge the acts giving rise to the funds against UK legislation, with which a UK professional is deemed to be entirely familiar? If that were the correct approach, the underlying acts may well be a 'crime' in the UK, whilst in reality only being subject to civil or administrative penalties in the 'home' country. A perverse result would ensue, as a UK AML offence could arise on the basis of the deeming that the acts would have been a crime in the UK albeit that the acts were *not* committed in the UK and the 'victim' *was not* based in the UK.

Wider issues affecting international private banking

7.8   The inclusion within the AML panoply of the proceeds of tax offences (domestic or foreign) raises as a significant industry issue the possible demise of international private banking.

International private banking ('IPB') has an Achilles heel in its general inability to deal with the customer or client's specific taxation profile in their 'home' country. In asset value terms this is a very significant issue for customers or clients from parts of South East Asia, the Indian sub-continent, Africa, Central America and South America (the proceeds of corruption are also within the AML statutes), but it is still also an issue in the European context.

Some individuals may be fortunate enough to live in countries without taxation such as Bermuda or Saudi Arabia. A smaller number of individuals may manage to construct their lives so they are not officially resident anywhere, which is achievable by spending time in a number of different countries without triggering the specific 'days spent' residence criteria of any one of them.

Some individuals may be fortunate enough to live in countries where taxation is only imposed on a territorial or 'source' basis, so that income or gains earned 'offshore' that country may not be subject to home country taxation either at all (as in Hong Kong) or if it is 'captured' in an offshore company, such as was the case in the US prior to the 1967 tax reform, and/or is not 'remitted' to the home country, as in Singapore. In response to this, many developing countries have recently introduced, or are in the process of introducing, controlled foreign corporation (US)/controlled foreign company (UK) -type legislation or anti-tax haven legislation. Anti-tax haven legislation involves publishing a prescribed 'blacklist' of jurisdictions and introducing rules that penalise transactions with such 'blacklisted' countries (for example, Mexico, Venezuela, Argentina and Brazil). For further information see Richard J Hay *Worldwide Taxation in Latin America: Strategies for Private Banks (2000)*.

However, the vast majority of individual private banking clients (both in numerical terms and in asset value terms) do officially reside somewhere, generally in countries with systems of taxation and a functioning tax administration. Typically, such an individual has accumulated funds in a bank in a country other than his/her home country, and typically those funds and/or the income and gains arising on them, have not been declared to the home country tax authorities. Indeed, one of the reasons most frequently advanced for *not* using the domestic banking sector in the home country is the lack of confidentiality, coupled with the risk of possible kidnap and financial blackmail.

Thus the international private banker from (say) Hong Kong, London, Luxembourg or New York is aware that the funds are 'undeclared' to the home country tax authorities, and it is unlikely that there is a detailed discussion of how to (or whether to) get back into compliance with the home country tax laws (private bankers usually make it clear to their clients that they do not give specific tax advice), unless some sort of tax amnesty becomes available (as has been the case recently in Italy and Germany).

Such funds therefore, on the UK analysis, constitute or include the 'proceeds of crime'.

In the European context, the Luxembourg private banker is in the same position vis-à-vis clients from (say) Germany or France. Although the European Directive on the Taxation of Savings Income (Council Directive 2003/48/EC of 3 June 2003, OJ L157, 26.06.2003 p 38) initiative will eventually resolve the 'black' status of most of such money for as long as it remains unstructured (ie, in accounts owned by individuals), the Directive does not address assets held within structures (offshore companies, trusts, etc).

Chief Justice Smellie of the Cayman Islands noted in a recent article (14 December 2000 – presented in December 2000 at the IBC):

'Nowadays, in the more advanced financial centres, it is my understanding that the more sophisticated practitioners routinely seek to clarify the true nature of the client's transactions and will inform the client that he or she must comply with domestic tax laws and that he or she is not prepared to assist in the evasion of such laws. Moreover, in appropriate cases practitioners will require tax opinions vouchsafing compliance with the tax laws of the clients' domicile. I believe that we can now all agree that there can be little, if any, objection to the imposition of a code of practice which discourages the breach of foreign tax laws as a concomitant to the principles and obligations of international comity'.

As 'onshore' governments (led by the UK) have now refocused their AML legislation so as to bring within its ambit anyone who assists with the concealment or retention of the proceeds of foreign tax evasion, it follows that the proceeds of tax evasion (whether domestic or foreign) are now comprised in the definition of the 'proceeds of ...serious crime' and are thus immediately reportable.

It also follows that the international private banker is by the UK definition participating in foreign tax evasion, and is in his/her own right committing a criminal money laundering offence punishable with a prison term. And at industry level, the employer company, namely the private banking institution itself, would likewise appear to be indulging in wholesale institutional money laundering, since the gathering in of cross border assets would have been central to its strategy over the last ten or fifteen years.

Clearly some protection can be gained by filing SARs. However, the real question is what the institution should do about its partially, or even wholly-tainted portfolio of IPB clients (see para 12.10 AND APPENDIX 7).

Chapter 8

The UK AML Framework – Technical Issues

'All crimes' offences

8.1   The definition of 'criminal conduct' in the Proceeds of Crime Act ('PoCA') 2002 refers to conduct comprising a criminal offence. There is no limitation of the type of predicate offence covered, and there is no requirement for the predicate offender to be convicted in order to support an anti-money laundering ('AML') prosecution against the AML defendant (see 8.2 below).

Recommendation 1 of the current FATF *Forty Recommendations* (issued 23 June 2003 – see APPENDIX 3) provides that predicate offences for money laundering should apply to 'all serious offences' and suggests either an 'all crimes' approach or (either) a list of offences, or a 'threshold' approach where the threshold is linked to the applicable penalty of imprisonment. If the threshold approach is used, the Recommendation suggests offences punishable by more than six months or one year's imprisonment.

The 'all crimes' approach is logical and clears up overlapping legislation, but will cause great difficulty in relation to fiscal and tax-related offences. The position may be relatively clear in relation to domestic offences, but analytical difficulties arise where the offence occurs overseas (see CHAPTER 7: THE UK AML FRAMEWORK – FISCAL OFFENCES AND FOREIGN TAX ENFORCEMENT and CHAPTER 14: APPLICATION OF AML PRINCIPLES OUTSIDE THE UK: THE SPECIFIC APPROACH TO FISCAL OFFENCES IN SELECTED JURISDICTIONS).

Territorial limits and 'dual criminality'

8.2   Complex and technical issues abound! In terms of territoriality, criminal law traditionally confines itself to offences where some element of the activities of the underlying crime occur within the territorial borders of the jurisdiction (although 'long arm' statutes are increasingly common). In other words, the basic principle is that there can be no extra-territorial application to AML laws.

The Proceeds of Crime Act ('PoCA') 2002 is for the most part consistent with this, in that it does not apply unless some element of the *actus reus* is connected with the UK, in the sense of either occurring in the UK, or (if it occurred elsewhere) then at least having the criminal proceeds enter the UK.

Section 340(2) PoCA 2002 contains a dual definition of 'criminal conduct', namely:

• conduct which constitutes an offence in any part of the UK; or

• in relation to conduct which occurs *outside* the UK – conduct which *would* constitute an offence *if it had* occurred in any part of the UK.

The concept of 'criminal property', as defined in s 340(3), links directly to the requirement of 'criminal conduct'.

In terms of 'dual criminality', the position is more obscure. The three principal anti-money laundering (AML) offences (see CHAPTER 3: THE UK AML FRAME-WORK – PRINCIPAL OFFENCES) clearly do not have 'dual criminality' requirements, so the conduct does not also need to be unlawful under the criminal law of the foreign country in which it occurred. In contrast, the drafting of the *Civil Recovery* definition of 'unlawful conduct' in s 241 curiously does require dual criminality.

Recommendation 1 of the FATF *Forty Recommendations* (20 June 2003 – see APPENDIX 3) provides that predicate offences for money laundering *should* extend to conduct that occurred in another country, which constitutes an offence in that country, and which would have constituted a predicate offence had it occurred domestically.

Despite the territorial limitation of the criminal law (see above), these provisions establish a high degree of extraterritoriality (although the *Home Office Circular* of March 2003 does not clarify the position), and enable property obtained through conduct abroad to be recovered, or cash so obtained to be forfeited, even if the conduct was lawful where it took place but provided only that it would have been unlawful in any part of the UK *had it occurred there*, which rather obviously, it did not (*see HKSAR v Look Kar Win [1999] 4 HKC 783 4* in CHAPTER 14: APPLICATION OF AML PRINCIPLES OUTSIDE THE UK: THE SPECIFIC APPROACH TO FISCAL OFFENCES IN SELECTED JURISDICTIONS, involving Hong Kong residents gambling in Thailand).

There is also no requirement for the predicate offender to be convicted in order to support an AML prosecution against an AML defendant, although human rights issues of 'legal certainty' and 'proportionality' may arise if no conviction was obtained in any country in relation to the underlying predicate offence.

Thus, in the context of securing an AML conviction for a foreign fiscal offence (see CHAPTER 14 relating to other jurisdictions) s 340(2) PoCA 2002 seems to necessitate a 'double deeming', not only that the offence was committed in the UK, but also that the 'deemed victim' was (presumably) the UK Inland Revenue (the actual 'victim' of course being a foreign revenue administration). Thus, the extraterritorial effect is enlarged, but with it the difficulties in applying the section to the offence.

Proceeds

8.3   There is also a debate about the concept of the 'proceeds' of a foreign tax crime.

Some argue that money laundering is a type of crime that does not directly result in any 'proceeds'. Clearly if an individual has an undisclosed fortune held on deposit offshore and substantial funds in a bank at home, there is an argument that the funds at home might primarily contain the 'proceeds' of the domestic tax offence committed through non-reporting of (and non-payment of tax on) the offshore fortune.

An alternative view is that the offshore fortune is also the proceeds of crime, at least partially and possibly pro rata the sum onshore, on the basis that the offshore fortune may 'directly or indirectly' represent them. Certainly the point is not free from doubt.

In the recent English criminal case *R v Foggon [2003] EWCA Crim 270* the Court of Appeal confirmed that tax avoided or attempted to be avoided could also be a pecuniary advantage (see *R v Moran [2002] 1 WLR 253*; and *R v Dimsey [2000] QB 744*) obtained by an accused (in the context of a confiscation order).

Time limits and retrospectivity

8.4   Although PoCA 2002 expressly provides that it is immaterial when the criminal conduct occurred, there is no apparent intention to create wholesale retrospectivity (in any event prohibited under European Convention on Human Rights Article 7, and see *Welch v United Kingdom (Application 17440/90) (1995) 20 EHHR 247*), and it is just the difference in time between the underlying predicate offence and the subsequent AML offence that is intended.

It is, however, clear that both the know-your-client ('KYC') and *due diligence* obligations, and the principal money laundering offences themselves, do extend backward in time without time limit in respect of all business whenever taken on. This position may be mitigated by local statute or regulation.

'Knowledge' and 'suspicion'

8.5   The requisite mental elements (*mens rea*) of the PoCA 2002 AML offences are 'knowledge' or 'suspicion' that the property in question constitutes or represents the benefit of criminal conduct. An understanding of the concepts of 'knowledge' or 'suspicion' is crucial as lawyers can attest how plain words do not always mean what they seem to mean. A more detailed consideration of the differing 'mental' elements of the offences follows; this becomes of particular relevance in relation to foreign (ie, non-UK) fiscal offences (see CHAPTER 7: THE UK AML FRAMEWORK – FISCAL OFFENCES AND FOREIGN TAX ENFORCEMENT).

'Knowledge' is an absolute – one either knows or one does not – hence the legislation includes the lesser requirement of mere 'suspicion' to cover the case where someone does not actually know but still has suspicions or doubts. The key to keeping a UK professional or financial institution from falling within the principal AML offences is therefore the requirement for there to be neither 'knowledge' nor 'suspicion' that the property in question emanates from criminal conduct.

Case law in the area of constructive trusts (see 12.5) shows there are various types of knowledge:

(a) actual knowledge;

(b) 'Nelsonian' knowledge – this would also suffice for the offence; and

(c) imputed or constructive knowledge – this introduces an objective standard of knowledge, whereby one might be deemed to 'know' something if it could have been ascertained from enquiries which 'the reasonable person' would have made in the same circumstances (see *Baden Delvaux v Société Générale 1992; Royal Brunei Airlines v Tan [1995] 2 AC 378* and *BCCI (Overseas) v Akindele [2000] 4 All ER 221*).

These are also referred to in the *Guidance Notes* (see 6.4 and 12.5).

Article 1 of the Second EU Money Laundering Directive (EU Directives 91/308 OJ L 166/77, 28 June 1991and 2001/97 OJ L 344/76, 28 December 2001) appears to favour an expansive test of knowledge, on the basis that it states:

'knowledge, intent or purpose required as an element of the above-mentioned activities may be inferred by objective factual circumstances'.

The standard of knowledge under PoCA 2002 is subjective. It is usually quite difficult to prove a person's actual knowledge, but if there is less than actual subjective knowledge, then there may still be a residual suspicion. The requisite 'suspicion' does not need to relate to the particular underlying crime that gave rise to the criminal proceeds, and it is sufficient simply to show that there was suspicion as to the tainted nature of the source of funds that gave rise to the 'property'. A 'suspicious activity' report or 'SAR' is what is then filed.

But 'suspicion' is a very unusual connecting factor for attributing criminal liability, let alone for something as important as an AML offence with a lengthy prison term attached. Suspicion is not an easy state of mind to define, and the difficulties for those working with the Act are exacerbated by the fact that there is no definition in the primary legislation.

Attempts have, however, been made to define suspicion in case law. In *Hussein v Chong Fook Kam [1969] 3 All ER 1626*, it was held that the word suspicion in its ordinary meaning is a state of conjecture or surmise where proof is lacking: 'I suspect, but I cannot prove'. Similarly, in the case of *Corporate Affairs Comr v Guardian Investments [1984] VR 1019* it was stated that the word 'suspect' requires a degree of satisfaction, not necessarily amounting to belief, but at least extending beyond speculation as to whether an event has occurred or not. In contrast, mere speculation was excluded in the case of *Walsh v Loughman [1991] 2 VR 351* where it was held that 'although the creation of suspicion requires a lesser factual basis than the creation of a belief it must nonetheless be built upon some foundation'.

As regards 'suspicion' in relation to foreign tax offences, the Joint Money Laundering Steering Group *Guidance Notes* 2003 concede that there is no requirement for institutions to have knowledge of the tax (or other) laws in the countries in which criminal conduct may have occurred (*Guidance Notes*, Appendix C, p 206).

In a House of Lords case (*Manifest Shipping Co v Uni-Polaris Shipping Co [2001] UKHLI*) in 2001 involving a marine insurance claim, Lord Scott of Foscote commented at para 116 that 'suspicion is a word that can be used to describe a state of mind that may, at one extreme, be no more than a vague feeling of unease, and at the other extreme reflect a firm belief in the existence of the relevant facts'.

A recent learned article (Ryan Myint 'Solicitors Beware: Money Laundering after R v Duff' [2003] JICTCP Vol 10 No 2) notes the difficulties inherent in such a broad definition in the context of the new statutory offence of failing to report a suspicion of money laundering (see CHAPTER 4: THE UK AML FRAME-WORK – OTHER OFFENCES).

Also note that in the current FATF *Forty Recommendations*, Recommendation 2 provides that the intent and knowledge required to prove an AML offence should be consistent with the standards set out in the Vienna Convention (Vienna Convention against *Illicit Traffic in Narcotic Drugs and Psychotropic Substances 1988*) and the Palermo Convention (the 2000 UN Convention on *Transnational Organised Crime*), including that such mental state can be inferred from objective factual circumstances (if so, a person could be convicted of any AML offence for being 'wilfully blind').

There should be a degressive scale, beginning with 'knowledge', then moving to 'belief', then 'strong suspicion' (or 'gut feel'), then to 'speculation', and finally to 'doubt' or 'uncertainty'. It is submitted that the latter two categories ('speculation' and 'doubt'/'uncertainty') cannot be constitutive of the required mental element. In any event, a 'speculation' or a doubt/ uncertainty should be resolved either way by some further action on the part of the professional, (such as directing specific questions to the client as to what is going on) and if the responses are unsatisfactory it automatically converts into an actual suspicion.

In this context, it is interesting to note that the August 2002 edition of Guernsey's 'Rainbow Book' also requires persons submitting SARs to provide 'full evidence to demonstrate why the suspicion has been raised'. Whilst it is clear what is meant, there may be difficulties in providing 'full evidence' of the type admissible in court proceedings. The fundamental distinction between 'knowledge' and 'suspicion' means that if the person only has a 'suspicion' then there is unlikely to be any 'full evidence', as if there was, the suspicion becomes 'knowledge' by corroboration.

The clear and present danger for professionals lies in allowing knowledge or suspicion to be judged with hindsight or objectively. If this does become the test (outside of the regulated sector offence of negligently failing to report), then it is no longer merely a question of what you actually knew (or did not know) or suspected (or did not suspect); what may matter is what the 'reasonable lawyer', 'reasonable private banker' or 'reasonable accountant' would have concluded if faced with the same circumstances. On the face of it, PoCA 2002 at present only introduces an objective test of suspicion for the offence of *failure to disclose* (see CHAPTER 4: THE UK AML FRAMEWORK – OTHER OFFENCES).

Most of the offshore centres have a subjective test (Hong Kong, Liechtenstein, and Singapore have a mixed test that is both objective and subjective). It is not yet clear if the subjective standard will stand alone, or if an objective element will be grafted on as well. In Bermuda, the Association of Bermuda Compliance Officers is lobbying the Bermuda Monetary Authority hard to keep the test objective, arguing that a clear definition of *mens rea* should be adopted since what a jury may regard as 'reasonable grounds to suspect', after the fact and in the light of evidence that may not have been obvious when the transaction took place, may not at the time have triggered suspicion from the employee concerned (*Bottom Line*, Bermuda, November/December 2003).

A decision of the UK Court of Appeal in 2000 (interlocutory proceedings *Walker v Stones [2000] 4 All ER 412*) on the definition of 'dishonesty' within the context of a trustee exemption clause shows the courts' willingness to substitute a 'hindsight' test for a subjective belief genuinely held in good faith. On the other hand, in a more recent House of Lords decision (*Twinsectra v Yardley [2002] UKHL 12*) a Surrey solicitor was found to have possibly been naive or misguided, but not dishonest. But the tests for establishing 'dishonesty' in a criminal trial, as laid down in *R v Ghosh [1982] 1 QB 1053*, are whether the accused's act was 'dishonest' by the standards of reasonable and honest men, and did the accused realise his act would be so regarded: thus a clear objective standard applies.

By way of contrast, in 1990 (some three years before the Criminal Justice Act 1993 amendments), the judge at first instance in *Agip (Africa) Ltd v Jackson [1990] Ch 265* (Millett J as he then was, now Lord Millett); affd [1991] Ch 547, CA considered the merits of an argument put forward on behalf of the accountants that they did not act dishonestly because what they suspected was 'only' a breach of exchange control or 'only' a case of tax evasion. This approach received a dusty answer from the judge. He said this at page 294H:

> 'What did Mr Jackson and Mr Griffin think was going on? There is some evidence of this in the minutes of the first meeting of the Directors of

Keclward Limited of 22 March 1984 and it will be wrong of me to ignore it. This suggests that they thought that their clerk was engaged in evading Tunisian Exchange Control, possibly with the connivance of the Plaintiffs and on their behalf – though the minutes do not say so. In my judgment, however, it is no answer for a man charged with having knowingly assisted in a fraudulent and dishonest scheme to say that he thought that it was "only" a breach of exchange control or "only" a case of tax evasion. It is not necessary that he should have been aware of the precise nature of the fraud or even of the identity of its victim. A man who consciously assists others by making arrangements which he knows are calculated to conceal what is happening from the third party, takes the risk that they are part of a fraud practised on that party'.

This is salutary advice. Once a professional sinks to a position of knowing that his client is involved in fraudulent activity, he will find it very difficult to argue that he was not sufficiently on notice of a fraud on a particular party.

While the courts are very reluctant to enforce, directly or indirectly, a foreign revenue law, they will not look kindly on professionals who get involved in what they know to be dishonest activity, even if the professional believes that it is 'only' a fraud on a foreign tax authority or exchange control authority. Commission of a money laundering offence is an automatic consequence, and a SAR should also be filed.

Overall therefore this area is fraught with dangers, and will remain so until further clarified by a higher level court in the UK.

Banking initiatives

The 'Wolfsberg Principles' of October 2000

8.6   On 30 October 2000, a group of the world's leading private banks (the participating institutions are ABN AMRO Bank, Barclays Bank plc, Banco Santander Central Hispano SA, The Chase Manhattan Private Bank, Citibank NA, Crédit Suisse Group, Deutsche Bank AG & Bankers Trust, HSBC plc; JP Morgan & Co, Société Générale SA, and UBS AG) published the 'Wolfsberg Anti-Money Laundering Principles' (so-called because important working sessions were held in the Wolfsberg Centre of UBS. See www.wolfsberg-principles.com) by way of their formal anti-money laundering policy statement. These global AML guidelines are aimed primarily at their international private bankers, including both relationship managers and those involved with fiduciary activities in the offshore havens. The principles were drawn up in conjunction with Transparency International, the global anti-corruption organisation (see CHAPTER 10: UK AML REPORTING PROCEDURES).

The principles are to some extent a response to scandals and events over the preceding two years (for example the 1.3 billion dollars belonging to the late

Sani Abacha (former President of Nigeria) held by various London banks; and see the *Levin Report* at 12.6). However, whatever their background, they are very much the latest word on appropriate KYC policies, guidelines for dealing with international HNWI and UHNWI clients, and identification and follow-up of unusual or suspicious transactions. For this reason, the Wolfsberg Principles are an important document, and are reproduced in APPENDIX 3.

Whilst a formal anti-money laundering policy statement is not necessarily a new idea, it is interesting to identify both the international banking groups which endorsed the principles, and by default those other international private banking ('IPB') and financial service groups which have not (yet) signed up to the principles.

To those with experience in IPB and the offshore field, the principles will seem pretty much like an exercise in common sense, and as such contain no surprises. The key points and procedural requirements are as follows:

(a) Accept only those clients whose source of wealth and funds can be reasonably established to be legitimate. Primary responsibility for this lies with the private banker who sponsors the client for acceptance, and mere fulfilment of internal review procedure does not relieve the private banker of this basic responsibility. In other words, slavishly following a checklist is insufficient.

(b) The identity of natural persons will be established by reference to official identity papers (note that identification documents must be current at the time).

(c) Beneficial ownership must be established for all accounts. Due diligence must be done on all principal beneficial owners identified in accordance with the following principles:

   (i) *individuals* – establish whether the client is acting on his/her own behalf. If doubt exists, establish the capacity in which and on whose behalf the account holder is acting;

   (ii) *offshore companies* – understand the structure of the company sufficiently to determine the provider of funds, principal owner(s) of the shares and those who have control over the funds (eg, the directors) and those with the power to give direction to the directors of the company;

   (iii) *trusts* – understand the structure of the trust sufficiently to determine the provider of funds (eg, the settlor), those who have control over the funds (eg, the trustees), and any persons or entities who have the power to remove the trustees (eg, a protector).

(d) Due diligence information must be collected and recorded covering the following categories:

   (i) purpose and reasons for opening the account;

   (ii) anticipated account activity;

    (iii)   source of wealth (description of the economic activity which has generated the net worth);

    (iv)   estimated net worth;

    (v)   source of funds (description of the origin and the means of transfer for monies that are accepted for the account opening); and

    (vi)   references or other sources to corroborate reputation information where available.

(e)   Unless other measures reasonably suffice to conduct the due diligence on a client (eg, favourable and reliable references), a client will be met prior to account opening.

(f)   Additional diligence/heightened scrutiny is required on clients and beneficial owners resident in and funds sourced from 'high-risk countries' (ie, countries having inadequate anti-money laundering standards, or representing a high risk for crime and corruption).

(g)   Additional diligence/heightened scrutiny is also required on clients and beneficial owners who hold public offices, who have (or have had) positions of public trust (such as government officials, senior executives of government corporations, politicians, important political party officials etc) and their families and close associates. These can be referred to as a politically exposed person ('PEP') or a politically sensitive person ('PSP').

(h)   Legitimate aids to identifying unusual or suspicious activities may include:

    (i)   monitoring of transactions;

    (ii)   client contacts (meetings, discussions, in-country visits, etc);

    (iii)   third-party information (eg, newspapers, Reuters, the Internet); and

    (iv)   knowledge of the client's environment (eg, the political situation in his/her country).

(i)   Record retention requirements for all anti-money laundering related documents are that these must be retained for a minimum of five years. An interesting question arises in relation to this concept, as most institutions will err on the side of caution and retain more paperwork rather than less, thus raising a similar issue to that discussed in relation to audits of qualified intermediaries (see CHAPTER 5: THE UK AML FRAMEWORK – ASSET RECOVERY AND FORFEITURE.)

The two areas ('f' and 'g' above) where 'additional diligence/heightened scrutiny' is required merit further comment.

Firstly, high-risk countries' is not a concept defined in a single list. The Financial Action Task Forces ('FATF') blacklist only covers countries with inadequate anti-money laundering standards. There are many countries that have never either been on or off the FATF blacklist, through never having been part of the FATF process in the first place. One such example is Latvia. Two more extreme examples are Libya and Cuba.

The Transparency International Corruption Perception's Index provides a clear ranking of countries in terms of the risk for crime and corruption. However, there is no 'brightline' or cut-off point on the scale, above which it is fine to deal, and below which it is not.

Know-your-client and due diligence requires professionals to be sure whether clients and beneficial owners are resident in, or funds are sourced from, such countries. Given that financial institutions dislike imprecision, many have taken to developing their own internal blacklists. Such lists will vary from institution to institution. And as it always prudent to err on the side of safety, many of such lists will go wider than may have been strictly necessary.

Secondly, the issue of PSPs/PEPs, namely clients and beneficial owners who hold public offices, who have (or have had) positions of public trust (such as government officials, senior executives of government corporations, politicians, important political party officials etc) and their families and close associates.

It is difficult to be sure one is not dealing with a PSP/PEP if there is no central database of such persons let alone of relationships such as their family members and close associates. Such a matrix list would be a key resource, provided it was accessible. At present, approaches to government agencies and regulators are generally met only with copies of published terrorism sanctions lists.

As far as concerns PSPs, the Director General of the Jersey Financial Services Commission proposed in July 2001 that banks and other institutions should have access to databases detailing at least the identity of ministers and senior public officials, and listing friends and associates of politicians in corrupt regimes. Some specialist companies have already started addressing this issue. On 16 July 2002 a consortium of big Wall Street and European financial businesses announced the set up of Regulatory DataCorp (see their website at www.citigroup.com/citigroup/press/020716b.htm). Whilst such an initiative could be potentially extremely useful, it would also seem to raise other concerns:

— To be truly useful, the information needs to be available to those in the industry as a whole. It is unclear who will be able to gain access and at what price. The private sector would benefit enormously from the information in avoiding being tainted by a genuine corruption case.

— The information must be of pinpoint accuracy. It is not difficult to imagine a payment being held up and a commercial opportunity or contractual obligation missed simply through a name being (wrongly as it might turn out) linked on such a database to being a business associate or even a relative of a government official.

— The issue of remedies for error become important. It is unclear whether individuals should have the right to inspect their entries and correct errors.

— There is an obvious issue of data protection and access to overcome. Data protection legislation has already been in place for several years, whilst human rights legislation is a more recent phenomenon. Data protection principles must be observed just as strictly, and should prevent any form of unauthorised access.

In marked contrast, a recent initiative between financial institutions in Hong Kong to share customer data was cancelled on grounds of data protection (see 9.4 for more information of blacklists and databases).

'Wolfsberg II' (January 2002)

8.7 In January 2002 the Wolfsberg Group of banks issued global guidelines on combating terrorist financing. In these the Group restated their commitment to co-operating with and assisting law enforcement and government agencies in their efforts to combat the financing of terrorism.

The Group also identified areas for further discussion with governments. Three areas merit particular note:

— Governments should be more precise in publishing name lists, as Arabic names published in the Roman alphabet are capable of being spelled in numerous different ways.

— Governments should include better details on official lists, such as (for individuals) date of birth, place of birth and passport number, and (for companies) place of incorporation and details of principals, and in all cases stating the reason for inclusion on the list.

— Governments should permit financial institutions to report unusual or suspicious transactions that may relate to terrorism without breaching any duty of customer confidentiality.

The Wolfsberg Group is continuing to evolve its guidelines.

EU initiatives

Introduction

8.8 The main elements of EU AML policy (the two AML Directives) come under internal market and comprise the 'first pillar' initiatives. Since the Amsterdam Treaty entered into force (1 May 1999) several key policy areas in the area of justice and home affairs, including organised crime, were moved from national level to EU level, and now comprise the third pillar' initiatives. The 'second pillar' deals with EU common foreign and security policy, so that EU legislation on terrorist financing, although strictly a 'first pillar' initiative, derives from 'second pillar' initiatives'.

The 1991 Directive

8.9   EC Money Laundering Directive 91/308/EEC was adopted on 16 June 1991. Its text is set out *in extenso* in *Butterworths Money Laundering Law* at. The EC Directive 91/308/EEC requires member states to prevent the use of their financial systems for money laundering. The Directive suggests three main steps to combat money laundering:

—   criminalise it;

—   take measures to identify laundered proceeds with a view to confiscation;

—   pass laws and establish systems to prevent the proceeds of crime being laundered in the first place.

The Directive also sets out requirements to be placed on financial businesses in the member states. This includes customer identification (KYC), and retention of records relating to identification and transactions for a period of five years. The Directive also requires member states to require such institutions to inform the authorities about suspected money laundering activity.

The FATF Annual Report on Typologies published on 1 February 2001, known as 'FATF-XII', (see 8.5) noted in its review of 2000–01 the anticipated expansion in the scope of the EU Directive (paragraph 37).

Extension of Directive

8.10   On 29 September 2000, the EU Council of Ministers voted to extend the AML rules in Directive 91/308/EEC (approved by the European Parliament on 5 April 2001) to cover all serious crimes, and 'to include notaries and other independent legal professionals (ie, lawyers) as well as accountants, auditors and other professionals' along with financial intermediaries.

This ties in to FATF initiatives, which had in tandem recommended including lawyers, notaries, accountants and other legal professionals (see further information on FATF-XII Typologies at 6.1 and 12.1). The KYC regime now extends to a broader range of businesses and professional or service activities, and no longer encompasses just 'financial businesses' as before.

As regards lawyers (legal professionals), the types of legal work that are now included within the scope of the Directive are:

—   Assisting in the planning or execution of transactions for a client concerning the:

  •   buying and selling of real property or business entities;

  •   managing of clients' money, securities or other assets;

  •   opening or management of bank, savings or securities accounts;

- • organisation of contributions necessary for the creation, operation or management of companies;

- • creation, operation or management of trusts, companies or similar structures.

— Acting on behalf of and for a client in any financial or real estate transaction.

The EU Commission was given a three-year delay to December 2003 to finalise the definition of serious crimes and criminal activities. 'Tax evasion' is not specifically included within the scope of the Directive, although the definition of 'criminal activity' is widely drafted, covering 'fraud, corruption or any other illegal activity'. Their final conclusions are still awaited at the date of publication of this book.

The European Commission is currently working on other EU initiatives in the AML area, including:

— a paper and recommendations on non-transparent financial and corporate structures in EU Member States, such as trusts and bearer share companies, where it is likely or possible these may obstruct international co-operation on AML; and

— a draft model agreement to form the basis of mutual assistance with third countries (such as the US) to combat money laundering, and covering *inter alia* exchange of information, suspension of banking secrecy, information on beneficial ownership, and freezing of assets. Once the EU Council adopts the model agreement it will authorise the opening of negotiations with third countries.

Chapter 9

Know-Your-Customer, Due Diligence and Compliance

Know-your-customer and due diligence

9.1   Since the events of 11 September 2001, lawmakers and regulators have significantly tightened up on their general anti-money laundering ('AML') policies and procedures as part of the exercise of eliminating the financial supports for terrorism. In the United Kingdom (and in the overseas dependencies and territories) it is now an absolute requirement for financial services and related businesses to be entirely clear that neither the *source* nor the *destination* of funds involves money laundering activity. This is not an easy task – a bit like looking for the proverbial needle in a haystack. A large bank might typically handle between 10,000 and 150,000 wire transfers per day. The enlargement of the scope of AML laws has been seen by some as simply making the haystack bigger (see 'Money laundering fight could hit the wrong targets' (2001) The Times, 2 October, www.thetimes.co.uk). It is a trite fact that it is often extremely difficult to make distinctions between good and bad customers or clients, and between acceptable or illicit transactions.

General requirements to 'know-your-customer' ('KYC') are an important element in this process. As a result, financial institutions both onshore and offshore, have for the last year or so been updating their KYC information. For example, in February 2002, Guernsey, Jersey and the Isle of Man announced new measures to strengthen their anti-money laundering regimes, the principal features of which are:

- to extend KYC requirements so that financial institutions are required to look beyond their direct customers (such as trusts and companies, as customers of banks and brokers) and identify the principals behind them;

- to tighten up due diligence procedures, in particular where the customer is referred by another institution; and

- to require financial institutions to embark upon a progressive risk prioritised programme to bring the records of existing customers up to current standards.

A joint position paper entitled 'Overriding principles for a revised KYC framework' was also issued, and is set out in APPENDIX 4. Also see the Guernsey Financial Services Commission website at www.gfsc.guernseyci.com

In the FSA discussion paper 'Reducing money laundering risk' (August 2003) the term 'identification' means the basic information (name and address) collected to meet the legal and regulatory identification requirements, while the term 'know-your-customer' or 'KYC' refers to the additional information (for example, occupation) that a firm may obtain for anti-money laundering risk management purposes.

For individuals this has been done by asking for passport copies (in a satisfactory form, as specified in *Kluwerpewrs' Passport Handbook*), and for proof of residence in the form of utility bills. Many institutions have forwarded detailed questionnaires for completion and return. APPENDIX 4 lists acceptable types of proof of address (a utility bill may be no more than proof of the place to where the bill is sent, and not of residency itself). The proposed Inland Revenue Guidance on implementing the EU Directive on the Taxation of Savings Income ('EUSD') contains detailed rules for establishing 'residence' for EUSD purposes, and in which the Inland Revenue state that 'the country of residence for tax purposes is not affected by these rules'. Such requirements will give some individuals difficulty if they have utility bills in the name of a company, or if they live in a country where the use of PO boxes is prevalent. Overall, the slavish demand for passports and gas bills has produced a high level of consumer irritation – and at the same time has probably failed to flush out a single al Qu'aeda supporter – but may just have succeeded in upsetting tax evaders facing the EUSD initiative.

When dealing with companies there is an important and immediately applicable distinction between public listed companies, and private unlisted companies. For public listed companies, no further evidence of identity is required if the company is listed on a recognised stock exchange, or is a subsidiary of such a listed company. For private unlisted companies, more detailed information is sought, requiring the identification of (and proof of residence items for) the principal shareholders. In some countries, this information may be obtainable through a search at the companies registry (companies house, etc) or register of commerce, where these are open to public inspection. There can be no indication in such registers if any shares are registered in nominee names, so this method is imperfect.

Many institutions have produces their own internal KYC checklists for individual or corporate clients and customers, in order to comply with the requirements of the Financial Services and Markets Act 2000 or similar applicable rules. A sample checklist is attached at APPENDIX 4.

In countries and jurisdictions where the registry is essentially private, the requirement to identify the influential shareholders or those who ultimately own and control the company may be less easy to satisfy to a level capable of extrinsic proof.

If two or more companies are involved in the chain of ownership, KYC requires 'piercing the veil' of all intermediate layers, so as to identify the individual(s) owner(s). The requirement essentially boils down to identifying one or more 'warm bodies' and obtaining the same identification and proof of residence items.

Finally, if a trust is included in the ownership structure, then it becomes necessary to identify both the *source* and the *destination* of the funds, in terms of both the settlor and the beneficiaries. Trusts and trustees are considered in more detail in 12.2.

In the private banking sector, The Wolfsberg AML Principles are of great assistance (see 8.6 and 8.7). On 30 October 2000, a group of the world's leading private banks published the 'Wolfsberg Anti-Money Laundering Principles' by way of their formal anti-money laundering policy statement. These global AML guidelines are aimed primarily at their international private bankers, including both relationship managers and those involved with fiduciary activities in the offshore havens. The Principles were drawn up in conjunction with Transparency International, the global anti-corruption organisation. The Principles were revised in May 2002, and the Wolfsberg Group's most recent statement on monitoring, screening and searching was published in September 2003. Their website, which can be found at www.wolfsberg-principles.com, also features a FAQ series on beneficial ownership, politically exposed persons and intermediaries. (See APPENDIX 3.)

Compliance

9.2   Anti-money laundering compliance is fundamental to the ongoing viability of a professional practice or a fiduciary business: it is mandatory, non-negotiable, and an integral part of any system of regulation or licensing supervision. Any institution connected with a money laundering scandal will certainly lose its good reputation in the market-place, whilst its licence will simply not be renewed in the face of blatant non-compliance. To help companies and professionals comply, a KYC range of products are published by Offshore Business News and Research Inc, see www.offshorealert.com

In the UK regulated sector, across-the-board compliance is essential in order to avoid conviction of the criminal offence (punishable by a maximum of two years' imprisonment and/ or a fine) of not maintaining the administrative procedures and staff training required under the Money Laundering Regulations (see CHAPTER 6: THE UK AML FRAMEWORK – THE MONEY LAUNDERING REGULATIONS AND GUIDANCE NOTES). This offence is capable of being committed *irrespective of* whether or not any substantive money laundering has taken place. As noted at 8.2, an AML conviction under ss 327–334 PoCA can occur even if there has been no conviction for the ultimate 'serious crime' from which the alleged 'proceeds' flowed. The situation is the same with the Regulations, in that non-compliance with the Regulations is a stand-alone offence.

As examples, the UK FSA has recently imposed substantial fines on financial institutions for AML offences. Royal Bank of Scotland was fined £750,000 in

December 2002, and Abbey National was fined £2,000,000 in December 2003. What is interesting about both of these cases was that, in imposing the fines, the Regulator specifically admitted that no actual money laundering had been detected, but that the fines were nevertheless being imposed as the two banks did not have adequate KYC and due diligence information concerning their customers' and their activities.

Risk-based approach

9.3   As noted above, the blanket collection of passport copies and two utility bills has led to a negative reaction. The latest Joint Money Laundering Steering Group ('JMLSG') *Guidance Notes* 2003 call for a risk-based approach, whereby each individual institution should assess the risk within their products and services, and tailor their AML procedures to reflect this evaluation. So it is hoped that banks etc will stop pestering their long-standing customers to 'prove their residential address' when in any event they have been sending such customers their own bank statements to their residential address for years, so, in the absence of a recent home move, the 'proof of residence' exists within their own database.

Another matter of concern is the possibility of a payment being mistakenly blocked, or a bank or investment account mistakenly frozen by a similarity in the name of the account owner and a name on the 'banned' list. For example, Yassin Quadi, a Saudi business had his UK assets frozen in October 2001 by the UK Treasury, he was then denied details or an explanation of the procedures to clear his name. This occurred in November 2001 in relation to three Islamic funds promoted by Pictet & Cie through their Luxembourg office, trading in which was halted by the Luxembourg authorities. For further information on the 'banned list' see www.ustreas.gov/offices/enforcement/ofac/sdn/index.html where the US Treasury Department's list of 'blocked persons' and specially designated name ('SDN') lists are available.

The spelling of Middle Eastern names can be a cause a problem as unfortunately there is no 'correct' equivalent spelling in English. Full Arabic names are often complex, and as there is no standard way of 'romanising' Arabic, one name can be rendered in English in many different ways.

A balance needs to be struck between requests for specific KYC information, and wider trawls for competitive or marketing information. For example, one UK bank that caters to some 16,000 racehorse owning customers, large numbers of whom are not based in the UK (at least from a domicile standpoint), sent a detailed questionnaire to its customers asking for details of marital status, residential status, other main bank accounts and credit cards held, employment details, income details, and details of their fixed monthly household expenditure: although the questions were asked in good faith in an effort to be ahead of the evolution of KYC requirements, many of their customers will simply have disregarded or returned the form incomplete, on grounds of intrusiveness.

Overall, therefore, a 'risk-based' approach is essential in order to create the AML regime where customer disruption is reduced to a minimum but intelligence value is raised to the maximum, and STR reports are a useful enforcement tool rather than just defensive bureaucracy. After all, the AML laws are government led, and their purpose is to catch AML offenders.

Blacklists and databases

9.4 In this context, blacklists and databases should be of great assistance in providing some sort of negative clearance on customers and clients. However, security concerns at government level, and data protection concerns at the private level, mean that practitioners and professionals are all but on their own when it comes to identifying potential AML offenders.

In terms of international transactions, a useful only publicly available blacklist is the FATF list of 'Non-Cooperative Countries and Territories' (a copy of which is included in the Appendix at A3.2). This provides a presumption that a transaction or payment involving a blacklisted country is automatically suspicious.

As far as concerns KYC and transactions of individuals and companies, at present the relevant databases are almost all owned and maintained by governments, and thus not available to or accessible by the private sector. It is thus particularly galling for the private sector to be made legally responsible on the one hand for monitoring and controlling AML prevention, while on the other hand being denied access to the very databases of information that would enable professionals etc to enquire as to a given individual or company's background. Governments and regulators have such tools at their own disposal. This is not a very level information or enforcement playing field, and results in the practitioner or professional being squeezed as the 'piggy in the middle'.

Some specialist companies have started to address this issue. On 16 July 2002 a consortium of big Wall Street and European financial businesses announced the set up of Regulatory DataCorp International whose new system, called GRID (the Global Regulatory Information Database) draws information from more than 20,000 sources worldwide. It is interesting to note that RDI has been operating since July 2003, while in contrast a 2002 initiative between financial institutions in Hong Kong to share customer data was cancelled on the grounds of data protection. For more information see www.citigroup.com/citigroup/press/020716b.htm

Whilst such an initiative is potentially extremely useful, it still raises other concerns:

— To be truly useful, the information needs to be available to those in the industry as a whole. It is unclear who will be able to gain access and at what price. The private sector would benefit enormously from the information in avoiding being tainted by a genuine corruption case.

— The information must be of pinpoint accuracy. It is not difficult to imagine a payment being held up and a commercial opportunity or contractual obligation missed simply through a name being (wrongly as it might turn out) linked on such a database to being a business associate or even a relative of a government official.

— The issue of remedies for error become important. It is unclear whether individuals should have the right to inspect their entries and correct errors.

— There is an obvious issue of data protection and access to overcome. Data protection legislation has already been in place for several years, whilst human rights legislation is a more recent phenomenon. Data protection principles must be observed just as strictly, and should prevent any form of unauthorised access.

There are also some private database services available. These include 'BEST-AML' software which cross-references to *Worldcheck* (see www.isys.ch/products/prods/aml_f.html) and *complinet* (see info@complinet.com – 14 day trial available to Society of Trust and Estate (STEP) members) which links to their KYC Check (in turn linked to the FSA, SEC and FBI databases However, their user subscriptions tend to be set at levels that make them attractive only to the larger institution.

As far as concerns politically sensitive persons (PSPs), the Director General of the JFSC proposed in July 2001 that banks and other institutions *should* have access to databases detailing at least the identity of ministers and senior public officials, and listing friends and associates of politicians in corrupt regimes. Again, this is in the category of excellent ideas, and Regulatory DataCorp International is assembling just such a list covering virtually every country in the world.

Proliferation of government databases

9.5   The brave new world of Regulatory DataCorp International will herald in an era of tighter enforcement, but this will likely be coupled with confusion and hard cases along the way.

The cancellation of BA 223 (and several Air France flights) just before Christmas 2003 and again in early February 2004 was initially justified as based on 'extremely detailed and explicit intelligence' provided to the French by the United States. However, in the pre-Christmas alert, the passenger suspected of being a Tunisian radical turned out to be a child who coincidentally shared the same name (see 9.3).

The United States, and no doubt other countries, regulatory agencies have so far been reluctant to coordinate their efforts. But the Homelands Security initiative that began in the US in January 2004 and involves foreign visitors to the US being photographed and fingerprinted, will lead to a 'searchable and integrated' master list of suspects, known as 'Tipoff'. This will be integrated with databases maintained by the FBI, the CIA, several Pentagon departments and other US Government bureaus.

The era of 'Big Brother' is clearly now approaching fast!

Chapter 10

Reporting Procedures

Introduction and reporting statistics

10.1   As noted in CHAPTER 9: KNOW-YOUR-CLIENT, DUE DILIGENCE AND COMPLIANCE, there are profound potential criminal and public relations risks for employees, professionals and financial institutions themselves in committing an offence of money laundering. The statutory procedure for obtaining exoneration from the principal anti-money laundering ('AML') offences appears straightforward, involving nothing more than the filing of a suspicious activity report (or SAR). On this basis one might think that the authorities would have been inundated with SARs.

However, over the last two years, the National Criminal Intelligence Service ('NCIS') (www.ncis.co.uk) has repeatedly criticised UK professionals for their alleged failure to ensure that their clients are honest people dealing with legitimate funds. From an initial 18,400 SARs in 2000, the numbers have steadily increased (to 31,250 in 2001, to 63,000 in 2002, and over 100,000 SARs in 2003). The significant jump in 2003 followed the coming into force of Proceeds of Crime Act (PoCA) 2002 in February 2003, and the Second EU Money Laundering Directive in June 2003 (see also the KPMG Report *Money Laundering: Review of the Reporting System*, prepared for NCCIS and published 1 July 2003, available in full on the NCIS website). After 1 March 2004, when UK Solicitors, Accountants and other 'relevant businesses' (see 6.1) became subject to the Money Laundering Regulations 2003, the rate of SAR reporting is likely to experience a huge jump. But despite that, overall numbers of SARs are small in relation to the number of financial professionals and activities/transactions in any twelve-month-period.

There is no doubt that many banks have been panicked into making large numbers of unnecessary 'defensive' SARs. But NCIS notes that of the 31,250 SARs in 2001 only 1% were from solicitors and only 0.35% from accountants. The Law Society has stated publicly that some city firms of solicitors are being used by money launderers, but expected reporting by solicitors to increase as firms become more diligent. Property/conveyancing departments of law firms are now within the AML net, current high valuation levels in the UK property market may in part be a result of money laundering activity through this sector (see 'The UK threat of serious and organised crime' NCIS Report 2003).

Know-your-client information and client reporting

10.2   While the know-your-client ('KYC') and due diligence process requires a proactive investigative role, it does not as such turn a professional into an informer – this only arises if a SAR is required.

In a suspicious activity report the professional's role is reactive, as an informant, and is probably subjective. The client is uninformed and is non-participative, and must be kept unaware because of the tipping-off rules.

There is an inherent conflict between a professional acting with professional confidentiality, and him/her filing a SAR. This conflict is explored more fully in CHAPTER 11: ISSUES FACING PROFESSIONALS AND PRACTITIONERS.

A solution to this is to make the prospective client aware at the 'prospect' stage of the possibility of a report being filed in the future, based on any future concerns, suspicions etc. Perhaps this is prudent; perhaps it is daydreaming. Some clients will accept the discussion and move along with their planning. Other clients will get up and leave.

The reporting process and procedures

10.3   Every professional firm, financial institution and fiduciary business is required to have a Money Laundering Reporting Officer ('MLRO'). This person should be sufficiently senior to command authority, and have considerable practical experience in the business.

The MLRO must also ensure that each relevant employee (meaning those employees who are in the areas of business relating to customers and their activities) knows:

—   who the MLRO is;

—   to whom he/she should report suspicions; and

—   that there is a clear reporting chain under which those suspicions will be passed without delay to the MLRO.

The internal reporting form should encourage employees to be as detailed as possible, even if their comments are wholly subjective.

If an employee makes a report to the MLRO, he/she is discharged from further individual responsibility under ss 337, 338, 339 PoCA 2002.

The MLRO or institution then has to determine whether or not to make a formal SAR. If after completing a review of the activity/ies reported (including discussions with the individual employee(s) concerned) the MLRO decides that the initial report does indeed give rise to a knowledge or suspicion of money laundering, then the MLRO must disclose this information to the appropriate law enforcement agency.

It is presumably open to an employee to 'go direct' if he/she is aware that the MLRO has not followed up, although such a course could be career altering.

Such a course would not be necessary in relation to the PoCA offences, but could still provide valuable protection in the case of common law AML crimes (see 10.4 below).

Within the UK, disclosure of suspicions should be made in the first instance to the financial unit of NCIS (www.ncis.co.uk). The financial unit is staffed by police and customs (inland revenue) officers. All disclosures must be made in a standard format, and NCIS has developed a web-based reporting system both to standardise reports and accelerate procedures. APPENDIX 5.2 sets out the two NCIS report disclosure templates (the 'Limited Intelligence Report' and the 'Standard Report') which are also available on the NCIS website.

NCIS provide technical support to financial services relating to SARs, and advice and assistance on reporting suspicions of money laundering. Interested persons should contact the Economic Crime Branch duty desk (during UK office hours) on +44 20 7238 8282 or 8607.

There can be no objection to the MLRO consulting outside professional legal advisors in reaching his/her conclusion as to whether to report. However, the advice of prudence will invariably be 'when in doubt, report'.

As noted at 3.5, it is a complete defence to the principal PoCA offences for the employee in question, and by extension his/her employer, to have reported his/her knowledge or suspicion.

However filing an SAR does *not* provide a defence, either to employee or the institution, in relation to AML offences arising as a result of common law offences such as fraud, false accounting or cheating the revenue, or the inchoate offences of conspiring or inciting, or aiding and abetting, counselling or procuring. Herein lies a dilemma – in the light of *P v P [2003] EWHC 2260 (Fam)* (see 11.4 and APPENDIX 6) it is unlikely that a court would be very sympathetic with an employer institution who failed to report externally, even if the employee who reported internally would have evidence justifying his/her exoneration.

Two-tier reporting

10.4   At the end of January 2004, the ICAEW announced that they had has been influential in advising NCIS to introduce abbreviated reporting for crimes of 'lesser intelligence value', reducing the burdens on those reporting money laundering.

In consultation with the Consultative Committee of Accountancy Bodies, the ICAEW called for two-tier reporting to help compensate for the lack of *de minimis* provisions in the legislation. The two-tier system recommended was introduced by the NCIS on 1 March 2004, and allows those reporting crimes of lesser intelligence value to fill in a shorter, less time-consuming form.

Consent or otherwise

10.5   The NCIS will acknowledge to the reporting business their receipt of the disclosure (SAR).

Section 335 PoCA requires NCIS to give or refuse *consent* within seven days. In most cases NCIS will give the reporting business their written *consent* to continue, or if NCIS have not responded within seven days, such *consent* is deemed to have been given.

In the case of the reporting business being a professional firm, the *consent* relates to continuing to process the particular transaction or activity. In the case of the reporting business being a bank, a fiduciary business, or other financial institution, the *consent* relates to continuing to operate the account or relationship.

In exceptional cases the reporting business will not receive such *consent*. In such a case, the information disclosed in the SAR will be allocated to trained professionals in Her Majesty's Customs and Excise ('HMC&E') or in the relevant Regional Crime Squad. Either of the latter will then follow up with the MLRO of the reporting business, and probably also with the individual employee(s) concerned. However, if NCIS do refuse to give *consent*, then for the 31-day-period from the date of the refusal the transaction or arrangement *may not* be proceeded with without the reporting business being at risk of committing an AML offence. Only at the end of this 'moratorium period' may the reporting business continue freely.

In 2002, a new multi-agency initiative was launched: the Concerted Inter-Agency Criminal Finances Action Group (CICFA), chaired by HMC&E, aims to improve the UK's response to the financial aspects of crime, particularly the recovery of criminal assets and the detection and prevention of money laundering. It is looking *inter alia* to capitalise on PoCA and the creation of the Assets Recovery Agency. CICFA members include the Association of Chief Police Officers (ACPO), the National Crime Squad and NCIS.

In other jurisdictions, in particular offshore financial centres, the position in terms of obtaining *consent* may be by no means as clear cut. Time frames and time limits are central to the UK system. If a different jurisdiction does not have corresponding time frames and time limits, then practical difficulties will ensue.

This was indeed the case in the recent offshore trust in Jersey involving the State of Qatar (see 12.5). That litigation began in July 2000, when the trustees filed an SAR, and continued until the day the Iraq war broke out in March 2003. There were concerns as to corruption arising by way of commissions paid to three Jersey trusts by arms companies. There were also concerns that the trust fund might properly be held on constructive trust for the State of Qatar, rather than for the individual beneficiaries of the trusts in question.

In response to an application brought by Sheikh Hamad (the then Foreign Minister of Qatar) as beneficiary of the trusts, the Royal Court apparently declared on 17 May 2001 that there was no breach of fiduciary duty owed to the State of Qatar, and no constructive trust in favour of the State of Qatar, or any other person.

This decision might have been expected to resolve matters, but the trustees were caught on the horns of a dilemma as they had made an SAR, but had not received any form of *consent* from the Jersey police. In fact the police were unwilling (ie, had refused) to grant *consent* to any distribution from the trusts at what was said to be an early stage of a complex enquiry. The effect of the police refusal to grant *consent* was to paralyse the administration of the trusts, and to expose the trustees to liability for breach of trust.

In around July 2001, Sheikh Hamad made a second application, seeking directions from the court 'that will enable the trustees to resume the administration of (the trusts) in accordance with their terms within such a time and to such an extent as may be reasonable in all the circumstances of the case'. The Jersey Attorney-General objected to this application, contending that it would be contrary to public policy to grant the Order sought, because the Sheikh's clear collateral purpose was to use any declaration granted to hinder any criminal investigation and any subsequent criminal proceedings (presumably by asking the trustees to transfer the trust assets out of Jersey). See 12.5 for a wider discussion of this litigation.

Indemnity

10.6   The reporting business may seek an indemnity from any possible law suit for breach of confidentiality instigated in the future by its customer of client in respect of whom the SAR was made. In order to obtain an indemnity, the reporting business should request a production order from the NCIS investigating team.

This issue is of course of extreme importance to professionals and practitioners, and is considered in greater detail in CHAPTER 11: ISSUES FACING PROFESSIONALS AND PRACTITIONERS and CHAPTER 12: ISSUES FACING TRUSTEES AND EXECUTORS.

According to NCIS, in the event the SAR leads to a criminal prosecution of the client or customer of the reporting business, the source of the SAR (ie, the identity of the reporting business) is protected. How much weight can in practice be attached to this promise remains to be seen, as some of the recent cases on SARs indicate that the identity of the parties may be revealed sooner rather than never.

Chapter 11

Issues Facing Professionals and Practitioners

Introduction

11.1   Anti-money laundering laws ('AML') and procedures have entirely changed the position of professionals and practitioners in terms of their traditional duty of confidentiality towards their clients.

Through being thrust to the forefront of AML's 'privatised' law enforcement initiatives aimed at stamping out money laundering by third parties, professionals and practitioners now for the first time ever, face an array of potential criminal offences, including both offences of commission and offences of omission, for the ultimate acts of other people, whether or not clients.

The know-your-client ('KYC') and due diligence processes are central to this, coupled with the requirement to file an suspicious activity report ('SAR') where knowledge or suspicion of an AML offence arises. As noted in 10.3, the KYC and due diligence process requires a proactive investigative role. The professional or practitioner becomes an informer where an SAR is required, while the client must be kept unaware because of the tipping-off rules.

Part of the solution now is to make prospective clients clearly aware at the 'prospect' stage that public duties now outweigh the duty of confidentiality: and probably also for existing clients (possibly advised by circular letter or notice attached to the next fee note). Thus, they need to be made aware of the possibility of an SAR being filed in the future, based on any future suspicions, etc relating either to the prospective client or indeed to third parties with whom the prospective client is (or was) engaged in a transaction. Such a procedure is prudent. Most prospective clients (and existing clients) will accept the discussion as not applicable to them, and will move along with their requirements. If the occasional prospect or client just ups and leaves, then the professional or practitioner may have succeeded in avoiding a problem further down the road.

Thus it may be prudent to include specific wording in the client care letter (or standard terms and conditions of business), stating clearly the position of the professional or practitioner in this regard.

In his recent article ('Self-Preservation v Professionalism' [2002] NLJ 11 October), English Barrister David Dabbs notes that the UK Parliament has now turned the 'gatekeepers' (a term coined used to describe accountants, lawyers, notaries and other professionals) into 'amateur detectives, expected now to actively participate in the detection and prevention of crime'.

Mr Dabbs has included in his article sample paragraphs for a client care letter. These read as follows:

'Under this retainer we shall abide by our professional duty to keep secret and in strict confidence information received from you concerning your personal, financial or other circumstances. We shall not disclose such information to any person without your consent; save where we have reached the conclusion (whether justified or not) that this information ("incriminating information") implies that you are, or were once, engaged in criminal activity of a kind proscribed by law. In such circumstances, we shall be entitled to conclude that our duty to the public outweighs our duty of confidence to you; and we reserve the right to disclose incriminating information to the proper authorities for the sake of our duty to comply with the law.

In such circumstances, either such disclosure will not amount to a breach of our duty of confidence; alternatively, in so far as such disclosure might otherwise amount to a breach, save where malice is proved, we will accept no liability whatsoever for any loss or damage, direct or indirect, and howsoever occasioned (death or serious injury aside) as a result of such disclosure'.

Interestingly, senior English solicitor John Rhodes of Macfarlanes attached as an appendix to his conference papers (*Reporting Suspicious Transactions* for the Offshore Trust and Tax Planning Summit, Miami, 23 October 2002) a letter to clients setting out the position in relation to legal professional privilege, foreign tax evasion and the effect of the (then anticipated) Proceeds of Crime Act 2002 (PoCA). His concluding paragraph wisely counselled, 'I suggest that we arrange to speak later on this week if you have any further questions arising from this analysis'.

Professional privilege and confidentiality – general position

11.2   It is helpful to review briefly the general position in terms of professional privilege and confidentiality, and then highlight how the AML laws (especially PoCA and *P v P*) have altered this.

There is an absolute privilege as to communications between a lawyer and a client in relation to legal proceedings, whereby information is inadmissible in evidence in a court of law, and the judge will not allow it to be elicited. As regards what is known as 'legal professional privilege', the key feature is that a communication passing between lawyer and client conveying legal advice or relating to the conduct of on-going litigation need not be given in evidence or disclosed by the client and, without the client's consent, may not be given in evidence or disclosed by the legal adviser. This especially covers anything disclosed to a lawyer in the context of a retainer to defend the client of a particular criminal offence.

The scope of legal professional privilege is broad (see P O'Hagan's article on the English Court of Appeal case *Barclays Bank v Eustice [1995] 4 All ER 511* in Private Client Business ([1997] PCB 131). Also see *Canada Trust Co v Century Holdings BVI July 1998, 1 ITELR 056*), in that it can also extend as between lawyer and client to legal advice outside the context of on-going litigation.

In the UK there is a statutory formulation of the privilege in the Police and Criminal Evidence Act 1984, s 10(1), which provides that:

'(1)   Subject to subsection (2) below in this Act "items subject to legal privilege" means:

  (a)   Communications between a professional legal adviser and his client or any person representing his client made in connection with the giving of legal advice to the client;

  (b)   Communications between a professional legal adviser and his client or any person representing his client or between such an adviser or his client or any such representative and any other person made in connection with or in contemplation of legal proceedings and for the purpose of such proceedings; and

  (c)   Items enclosed with or referred to in such communications and made:

    (i)   In connection with the giving of legal advice; or

    (ii)   In connection with or in contemplation of legal proceedings and for the purpose of such proceedings; when they arc in the possession of a person who is entitled to possession of them'.

This section has been authoritatively stated to reproduce the common law of the UK (see Lord Goff in *R v Central Criminal Court, ex p Francis and Francis [1989] AC 346* and *Cross and Tapper on Evidence* (9th edn, 2003) Butterworths).

The professional duty of confidentiality is (or was) the essence of a lawyer's function. The Law Society's *Guide to Professional Conduct* declares confidentiality to be 'a primary and fundamental right and duty of the lawyer' (Principle 2.3.2).

In the recent House of Lords case *Prince Jefry Bolkiah v KPMG [1999] 2 AC 222*, the professional duty of confidentiality was considered in detail. Lord Hope stated that it '... extends well beyond that of refraining from deliberate disclosure ...'. And Lord Millett said (at p 236):

'It is of overriding importance to the proper administration of justice that a client should be able to have complete confidence that what he tells his solicitor will remain secret. This is a matter of perception as well as substance.' See *Koch Shipping v Richards Butler [2002] Lloyd's Rep PN 201.*

In the more recent House of Lords Case *R v Special Comrs & Anor ex p Morgan Grenfell [2002] UKHL 21* Lord Hoffmann restated that 'the policy of legal professional privilege requires that the client should be secure in the knowledge that protected documents and information will not be disclosed at all'.

It should be noted that a common law 'crime/fraud exception' has existed for some decades. This is referred to in paragraphs 4.12–4.14 of the *Money Laundering: Guidance for Solicitors (Pilot January 2004)*.

As is demonstrated in 11.3 below, the PoCA and its aftermath has very much changed the rules.

Professional privilege and confidentiality issues post PoCA

11.3   Although the 'crime/fraud exception, (see 11.2) has existed for some decades, the concept of a 'statutory exception' to the common law professional duty of confidentiality is entirely the result of AML legislation. It started with the Drug Trafficking Act 1994, and was expanded, first of all by the Terrorism Act 2000 (as amended), and more recently by ss 337 and 338 PoCA.

Sections 331 and 332 PoCA create offences of failure of a Money Laundering Reporting Officer ('MLRO') (whether or not in the regulated sector) to disclose to the authorities any knowledge or reasonable suspicion of the client's receipt or dealing in the proceeds of any of the scheduled offences – see 3.2 and also 11.5 below in relation to 'authorised disclosure' under s 338 and 'protected disclosure' under s 337 PoCA.

The Money Laundering Regulations 2003 (see CHAPTER 6: THE UK AML FRAMEWORK – THE MONEY LAUNDERING REGULATIONS AND GUIDANCE NOTES) have extended the definition of 'relevant financial business' so that solicitors and accountants are now subject to these provisions. They also now apply to those engaged in investment business, to tax advisers (persons 'providing tax advice'), and to trustees (see CHAPTER 12: ISSUES FACING TRUSTEES AND EXECUTORS). Thus, the duty of confidentiality is no longer an absolute, but is outweighed by an overriding positive duty to the state, to protect the public interest.

Just as s 330(10) PoCA contains an exception for the need to report privileged information, Regulation 7(3) of the Money Laundering Regulations 2003 (see 6.1) also provides that the obligation to report to the MLRO does not apply where the person carrying on the relevant business is a professional legal adviser, and the knowledge or suspicion is based on information or some other matter which came to him in privileged circumstances.

However, as s 330(11) excludes from the 'privilege defence' information or other matters which are communicated or given with the intention of furthering a criminal purpose, Regulation 7(5) contains similar provisions which restrict the operation of privilege. Privilege has always been vitiated by a criminal purpose, and it is the purpose of the person whom communicates the information (which need not be shared by the person receiving it) which is important – see *R v Central Criminal Court, ex p Francis and Francis [1989] 1 AC 346*. This means that before a lawyer can decide not to report knowledge or suspicion, on the grounds of privilege, he will have to first satisfy himself as to the reason he was given the information.

This overriding duty to the state is reflected in The Law Society's *Guide to Professional Conduct* which allows a solicitor to report his client to the authorities rather than be dragged into providing assistance in the perpetration of a crime (see Principle 16.02).

Thus, while these may be more of a concern to solicitors than accountants, there is a general concern within both professions in the apparent conflict created by the AML legislation in requiring disclosure by a SAR of details a client's affairs where the professional has concerns as to AML issues.

Non-disclosure is not a practical option, as there are severe penalties for such a course of action or inaction.

It is perhaps a result of the UK not having a written constitution that has allowed such a long-standing common law principle effectively to be swept aside. See in contrast two recent Canadian cases where the statutory AML provisions requiring disclosure were themselves held to be unconstitutional. See Canadian Supreme Court in *Lavalee Rackel and Heintz v Canada (A-G) [2002] SCC 61, 12 September 2002*; also British Columbia Supreme Court in *Law Society of British Columbia v A-G of Canada [2000] BC Supreme Court 1593*.

Robert Pang v Comr of Police 2 December 2002 (unreported) is an important Hong Kong case in relation to issues of legal professional privilege. The applicant, a well-known barrister, sought four Declarations, and obtained two, in the context of his arrest under s 25A(1) Organised and Serious Crimes Ordinance ('OSCO'). The declarations sought were in the following terms:

— that on the true construction of s 25A of OSCO, it does not cover information and communications communicated to counsel which are covered by legal professional privilege when taking instructions and rendering legal advice (Declaration granted);

— further or alternatively, that s 25A of OSCO, insofar as it relates to information and communications communicated to counsel which are covered by legal professional privilege contravenes articles 35, 39 and 87 of the Basic Law and article 14 of the International Covenant on Civil and Political Rights 1996 (Declaration not granted);

— further or in the further alternative, that s 25A of OSCO, insofar as it requires a barrister of Hong Kong to disclose any matters which are covered by legal professional privilege contravenes articles 35, 39 and 87 of the basic law and article 14 of the International Covenant on Civil and Political Rights 1996 (Declaration not granted); and

— that the arrest and detention of the applicant on 14 March 2002 was arbitrary and unlawful (Declaration granted).

P v P

11.4   The landmark case of *P v P [2003] EWHC 2260 (Fam), [2003] 4 All ER 843* was decided on the 8th October 2003 in the UK High Court (Family Division). The factual background was relatively simple, concerning matrimonial proceedings where in the course of the negotiations on financial relief for the wife, her solicitors became aware via the husband's disclosures, that part of his substantial assets were derived from untaxed income. As such, the wife's solicitors became concerned that they might be committing an offence under s 328 PoCA. The judgement is set out in full in APPENDIX 6 and is required reading.

Two main issues arose in the proceedings:

— whether and in what circumstances it is permitted to act in relation to an arrangement; and

— whether and in what circumstances a legal adviser, having made an authorised disclosure, is permitted to tell others of the fact that he/she has done so.

The judgment of the President of the Family Division, Dame Justice Butler-Sloss, contains valuable guidance on a number of vexed issues, including:

● the extent to which a solicitor handling a divorce case for a client might come within the ambit of s 328 PoCA (arrangements etc) in relation to a proposed financial settlement where part of the funds had not been declared for tax;

● whether the facts should be disclosed to National Criminal Intelligence Service ('NCIS') in the form of a SAR;

● the seeking of a consent order under s 335 PoCA;

● that there is no professional privilege exemption under ss 327, 328 or 329 PoCA (although there is under s 330(6)(b)); and

● that ss 333 and 342 PoCA provide an exemption from the offence of 'tipping-off' where the mere fact of the SAR would suffice to tip off the client.

Because of the importance of the issues raised in relation both to SAR disclosures, and to the conflicting issues of disclosure thereof versus the 'tipping-off' provisions in PoCA, a number of third parties to the matrimonial proceedings intervened in the case by way of written submissions, namely NCIS, both The Law Society and The Bar Council, and the Inland Revenue.

In paragraph 64 of the judgment the judge discusses the provisions of ss 333 and 342 PoCA in relation to the duty of disclosure and the effect of tipping-off a client:

'Sections 333 and 342 specifically recognise a legal adviser's duty in ordinary circumstances to make the relevant disclosures, even where the result would be to tip off their client, where to do so would fall within the ambit of being in connection with the giving of legal advice or with legal proceedings actual or contemplated. A central element of advising and representing a client must be, in my view, the duty to keep one's client informed and not to withhold information from him/her. (See *Halsbury's Law of England*, above). Since the function of the Act is to regulate the proceeds of criminal behaviour, it is clear that in every circumstance where a solicitor believes an authorised disclosure to the NCIS is necessary there will be at least a suspicion of criminal purpose. If, as the NCIS suggests, sections 333(4) and 324(5) bite every time a party who is suspected of holding a criminal purpose is given notice that a disclosure has been or will be made to the NCIS (ie, "is tipped-off"), then the legal professional exemptions in sections 333(3) and 324(4) would be rendered meaningless. Sections 333(4) and 342(5) must have some purpose and the interpretation suggested by the NCIS cannot in my view be correct. The exemption is lost if a disclosure to a client is made "with the intention of furthering a criminal purpose". The natural meaning of those words would seem to be clear. The approach which the House of Lords took to the word "held" in *Francis* should not be transposed into this context in relation to the word "made", nor would it be necessary or proper to attempt to do so. Whereas the purpose of holding documents can be tainted by the intention of any number of people (including client and third parties), the intention of a legal adviser in choosing to make a disclosure would seem to belong to the adviser alone. The context and purpose of this particular section of the PoCA is distinguishable from that in *Francis,* not least because the PoCA has specifically underlined the duty of disclosure by legal advisers'.

The Judge also found (para 56) that there is no distinction between degrees of criminal property, whether the illegally obtained sum is ten or a million pounds.

'Whatever may be the resource implications, the legal profession would appear to be bound by the provisions of the Act in all cases, however big or small.'

An article published on 10th October 2003 by the legal correspondent of *The Times* commented that, according to a number of practitioners, PoCA '… now appears to reach far beyond its original purpose, and needs to have its scope restricted'.

Confidentiality issues, conflicts and reporting – post *P v P*

11.5   As noted at 6.1, the Money Laundering Regulations 2003 were published in November 2003, and are generally in force as of 1st March 2004 (although certain activities come into force on later dates) The new Regulations apply to every 'relevant business', which broadly includes lawyers (Regulation 2(2)(l)), accountants (Regulation 2(2)(j)) and tax advisors (Regulation 2(2)(i)).

As a result of *P v P*, The Law Society of England and Wales, which intervened in the case by way of written submissions, has provided detailed clarification on the case in paras 4.59 to 4.81 of the *Money Laundering: Guidance for Solicitors (Pilot January 2004)*.

In an appendix to the judgment, NCIS gave guidance in guidance in relation to disclosures by the legal profession:

'Part 7 Proceeds of Crime Act 2002

12. The NCIS would wish the legal profession to note that subject to s 333(4), under s 333(3) PoCA there is no restriction on the legal advisor informing any person of the fact that they have made a report to the NCIS if such a disclosure is to a client or his representative in connection with the giving of legal advice to the client or the disclosure is made in connection with legal proceedings or contemplated legal proceedings.

Part 8 Proceeds of Crime Act 2002

However, if a legal advisor takes the view that he should inform his client (or any other person) of a disclosure to the NCIS, then he must also have regard to s 342. The section provides that if a person including a legal advisor at least suspecting that a person responsible for investigation under the Act is acting or proposing to act in connection with a confiscation, money laundering or civil recovery investigation which is being or is about to be conducted the offence of prejudicing an investigation is made out if a disclosure is made which is likely to prejudice such an investigation, whether or not there has been a disclosure to the NCIS. The legal advisor will note the defence contained in s 342(3) which permits disclosures to a client or to any person in connection with legal proceedings or the giving of legal advice. This would have to be borne in mind when considering whether or not it was necessary to inform a client or another person of a disclosure whether actual or contemplated'.

Thus, the overall position is finely balanced, and there may be further changes if the Solicitors Family Law Association's challenge to *P v P* is successful.

Constructive trust issues

11.6   Of great importance is the issue of a professional/practitioner or fiduciary being found liable as a constructive trustee, and having to return (or reimburse) funds after the event to their 'proper' owner.

In an ideal world, adequate know-your-customer and due diligence procedures would highlight the most blatant cases of a so-called client in fact dealing with property belonging to another. But it would be naïve to think that all such cases can be prevented from the outset.

And the AML reporting regime does not assist in exonerating a professional/ practitioner or fiduciary against this risk area; constructive trusteeship arises through application of trust law and principles of equity, and has nothing to do with money laundering as such. The two issues only overlap where funds that are found to be subject to a constructive trust are at the same time identified as having passed under the possession or control of the 'client' through some fraud or deception practiced on the true owner. At that stage money laundering issues arise, and a suspicious transaction report is appropriate.

Note that the NCIS disclosure template has at its data box at top left an item entitled 'constructive trust'.

Constructive trusts are discussed more fully at 12.5.

Prosecutions and cautionary tales

11.7 The 'all crimes' nature of the AML offences under PoCA 2002 (and in many of the offshore jurisdictions) should simplify prosecution procedures. However, to date there have been few prosecutions or convictions for money laundering offences on a stand-alone basis. Law enforcement agencies prefer to prosecute the more substantive related crime (eg, drug trafficking etc), and are understandably reluctant to get involved in the complexities of pure AML offences. This may be due to a combination of factors, including under-resourcing, and local political sensitivities in having the local Regional Crime Squad being seen to prioritise tackling higher profile street crimes. Nevertheless there are already a number of cautionary tales for practitioners.

Recently an English solicitor, Jonathan Duff, was imprisoned for six months by the Manchester Crown Court for the AML offence of failing to report his suspicion in relation to money paid to his firm by a commercial client who was then convicted of drug trafficking. Duff did take independent advice in relation to reporting suspicion, but evidently decided that he had no such reportable suspicion. His misunderstanding may have been based on ambiguous wording in the statute, but despite accepting his was a genuine mistake of law, the judge sent Duff to prison for his act of omission.

As noted at 8.5, a recent article in the Journal of International Trust and Corporate Planning (Ryan Myint, 'Solicitors Beware: Money Laundering after R v Duff' [2003] Vol 10 No 2) analyses the *Duff* case. The article merits a careful read. However, two points in the case stand out as curious:

- the transactions which Duff failed to report involved some highly suspicious circumstances, but Duff seems to have missed all of the warning signals; and

- Duff was prosecuted under s 52(1) Drug Trafficking Act 1994, which provided that a person who fails to disclose knowledge or suspicion of drug money laundering is guilty of an offence (PoCA introduces a similar offence, but on an 'all crimes' basis). Neither the trial judge nor the Court of Appeal clarified why the s 52(2) exception did not apply to Duff. Section 52(2) provides an exception to s 52(1) where the information came to the professional legal advisor in privileged circumstances. Clearly, therefore, there must not have been any element of 'legal advice' being given.

In the United States a Miami lawyer, Donald Ferguson, was sentenced to over two years' imprisonment for AML offences for accepting a client's legal fees from a friend of the client who was involved in the Cali, Colombia, drug cartels. The court showed that Ferguson knew or should have known that the money came from illegal activity, even though his own client was not part of the cartels, and the money was paying for legitimate legal services. Ferguson was disbarred.

Also in the United States, former English solicitor Andrew Rutherford is awaiting trial, following his extradition (Law Society Gazette [2003] 25 April). Mr Rutherford has been indicted for money laundering in 1999, and is accused of violating securities, banking and tax laws, and using corporations which he had set up in offshore jurisdictions, which are alleged to be 'bogus', on the grounds presumably that themselves or their business transactions might be susceptible to a successful 'sham' attack.

There will often be cases where an AML offence will automatically arise in consequence of conviction of a predicate offence – even though, as noted at 8.2, a conviction for the predicate offence is not required to support an AML prosecution. This might include Heidi Fleiss (who spent 21 months in prison for conspiracy, tax evasion and money laundering); or Benazir Bhutto who received a six-month suspended prison sentence in Switzerland for laundering 11 million dollars through Swiss accounts. However, it is noteworthy that AML prosecutions do not seem to have followed.

Chapter 12

Issues Facing Trustees and Executors

Introduction

12.1 By way of introduction and background, it is clear from many of the international initiatives of supranational organisations such as Financial Action Task Force ('FATF') and the Organisation for Economic Co-operation and Development ('OECD') over the last few years' that offshore trusts (and offshore companies) are regarded as having a high degree of risk from a money laundering standpoint. This may in part result from the fact that structures involving trusts and companies are often complex and difficult to understand. Thus, they also require greater initial know-your-client (KYC) work by institutions to identify beneficiaries and controllers (see 12.3).

In evidence of this point paragraph 29 of the FATF 'Report on Money Laundering Typologies 2000–2001' published on 1 February 2001, states:

> '29. This year's typologies exercise was the first to focus on trusts as another legal mechanism that could be misused for money laundering purposes. In many ways, this use is similar to and associated with the role of corporate entities and company formation agents discussed in earlier typologies studies. Consequently, the actions proposed by the experts this year for dealing with trusts should also be viewed in the larger context of confronting the misuse of all legal mechanisms for money laundering purposes, increasing transparency with regard to such formations, more closely ensuring the integrity of the professionals involved in the creation of these mechanisms, and working toward some universal standards that could preclude the establishment of systems in certain jurisdictions that facilitate and protect such misuse'.

Offshore structures certainly can be used to enable (or assist) people to hide income and assets, just as motor vehicles can be used to kill – although that is not the primary purpose of either. Private offshore companies such as an international business corporation ('IBC') can provide highly effective vehicles for criminals to hide the proceeds of crime of all sorts, and for others to hide assets from family members, future creditors and others with legitimate expectations. Yet this is by no means exclusively an offshore problem, as shown by the burgeoning number of limited liability company (limited life company) incorporations in Delaware and other states of the United States.

The fallacy in these reports and studies is that just because something is *capable* of being abused does not automatically mean that the vast majority of people will or do abuse it. The vast majority of trusts are perfectly legitimate.

To take one such report as an example, the OECD's *BCV Report* examines the misuse of a variety of 'corporate vehicles'. This primarily refers to companies, especially private companies, although trusts are also specifically included in the remit.

The *BCV Report* contains kind words about the *bona fide* use of both offshore international business corporations (IBCs) and trusts:

- As regards IBCs, it notes at page 24 that IBCs are used for many legitimate commercial activities, including holding intellectual property, legally obtaining the benefits of tax treaties, and serving as a holding company.

- As regards trusts, it notes at paragraph 25 that a trust is an important, useful, and legitimate vehicle for the transfer and management of assets.

However the report also notes the 'dark side', whereby these entities are, under certain conditions, misused for illicit purposes, including money laundering, bribery/corruption, hiding and shielding assets from creditors, illicit tax practices, self-dealing/defrauding assets/diversion of assets, market fraud, circumvention of disclosure requirements, and other forms of illicit behaviour:

— As regards IBCs, the *BCV Report* states that 'the vulnerability of IBCs to misuse for illicit purposes depends to a considerable extent on their "anonymity" features and the type of regulatory regime to which they are subject. In many OFCs, IBCs employ nominee shareholders and nominee directors to disguise ownership and control. IBCs are subject to little or no formal supervision, with no requirement to file annual returns or annual accounts' (page 24).

— As regards trusts, the *BCV Report* states that 'as with other types of corporate vehicles, trusts can also be misused for illicit purposes. Part of the attractiveness of misusing trusts lies in the fact that trusts enjoy a greater degree of privacy and anonymity than other corporate vehicles. Given the private nature of trusts and the fact that a trust is essentially a contractual agreement between two private persons, virtually all jurisdictions recognising trusts have purposely chosen not to regulate trusts like other corporate vehicles such as corporations. This also means that, unlike corporations, there are no registration requirements or central registries and there are no authorities charged with overseeing trusts' (page 25).

So it is against this negative background that we examine AML measures as they apply to trusts and trustees. The emphasis of this chapter will primarily on 'offshore' trusts, but with consideration as appropriate of onshore trusts and trustees.

KYC and due diligence

12.2   Within the UK, trustees are now within the regulated sector. As noted in Chapter 6: THE UK AML FRAMEWORK – THE MONEY LAUNDERING REGULA-

TIONS AND GUIDANCE NOTES, the Money Laundering Regulations 2003 were published in November 2003, and are generally in force as of 1 March 2004 (although certain activities come into force on later dates).

The new Regulations apply to every 'relevant business', which includes UK fiduciaries and corporate service provider's ('CSP's), as by virtue of Regulation 2(2)(m), this specifically includes:

'... the provision by way of business of services in relation to the formation, operation or management of a company of trust'.

As noted in 9.1, if a trust is somewhere included in an ownership structure, then it is necessary to identify both the *source* and the *destination* of the funds, in terms of both the settlor and the beneficiaries. The question has long been raised as to who is the 'owner' or 'economic owner' of a trust. The Swiss have long required a name or names for the mandatory *Form A* disclosure on opening a bank account for a trust; and in Luxembourg, a similar question has been put to trustees for the last twelve or more years.

This question, among others, has now been answered by the Society of Trust and Estate Practitioners ('STEP') in their *STEP Commentary* (see 12.3 below).

STEP anti-money laundering commentary

12.3 The text of the *STEP Commentary* is set out in APPENDIX 7. As a published industry standard, the *STEP Commentary* is a helpful reference point. It could also assist a practitioner in a difficult case to establish a defence to an AML charge on the basis that the standard in the industry was adhered to.

The commentary addresses the issue of who is the 'owner' or 'economic owner' of a trust. The following passages from section 3 should be noted:

'The "beneficial owner" is generally to be construed as the beneficiaries of the trust. Efforts should be made to identify every beneficiary. Only in exceptional cases, and where the trust instrument is essentially silent on the intended beneficiaries, reference may need to be made to letters of wishes to identify those actually intended to benefit.

Often, for drafting reasons a trust deed will include a wide class of beneficiaries, many of whom are not entitled to benefit from the trust fund other than in remoter circumstances. Instructions to verify every future contingent beneficiary might be unduly onerous and in certain circumstances impossible. Recommendation 5 [of the Forty Recommendations] allows financial institutions to determine the extent of the customer due diligence measures on a risk sensitive basis depending on the type of customer, business relationship or transaction.

In low risk cases and in order not to interrupt the normal conduct of business, practitioners should be permitted to undertake the verification of beneficiaries after having established the business relationship. However, in all such cases, verification of beneficiaries should occur prior to a distribution of assets.

For example in the case of a beneficiary in a discretionary trust who is entitled to a distribution when he or she reaches the age of twenty-one and who is presently a minor, there would be no verification process required until distribution was expected. Since the aim is to prevent criminals from having access to the trust assets, this effectively manages the money laundering risks

However verification should be initiated at the outset where the money laundering risk is considered high even if a distribution is not in immediate prospect. For example, if a beneficiary is from a jurisdiction on the Financial Action Task Force (FATF) blacklist'.

A point of clarification is required at section 4, which discusses the distinction between 'identification' and 'verification'. The text suggests that 'identification' involves getting details of full name, date of birth, nationality and address, whereas 'verification' involves proving 'identification' by for example a copy passport.

This may be the wrong emphasis, and may not be the correct place to draw the dividing line, for the following reasons:

- *Identification*. Trust law already requires 'certainty of objects' (see *McPhail v Doulton [1971] AC 424* and more recently *Re Rosewood [2003] UKPC 26*) so it is not going far beyond pre-existing law to require the full name and date of birth of discretionary beneficiaries. This can be easily proved by a birth certificate copy (coupled as the case may be with a subsequent marriage certificate or change of name deed).

- *Nationality* is only provable by means of an official document such as a passport or national identity card.

- *Addresses* can and do change, although in the case of adult beneficiaries there are a number of acceptable ways of establishing proof of residence (see APPENDIX 4).

As a pragmatic assist for practitioners (STEP members) in the case of a family trust (established typically by a parent) and including minor children in the beneficiary group, the trustees should do whatever they feel is sensible to define with certainty the identities of the minor beneficiaries. If the settlor is a parent there can be no difficulty in getting a copy birth certificate, as it is their legal obligation to register the birth.

There may be no passport for a number of years until a child starts to travel internationally, but there is no real difficulty nowadays in getting passports for minor beneficiaries over four or five years old – possibly just inconvenience.

It may be more difficult for a relative or god-parent (as settlor) to get a copy birth certificate, but is still good practice to seek such an official confirmation of identity. A birth announcement from a reputable newspaper would also suffice.

Verification is different. Given the focus on terrorist AML, it becomes essential to apply due diligence to a beneficiary recipient at the time of (and in advance of) receipt of a trust distribution. Who is to know if the fresh-faced three-year-old cherub smiling out of a baby passport page might not grow up at age 22 into a manic sociopath.

The process of 'verification' should be a much more profound exercise than just getting a 'current valid passport'.

It may therefore be risky for a STEP member simply to rely on the commentary (as presently drafted), as they may be falling short of the proactive role professionals are now cast into, and could face a fine or prison sentence if they got it wrong by an over literal approach.

As noted at 12.6, nationality and country of residence may anyway serve as further 'alerts' to the possibility of money laundering. The problem is certainly not insuperable, and primarily involves an increased administrative burden imposed on trustees. (See also JMLSG *Guidance Notes* 2003 at 4.124 – 4.147).

Constructive trust issues

12.4   The risk of being found liable as a constructive trustee is of great importance. The funding of a trust with property not belonging to the 'settlor' raises complex tracing rights and remedies, and in such circumstances, the trustees could find themselves holding a trust fund on constructive trust for the defrauded party (for cases on constructive trusts see *Paragon Financier plc v D B Thakerar & Co [1999] 1 All ER 400, CA* and *Foskett v McKeown [2000] 3 All ER 97, HL*). As the funds themselves are the proceeds of the fraud, they constitute laundered money, and an suspicious activity report ('SAR') is appropriate. If they have in the meantime paid the funds away, they may be liable to reinstate the true owner in the full amount, thus being exposed to a financial double jeopardy.

Even partial funding with property not belonging to the settlor raises the same issues of constructive trust for the defrauded party, or the foreign revenue authority that is due the unpaid tax. This position will always arise in the event of proven criminality, in contrast, a settlor's pre-existing civil indebtedness, or civil judgment debt, will only give rise to a constructive trusteeship in narrowly defined circumstances. For further information on this subject see *Tolley's International Tax Planning*, (5th edn, 2002) pp 2–1 to 2–58.

Constructive trust issues arose in *Bank of Scotland v A Ltd [2001] EWCA Civ 52* which illustrates the tensions between criminal law provisions relating to tipping-off and the potential civil liability that may arise if an institution deals with the proceeds of a serious crime. In this case, the bank applied to the courts for directions as to what it should do, and the court made an order freezing the accounts. The customer whose account had been frozen (and who had not been notified of the reason) brought proceedings for the release of the funds.

At first instance, Laddie J laid down guidelines as to what an institution should do in the future, either if it wants to make payments from the account, or if it does not. The Court of Appeal did not endorse the guidelines, but did confirm the likelihood of a constructive trust arising in circumstances of suspicion of its customer's dishonesty. However, the court suggested that the Serious Fraud Office should have been made a party to the directions application.

The standard of 'knowledge' is central to the 'constructive trustee' issue (as noted at 8.5). Case law on constructive trusts identifies different degrees of knowledge:

* actual knowledge;

* 'Nelsonian' knowledge; and

* imputed or constructive knowledge (see *Baden Delvaux v Société Générale 1992; Royal Brunei Airlines v Tan [1995] 2 AC 378 and BCCI (Overseas) v Akindele [2000] 4 All ER 221*).

In the *State of Qatar* case (see 12.5) a trust beneficiary brought an application and obtained confirmation of the Jersey Royal Court that there was no constructive trust in favour of the State of Qatar or any other person. This is a highly unusual form of application, but shows what can be done if the circumstances require unusual action.

The Joint Money Laundering Steering Group (UK) (JMLSG) *Guidance Notes* 2003 contains guidance on constructive trust issues (see 6.3).

The *Esteem (Abacus (CI)) Ltd, Trustee of the Esteem Settlement v Grupo Torras SA [2003] JCR 092)* case in Jersey is a graphic example of claims against a trust alleging assets tainted by fraud, infringement of public policy, and seeking a remedial constructive trust to be grafted on so as to provide restitution to the victim of the fraud. Wherever a constructive trust is found, a SAR should not be far behind (see the discussion on *Tracing* in 5.7).

Reporting by trustee

12.5   In the *Nearco* case in Jersey (Royal Court, 6th August 2002) the Deputy Bailiff had to consider the consequences of a fiduciary business filing a SAR in response to a client instruction for them to resign all positions and transfer the company to another jurisdiction. Paragraph 17 of the judgment found as follows: '[w]e fully accept that Quorum acted in good faith, but in our judgement it was wholly mistaken in the attitude that it adopted'.

In other words, they could not (with judicial hindsight) have had a suspicion, and should not have filed a SAR. In consequence the fiduciary business was ordered to bear the costs of the hearing.

A more recent offshore trust case involving a SAR is the Jersey case involving the State of Qatar. Litigation began in July 2000, when the trustees filed an SAR, and continued until the day the Iraq war broke out in March 2003. There were two main sets of concerns: first as to corruption arising by way of commissions paid to three Jersey trusts by arms companies; and second that the trust fund might properly be held on constructive trust for the State of Qatar, rather than for the individual beneficiaries of the trusts in question.

In response to an application brought by Sheikh Hamad (the then Foreign Minister of Qatar), as beneficiary of the trusts, the Jersey Royal Court apparently declared on 17 May 2001 that there was no breach of fiduciary duty owed to the State of Qatar, and there was no constructive trust in favour of the State of Qatar or any other person.

However, as the trustees had made an SAR, but had not received any form of *consent* from the Jersey police, they were caught on the horns of a dilemma. The Jersey police were unwilling (ie, had refused) to grant *consent* to any distribution from the trusts at what was said to be an early stage of a complex enquiry. The effect of the police refusal to grant *consent* was in effect to paralyse the administration of the trusts, and to expose the trustees to liability for breach of trust.

In the summer of 2001, Sheikh Hamad made a second application, seeking directions from the Court:

> '… that will enable the trustees to resume the administration of [the trusts] in accordance with their terms within such a time and to such an extent as may be reasonable in all the circumstances of the case'.

The Jersey Attorney-General objected to this application, contending that it would be contrary to public policy to grant the Order sought, because the Sheikh's clear collateral purpose was to use any declaration granted to hinder any criminal investigation and any subsequent criminal proceedings (presumably by asking the trustees to transfer the trust assets out of Jersey).

An article entitled 'The State of Qatar and Jersey – the litigation and the lessons for trustees' by Simon Gould and David Hopwood of Mourant du Feu & Jeune, Jersey (STEP Journal Quarterly Review – Issue 2 Vol 3 of 2003, pg 17) notes how the trustee found itself on the horns of a dilemma between the risk of prosecution for a money laundering offence, and liability for a breach of trust:

> 'On the assumption that a trustee will normally risk civil liability for a breach of trust rather than a criminal prosecution, this also means that the police have, in effect, acquired the ability to freeze assets which are suspected to be the proceeds of criminal conduct, for an indefinite period, simply by refusing a trustee's request for consent to distribute those assets'.

Given the formal procedures and safeguards that exist in Jersey for the Attorney-General to apply for a *saisie judiciaire*, this short-cut method is unusually oppressive, and provides a vivid example of where the offshore jurisdictions need to emulate the strict time frames that are already laid down in the UK – see 10.3.

The article also notes how unsatisfactory it is that the law 'should place professional trustees in such a dilemma when they are endeavouring to assist the criminal justice system'.

The article ends with a review of possible countermeasures a trustee can adopt to resolve being caught in such a dilemma. One interesting suggestion, echoing those in 11.1, 11.4 and 11.5 of this handbook is that fiduciaries should arrange for a release from liability for breaches of trust in the event an SAR is made on reasonable grounds. Whilst it would certainly be wise for corporate service providers to amend their terms of business accordingly, it is less easy for trustees to do so, as to be most effective the provision would have to be included within the trust itself, which may not be capable of being amended without the consent of the court.

Industry issues and common failings

12.6   A first rule of money laundering prevention may be to recognise and deal with one's own weaknesses. Once you understand why you or your business is attractive to the wrong type of client, you are well placed to erect meaningful AML defences.

Conversely, the more control over a trust or company that is delegated to a client, the more vulnerable you become to money laundering risk. Therefore fiduciaries should avoid common forms of delegated control such as powers of attorney, bank signatory rights and direct access to funds via, for example, credit cards.

At a macro level, there is a presumption of 'suspicion' in any transaction involving a country on the current FATF blacklist, this is set out in A3.2, and the FATF website should be checked for updates (see www.fatf-gafi.org).

There should also be a presumption of 'suspicion' in any transaction involving a politically sensitive person ('PSP'). This may be a more difficult issue to check, although recourse can now be to the database services referred to in 9.5. Although major public figures are a household name (especially in their home countries), monitoring all possibilities of relationship is difficult, as the PSP concept extends not only a government official, but also to relatives of a government official, or even to their business associates.

Bribery and corruption is also an money laundering issue (see *Corporacion Nacional del Cobra de Chile v Interglobal Inc [2002] CILR 298 Grand Court of Cayman*). The *Levin Report* entitled 'Private banking and money laundering – a case study of opportunities and vulnerabilities' (published 9 November 1999) examines the vulnerability of private banking operations to such money laundering and contains four illustrative case histories at Citibank Private Bank. One of the case histories concerned Asif Ali Zardari, the husband of Benazir Bhutto, the former Prime Minister of Pakistan. Ms Bhutto was elected Prime Minister in 1988 and dismissed for alleged corruption in 1990. She was re-elected Prime Minister in October 1993 and dismissed again in November 1996. At various times Mr Zardari held political office, and in the period between the two Bhutto administrations he was imprisoned for corruption.

The *BCV Report* defines 'illicit activity' broadly as including *inter alia* bribery and corruption, which are tested as being 'illicit' only according to the laws of the perpetrator's country of citizenship, domicile or residence.

Any transaction involving the *proceeds of corruption*, or payments under a sham or false document, will also be *prima facie* 'suspicious' and may merit filing a SAR. As there are clear possibilities that offshore trusts and offshore companies can be used in connection with receiving or paying bribes or corrupt payments, fiduciaries must exercise enhanced vigilance, depending on the profile of the client or customer involved. See US 'Guidance on Enhanced Scrutiny for Transactions that may involve the Proceeds of Foreign Official Corruption' at APPENDIX 3.

The slippery slope for the offshore industry lies in where the definition and concept of the AML 'proceeds of crime' test will extend, as it would appear to bring within its scope any of the following types of payment either arising out of false or sham documentation, or where the recipient of the funds is not clearly reporting them for tax:

— commissions;

— fees;

— brokers' fees and other similar remuneration;

— sub-contract payments; or

— consulting agreements.

If these 'proceeds' can be the 'proceeds of crime' for AML purposes, then professionals and practitioners involved with offshore trusts and offshore companies (and the bankers to offshore trusts and offshore companies) must exercise the utmost vigilance.

Case studies – 'trustees as money launderers'

12.7 On 27 January 2004 members of Law Society of Hong Kong were given a presentation by James Wadham and Shane Kelly entitled *Trustees as money launderers*. This title was chosen deliberately to get the attention of solicitors in Hong Kong, many of whom may not have hitherto realised the scope of the AML legislation. Whilst OSCO in Hong Kong derives from different sources than the UK PoCA, its effect is broadly similar.

APPENDIX 7 contains some of the case studies used in the presentation. These are taken very much from day-to-day fiduciary life in Hong Kong. They merit careful study, as some of the types of client, the planning structures adopted, and the behaviour of the fiduciaries involved (trustees or CSPs) can be found in just about any jurisdiction, both onshore and offshore.

In addition, consider the AML aspects of a fiduciary becoming involved with sham or false documentation, whether a sham trust, or bogus commercial agreements (so-called consultancy agreements, agency commission agreements, loan agreements, etc).

In relation to international trading activities, private trading companies (PTCs) may be used in customs fraud, by under- (or over-) invoicing, or by relying on forged documents such as false certificates of origin or bills of lading. Reinvoicing operations by a PTC also raises AML and reporting issues.

Lord Millett's reasoning in the *Agip (Africa) Ltd* case (see quote at 8.5) is equally applicable in current AML era to any sort of arrangement that facilitates 'just' foreign tax evasion. Lord Millett's speech in the recent stamp duty case in the Hong Kong court of Final Appeal – *Comr of Stamp Revenue v Arrowtown Assets Ltd, 4 December 2003* – is also illustrative. Offshore fiduciaries should tremble and beware!

Regulation of trustees and on site inspection visits

12.8   Trust (or 'fiduciary') businesses are now regulated in a number of offshore jurisdictions. As part of the licensing process, their regulator has the right to make annual or occasional on site inspection visits.

An element of such visits involves checking the extent to which the fiduciary business is complying with the applicable Regulation and Guidance Notes (see CHAPTER 13: APPLICATION OF AML PRINCIPLES OUTSIDE THE UK: THE GENERAL APPROACH IN OTHER SELECTED JURISDICTIONS). It might also involve substantive checking of trust documents or corporate minutes to see if documents are correctly drawn up, dated currently etc. 'Sham' documents will be difficult to detect, but evidence of sham behaviour may be sought.

It is interesting to note a leading Bermuda attorney firm has objected to the very concept of 'on site' inspections as not being accompanied by an adequate indemnification in the trustees' favour against resulting loss or damage.

Executors and probate

12.9   For completeness, it is appropriate to look briefly at executorships and will trusts. (See also JMLSG *Guidance Notes* 2003, 4.150–4.153).

In the UK probate business is not a 'regulated sector' unless the executor is, or is advised by, a legal professional. In any event a court approved Grant of Probate or Letters of Administration is first required.

The likelihood of money laundering occurring in connection with a deceased's estate is extremely low, as death is generally not a premeditated 'transaction'. Nevertheless, AML rules will still generally apply, so that those involved should still consider filing an SAR if they have relevant suspicions.

Perhaps persons named as executors in a will, who discover the appointment only after the death of the testator, will have to conduct retroactive due diligence on the business and affairs of the deceased prior to accepting the appointment, however, it is always open to them to renounce.

There should also be a general *caveat* in respect of legacies or donations to minor or obscure charities established in jurisdictions where there is little or no charitable regulation. In this regard the FATF recommendations on *charities* should be noted (see APPENDIX 3).

The problem of institutional tax evasion

12.10   Paragraph 7.7 looked at the wider issues that affect international private banking. It is now appropriate to look at the same wider issues as they affect offshore fiduciaries and CSPs. In this regard, we refer to John Nugent's most illuminating paper to the STEP winter conference in December 2003 entitled *Practical implications of Money Laundering Regulations – tax evasion* extracts of which are set out in APPENDIX 7.

In his paper, Mr Nugent examines the potential implications of advance money laundering legislation for organisations that have, perhaps unconsciously, assisted in the evasion of taxes. Mr Nugent notes that tax evasion involves some blameworthy act or omission *and is in reality equivalent to fraud*. In essence tax evasion involves the concealment of the true facts of an arrangement, in contrast to tax avoidance.

Mr Nugent notes that while regulation of trustees, know-your-customer, and exchange of information is undermining offshore tax evasion, the type of legislation found in the Proceeds of Crime Act ('PoCA') will work to greater effect than anything that can be imposed on the offshore world. PoCA-style legislation has fatally wounded 'institutionalised tax evasion', namely mass tax evasion facilitated by organisations who honestly do not know; or turn a blind eye to; or do not care about; or actively encourage the fact that their clients and customers are evading taxes. These organisations are normally based in off-shore centres, although they may be owned by or have related entities in the onshore jurisdictions, those most immediately affected will be medium to large size organisations who have wide-ranging business interests beyond the entity containing the tax evasion arrangements.

Mr Nugent recommends that offshore organisations which provide offshore arrangements should urgently review the services they provide, to ensure that they are not running the risk of attracting new tax evasion arrangements and to analyse their existing clients and customers to identify any existing tax evasion arrangements. These organisations could be considered as 'critically ill' depending on the extent of their infection with tax evasion. If they are critically ill (ie, a very substantial proportion of their business could be classed as tax evasion) they face serious and urgent problems. Prosecution could follow if tax evasion monies have been actively sought or the organisations welcomed such business when it arrived.

Perhaps the most chilling comment is that 'although incomprehensible to most onshore professionals, the fact is that such organisations do exist. And the fact is though that some onshore parents may not be fully aware of the deep seated problem that their seemingly successful offshore children have stored up'. Mr Nugent concludes that sale of such a business is unlikely to be viable as there may not be much worth selling, and the market for certain sorts of businesses has already evaporated, so there may therefore be no choice but to break up the business.

These are harsh views indeed, but they simply describe the observed reality in most if not all of the offshore financial centres. The reality check in Mr Nugent's paper lies in the fact that the two-track approach within EUSD means that different standards will continue to apply both within the EU and as regards key third countries.

Chapter 13

Application of AML Principles Outside the UK: General Approach

Introduction

13.1　For understandable constitutional reasons, the UK anti-money laundering ('AML') rules, as originally defined in the Criminal Justice Act ('CJA') 1988 and 1993, and as now set out in Proceeds of Crime Act ('PoCA'), form the basis of the statutory AML regimes in the Crown dependencies and overseas territories.

The AML rules in other jurisdictions such as the United States and Canada, being less connected with the UK, have evolved differently.

There are subtle differences in the approaches some of the offshore jurisdictions have adopted in implementing their AML legislation. It is beyond the scope of this chapter to provide a comprehensive comparative analysis. Nevertheless, the salient features and differences can be noted by reference to APPENDIX 2 which contains summaries of the AML laws of the following key jurisdictions:

—　Bahamas;

—　Canada;

—　Cayman Islands;

—　Guernsey;

—　Jersey;

—　Hong Kong;

—　Isle of Man;

—　United States.

These summaries have been extracted from *Butterworths International Guide to Money Laundering Law and Practice* (2nd edn, 2002). Please note that, in the interests of brevity, and so as to remain consistent with the main focus of this Guide, the extracted sections do not include references to materials dealing with terrorist AML or drug AML.

Finally, CHAPTER 14: APPLICATION OF AML PRINCIPLES OUTSIDE THE UK: THE APPROACH TO FISCAL OFFENCES IN SELECTED JURISDICTIONS contains a more detailed summary of the attitude to the AML treatment of fiscal offences in various jurisdictions, together with a list of the principal statutes.

Chapter 14

Application of AML Principles Outside the UK: Specific Approach to Fiscal Offences

Introduction

14.1   As noted in CHAPTER 13: APPLICATION OF PRINCIPLES OUTSIDE THE UK: THE GENERAL APPROACH IN OTHER SELECTED JURISDICTIONS, the United Kingdom anti-money laundering rules ('AML') form the basis of the statutory AML regimes in the Crown dependencies and overseas territories, while the AML rules in other jurisdictions less connected with the UK, have evolved differently.

While it is beyond the scope of this chapter to provide a comprehensive comparative analysis, nevertheless, some salient features and differences in their particular attitude to the AML treatment of fiscal offences should be noted.

The approach in selected jurisdictions

The Bahamas

14.2   The Bahamas' AML code is contained in the Financial Transactions Reporting Act 2000 and the Proceeds of Crime Act 2000 ('PoCA'). The Commonwealth of the Bahamas, which is an independent sovereign nation, has modelled its substantive AML offences on the UK Criminal Justice Act ('CJA') offences. The scope of the offences covered includes any other offence triable in the Bahamas Supreme Court. As regards fiscal offences, there is no direct taxation in the Bahamas – foreign tax evasion is not regarded as a predicate offence, but as foreign tax evasion is frequently accompanied by a charge of fraud or a related offence, this would fall into PoCA 2000 Schedule, paragraph 'd'. Note that the Bahamas' Tax Information Exchange Agreement ('ITEA') with the United States (signed on 25 January 2002) defines 'criminal matter' as 'an examination, investigation or proceeding concerning conduct that constitutes a criminal tax offence' under US law.

AML laws and regulations include:

— Proceeds of Crime Act 2000;

— Proceeds of Crime (Money Laundering) Regulations 2000;

—   Financial Intelligence Unit Act 2000;

—   Financial Transaction Reporting Act 2000 (and amendments);

—   Criminal Justice (International Co-operation) Act 2000;

—   Money Laundering (Proceeds of Crime) (Amendment) Act 2000;

—   Criminal Justice (International Co-operation) Act 2000;

—   Dangerous Drugs Act 2000;

—   Tax Information Exchange Agreement (with the US) dated January 2002.

Bermuda

14.3   Bermuda's principal AML statute is the Proceeds of Crime Act 1997 (as amended). The Taxes Management Amendment Act and the Proceeds of Crime (Amendment) Act 2000 broadened the scope by redefining 'relevant offence' to cover all serious crime, including fraudulent tax evasion which occurs outside Bermuda if such evasion is actively facilitated within Bermuda. Thus the overseas commission of a tax offence can fall within the definition of 'suspicious transaction' reporting (it should be noted that there is a three-year cut off date). Under the Taxes Management Amendment Act 2000 the definition of criminal tax evasion was revised, and 'tax fraud' is defined as 'any deliberate or wilful act by a person with intent to defraud where that person knows that a substantial amount of tax would otherwise be due, and the conduct involved constitutes a *systematic effort or pattern of activity* (a definition which is similar to that of 'tax offence' contained in other US TIEAs, for example, with the Cayman Islands – see 14.5 below) designed to falsify material records to the relevant authorities'. The US-Bermuda Tax Information Exchange Agreement ('TIEA') of July 1986 provides for disclosure in cases of tax fraud and the evasion of taxes.

The AML laws and regulations in Bermuda include:

—   Proceeds of Crime Act 1997 (and amendments of 2000);

—   Proceeds of Crime (Money Laundering) Regulations 1998;

—   Taxes Management (Amendment) Act 1999;

—   Tax Information Exchange Act (with the US) dated 1986;

Canada

14.4   The Canadian AML framework is contained in the Proceeds of Crime (Money Laundering) Act 2000, and related regulations. The provisions follow loosely the UK CJA provisions, and encompass the proceeds of a 'designated offence' committed in Canada or an offence committed elsewhere which would constitute a 'designated offence' had it been committed in Canada. A 'designated offence' is essentially an indictable offence. There is thus a high element of extra-territoriality. However, offences under the Canadian Income Tax Act are excluded from the definition of 'designated offence' as the statutes already provide for specific rules and penalties for dealing with tax evasion and recovering any unpaid tax. For this reason, practitioners do not see that the Canadian AML regime can be extended to cover tax evasion against non-Canadian tax authorities committed outside Canada (see also 11.3).

The AML laws and regulations include:

—   Proceeds of Crime (Money Laundering) Act 2000;

—   Proceeds of Crime (Money Laundering) Suspicious Transaction Reporting Regulations;

—   Proceeds of Crime (Money Laundering) And Terrorist Financing Act 2001;

—   Proceeds of Crime (Money Laundering) And Terrorist Financing Regulations.

The Cayman Islands

14.5   The Cayman Islands AML provisions are contained in the Proceeds of Criminal Conduct Law (as amended), they follow the UK model. There is no need for dual criminality in the substantive law, but the Regulations contain a dual criminality approach. It should be noted that The Cayman Islands' TIEA with the US (signed on 27 November 2001) defines 'criminal tax evasion' in article 4 as 'wilfully, with dishonest intent to defraud the public revenue, evading or attempting to evade any tax liability …[which] must be of a significant or substantial amount …and the conduct involved must constitute a systematic effort or pattern of activity designed or tending to conceal pertinent facts from the tax authorities'. The TIEA signed between the US and the British Virgin Islands on 3 April 2002 contains a similar definition.

The AML laws and regulations in the Caymans include:

—   Proceeds of Criminal Conduct Law 2001 Revision;

—   Misuse of Drugs Law 2000 Revision;

—   Misuse of Drugs (International Co-operation) Law;

—   Narcotics Drugs (Evidence) (USA) Law 1984;

—   Proceeds of Criminal Conduct (Amendment) (Money Laundering Regulations) Law 2000;

—   Proceeds of Criminal Conduct Law (2000 Revision) Money Laundering (Amendment) Client Identification) Regulations 2001;

—   Proceeds of Criminal Conduct (Amendment) (Financial Intelligence Unit) Law 2001;

—   The Money Laundering Regulations 2000;

— Code of Practice (March 2000);

— Guidance Notes on the Prevention and Detection of Money Laundering (2001);

— Tax Information Exchange Agreement (with the US) dated November 2001.

Guernsey

14.6 The Guernsey AML provisions are contained in The Criminal Justice (Proceeds of Crime) (Bailiwick of Guernsey) Law 1999 as amended, which is closely based on the UK model. The Guernsey position on fiscal offences (domestic or foreign) is broadly the same as in Jersey (see 14.9 below), it is a common law offence in Guernsey to cheat the Guernsey Revenue, and the Guidance Notes 2002 state expressly that proceeds of a tax-related offence may fall within the AML offences. The position on foreign fiscal offences is less clear. It should be noted that Guernsey signed a TIEA with the US in September 2002 which (following the OECD commitment) requires exchange if information in criminal tax matters as of 1 January 2004, and in civil/administrative tax matters as of 1 January 2006.

The AML laws and regulations for Guernsey are:

— Money Laundering (Disclosure of Information) (Guernsey) Law 1995;

— The Criminal Justice (Proceeds of Crime) (Bailiwick of Guernsey) Law 1999 (as amended);

— The Criminal Justice (Proceeds of Crime) Regulations 1999 (as amended 2001);

— The Criminal Justice (Proceeds of Crime) (Bailiwick of Guernsey) (Enforcement of Overseas Confiscation Orders) Ordinance, 1999;

— Terrorism And Crime (Guernsey) Law 2002;

— Drug Trafficking Law 2000;

— The Criminal Justice (International Co-operation) Law 2001;

— Guidance Notes on the Prevention of Money Laundering;

— Tax Information Exchange Agreement (with the US) dated April 2002.

Hong Kong

14.7 The Hong Kong AML framework, contained in the Organized and Serious Crimes Ordinance ('OSCO') (as amended), is not based on the UK model, reflective of Hong Kong's autonomous status since July 1997. The AML offences are linked to the proceeds of indictable offences, irrespective of where the offence was committed. The position on fiscal offences is unclear, but is likely to follow the common law position.

Hong Kong has had recent money laundering cases of interest. In *HKSAR v Li Ching [1997] 4 HKC 108* the Court of Appeal held in December 1997 that it was sufficient to constitute an AML offence if the defendant believed he was dealing with property representing the proceeds of an indictable offence (which would include tax evasion), even if as it turned out, he was not. The case also confirmed that under OSCO it is not necessary for there to be a successful prosecution of the underlying serious crime, Justice Mayo holding that '… it is obviously the case that tax evasion must be a crime in China'.

In *HKSAR v Look Kar Win [1999] 4 HKC 783 4* the Court held in October 1999 that a football match-fixing that occurred in Thailand (where it may not have been illegal) could be prosecuted under corruption laws in Hong Kong, as the offence could be deemed to have taken place in Hong Kong (where it would have been illegal). The *Lam Yiu Chung* case was a money laundering case brought following an ICAC investigation, where the prosecution argued that 'it was reasonable for anyone involved in the operation to assume the cash was either illegitimate or evading the tax man'. And the *Robert Pang v Cmr of Police [2002], 2 December* case is also important in relation to issues of legal professional privilege – see CHAPTER 11: ISSUES FACING PROFESSIONALS AND PRACTITIONERS.

The AML laws and regulations are:

— Drug Trafficking (Recovery of Proceeds) Ordinance (Cap 405) ('DTRPO');

— Organised and Serious Crimes Ordinance (Cap 455) ('OSCO').

Isle of Man

14.8   The principal AML statute in the Isle of Man is the Criminal Justice (Money Laundering Offences) Act, which is directly modelled on the UK CJA. The Isle of Man position on whether a fiscal offence can constitute an AML offence is similar to that in the Channel Islands (see 14.6 above). Any conduct, wherever transacted, that is sufficiently serious to be triable 'on information' is caught by the Act. As offences under the Isle of Man Income Tax Acts are triable only summarily, at present they fall outside the scope of the AML offences. It is also unclear whether there are Manx equivalents to the UK common law offences of defrauding and/or cheating the revenue which are triable either summarily or on information. On the other hand, false accounting, which may be part of a tax evasion scheme, is an offence under the Manx Theft Act 1981, thus falling within the scope of the Manx AML code. It seems likely that the Isle of Man Courts would extend the statutory AML provisions to cover fiscal offences.

The AML laws and regulations include:

— Prevention of Terrorism Act 1990;

— Criminal Justice Act 1990;

— Drug Trafficking Act 1996;

— Criminal Justice (Money Laundering Offences) Act 1998;

— Anti-Money Laundering Code 1998.

Jersey

14.9   Jersey's Proceeds of Crime (Jersey) Law also follows the UK model. It defines 'criminal conduct' as conduct which, if committed in Jersey, might lead to a sentence of imprisonment of one year or more. As regards fiscal offences, since tax evasion in Jersey (in the sense of negligently or fraudulently making incorrect statements in connection with a tax return) is punishable under the Income Tax (Jersey) Law by a fine rather than imprisonment, it appears that fiscal offences do not fall within the scope of the AML offences. However, if a tax-related offence is accompanied by a common law offence (see 14.3, 14.5 above) such as forgery, fraud or false accounting – see *Foster v A-G 1992 JLR 6* – the position may differ. The Jersey *Guidance Notes* also confirm this at paragraph 2.04, stating that:

> '[a] tax related offence would constitute 'criminal conduct' where there is conduct amounting to the customary law offence of fraud [which] requires the existence of acts constituting a deliberate false representation causing actual prejudice to another and actual gain to the person accused. Although a tax-related offence committed outside of the Island may be within the definition of "criminal conduct" for the purposes of the Law, not all overseas tax offences will necessarily amount to such conduct'.

Note that Jersey also signed a TIEA with the US in September 2002 following joint negotiations with Guernsey.

The AML laws and regulations for Jersey include:

— Drug Trafficking Offences (Jersey) Law 1988 (as amended);

— Terrorism (Jersey) Law 2002;

— Proceeds of Crime (Jersey) Law 1999;

— Money Laundering (Jersey) Order 1999;

— Criminal Justice (International Co-operation) (Jersey) Law 2001;

— Tax Information Exchange Agreement (with the US) dated April 2002.

Singapore

14.10   Singapore's AML framework is contained in The Corruption, Drug Trafficking and other Serious Crimes (Confiscation of Benefits) Act, which is only loosely based on the UK model. Singapore does not at present regard foreign tax evasion as part of their AML offences.

The United States

14.11   In the US, the AML framework is currently being updated, and the US is moving in the same direction as the UK in its interpretation of AML laws as covering the proceeds of all crimes, including fiscal offences, but with the same academic issues that were encountered in the UK some ten years ago. The American College of Trust and Estate Counsel take the view that tax offences are not and should not be understood to be the type of criminal acts that can be held to produce 'proceeds of crime' for AML purposes, and that international transactions that led to underpayment or non-payment of tax should not be criminalised or made part of the AML STR structure. The IRS Code ss 1956 and 1957 have for some years prohibited engaging in a financial transaction knowing or being wilfully blind to the fact that the property involved represents the proceeds of 'some form of unlawful activity', where the person *inter alia* intends to engage in tax fraud or tax evasion of either US or non-US taxes. Recent cases in the US have held that evasion of non-US taxes and exchange control violations is an AML offence.

On 26 October 2001, in rapid response to the terrorist outrages of 11 September 2001, President George W Bush signed into law 'The Patriot Act' of 2001 ('Uniting and Strengthening America by Providing the Appropriate Tools Required to Intercept and Obstruct Terrorism (USA)) which *inter alia* requires US financial institutions to identify the foreign beneficial owners of accounts with them. These measures, which are being applied strictly, are producing anomalous results. In some cases institutions are requiring compulsory redemption or closure of an existing relationship if the name(s) is/are not provided. The Patriot Act measures also seem to run counter to the position under US Qualified Jurisdictions and Qualified Intermediaries programme, where the 'beneficial owner' concept stops at a 'real' company (ie, one that is not a nominee or pass through entity) and does not seek to pierce through to the ultimate individual beneficial owners.

The recent *Pasquantino* case *(United States of America v David Pasquantino US App LEXIS 14453 (2003))* confirms that the US Courts have also moved to expand the territorial limitation to enforcing foreign revenue laws (similar to the UK – see 7.2). The decision in *US v Hebroni* is noteworthy, as the US courts secured a conviction of money laundering and conspiracy to launder drugs money. The case was exceptional as all of the trading activities had taken place in Panama. The accused mainly seems to have sold jewellery to drug barons, knowing that it was being paid for with the proceeds of drug trafficking.

The US AML laws and regulations include:

—   Money Laundering Control Act 1986;

—   Patriot Act 2001.

Chapter 15

Conclusions

15.1   The anti-money laundering regimes that are in place or are being developed in various countries give rise to two main dilemmas:

- the issue of reporting a client (see CHAPTER 10: UK AML REPORTING PROCEDURES); and

- the issue of foreign tax evasion (see CHAPTER 7: THE UK AML FRAME-WORK – FISCAL OFFENCES AND FOREIGN TAX ENFORCEMENT).

Despite these, it seems likely that human nature will cause individuals and families to continue to diversify their assets and investments across more than one country or jurisdiction, so as to provide a hedge against political or economic risks. Tax avoidance and tax mitigation planning will thus continue, but overly aggressive tax planning will require extreme caution, as harsh cases will be subject to heavy penalties. In the UK, the Inland Revenue is increasingly using criminal prosecutions to combat tax evasion and also to counter tax avoidance (see *R v Stannard [2002] All ER (D) 162 (Feb)*. This case is discussed in detail in James Kessler's article 'What lessons to learn', which appears in two parts in Taxation (7 and 14 June 2001). See also *R v Dimsey [2001] UKHL 46* and *R v Allen [2000] QB 774*).

The offshore sector has undergone radical change since the events of 11 September 2001. Some offshore financial centres will remain part of the global financial system. Others will wither away. Internationally, anti-money laundering laws ('AML') coupled with increased exchange of information ('EoI') will curtail the worst excesses of offshore tax evasion. Those who assist in barefaced tax evasion will do so at their peril and in full knowledge of the issues involved (criminalisation, extradition, prison). Existing tax evasionary clients and customers should be jettisoned, and such future prospective clients should simply not be taken on (see 7.7 and John Nugent's talk given at the STEP winter conference in 2003 in APPENDIX 7).

The continuing evolution of AML legislation has placed greater powers of asset forfeiture and asset recovery in the hands of prosecutors and revenue gatherers, a recent example being the Assets Recovery Agency powers under PoCA 2002. It is inevitable that human rights issues will be increasingly invoked in AML proceedings, both in connection with forfeiture and on the wider issue of EoI generally.

FATF's *Forty Recommendations*, republished in revised form on 23 June 2003 require that 'strict safeguards should be established to ensure that this EoI is consistent with national and international provisions on privacy and data protection'. Human rights law is a relatively recent newcomer to the UK legal arena, but the human rights that are worthy of protection in relation to AML legislation are fundamental, and include the right of privacy, the right of property, and the right to a fair trial.

Application of the new post 11 September 2001 anti-terrorist laws also requires a careful balancing of traditional democratic freedoms with the new security requirements (for a more in-depth discussion than this title allows, see Baroness Helena Kennedy QC *Just Law* (2004)). All new laws and regulations require a settling in period, but the AML regime has coincided with both the introduction of human rights principles and their curtailment as a result of the events of 11 September 2001. This has left practitioners and their clients with uncertainties on the scope of the AML regime and the strength of the human rights protections and remedies.

Has the pendulum swung too far? The risk of over-reaction in seeking to apply AML laws to stamp out terrorism through striking at terrorist finances must be noted. (See Lord Hurd 'Lets not pretend we can be safe from terrorism' (2003) Financial Times, 3 December).

Can the pendulum ever swing back? A United Nations report of August 2002 noted that al Qu'aeda finances were still in good shape despite nearly 12 months of focused application of AML laws. This should not come as a surprise, as it is likely that only a tiny percentage of money destined for or owned by terror organisations such as al Qu'aeda actually flow through co-operative countries or territories (in FATF terms). So it is unlikely the pendulum will swing back whilst worldwide security threats remain so high.

Thus, the AML regime raises broad issues of concern. These include the concept of 'extraterritoriality', and the all too evident deficiencies in due process and matching issues of human rights.

Appendices

Contents

Appendix 1

Statutory Provisions

A1.1 Proceeds of Crime Act 2002

2002 Chapter 29

PROCEEDS OF CRIME ACT 2002

Interpretation

75 Criminal lifestyle

(1) A defendant has a criminal lifestyle if (and only if) the following condition is satisfied.

(2) The condition is that the offence (or any of the offences) concerned satisfies any of these tests—

    (a)   it is specified in Schedule 2;

    (b)   it constitutes conduct forming part of a course of criminal activity;

    (c)   it is an offence committed over a period of at least six months and the defendant has benefited from the conduct which constitutes the offence.

(3) Conduct forms part of a course of criminal activity if the defendant has benefited from the conduct and—

    (a)   in the proceedings in which he was convicted he was convicted of three or more other offences, each of three or more of them constituting conduct from which he has benefited, or

    (b)   in the period of six years ending with the day when those proceedings were started (or, if there is more than one such day, the earliest day) he was convicted on at least two separate occasions of an offence constituting conduct from which he has benefited.

(4) But an offence does not satisfy the test in subsection (2)(b) or (c) unless the defendant obtains relevant benefit of not less than £5000.

(5) Relevant benefit for the purposes of subsection (2)(b) is—

(a)   benefit from conduct which constitutes the offence;

(b)   benefit from any other conduct which forms part of the course of criminal activity and which constitutes an offence of which the defendant has been convicted;

(c)   benefit from conduct which constitutes an offence which has been or will be taken into consideration by the court in sentencing the defendant for an offence mentioned in paragraph (a) or (b).

(6) Relevant benefit for the purposes of subsection (2)(c) is—

(a)   benefit from conduct which constitutes the offence;

(b)   benefit from conduct which constitutes an offence which has been or will be taken into consideration by the court in sentencing the defendant for the offence mentioned in paragraph (a).

(7) The Secretary of State may by order amend Schedule 2.

(8) The Secretary of State may by order vary the amount for the time being specified in subsection (4).

NOTES

Initial Commencement

To be appointed
To be appointed: see s 458(1).

Appointment
Appointment: 24 March 2003: see SI 2003/333, art 2(1), Schedule; for transitional provisions see art 7 thereof (as amended by SI 2003/531, arts 2, 3).

Extent
This Part does not extend to Scotland: see s 461(1).

76   Conduct and benefit

(1) Criminal conduct is conduct which—

(a)   constitutes an offence in England and Wales, or

(b)   would constitute such an offence if it occurred in England and Wales.

(2) General criminal conduct of the defendant is all his criminal conduct, and it is immaterial—

(a)   whether conduct occurred before or after the passing of this Act;

(b)   whether property constituting a benefit from conduct was obtained before or after the passing of this Act.

(3) Particular criminal conduct of the defendant is all his criminal conduct which falls within the following paragraphs—

(a)   conduct which constitutes the offence or offences concerned;

(b)   conduct which constitutes offences of which he was convicted in the same proceedings as those in which he was convicted of the offence or offences concerned;

(c)   conduct which constitutes offences which the court will be taking into consideration in deciding his sentence for the offence or offences concerned.

(4) A person benefits from conduct if he obtains property as a result of or in connection with the conduct.

(5) If a person obtains a pecuniary advantage as a result of or in connection with conduct, he is to be taken to obtain as a result of or in connection with the conduct a sum of money equal to the value of the pecuniary advantage.

(6) References to property or a pecuniary advantage obtained in connection with conduct include references to property or a pecuniary advantage obtained both in that connection and some other.

(7) If a person benefits from conduct his benefit is the value of the property obtained.

NOTES

Initial Commencement

To be appointed
To be appointed: see s 458(1).

Appointment
Appointment: 24 March 2003: see SI 2003/333, art 2(1), Schedule; for transitional provisions see art 9 thereof.

Extent
This Part does not extend to Scotland: see s 461(1).

Part 5   Civil Recovery of the Proceeds etc of Unlawful Conduct

Chapter 1 Introductory

240   General purpose of this Part

(1) This Part has effect for the purposes of—

(a)   enabling the enforcement authority to recover, in civil proceedings before the High Court or Court of Session, property which is, or represents, property obtained through unlawful conduct,

(b)   enabling cash which is, or represents, property obtained through unlawful conduct, or which is intended to be used in unlawful conduct, to be forfeited in civil proceedings before a magistrates' court or (in Scotland) the sheriff.

(2) The powers conferred by this Part are exercisable in relation to any property (including cash) whether or not any proceedings have been brought for an offence in connection with the property.

NOTES

Initial Commencement

To be appointed
To be appointed: see s 458(1), (2).

Appointment
Appointment: 30 December 2002: see SI 2002/3015, art 2, Schedule.

241 "Unlawful conduct"

(1) Conduct occurring in any part of the United Kingdom is unlawful conduct if it is unlawful under the criminal law of that part.

(2) Conduct which—

(a)   occurs in a country outside the United Kingdom and is unlawful under the criminal law of that country, and

(b)   if it occurred in a part of the United Kingdom, would be unlawful under the criminal law of that part,

is also unlawful conduct.

(3) The court or sheriff must decide on a balance of probabilities whether it is proved—

(a)   that any matters alleged to constitute unlawful conduct have occurred, or

(b)   that any person intended to use any cash in unlawful conduct.

NOTES

Initial Commencement

To be appointed
To be appointed: see s 458(1), (2).

Appointment
Appointment: 30 December 2002: see SI 2002/3015, art 2, Schedule.

242 "Property obtained through unlawful conduct"

(1) A person obtains property through unlawful conduct (whether his own conduct or another's) if he obtains property by or in return for the conduct.

(2) In deciding whether any property was obtained through unlawful conduct—

(a) it is immaterial whether or not any money, goods or services were provided in order to put the person in question in a position to carry out the conduct,

(b) it is not necessary to show that the conduct was of a particular kind if it is shown that the property was obtained through conduct of one of a number of kinds, each of which would have been unlawful conduct.

NOTES

Initial Commencement

To be appointed
To be appointed: see s 458(1), (2).

Appointment
Appointment: 30 December 2002: see SI 2002/3015, art 2, Schedule.

Chapter 2 Civil Recovery in the High Court or Court of Session

Proceedings for recovery orders

243 Proceedings for recovery orders in England and Wales or Northern Ireland

(1) Proceedings for a recovery order may be taken by the enforcement authority in the High Court against any person who the authority thinks holds recoverable property.

(2) The enforcement authority must serve the claim form—

(a) on the respondent, and

(b) unless the court dispenses with service, on any other person who the authority thinks holds any associated property which the authority wishes to be subject to a recovery order,

wherever domiciled, resident or present.

(3) If any property which the enforcement authority wishes to be subject to a recovery order is not specified in the claim form it must be described in the form in general terms; and the form must state whether it is alleged to be recoverable property or associated property.

(4) The references above to the claim form include the particulars of claim, where they are served subsequently.

NOTES

Initial Commencement

To be appointed
To be appointed: see s 458(1), (2).

Appointment
Appointment: 24 February 2003: see SI 2003/120, art 2(1), Schedule.

Chapter 4 General

Recoverable property

305 Tracing property, etc

(1) Where property obtained through unlawful conduct ("the original property") is or has been recoverable, property which represents the original property is also recoverable property.

(2) If a person enters into a transaction by which—

(a) he disposes of recoverable property, whether the original property or property which (by virtue of this Chapter) represents the original property, and

(b) he obtains other property in place of it,

the other property represents the original property.

(3) If a person disposes of recoverable property which represents the original property, the property may be followed into the hands of the person who obtains it (and it continues to represent the original property).

NOTES

Initial Commencement

To be appointed
To be appointed: see s 458(1), (2).

Appointment
Appointment: 30 December 2002: see SI 2002/3015, art 2, Schedule.

308 General exceptions

(1) If—

(a) a person disposes of recoverable property, and

(b) the person who obtains it on the disposal does so in good faith, for value and without notice that it was recoverable property, the property may not be followed into that person's hands and, accordingly, it ceases to be recoverable.

(2) If recoverable property is vested, forfeited or otherwise disposed of in pursuance of powers conferred by virtue of this Part, it ceases to be recoverable.

(3) If—

    (a)   in pursuance of a judgment in civil proceedings (whether in the United Kingdom or elsewhere), the defendant makes a payment to the claimant or the claimant otherwise obtains property from the defendant,

    (b)   the claimant's claim is based on the defendant's unlawful conduct, and

    (c)   apart from this subsection, the sum received, or the property obtained, by the claimant would be recoverable property,

the property ceases to be recoverable.

In relation to Scotland, "claimant" and "defendant" are to be read as "pursuer" and "defender".

(4) If—

    (a)   a payment is made to a person in pursuance of a compensation order under Article 14 of the Criminal Justice (Northern Ireland) Order 1994 (SI 1994/2795 (NI 15)), section 249 of the Criminal Procedure (Scotland) Act 1995 (c 46) or section 130 of the Powers of Criminal Courts (Sentencing) Act 2000 (c 6), and

    (b)   apart from this subsection, the sum received would be recoverable property,

the property ceases to be recoverable.

(5) If—

    (a)   a payment is made to a person in pursuance of a restitution order under section 27 of the Theft Act (Northern Ireland) 1969 (c 16 (NI)) or section 148(2) of the Powers of Criminal Courts (Sentencing) Act 2000 or a person otherwise obtains any property in pursuance of such an order, and

    (b)   apart from this subsection, the sum received, or the property obtained, would be recoverable property,

the property ceases to be recoverable.

(6) If—

    (a)   in pursuance of an order made by the court under section 382(3) or 383(5) of the Financial Services and Markets Act 2000 (c 8) (restitution orders), an amount is paid to or distributed among any persons in accordance with the court's directions, and

    (b)   apart from this subsection, the sum received by them would be recoverable property,

the property ceases to be recoverable.

(7) If—

    (a)   in pursuance of a requirement of the Financial Services Authority under section 384(5) of the Financial Services and Markets Act 2000 (power of authority to require restitution), an amount is paid to or distributed among any persons, and

    (b)   apart from this subsection, the sum received by them would be recoverable property,

the property ceases to be recoverable.

(8) Property is not recoverable while a restraint order applies to it, that is—

    (a)   an order under section 41, 120 or 190, or

    (b)   an order under any corresponding provision of an enactment mentioned in section 8(7)(a) to (g).

(9) Property is not recoverable if it has been taken into account in deciding the amount of a person's benefit from criminal conduct for the purpose of making a confiscation order, that is—

    (a)   an order under section 6, 92 or 156, or

    (b)   an order under a corresponding provision of an enactment mentioned in section 8(7)(a) to (g),

    and, in relation to an order mentioned in paragraph (b), the reference to the amount of a person's benefit from criminal conduct is to be read as a reference to the corresponding amount under the enactment in question.

(10) Where—

    (a)   a person enters into a transaction to which section 305(2) applies, and

    (b)   the disposal is one to which subsection (1) or (2) applies,

    this section does not affect the recoverability (by virtue of section 305(2)) of any property obtained on the transaction in place of the property disposed of.

NOTES

Initial Commencement

To be appointed
To be appointed: see s 458(1), (2).

Appointment
Appointment: 30 December 2002: see SI 2002/3015, art 2, Schedule.

Part 7   Money Laundering

Offences

327   Concealing etc

(1) A person commits an offence if he—

    (a)   conceals criminal property;

    (b)   disguises criminal property;

    (c)   converts criminal property;

    (d)   transfers criminal property;

    (e)   removes criminal property from England and Wales or from Scotland or from Northern Ireland.

(2) But a person does not commit such an offence if—

    (a)   he makes an authorised disclosure under section 338 and (if the disclosure is made before he does the act mentioned in subsection (1)) he has the appropriate consent;

    (b)   he intended to make such a disclosure but had a reasonable excuse for not doing so;

    (c)   the act he does is done in carrying out a function he has relating to the enforcement of any provision of this Act or of any other enactment relating to criminal conduct or benefit from criminal conduct.

(3) Concealing or disguising criminal property includes concealing or disguising its nature, source, location, disposition, movement or ownership or any rights with respect to it.

NOTES

Initial Commencement

To be appointed
To be appointed: see s 458(1).

Appointment
Appointment: 24 February 2003: see SI 2003/120, art 2(1), Schedule; for transitional provisions and savings see arts 1(2)(d), (e), 3 thereof (as amended by SI 2003/333, art 14).

328   Arrangements

(1) A person commits an offence if he enters into or becomes concerned in an arrangement which he knows or suspects facilitates (by whatever means) the acquisition, retention, use or control of criminal property by or on behalf of another person.

(2) But a person does not commit such an offence if—

    (a)   he makes an authorised disclosure under section 338 and (if the disclosure is made before he does the act mentioned in subsection (1)) he has the appropriate consent;

    (b)   he intended to make such a disclosure but had a reasonable excuse for not doing so;

    (c)   the act he does is done in carrying out a function he has relating to the enforcement of any provision of this Act or of any other enactment relating to criminal conduct or benefit from criminal conduct.

NOTES

Initial Commencement

To be appointed
To be appointed: see s 458(1).

Appointment
Appointment: 24 February 2003: see SI 2003/120, art 2(1), Schedule; for transitional provisions and savings see arts 1(2)(d), (e), 3 thereof (as amended by SI 2003/333, art 14).

329   Acquisition, use and possession

(1) A person commits an offence if he—

    (a)   acquires criminal property;

    (b)   uses criminal property;

    (c)   has possession of criminal property.

(2) But a person does not commit such an offence if—

    (a)   he makes an authorised disclosure under section 338 and (if the disclosure is made before he does the act mentioned in subsection (1)) he has the appropriate consent;

    (b)   he intended to make such a disclosure but had a reasonable excuse for not doing so;

    (c)   he acquired or used or had possession of the property for adequate consideration;

    (d)   the act he does is done in carrying out a function he has relating to the enforcement of any provision of this Act or of any other enactment relating to criminal conduct or benefit from criminal conduct.

(3) For the purposes of this section—

(a) a person acquires property for inadequate consideration if the value of the consideration is significantly less than the value of the property;

(b) a person uses or has possession of property for inadequate consideration if the value of the consideration is significantly less than the value of the use or possession;

(c) the provision by a person of goods or services which he knows or suspects may help another to carry out criminal conduct is not consideration.

NOTES

Initial Commencement

To be appointed
To be appointed: see s 458(1).

Appointment
Appointment: 24 February 2003: see SI 2003/120, art 2(1), Schedule; for transitional provisions and savings see arts 1(2)(d), (e), 3 thereof (as amended by SI 2003/333, art 14).

330 Failure to disclose: regulated sector

(1) A person commits an offence if each of the following three conditions is satisfied.

(2) The first condition is that he—

(a) knows or suspects, or

(b) has reasonable grounds for knowing or suspecting,

that another person is engaged in money laundering.

(3) The second condition is that the information or other matter—

(a) on which his knowledge or suspicion is based, or

(b) which gives reasonable grounds for such knowledge or suspicion,

came to him in the course of a business in the regulated sector.

(4) The third condition is that he does not make the required disclosure as soon as is practicable after the information or other matter comes to him.

(5) The required disclosure is a disclosure of the information or other matter—

(a) to a nominated officer or a person authorised for the purposes of this Part by the Director General of the National Criminal Intelligence Service;

(b)   in the form and manner (if any) prescribed for the purposes of this subsection by order under section 339.

(6) But a person does not commit an offence under this section if—

(a)   he has a reasonable excuse for not disclosing the information or other matter;

(b)   he is a professional legal adviser and the information or other matter came to him in privileged circumstances;

(c)   subsection (7) applies to him.

(7) This subsection applies to a person if—

(a)   he does not know or suspect that another person is engaged in money laundering, and

(b)   he has not been provided by his employer with such training as is specified by the Secretary of State by order for the purposes of this section.

(8) In deciding whether a person committed an offence under this section the court must consider whether he followed any relevant guidance which was at the time concerned—

(a)   issued by a supervisory authority or any other appropriate body,

(b)   approved by the Treasury, and

(c)   published in a manner it approved as appropriate in its opinion to bring the guidance to the attention of persons likely to be affected by it.

(9) A disclosure to a nominated officer is a disclosure which—

(a)   is made to a person nominated by the alleged offender's employer to receive disclosures under this section, and

(b)   is made in the course of the alleged offender's employment and in accordance with the procedure established by the employer for the purpose.

(10) Information or other matter comes to a professional legal adviser in privileged circumstances if it is communicated or given to him—

(a)   by (or by a representative of) a client of his in connection with the giving by the adviser of legal advice to the client,

(b)   by (or by a representative of) a person seeking legal advice from the adviser, or

(c)   by a person in connection with legal proceedings or contemplated legal proceedings.

(11) But subsection (10) does not apply to information or other matter which is communicated or given with the intention of furthering a criminal purpose.

(12) Schedule 9 has effect for the purpose of determining what is—

    (a)   a business in the regulated sector;

    (b)   a supervisory authority.

(13) An appropriate body is any body which regulates or is representative of any trade, profession, business or employment carried on by the alleged offender.

NOTES

Initial Commencement

To be appointed
To be appointed: see s 458(1).

Appointment
Appointment: 24 February 2003: see SI 2003/120, art 2(1), Schedule; for transitional provisions and savings see arts 1(2)(b), (c), 4 thereof.

Subordinate Legislation
Proceeds of Crime Act 2002 (Failure to Disclose Money Laundering: Specified Training) Order 2003, SI 2003/171 (made under sub-s (7)(b)).

331   Failure to disclose: nominated officers in the regulated sector

(1) A person nominated to receive disclosures under section 330 commits an offence if the conditions in subsections (2) to (4) are satisfied.

(2) The first condition is that he—

    (a)   knows or suspects, or

    (b)   has reasonable grounds for knowing or suspecting,

that another person is engaged in money laundering.

(3) The second condition is that the information or other matter—

    (a)   on which his knowledge or suspicion is based, or

    (b)   which gives reasonable grounds for such knowledge or suspicion,

came to him in consequence of a disclosure made under section 330.

(4) The third condition is that he does not make the required disclosure as soon as is practicable after the information or other matter comes to him.

(5) The required disclosure is a disclosure of the information or other matter—

    (a)   to a person authorised for the purposes of this Part by the Director General of the National Criminal Intelligence Service;

    (b)   in the form and manner (if any) prescribed for the purposes of this subsection by order under section 339.

(6) But a person does not commit an offence under this section if he has a reasonable excuse for not disclosing the information or other matter.

(7) In deciding whether a person committed an offence under this section the court must consider whether he followed any relevant guidance which was at the time concerned—

  (a)   issued by a supervisory authority or any other appropriate body,

  (b)   approved by the Treasury, and

  (c)   published in a manner it approved as appropriate in its opinion to bring the guidance to the attention of persons likely to be affected by it.

(8) Schedule 9 has effect for the purpose of determining what is a supervisory authority.

(9) An appropriate body is a body which regulates or is representative of a trade, profession, business or employment.

NOTES

Initial Commencement

To be appointed
To be appointed: see s 458(1).

Appointment
Appointment: 24 February 2003: see SI 2003/120, art 2(1), Schedule; for transitional provisions and savings see arts 1(2)(b), (c), 4 thereof.

332   Failure to disclose: other nominated officers

(1) A person nominated to receive disclosures under section 337 or 338 commits an offence if the conditions in subsections (2) to (4) are satisfied.

(2) The first condition is that he knows or suspects that another person is engaged in money laundering.

(3) The second condition is that the information or other matter on which his knowledge or suspicion is based came to him in consequence of a disclosure made under section 337 or 338.

(4) The third condition is that he does not make the required disclosure as soon as is practicable after the information or other matter comes to him.

(5) The required disclosure is a disclosure of the information or other matter—

  (a)   to a person authorised for the purposes of this Part by the Director General of the National Criminal Intelligence Service;

  (b)   in the form and manner (if any) prescribed for the purposes of this subsection by order under section 339.

(6) But a person does not commit an offence under this section if he has a reasonable excuse for not disclosing the information or other matter.

NOTES

Initial Commencement

To be appointed
To be appointed: see s 458(1).

Appointment
Appointment: 24 February 2003: see SI 2003/120, art 2(1), Schedule; for transitional provisions and savings see arts 1(2)(b), (c), 4 thereof.

333   Tipping off

(1) A person commits an offence if—

    (a)   he knows or suspects that a disclosure falling within section 337 or 338 has been made, and

    (b)   he makes a disclosure which is likely to prejudice any investigation which might be conducted following the disclosure referred to in paragraph (a).

(2) But a person does not commit an offence under subsection (1) if—

    (a)   he did not know or suspect that the disclosure was likely to be prejudicial as mentioned in subsection (1);

    (b)   the disclosure is made in carrying out a function he has relating to the enforcement of any provision of this Act or of any other enactment relating to criminal conduct or benefit from criminal conduct;

    (c)   he is a professional legal adviser and the disclosure falls within subsection (3).

(3) A disclosure falls within this subsection if it is a disclosure—

    (a)   to (or to a representative of) a client of the professional legal adviser in connection with the giving by the adviser of legal advice to the client, or

    (b)   to any person in connection with legal proceedings or contemplated legal proceedings.

(4) But a disclosure does not fall within subsection (3) if it is made with the intention of furthering a criminal purpose.

NOTES

Initial Commencement

To be appointed
To be appointed: see s 458(1).

Appointment
Appointment: 24 February 2003: see SI 2003/120, art 2(1), Schedule; for transitional provisions and savings see arts 1(2)(b)–(e), 3, 4, thereof (as amended by SI 2003/333, art 14).

334   Penalties

(1) A person guilty of an offence under section 327, 328 or 329 is liable—

> (a)   on summary conviction, to imprisonment for a term not exceeding six months or to a fine not exceeding the statutory maximum or to both, or

> (b)   on conviction on indictment, to imprisonment for a term not exceeding 14 years or to a fine or to both.

(2) A person guilty of an offence under section 330, 331, 332 or 333 is liable—

> (a)   on summary conviction, to imprisonment for a term not exceeding six months or to a fine not exceeding the statutory maximum or to both, or

> (b)   on conviction on indictment, to imprisonment for a term not exceeding five years or to a fine or to both.

NOTES

Initial Commencement

To be appointed
To be appointed: see s 458(1).

Appointment
Appointment: 24 February 2003: see SI 2003/120, art 2(1), Schedule; for transitional provisions and savings see arts 1(2)(b)–(e), 3, 4, thereof (as amended by SI 2003/333, art 14).

SCHEDULE 2

LIFESTYLE OFFENCES: ENGLAND AND WALES

Section 75

Drug trafficking

1   (1) An offence under any of the following provisions of the Misuse of Drugs Act 1971 (c 38)—

> (a)   section 4(2) or (3) (unlawful production or supply of controlled drugs);

> (b)   section 5(3) (possession of controlled drug with intent to supply);

> (c)   section 8 (permitting certain activities relating to controlled drugs);

> (d)   section 20 (assisting in or inducing the commission outside the UK of an offence punishable under a corresponding law).

(2) An offence under any of the following provisions of the Customs and Excise Management Act 1979 (c 2) if it is committed in connection with a

prohibition or restriction on importation or exportation which has effect by virtue of section 3 of the Misuse of Drugs Act 1971—

    (a)   section 50(2) or (3) (improper importation of goods);

    (b)   section 68(2) (exploration of prohibited or restricted goods);

    (c)   section 170 (fraudulent evasion).

(3) An offence under either of the following provisions of the Criminal Justice (International Co-operation) Act 1990 (c 5)—

    (a)   section 12 (manufacture or supply of a substance for the time being specified in Schedule 2 to that Act);

    (b)   section 19 (using a ship for illicit traffic in controlled drugs).

Money laundering

2   An offence under either of the following provisions of this Act—

    (a)   section 327 (concealing etc criminal property);

    (b)   section 328 (assisting another to retain criminal property).

Directing terrorism

3   An offence under section 56 of the Terrorism Act 2000 (c 11) (directing the activities of a terrorist organisation).

People trafficking

4   (1) An offence under section 25, 25A or 25B of the Immigration Act 1971 (c 77) (assisting unlawful immigration etc).

(2) *An offence under section 145 of the Nationality, Immigration and Asylum Act 2002 (traffic in prostitution)*

[(2) An offence under any of sections 57 to 59 of the Sexual Offences Act 2003 (trafficking for sexual exploitation).]

Arms trafficking

5   (1) An offence under either of the following provisions of the Customs and Excise Management Act 1979 if it is committed in connection with a firearm or ammunition—

    (a)   section 68(2) (exportation of prohibited goods);

    (b)   section 170 (fraudulent evasion).

(2) An offence under section 3(1) of the Firearms Act 1968 (c 27) (dealing in firearms or ammunition by way of trade or business).

(3) In this paragraph "firearm" and "ammunition" have the same meanings as in section 57 of the Firearms Act 1968 (c 27).

Counterfeiting

6   An offence under any of the following provisions of the Forgery and Counterfeiting Act 1981 (c 45)—

    (a)   section 14 (making counterfeit notes or coins);

    (b)   section 15 (passing etc counterfeit notes or coins);

    (c)   section 16 (having counterfeit notes or coins);

    (d)   section 17 (making or possessing materials or equipment for counterfeiting).

Intellectual property

7   (1) An offence under any of the following provisions of the Copyright, Designs and Patents Act 1988 (c 48)—

    (a)   section 107(1) (making or dealing in an article which infringes copyright);

    (b)   section 107(2) (making or possessing an article designed or adapted for making a copy of a copyright work);

    (c)   section 198(1) (making or dealing in an illicit recording);

    (d)   section 297A (making or dealing in unauthorised decoders).

(2) An offence under section 92(1), (2) or (3) of the Trade Marks Act 1994 (c 26) (unauthorised use etc of trade mark).

Pimps and brothels

8   *(1) An offence under any of the following provisions of the Sexual Offences Act 1956 (c 69)—*

    (a)   *section 2 (procuring a woman by threats);*

    (b)   *section 3 (procuring a woman by false pretences);*

    (c)   *section 9 (procuring a defective woman to have sexual intercourse);*

    (d)   *section 22 (procuring a woman for prostitution);*

    (e)   *section 24 (detaining a woman in a brothel);*

    (f)   *section 28 (causing or encouraging prostitution etc of girl under 16);*

    (g)   *section 29 (causing or encouraging prostitution of defective woman);*

    (h)   *section 30 (man living on earnings of prostitution);*

    (i)   *section 31 (woman exercising control over prostitute);*

 (j) *section 33 (keeping a brothel);*

 (k) *section 34 (letting premises for use as brothel).*

(2) An offence under section 5 of the Sexual Offences Act 1967 (c 60) (living on the earnings of male prostitute).

Prostitution and child sex

8 (1) An offence under section 33 or 34 of the Sexual Offences Act 1956 (keeping or letting premises for use as a brothel).

(2) An offence under any of the following provisions of the Sexual Offences Act 2003—

 (a) section 14 (arranging or facilitating commission of a child sex offence);

 (b) section 48 (causing or inciting child prostitution or pornography);

 (c) section 49 (controlling a child prostitute or a child involved in pornography);

 (d) section 50 (arranging or facilitating child prostitution or pornography);

 (e) section 52 (causing or inciting prostitution for gain);

 (f) section 53 (controlling prostitution for gain).

Blackmail

9 An offence under section 21 of the Theft Act 1968 (c 60) (blackmail).

Inchoate offences

10 (1) An offence of attempting, conspiring or inciting the commission of an offence specified in this Schedule.

(2) An offence of aiding, abetting, counselling or procuring the commission of such an offence.

NOTES

Initial Commencement

To be appointed
To be appointed: see s 458(1).

Appointment
Appointment: 24 March 2003: see SI 2003/333, art 2(1), Schedule; for transitional provisions see art 7 thereof (as amended by SI 2003/531, arts 2, 3).

Amendment
Para 4: substituted by the Nationality, Immigration and Asylum Act 2002, s 114(3), Sch 7, para 31.
 Date in force: 10 February 2003: see SI 2003/1, art 2, Schedule.

Para 4: sub-para (2) substituted by the Sexual Offences Act 2003, s 139, Sch 6, para 46(1), (2).
Date in force: to be appointed: see the Sexual Offences Act 2003, s 141(1).
Para 8: substituted by the Sexual Offences Act 2003, s 139, Sch 6, para 46(1), (3).
Date in force: to be appointed: see the Sexual Offences Act 2003, s 141(1).

Extent
This Schedule does not extend to Scotland: see s 461(1).

Appendix 1.2

Money Laundering Regulations 2003, Part II

SI 2003 No 3075

Part II   Obligations on Persons who Carry on Relevant Business

3   Systems and training etc to prevent money laundering

(1) Every person must in the course of relevant business carried on by him in the United Kingdom—

    (a)   comply with the requirements of regulations 4 (identification procedures), 6 (record-keeping procedures) and 7 (internal reporting procedures);

    (b)   establish such other procedures of internal control and communication as may be appropriate for the purposes of forestalling and preventing money laundering; and

    (c)   take appropriate measures so that relevant employees are—

        (i)   made aware of the provisions of these Regulations, Part 7 of the Proceeds of Crime Act 2002 (money laundering) and sections 18 and 21A of the Terrorism Act 2000; and

        (ii)   given training in how to recognise and deal with transactions which may be related to money laundering.

(2) A person who contravenes this regulation is guilty of an offence and liable—

    (a)   on conviction on indictment, to imprisonment for a term not exceeding 2 years, to a fine or to both;

    (b)   on summary conviction, to a fine not exceeding the statutory maximum.

(3) In deciding whether a person has committed an offence under this regulation, the court must consider whether he followed any relevant guidance which was at the time concerned—

    (a)   issued by a supervisory authority or any other appropriate body;

    (b)   approved by the Treasury; and

(c)   published in a manner approved by the Treasury as appropriate in their opinion to bring the guidance to the attention of persons likely to be affected by it.

(4) An appropriate body is any body which regulates or is representative of any trade, profession, business or employment carried on by the alleged offender.

(5) In proceedings against any person for an offence under this regulation, it is a defence for that person to show that he took all reasonable steps and exercised all due diligence to avoid committing the offence.

(6) Where a person is convicted of an offence under this regulation, he shall not also be liable to a penalty under regulation 20 (power to impose penalties).

4   Identification procedures

(1) In this regulation and in regulations 5 to 7—

(a)   "A" means a person who carries on relevant business in the United Kingdom; and

(b)   "B" means an applicant for business.

(2) This regulation applies if—

(a)   A and B form, or agree to form, a business relationship;

(b)   in respect of any one-off transaction—

(i)   A knows or suspects that the transaction involves money laundering; or

(ii)   payment of 15,000 euro or more is to be made by or to B; or

(c)   in respect of two or more one-off transactions, it appears to A (whether at the outset or subsequently) that the transactions are linked and involve, in total, the payment of 15,000 euro or more by or to B.

(3) A must maintain identification procedures which—

(a)   require that as soon as is reasonably practicable after contact is first made between A and B—

(i)   B must produce satisfactory evidence of his identity; or

(ii)   such measures specified in the procedures must be taken in order to produce satisfactory evidence of B's identity;

(b)   take into account the greater potential for money laundering which arises when B is not physically present when being identified;

(c) require that where satisfactory evidence of identity is not obtained, the business relationship or one-off transaction must not proceed any further; and

(d) require that where B acts or appears to act for another person, reasonable measures must be taken for the purpose of establishing the identity of that person.

5 Exceptions

(1) Except in circumstances falling within regulation 4(2)(b)(i), identification procedures under regulation 4 do not require A to take steps to obtain evidence of any person's identity in any of the following circumstances.

(2) Where A has reasonable grounds for believing that B—

(a) carries on in the United Kingdom relevant business falling within any of sub-paragraphs (a) to (e) of regulation 2(2), is not a money service operator and, if carrying on an activity falling within regulation 2(2)(a), is an authorised person with permission under the 2000 Act to carry on that activity;

(b) does not carry on relevant business in the United Kingdom but does carry on comparable activities to those falling within sub-paragraph (a) and is covered by the Money Laundering Directive; or

(c) is regulated by an overseas regulatory authority (within the meaning given by section 82 of the Companies Act 1989) and is based or incorporated in a country (other than an EEA State) whose law contains comparable provisions to those contained in the Money Laundering Directive.

(3) Where—

(a) A carries out a one-off transaction with or for a third party pursuant to an introduction effected by a person who has provided a written assurance that evidence of the identity of all third parties introduced by him will have been obtained and recorded under procedures maintained by him;

(b) that person identifies the third party; and

(c) A has reasonable grounds for believing that that person falls within any of sub-paragraphs (a) to (c) of paragraph (2).

(4) In relation to a contract of long-term insurance—

(a) in connection with a pension scheme taken out by virtue of a person's contract of employment or occupation where the contract of long-term insurance—

(i) contains no surrender clause; and

        (ii)   may not be used as collateral for a loan; or

   (b)   in respect of which a premium is payable—

        (i)   in one instalment of an amount not exceeding 2,500 euro; or

        (ii)   periodically and where the total payable in respect of any calendar year does not exceed 1,000 euro.

(5) Where the proceeds of a one-off transaction are payable to B but are instead directly reinvested on his behalf in another transaction—

   (a)   of which a record is kept; and

   (b)   which can result only in another reinvestment made on B's behalf or in a payment made directly to B.

6   Record-keeping procedures

(1) A must maintain procedures which require the retention of the records prescribed in paragraph (2) for the period prescribed in paragraph (3).

(2) The records are—

   (a)   where evidence of identity has been obtained under the procedures stipulated by regulation 4 (identification procedures) or pursuant to regulation 8 (casinos)—

        (i)   a copy of that evidence;

        (ii)   information as to where a copy of that evidence may be obtained; or

        (iii)   information enabling the evidence of identity to be re-obtained, but only where it is not reasonably practicable for A to comply with paragraph (i) or (ii); and

   (b)   a record containing details relating to all transactions carried out by A in the course of relevant business.

(3) In relation to the records mentioned in paragraph (2)(a), the period is—

   (a)   where A and B have formed a business relationship, at least five years commencing with the date on which the relationship ends; or

   (b)   in the case of a one-off transaction (or a series of such transactions), at least five years commencing with the date of the completion of all activities taking place in the course of that transaction (or, as the case may be, the last of the transactions).

(4) In relation to the records mentioned in paragraph (2)(b), the period is at least five years commencing with the date on which all activities taking place in the course of the transaction in question were completed.

(5) Where A is an appointed representative, his principal must ensure that A complies with this regulation in respect of any relevant business carried out by A for which the principal has accepted responsibility pursuant to section 39(1) of the 2000 Act.

(6) Where the principal fails to do so, he is to be treated as having contravened regulation 3 and he, as well as A, is guilty of an offence.

(7) "Appointed representative" has the meaning given by section 39(2) of the 2000 Act and "principal" has the meaning given by section 39(1) of that Act.

7 Internal reporting procedures

(1) A must maintain internal reporting procedures which require that—

(a) a person in A's organisation is nominated to receive disclosures under this regulation ("the nominated officer");

(b) anyone in A's organisation to whom information or other matter comes in the course of relevant business as a result of which he knows or suspects or has reasonable grounds for knowing or suspecting that a person is engaged in money laundering must, as soon as is practicable after the information or other matter comes to him, disclose it to the nominated officer or a person authorised for the purposes of these Regulations by the Director General of the National Criminal Intelligence Service;

(c) where a disclosure is made to the nominated officer, he must consider it in the light of any relevant information which is available to A and determine whether it gives rise to such knowledge or suspicion or such reasonable grounds for knowledge or suspicion; and

(d) where the nominated officer does so determine, the information or other matter must be disclosed to a person authorised for the purposes of these Regulations by the Director General of the National Criminal Intelligence Service.

(2) Paragraph (1) does not apply where A is an individual who neither employs nor acts in association with any other person.

(3) Paragraph (1)(b) does not apply in relation to a professional legal adviser where the information or other matter comes to him in privileged circumstances.

(4) Information or other matter comes to a professional legal adviser in privileged circumstances if it is communicated or given to him—

(a) by (or by a representative of) a client of his in connection with the giving by the adviser of legal advice to the client;

(b) by (or by a representative of) a person seeking legal advice from the adviser; or

    (c)   by a person in connection with legal proceedings or contemplated legal proceedings.

(5) But paragraph (4) does not apply to information or other matter which is communicated or given with the intention of furthering a criminal purpose.

(6) "Professional legal adviser" includes any person in whose hands information or other matter may come in privileged circumstances.

Schedule

Part II   Obligations on Persons who Carry on Relevant Business

4 Identification procedures

(1) In this regulation and in regulations 5 to 7—

    (a)   "A" means a person who carries on relevant business in the United Kingdom; and

    (b)   "B" means an applicant for business.

(2) This regulation applies if—

    (a)   A and B form, or agree to form, a business relationship;

    (b)   in respect of any one-off transaction—

        (i)   A knows or suspects that the transaction involves money laundering; or

        (ii)   payment of 15,000 euro or more is to be made by or to B; or

    (c)   in respect of two or more one-off transactions, it appears to A (whether at the outset or subsequently) that the transactions are linked and involve, in total, the payment of 15,000 euro or more by or to B.

(3) A must maintain identification procedures which—

    (a)   require that as soon as is reasonably practicable after contact is first made between A and B—

        (i)   B must produce satisfactory evidence of his identity; or

        (ii)   such measures specified in the procedures must be taken in order to produce satisfactory evidence of B's identity;

    (b)   take into account the greater potential for money laundering which arises when B is not physically present when being identified;

(c)   require that where satisfactory evidence of identity is not obtained, the business relationship or one-off transaction must not proceed any further; and

(d)   require that where B acts or appears to act for another person, reasonable measures must be taken for the purpose of establishing the identity of that person.

Appendix 2

International Money Laundering Law

Appendix 2.1

The Bahamas

Dr Peter D Maynard – Counsel and Attorney at Law

Money laundering

Money laundering was made a criminal offence under the now repealed Money Laundering Act 1996. Currently, under the financial architecture, PoCA 2000, Pt V contains the key money laundering offences, in PoCA 2000, ss 40–44, namely:

- concealing, transferring or dealing with the proceeds of criminal conduct;
- assisting another to retain proceeds of criminal conduct;
- acquisition, possession or use of proceeds of criminal conduct;
- failure to disclose knowledge or suspicion of money laundering; and
- tipping off.

PoCA 2000, s 40(1) and (2) set out the *actus reus* of offences of concealing, transferring or dealing with the proceeds of criminal conduct. The language is quite comprehensive.

PoCA 2000, s 40 reads as follows:

'40(1) A person is guilty of an offence of money laundering if he—

(a) uses, transfers, sends or delivers to any person or place any property which, in whole or in part directly or indirectly represents his proceeds of criminal conduct; or

(b) disposes, converts, alters or otherwise deals with in any manner and by any means that property, with the intent to conceal or disguise such property.

(2) A person is guilty of an offence of money laundering if, knowing, suspecting or having reasonable grounds to suspect that any property in whole or in part directly or indirectly represents, another person's proceeds of criminal conduct, he—

(a) uses, transfers, sends or delivers to any person or place that property; or

(b) disposes of or otherwise deals with in any manner by any means that property, with the intent to conceal or disguise such property.

(3) In this section the references to concealing or disguising any property include references to concealing or disguising its nature, source, location, disposition, movement or ownership or any rights with respect to it.'

The common *mens rea* is the intent to conceal or disguise property. PoCA 2000, s 40(2) gives an additional provision for the *mens rea*: knowing, suspecting or having reasonable grounds to suspect that any property in whole or in part, directly or indirectly represents, another person's proceeds of criminal conduct.

'Assisting' is covered by PoCA 2000, s 41(1), which states:

'41(1) Subject to subsection (3), a person is guilty of an offence if he enters into or is otherwise concerned in an arrangement whereby—

(a) the retention or control by or on behalf of another person ("A") of A's proceeds of criminal conduct is facilitated (whether by conceal-ment, removal from the jurisdiction, transfer to nominees or other-wise); or

(b) A's proceeds of criminal conduct—

(i) are used to secure that funds are placed at A's disposal; or

(ii) are used for A's benefit to acquire property, and he knows, suspects, or has reasonable grounds to suspect that A is a person who is or has been engaged in or has benefited from criminal conduct.'

'Acquisition of criminal proceeds' is dealt with by PoCA 2000, s 42 (1), which reads:

'42(1) A person is guilty of an offence if, knowing, suspecting or having reasonable grounds to suspect that any property is, or in whole or in part directly or indirectly represents, another person's proceeds of criminal conduct, he acquires or uses that property or has been of it.'

In addition, the offence of failure to disclose knowledge or suspicion of money laundering is set out in PoCA 2000, s 43(2). A person is guilty of an offence if they fail to disclose to the Financial Intelligence Unit ('FIU') or to a police officer, as soon as reasonably practicable, their knowledge or suspicion that another person is engaged in money laundering. This provision is the basis for the suspicious transaction reporting system directed by the FIU.

The Bahamas has all crimes money laundering offences. The offences governed by PoCA 2000 and set out in PoCA 2000, Sch include:

'(a) an offence under the Prevention of Bribery Act, Chapter 81;

(b)   an offence under section 40, 41, or 42 (money laundering);

(c)   an offence which may be tried on information in The Bahamas other than a drug trafficking offence;

(d)   an offence committed anywhere that, if it had occurred in The Bahamas, would constitute an offence in The Bahamas as set out in this Schedule.'

What crimes are predicate offences for money laundering purposes? In PoCA 2000, Sch, as indicated above, money laundering offences are referred to in para (b). However, a comprehensive range of predicate offences is covered in paras (a), (c) and (d). The limitation is that the offence is to be mutual or reciprocal, as suggested by the language of (d).

Is foreign corruption a predicate offence? The Bahamas is a party to the relevant international and regional conventions and resolutions. But there is no specific offence of foreign (or local) corruption. However, applying PoCA 2000, Sch, para (d) (see above), it is likely that such an offence would be caught under bribery, stealing, fraud or related offences. Therefore, such an offence would qualify as a predicate offer.

Is foreign tax evasion a predicate offence? Under international law, The Bahamas is not required to enforce the tax and revenue laws of other countries. The Bahamas has not entered into treaties with other countries, except the Tax Information Exchange Agreement with the US, concluded on 25 January 2002, which creates an obligation to assist the US in obtaining tax information which may be the foundation of a charge in the US of tax evasion. In any event, tax evasion is frequently accompanied by a charge of fraud or a related offence which is reciprocal, and which would fall into PoCA 2000, Sch, para (d).

How is terrorism defined? The Bahamas is a party to UN and other multilateral anti-terrorism conventions and resolutions. It has participated in the drafting of them over the years. But, prior to the terrorist attacks in the US on 11 September 2001, as elsewhere, this was not the most pressing issue on the national legislative agenda. Since then, an Executive Order to facilitate the freezing of assets of terrorists and their associates has been issued. Banking records have been examined to determine whether any accounts belong to any individual or organisation included in the list provided by the US government. No accounts in the names of such individuals or organisations were found. In addition, it is noteworthy that new anti-terrorism legislation is being considered by the Parliament of the Bahamas.

Does the predicate offence have to be proved to a criminal or civil standard of proof? The criminal standard of proof would apply to the predicate offences, as it would apply to all offences in The Bahamas.

It may be asked whether The Bahamas has a suspicion-based reporting system or a transaction based reporting system (or hybrid of the two). The reporting system is suspicion-based. Transaction-based systems are regarded as even more costly and ineffective than suspicion-based systems.

What is the definition of suspicious? Is the definition of suspicion objective or subjective, and what is a suspicious transaction for these purposes? There is no definition of 'suspicious' in the legislation. It is intended to have its ordinary meaning, and is subjective. However, due diligence and Know Your Customer rules have been in place for a considerable time. In addition, voluminous manuals of suspicious transaction and anti-money guidelines have been issued by the FIU which contain examples of suspicious transactions. A transaction, as defined in the Financial Transactions Reporting Act 2000, s 2:

'(a) means any deposit, withdrawal, exchange or transfer of funds (in whatever currency denominated), whether

(i) in cash,

(ii) by cheque payment order or other instrument, or

(iii) by electronic or other non-physical means; and

(b) without limiting the generality of its foregoing, includes any payment made in satisfaction, in whole or in part, or any contractual or other legal obligation;

but does not include any of the following—

(c) the placing of any bet;

(d) participation in any game of chance defined in the Lotteries and Gaming Act;

(e) any transaction that is exempted from the provisions of this Act by or under regulations made under section 42 [sic].'

It is the Financial Transactions Reporting Act 2000, s 50 that empowers the minister to make regulations.

Separate suspicious transaction and anti-money laundering guidelines, tailored for particular sectors, have been issued to each of the following groups: banks and trust companies; financial service providers; co-operative societies; the insurance sector; the securities industry; and licensed casino operators. They contain copious examples of suspicious transactions and are designed to be used as a reference and a training tool.

For additional guidance, the prescribed form of a suspicious transaction report ('STR') is set out in FTRA 2000, Sch 2. The details to be included in the report are set out in that form and in FTRA 2000, s 14.

Disclosure of money laundering and suspicions thereof is mandatory in relation to all offences. There is also an obligation to maintain anti-money laundering procedures. This obligation applies to all financial institutions. Under FTRA 2000, s 3(1), a financial institution means:

'(a) bank or trust company, being a bank or trust company licensed under the Banks and Trust Companies Regulation Act, 2000;

(b)   a company carrying on life assurance business as defined in section 2 of the Insurance Act;

(c)   a co-operative society registered under the Co-operative Societies Act;

(d)   a friendly society enroled under the Friendly Societies Act;

(e)   a licensed casino operator within the meaning of the Lotteries and Gaming Act;

(f)   a broker-dealer within the meaning of section 2 of the Securities Industry Act;

(g)   a real estate broker, but only to the extent that the real estate broker receives funds in the course of the person's business for the purpose of settling real estate transactions;

(h)   a trustee or administration manager of investment manager of a superannuation scheme;

(i)   a mutual fund administrator or operator of a mutual fund within the meaning of the Mutual Funds Act, 1995;

(j)   any person whose business consists of any of the following: (i) borrowing or lending or investing money, (ii) administering or managing funds on behalf of other persons, (iii) acting as trustee in respect of funds of other persons, (iv) dealing in life assurance policies, (v) providing financial services that involve the transfer or exchange of funds, including (without limitation) services relating to financial leasing, money transmissions, credit cards, debit cards, treasure certificates, bankers draft and other means of payment, financial guarantees, trading for account of others (in money market instruments, foreign exchange, interest and index instruments, transferable securities and futures), participation in securities issues, portfolio management, safekeeping of cash and liquid securities, investments related insurance and money changing; but not including the provision of financial services that consist solely of the provision of financial advice;

(k)   a counsel and attorney, but only to the extent that the counsel and attorney receives funds in the course of that person's business (i) for the purposes of deposit or investment, (ii) for the purpose of settling real estate transactions; or (iii) to be held in a client account;

(l)   an accountant, but only to the extent that the accountant receives funds in the course of that person's business for the purpose of deposit or investment.'

With reference to the 11 principal statutes which make up the new anti-money laundering financial architecture (see above) which took effect on 29 December 2000 (apart from the Insurance Act 2000 and Co-operative Societies Act 2000, which came into force in mid-2000), all have some bearing to the government's anti-money laundering campaign and its response to the pressure of the OECD.

They should be read together with the other statutes which make up the new financial architecture and the related statutes.

Proceeds of Crime Act 2000

The keystone anti-money laundering statute is PoCA 2000, which consists of seven Parts: preliminary; confiscation orders; enforcement of confiscation orders; information gathering powers; money laundering; seizure of cash; and miscellaneous and supplemental. It contains 64 sections and a Schedule.

PoCA 2000, s 3 provides for the interpretation of several expressions used in the legislation, such as 'drug trafficking', 'drug trafficking offence' and 'proceeds of criminal conduct'. As for what is a relevant offence under the Act, s 3 refers to PoCA 2000, Sch which sets out a relevant offence as follows:

'(a)   an offence under the Prevention of Bribery Act, Chapter 81;

(b)   an offence under section 40, 41, or 42 of this Act (money laundering);

(c)   an offence which may be tried on information in The Bahamas other than a drug trafficking offence;

(d)   an offence committed anywhere that, if it had occurred in The Bahamas, would constitute an offence in The Bahamas as set out in this Schedule.'

PoCA 2000, s 4 defines property and realisable property.

PoCA 2000, s 5 makes provisions for the valuation of property which shall be the market value of the property, taking into consideration any amount required to discharge an incumbrance. PoCA 2000, s 6 provides retroactively that a gift is caught by the legislation. A gift is caught if it was made by the defendant at any time from the beginning of the period of six years after the proceedings were instituted or when an application for a charging or restraint order was made; or if it was made by the defendant at any time and was a gift of property received by the defendant in connection with drug trafficking carried on by them or another person, or which property in whole or in part directly or indirectly represented in the defendant's hands property received by them in that connection.

PoCA 2000, s 7 provides for the definition of other terms used in the legislation, including 'items subject to legal privilege': attorney-client communications in respect of legal advice to the client, and communications between attorney and client and any other person in connection with or in contemplation and for the purpose of legal proceedings. However, privilege does not apply if the communications are not in the possession of a person entitled to possession of them. Items resulting from criminal conduct or held with the intention of furthering a criminal purpose are not subject to legal privilege, and legal privilege does not extend to information regarding the identity or address of the client or principal.

'Money laundering' is defined as doing an act which constitutes an offence under PoCA 2000, s 40, 41 or 42, or which would constitute such an offence if done in The Bahamas. For these purposes, having possession of any property is taken to be doing an act in relation to it.

PoCA 2000, ss 40–44 provide for the five offences relating to money laundering. These offences are concealing or transferring proceeds of criminal conduct; assisting another to retain proceeds of criminal conduct; acquisition, possession or use of proceeds of criminal conduct; disclosure of knowledge or suspicion of money laundering; and tipping off. The former three offences are discussed above, and the latter two below.

Financial Transactions Reporting Act 2000

The legislation is aimed not only at punishing money laundering, but also at preventing it. FTRA 2000 plays an important role in this scheme. The Act consists of six Parts, 51 sections and two Schedules. Of note among the preliminary provisions is the definition of 'financial institution' which is given a comprehensive meaning under FTRA 2000, s 3 (see above). A financial 'transaction' means any deposit, withdrawal, exchange or transfer of funds (FTRA 2000, s 2).

FTRA 2000, Pt II deals with obligations of financial institutions to verify the identity of persons. Where any request is made to a financial institution for a person to become a 'facility holder' as defined in FTRA 2000, s 2, the financial institution is required to verify the identity of the person (FTRA 2000, s 6).

Where any person conducts an 'occasional transaction', as defined in FTRA 2000, s 2, the financial institution is required to verify the identity of the person if the amount of funds involved in the transaction exceeds a prescribed amount (FTRA 2000, s 7). The prescribed amount under FTRA 2000, Pt II is US $10,000.

Under FTRA 2000, ss 8 and 9, financial institutions are also required to verify the identity of any person who conducts a transaction on behalf of another person. Where a financial institution is required to verify the identity of any person, such verification must be done by means of documentary or other evidence as is reasonably capable of establishing the identity of that person (FTRA 2000, s 11).

FTRA 2000, s 12 sets out penalties against persons who commit offences against FTRA 2000, Pt II. According to the regulations, where a financial institution is required to verify the identity of any person, the following information is required:

1   full and correct name of the person;

2   their permanent address;

3   their telephone and fax number (if any);

4   their date and place of birth;

5   their nationality;

6   their occupation and name of employer (if self-employed, the nature of the self-employment);

7   a copy of the first four pages of their passport or a copy of their national identity card showing the following details–

   (i)   number and country of issuance,

   (ii)   issue date and expiry date, and

   (iii) signature of the person;

8   their signature;

9   the purpose of the account and the potential account activity;

10   their written authority to obtain independent verification of any information provided;

11   their source of income or wealth;

12   their written confirmation that all credits to the account are and will be beneficially owned by the facility holder; and

13   such documentary or other evidence as is reasonably capable of establishing the identity of that person. Written confirmation of ownership indicated at 12 applies to the verification of identity of the beneficial owners of all facilities.

As regards verification of corporate entities, where a financial institution is required to verify the identity of any corporate entity, whether incorporated in The Bahamas or elsewhere, the following information is required:

1   a certified copy of the certificate of incorporation;

2   a certified copy of the Memorandum and Articles of Association of the entity;

3   the location of the registered office or registered agent of the corporate entity;

4   the resolution of the Board of Directors authorising the opening of the account and conferring authority on the person who will operate the account;

5   confirmation that the corporate entity has not been struck off the register or is not in the process of being wound up;

6   the names and addresses of all officers and directors of the corporate entity;

7   the names and addresses of the beneficial owners of the corporate entity, except a publicly traded company;

8   a description and nature of the business, including the date of commencement of business, products or services provided and the location of principal business;

9   the purpose of the account and the potential parameters of the account, including the size (in the case of investment and custody accounts) balance ranges (in the case of deposit accounts) and the expected transaction volume of the account;

10   written authority to obtain independent verification of any information provided;

11   written confirmation that all credits to the account are and will be beneficially owned by the facility holder; and

12   such other official document and other information as is reasonably capable of establishing the structural information of the corporate entity.

FTRA 2000, Pt III deals with the obligation to report suspicious transactions. Where a financial institution has reasonable grounds to suspect that a transaction is relevant to the enforcement of PoCA 2000, the financial institution is required to report the transaction to the FIU (FTRA 2000, s 14).

Auditors are also required to report suspicious transactions to the police (FTRA 2000, s 15). Persons who report suspicious transactions are protected from civil, criminal or disciplinary proceedings in respect of such disclosure (FTRA 2000, s 16). However, counsel and attorneys are not required to disclose any communication made to them in their professional capacity (FTRA 2000, s 17). The identity of persons making suspicious transactions reports is protected by FTRA 2000, s 19.

FTRA 2000, Pt IV deals with the retention of records. Every financial institution is required to keep records so as to enable the FIU to reconstruct any transaction that is conducted through that institution (FTRA, s 23).

Every financial institution is required to keep records so as to enable the FIU to ascertain the nature of the evidence used by the institution to verify the identity of a person (FTRA 2000, s 24). FTRA 2000, s 30 sets out penalties against persons who commit offences against FTRA 2000, Pt IV.

FTRA 2000, Pt V deals with search warrants. This Part sets out provisions for the issuing and execution of search warrants for anything upon or in respect of which any offence against FTRA 2000 has been committed.

FTRA 2000, s 39 sets out the liabilities of employers and employees and directors and officers of bodies corporate. FTRA 2000, s 42 gives the Minister power to make regulations for the purposes of the Act.

Disclosure and tipping-off

How is a disclosure report made? To what agency? As for the procedures, as set out, for example, in the guidelines for financial and corporate service providers, employees are required to report suspicious transactions to the Money Launder-ing Reporting Officer ('MLRO'), an internal officer to be appointed by each financial institution. If the employee has reported their suspicion to the MLRO, they have satisfied this obligation. The financial institution must ensure that prospective suspicions are passed without delay to the MLRO, who facilitates the expeditious reporting to the FIU, which is the national reception point for the disclosure of STRs. The MLRO, who may be a senior member of the compliance, internal audit or fraud department or, indeed, the chief executive in smaller institutions, determines whether the information rises to the level of knowledge or suspicion of money laundering.

Do they apply to operations abroad? No – they apply only to financial institu-tions within the jurisdiction.

Could disclosure result in a breach of customer confidentiality? Yes. However, the legislation requires that no civil liability will arise as a result of a disclosure.

Does the agency consent to transactions? No. The system is not based on transaction reporting. However, on the basis of an STR, the FIU may object to a transaction and take other steps, such as issuing a monitoring, restraining or freezing order.

How much feedback is given? The FIU must give feedback to the reporting institution. A form has been developed by the FIU for this purpose. What use is made of the intelligence obtained? The information may be the foundation of a charge for a criminal offence. For the purpose of laying a charge, the FIU works in co-ordination with the Attorney-General's Office. The information may also be used for interim measures by the FIU, such as the orders referred to above.

PoCA 2000, s 44(1) and (2) deal with the offence of tipping off. Section 44 reads in the relevant part as follows:

'44(1) A person is guilty of an offence if—

(a) he knows, suspects or has reasonable grounds to suspect that a police officer is acting, or is proposing to act, in connection with an investigation which is being, or is about to be, conducted into money laundering; and

(b) he discloses to any other person information or any other matter which is likely to prejudice that investigation.

(2) A person is guilty of an offence if—

(a) he knows, suspects or has reasonable grounds to suspect that a disclosure has been made to a police officer or, to an appropriate person under section 41, 42 or 43; and

(b) he discloses to any other person information or any other matter which is likely to prejudice any investigation which might be conducted following such a disclosure.'

As for the offence of tipping off, the tipping off provisions do not conflict with principles governing liability for knowing assistance. The leading cases on dishonest assistance (eg, *Royal Brunei Airlines Sdn Bhd v Tan [1995] 2 AC 378, PC; Barnes v Addy (1874) 9 Ch App 244)*suggest that, where a third party dishonestly assists a trustee to commit a breach of trust, the third party is liable to the beneficiary for the loss, even if the third party has not received any trust property and the trustee has not actually been dishonest. Therefore, there is no conflict with tipping off as provided in the Bahamian legislation.

Appendix 2.2

Canada

Marc Duquette – Partner, Ogilvy Renault, Montreal

Martin Theriault – Associate, Ogilvy Renault, Montreal

New legislation

The new legislation, called 'An Act to facilitate combating the laundering of proceeds of crime and to establish the Financial Transactions and Reports Analysis Centre of Canada' was enacted on 5 July 2000. The Act (whose short title was the Proceeds of Crime (Money Laundering) Act, referred to hereinafter as 'PC(ML)A 2000') built on the previous legislation by introducing a requirement to report certain suspicious financial transactions as well as cross border movements of currency.

New Regulations

The government next proceeded to adopt the first of a series of Regulations prescribing the conditions pertaining to the application of PC(ML)A 2000. Upon the adoption of the Proceeds of Crime (Money Laundering) Suspicious Transaction Reporting Regulation (SOR/2002–184) (the Suspicious Transaction Regulations), a portion of the substantive provisions of PC(ML)A 2000, Pt I came into force on 8 November 2001. The legislation thus now requires financial institutions and other designated persons and entities to report suspicious transactions, ie financial transactions which they reasonably suspect are related to the commission of a money laundering offence.

Subsequently, on 9 May 2002, additional Regulations, known as the Proceeds of Crime (Money Laundering) and Terrorist Financing Regulations (SOR/2002–184) (the Money Laundering Regulations) were published to address, *inter alia*, the reporting of large cash transactions and the record-keeping thereof.

Overview of money laundering legislation

In Canada, criminal law and international affairs fall within the exclusive jurisdiction of the federal Parliament. The laws dealing with such matters and with money laundering may be categorised in the following manner:

1   *Substantive legislation*: these are the laws under which the criminal offences are created, including the Criminal Code, and which are discussed at below.

2   *Money laundering legislation* (record keeping, reporting and other): these laws have recently been the object of in-depth revision by the federal legislative authority and the Proceeds of Crime (Money Laundering) Act, originally enacted in 1991, is now almost entirely replaced by PC(ML)TFA 2001. These laws are covered at below.

3   *Complementary legislation*: these laws consist essentially of the Mutual Legal Assistance in Criminal Matters Act 1988 and the Seized Property Management Act 1993, together with certain provisions of the Criminal Code pertaining to search, seizure and detention of proceeds of crime. The complementary legislation is discussed at below.

Substantive legislation

Offence of laundering proceeds of crime

The relevant offences are found in the Criminal Code (Criminal Code, s 462.31), which defines the offence of 'laundering proceeds of crime'. According to the Criminal Code, everyone commits an offence who uses, transfers the possession of, sends or delivers to any person or place, transports, transmits, alters, disposes of or otherwise deals with, in any manner and by any means, any property or any proceeds of any property with intent to conceal or convert that property or those proceeds, knowing or believing that all or a part of that property or of those proceeds was obtained or derived directly or indirectly as a result of (a) the commission in Canada of a designated offence, or (b) an act or commission anywhere that, if it has occurred in Canada, would have constituted a designated offence.

Under the Criminal Code (s 462.31(2)), everyone who commits a money laundering proceeds of crime offence is guilty of an indictable offence and liable to imprisonment for a term not exceeding ten years.

Designated offence

Recent amendments have been made to the Criminal Code to introduce the concept of designated offence. As stated in the Criminal Code, s 462.3(1), a designated offence means (a) an indictable offence under the Criminal Code or any other Act of Parliament, other than an indictable offence prescribed by regulation, or (b) a conspiracy or an attempt to commit, being an accessory in relation to, or any counselling in relation to, an offence referred to in para (a). A new set of Regulations relating to the Criminal Code, s 462.3(1)(a) was adopted, which state that the indictable offences under the following Acts are excluded from the definition of designated offence: the Budget Implementation Act, 2000, the Canada Agricultural Products Act, the Copyright Act, the Excise Act (except for specific indictable offences thereunder), the Excise Tax Act, the Feeds Act, the Fertilizers Act, the Foreign Publishers Advertising Services Act, the Health of Animals Act, the Income Tax Act, the Meat Inspection Act, the Nuclear Safety and Control Act (except for an indictable offence hereunder), the Plant Protection Act and the Seeds Act. Further to the introduction of this new concept of designated offence under the Criminal Code, s 462.31, the offence of laundering proceeds of crime now extends to all indictable offences under the Criminal Code and other Acts of Parliament, other than the exceptions listed above. Prior to this amendment, the laundering proceeds of crime offence applied only to a limited list of indictable offences.

According to statements published as part of the Regulations Excluding Certain Indictable Offences from the Definition of 'Designated Offence' (Regulations Excluding Certain Indictable Offences from the Definition of 'Designated Offence', see section entitled 'Regulatory Impact Analysis Statement' therein.), the offences excluded from the definition of designated offence are regarded as inappropriate for inclusion in the Criminal Code proceeds of crime scheme for a number of reasons. In some instances, the proceeds derived from the commission of the excluded offence are subject to particular procedures contained in the statute in which that offence is found. As an example, offences under the Income Tax Act, the Excise Act and the Excise Tax Act are excluded, since the statutes already provide for specific rules and penalties for dealing with tax evasion and recovering any unpaid tax. Another reason for excluding offences from the definition of designated offence comes from the fact that certain offences are part of a regulatory context based on enforcement involving an administrative and monetary penalty structure. This is the case with a number of statutes that are subject to the Agriculture and Agri-Food Administrative Monetary Penalties Act, such as the Feeds Act, the Fertilisers Act, the Meat Inspections Act, and certain other Acts.

Extra-territorial application

As can be seen from the above, a money laundering offence generally involves concealing or converting property from the proceeds of property, knowing or believing that these were derived from the commission of an offence referred to as the 'laundering of proceeds of crime offence' as defined in the Criminal Code and described above. It should be noted that a number of these offences have extra-territorial application and that these offences will constitute an offence in Canada even if they were not committed in Canada where the act or omission, if it had occurred in Canada, would have constituted an offence therein as described above. For instance, the offence of corruption of a foreign official referred to in the Corruption of Foreign Public Officials Act (s 5) is an example. Under this provision, every person commits an offence if they use, transmit or otherwise deal with, in any manner, any property or any proceeds of any property with the intent to conceal or convert that property, knowing that the property was obtained as a result of (i) the commission of the offence of bribing a foreign public officer or (ii) an act or omission anywhere that, if it had occurred in Canada, would have constituted the offence of bribing a foreign public officer. The offence of bribing a foreign public officer is made by anyone who, in order to obtain or retain an advantage in the course of business, gives or offers a loan or benefit of any kind to a foreign public official as a consideration for an act by the official in connection with the performance of the official's duties or functions, or to induce the official to use his or her position to influence any acts of the foreign state or public international organisation for which the official performs duties or functions.

Money laundering legislation

PC(ML)TFA 2001 and its Regulations is gradually coming into force, and parts of the Act and certain of its Regulations are already effective. The Act is divided in separate Parts, covering:

1   *Part I* record keeping and reporting of suspicious transactions;

2   *Part II* reporting of currency and monetary instruments;

3   *Part III* financial transactions and reports analysis centre of Canada; and

4   *other separate Parts* dealing with Regulations, and offences and punishments.

One of the major amendments to the previous legislative frame was introduced by PC(ML)TFA 2001, Pt I with its reporting and record keeping requirements and the introduction of the reporting of suspicious transactions.

Prescribed parties

PC(ML)TFA 2001, Pt I applies to the following persons and entities, *inter alia*:

1   authorised foreign banks within the meaning of the Bank Act, s 2 in respect of their business in Canada, or banks to which the Bank Act applies;

2   co-operative credit societies, savings and credit unions and *caisses populaires* (a local type of credit union) regulated by a provincial Act and associations regulated by the Co-operative Credit Associations Act;

3   life companies or foreign life companies to which the Insurance Companies Act applies or life insurance companies regulated by a provincial Act;

4   companies to which the Trust and Loan Companies Act applies;

5   trust companies regulated by a provincial Act;

6   loan companies regulated by a provincial Act;

7   persons and entities authorised under provincial legislation to engage in the business of dealing in securities, or to provide portfolio management or investment counselling services;

8   persons and entities engaged in the business of foreign exchange dealing;

9   persons and entities engaged in a business, profession or activity described in Regulations made under PC(ML)TFA 2001;

10   persons and entities engaged in a business or profession described in Regulations made under PC(ML)TFA 2001, while carrying out the activities described in the Regulations;

11   casinos, including those owned or controlled by Her Majesty (many casinos in Canada are owned and operated by provincial governments.);

12   departments and agents of Her Majesty in right of Canada or of a province that are engaged in the business of accepting deposit liabilities or that sell money orders to the public, while carrying out the activities described in Regulations made under PC(ML)TFA 2001; and

13   for the purposes of reporting suspicious transactions, employees of a person or entity referred to above (collectively, the 'Prescribed Parties' and, individually, a 'Prescribed Party').

In relation to point 13 at above, it should be noted that an offence may be committed under PC(ML)TFA 2001 either by an entity or by its individual employees. For example, a bank may be liable for the actions of its employees, and it is sufficient proof of the offence when prosecuting the bank to establish that the offence was committed by an employee or agent of the bank, whether or not the employee or agent is identified or has been prosecuted for the offence. It is, however, a valid defence for the entity to establish that it has exercised due diligence to prevent the commission of the offence (s 79). It should also be noted that where a person or entity (ie, a bank) commits an offence, any officer, director or agent of the entity who directed, authorised, assented to, acquiesced in or participated in its commission is a party to and guilty of the offence, and liable on conviction to the punishment provided for the offence, whether or not the person or entity has been prosecuted or convicted (s 73). No employee of the entity, however, shall be convicted of the offence of failing to report a suspicious transaction where the employee had reported the transaction to its superior (s 75(2)).

Money laundering offence

According to PC(ML)TFA 2001, a money laundering offence means an offence under the Criminal Code, s 462.31(1), as more fully described at above (s 2).

Record keeping

Records to be kept

The records that financial entities are required to keep, where a person or entity opens an account, is a signature card in respect of each account holder for that account or, in respect of an account opened by a corporation, a copy of the document relating to the power to bind a corporation in respect of the account. Under the Money Laundering Regulations (s 1(2)) and the Suspicious Transaction Regulations (s 1(1)), financial entities mean the persons and entities listed under points 1, 2, 4, 5, 6 and 12 above. In the case of point 12 however, only for specific activities listed in the said Regulations (Financial Entities).

Other documents to be kept include copies of operating agreements, deposit slips, debit and credit memos, account statements sent to the clients, every cleared cheque drawn on or deposited to the account, unless certain conditions are met, client credit files and transaction tickets in respect of every foreign currency exchange transaction. Additional conditions are also prescribed for particular classes of Prescribed Parties, such as life insurance companies and life insurance brokers or agents, securities dealers, persons or entities engaged in the business of foreign exchange dealings, money services businesses, legal counsel and legal firms, accountants and accounting firms, real estate brokers or sales representatives, casinos and even certain government departments and agents.

Ascertaining identity

Every person or entity required to keep and retain a large cash transaction record under the Money Laundering Regulations must also ascertain the identity of every individual with whom the person or entity conducts a transaction in respect of which that record must be kept, other than a deposit to a corporate account or by means of an automated banking machine (s 53). Certain exceptions, however, apply: see Money Laundering Regulations, ss 62 and 63. The Regulations also prescribe certain measures for ascertaining identity.

Acting for a third party

Every person or entity required to keep large cash transaction records must take reasonable measures to determine whether the individual who in fact gives the cash in respect of which the record is kept is acting on behalf of a third party. Where the person or entity determines that the individual is acting on behalf of a third party, the person or entity must keep a record setting out details such as the third party's name and address, the nature of the principal business or occupation of the third party, the nature of the relationship between the third party and the individual who gives the cash to the Prescribed Party, etc. Other provisions pertaining to persons or entities required to keep a signature card or an account operating agreement also prescribe the same, such that they shall, at the time that the account is opened, take reasonable measures to determine whether the account is to be used by, or on behalf of, the third party (Money Laundering Regulations, ss 8 and 9).

Conservation of records

Finally, the prescribed records must be kept in a machine-readable or electronic form and must be retained for a period of at least five years following the day of the closing of the account to which it relates or, in other cases, five years from the day on which it was created. In addition, every record that is required to be kept shall be retained in such a way that it can be provided for examination by an authorised person within 30 days of the request (Money Laundering Regulations, ss 68–70).

Reporting prescribed transactions

PC(ML)TFA 2001 contains an obligation for the Prescribed Parties to report certain prescribed transactions to FINTRAC (PC(ML)TFA 2001, s 9). Such reporting requirement is scheduled to come into effect on 30 November 2002 and, as set forth in the Money Laundering Regulations, it requires each Prescribed Party to report to FINTRAC, in a specified form and manner, such prescribed transactions occurring in the course of their activities. Every Financial Entity must report to FINTRAC any receipt from a client of an amount in cash of CDN $10,000 or more in the course of a single transaction, together with prescribed information, unless the cash is received from another Financial Entity or a public body (see the Money Laundering Regulations, s 12(a)). The prescribed information to be provided by the Financial Entity includes information on the place of business where the transaction occurred, information on the actual transaction (including details of the transaction, type of funds, amount of transaction, currency of transaction and names of other institutions and account numbers involved, as well as details of the disposition of funds), account information (including full name of each account holder), information on persons conducting the transaction (such as the person's full name, address, country of residence, telephone numbers, citizenship and identifier, date of birth, occupation, employer, etc) and information on the entity or person on whose behalf the transaction is conducted (if applicable).

Obligations of the Financial Entities also include reporting to FINTRAC the sending out of Canada or the receipt from outside Canada, at the request of a client, of an electronic fund transfer of CDN $10,000 or more in the course of a single transaction, together with certain required information which includes, *inter alia*, transaction information, information on a client ordering payment of an electronic fund transfer, information on the person or entity that sends payment instruction or that orders funds transfer on behalf of a client, information on sender's correspondent acting as reimbursement bank for sender (if applicable) and information on any intermediary institution (Money Laundering Regulations, s 12(b) and (c)).

Prescribed Parties other than Financial Entities such as life insurers, life insurance brokers or agents, securities dealers, persons or entities engaged in the business of foreign exchange dealings, money services businesses, legal counsel and legal firms, accountants and accounting firms, real estate brokers and sales representatives and casinos are subject to particular reporting obligations in respect of described transactions which, for the most part, relate to receipt of amounts in cash, but not to electronic fund transfers of CDN $10,000 or more, which are typically handled only by Financial Entities.

Financial Entities are not required to report prescribed transactions if certain conditions are met. These include situations where their client has, for at least 24 months, had an account in respect of that business with a single Financial Entity, whether it be the Financial Entity receiving the deposit or another Financial Entity.1 Other exceptions include where cash deposits made by a client are consistent with its usual practice in respect of the business and where the Financial Entity has taken reasonable measures to determine the source of the cash for those deposits. These exceptions to the obligation to report prescribed transactions do not apply however to corporations carrying on a business related to pawn broking or corporations whose principal business is the sale of vehicles, vessels, farm machinery, aircraft, mobile homes, jewellery, precious gems or metals, antiquities or art (Money Laundering Regulations, s 50). Finally, a Financial Entity having provided FINTRAC with certain prescribed information on a particular client may be exempted, except for the obligation to send an annual report or a report in cases where a change occurs, from sending reports to FINTRAC each time a transaction is made by such client, where the client qualifies for the exemption (Money Laundering Regulations, s 50(2)).

Reporting suspicious transactions relating to money laundering

Reporting requirement

Another reporting requirement introduced by PC(ML)TFA 2001 (s 7) consists of the obligation for each Prescribed Party to report to FINTRAC, in the prescribed form and manner, every financial transaction that occurs in the course of their activities and in respect of which there are reasonable grounds to suspect that the transaction is related to the commission of a money laundering offence or to the commission of a terrorist activity financing offence (the latter is discussed below).

Reasonable grounds to suspect

PC(ML)TFA 2001 does not contain any indication as to what should be reasonable grounds to suspect that a transaction is related to the commission of a money laundering offence. Rather, specific guidelines regarding suspicious transactions have been published (the 'Guidelines'). According to the Guidelines, 'reasonable grounds to suspect' may be determined by what is reasonable in the circumstances of each Prescribed Party, such as normal business practices and systems within the industry of such Prescribed Party. Transactions may give rise to reasonable grounds to suspect that they are related to money laundering regardless of the sum of money involved.

Common indicators

As a general rule, the Guidelines indicate that a transaction may be connected to money laundering when it raises questions or gives rise to discomfort, apprehension or mistrust. The context in which the transaction occurs is a significant factor in assessing suspicion. Transactions should be evaluated in terms of what seems appropriate and is within practices in a particular line of business. The fact that the transactions do not appear to be in keeping with normal industry practices may be a relevant factor for determining whether there are reasonable grounds to suspect that the transactions are related to money laundering.

An assessment of suspicion should be based on a reasonable evaluation of relevant factors, including the knowledge of the customers' business, financial history, background and behaviour.

The Guidelines list over 75 such general indicators. While we do not purport to list them all here, a few selected examples may be of interest. For example, signs of reluctance on the part of a client to have correspondence sent to a home address; appearing to have accounts with several financial institutions in one area for no apparent reason; showing uncommon curiosity about internal systems, controls and policies; presenting confusing details about the transaction; being secretive and reluctant to meet in person; being involved in an activity out of keeping for that individual or business; insisting that a transaction be done quickly; inconsistencies in the client's presentation of the transaction; attempting to develop close rapport with staff; using aliases or different addresses or a post office box; or offering money, gratuities or unusual favours for the provision of services that may appear unusual or suspicious are all common indicators. An indication by a client of a desire not to report or complete any document required for the transaction, refusing to produce personal identification documents, inordinately delaying presenting corporate documents, consistently making cash transactions that are just under the reporting threshold, frequently purchasing foreign currency drafts when outside of normal activity for the client or making a transaction which seems inconsistent with the client's apparent financial standing or usual activities are also signs.

A transaction that is unnecessarily complex with no stated purpose or that is inconsistent with what would be expected from the declared business is also a common indicator. Accounts with a large number of small cash deposits and a small number of large cash withdrawals should also raise suspicion. Inactive or dormant accounts which suddenly show significant activity, transactions across many international lines or with ties to a country where illicit drug production or exporting may be prevalent or where there is no effective anti-money-laundering system should also be considered.

Clients and other parties to the transaction having no apparent ties to Canada, transactions involving a country known for highly secretive banking or corporate laws, or loans secured by obligations from offshore banks are also identified. Specifically, offers of multimillion-dollar deposits from a confidential source to be sent from an offshore bank or somehow guaranteed by an offshore bank or involving an offshore 'shelf' bank whose name may be very similar to the name of a major legitimate institution should also raise suspicion. So are the use of letters of credit and other methods of trade financing to move money between countries when such trade is inconsistent with the client's business.

Compliance regime

The Money Laundering Regulations set out a series of compliance requirements to be implemented by all Prescribed Parties (Money Laundering Regulations, s 71). According to these draft Regulations, the compliance regime to be adopted will have to include:

1   the appointment of an individual to be responsible for the implementation of the compliance regime;

2   the development and application of compliance policies and procedures;

3   a review as often as is necessary of said policies and procedures to test their effectiveness, which review shall be conducted by an internal or external auditor; and

4   where the Prescribed Party has employees, an ongoing employee compliance training programme.

Non-compliance with such requirements may result in penalties of up to CDN $500,000 or a maximum of five years' imprisonment (PC(ML)TFA 2001, s 74).

Tipping-off

PC(ML)TFA 2001 also prohibits Prescribed Parties to disclose that they have made a report regarding suspicious transactions or disclose the content of such a report with the intent to prejudice a criminal investigation, whether or not a criminal investigation has begun (PC(ML)TFA 2001, s 8).

Immunity

PC(ML)TFA 2001 also contains an immunity provision (s 10) to the effect that no criminal or civil proceedings lie against a Prescribed Party for making a report in good faith with respect to suspicious transactions or prescribed transactions. A specific provision (s 11) of PC(ML)TFA 2001 also confirms that nothing in PC(ML)TFA 2001, Pt I requires a legal counsel to disclose any communication that is subject to solicitor-client privilege.

Privileged information

Notwithstanding the fact that PC(ML)TFA 2001, s 11 states that nothing in PC(ML)TFA 2001, Pt I requires a legal counsel to disclose any communication that is subject to solicitor-client privilege, the lack of definition in PC(ML)TFA 2001 of expressions such as 'communication' or 'solicitor-client privilege' does not provide a clear protection of the solicitor-client privilege. Whether any information or document is protected by solicitor-client privilege will be a question of fact to be addressed in each case, thus rendering the situation problematic. A constitutional challenge of the application of reporting requirements under PC(ML)TFA 2001 to lawyers is presently being made before the courts of various provinces of Canada (as discussed above).

Appendix 2.3

The Cayman Islands

Greg Link – Quin & Hampson, George Town, Grand Cayman

All crimes legislation: the Proceeds of Criminal Conduct Law

As part of their continuing commitment to the fight against crime and money laundering, the Cayman Islands introduced all crimes money laundering legislation in 1996 (latest revision being in 2001). This was the first all-crimes money laundering legislation in the region and enacted in substance the 'suspicious transaction' reporting obligations and onward disclosure practice of the UK Criminal Justice Act 1993. The 'all crimes' description is tempered by the requirement of dual criminality. In other words, if the predicate offence occurred in a foreign jurisdiction, the offence must be one that would similarly be an offence in the Cayman Islands. Criminal conduct is defined in PCCL 2001 as 'conduct which constitutes an offence to which this law applies or would constitute such an offence if it had occurred in the Islands' (PCCL 1996, s 22(10)).

The Proceeds of Criminal Conduct Law orders

PCCL 2001 contains three orders that relate to the proceeds of criminal conduct. These are the confiscation order, restraint order and charging order.

The confiscation order allows the Grand Court to make an order against an offender requiring them to pay such sum as the court thinks fit (s 5(1), where they are found guilty of any offence to which this law applies (s 5(2)) and they have benefited from that offence (s 5(2)(b)(i)) and the benefit is at least the minimum amount (PCCL 2001, s 5(2)(b)(ii)).

Although reference is made to a 'minimum amount', such an amount is not defined. The Attorney-General, in the Second Reading of the Bill, stated 'there is no minimum amount for domestic offences'. This anomaly is due to the fact that PCCL 2001 is largely a transposition of the equivalent UK legislation. The fact that references to the minimum amount have remained in PCCL 2001, whilst not indicative of careful drafting, should not pose any practical problems.

To prevent a person dealing with funds that may become subject to a confiscation order, the Grand Court has the power to impose restraint or charging orders where proceedings have been instituted against the defendant (PCCL 2001, s 9(1)(a)), the proceedings have not been concluded (PCCL 2001, s 9(1)(b)) and either a confiscation order has been made or it appears to the court that there are reasonable grounds for thinking that a confiscation order may be made (PCCL 2001, s 9(1)(c)). These powers are also exercisable where the court is satisfied that proceedings will be instituted against a person within 21 days of the granting of a restraint or charging order, or such longer period as the court may grant (PCCL 2001, s 9(2)(a)), and it appears to the court that a confiscation order may be made in proceedings for the offence. Originally, the court had to be satisfied that proceedings would be instigated against a person within seven days of the application for the restraint or charging order. PCCL 2001 is now more in line with the UK provisions, which require proceedings to be instituted within a reasonable time (Criminal Justice Act 1988, s 76(4)). Whilst ostensibly an inconsequential change, in *In The Matter of WJ McCorkle and C McCorkle* ([1998] CILR 1), a restraint order was removed when the proceedings were brought eight days after the restraint order was made. PCCL 2001 now has greater flexibility in regard to the timing of the bringing of proceedings.

Further, where a restraint order has been imposed, a receiver may also be appointed over the assets. The detrimental effect to a person's business and/or personal circumstances can be enormous where a restraint order is granted, and devastating when combined with the appointment of a receiver. Due to the draconian nature of the restraint order (and the costs incurred when a receiver is appointed), PCCL 2001 allows for compensation to be paid where the proceedings do not result in a conviction, or that conviction is quashed, or a pardon is granted (PCCL 2001, s 19(1)(a) and (b)). For an order for compensation to be granted, the Grand Court must be satisfied that there was serious default on the part of a person concerned in the investigation or prosecution of the offence concerned (PCCL 2001, s 19(2(a)) and the applicant has suffered substantial loss (PCCL 2001, s 19(2)(b)).

The Proceeds of Criminal Conduct Law offences

PCCL 2001 contains offences aimed at actively discouraging bankers and other professionals from remaining oblivious to the source of wealth of their clients. These offences are discussed below.

Assisting another to retain the benefit of criminal conduct

PCCL 2001, s 22(1) reads:

'Subject to subsection (3), whoever enters into or is otherwise concerned in an arrangement whereby—

(a) the retention or control by or on behalf of another (A) of property which is the proceeds of A's criminal conduct is facilitated (whether by concealment, removal from the jurisdiction, transfer to nominees or otherwise); or

(b) property which is the proceeds of A's criminal conduct—

(i) are used to secure that funds are placed at A's disposal; or

(ii) is used for A's benefit to acquire property by way of investment, knowing or suspecting that A is a person who is or has been engaged in criminal conduct or has benefited from criminal conduct is guilty of an offence.'

PCCL 2001, s 22(3) concerns the disclosure to the Reporting Authority of a suspicion or belief that funds or investments are derived from, or used in connection with, criminal conduct (see below).

The *mens rea* of this offence is 'knowing or suspecting that 'A' is a person who is or has been engaged in criminal conduct or has benefited from criminal conduct'.

The meaning of knowledge was discussed in *Baden v Société Générale pour Faroviser le Developpement du Commerce et de l'Industrie en France SA [1992] 4 All ER 161*. Although this case was concerned with the requisite knowledge of a constructive trust, the concepts are relevant. Five different mental states were set out:

(i)   actual knowledge;

(ii)   wilfully shutting one's eyes to the obvious;

(iii) wilfully and recklessly failing to make such inquiries as an honest and reasonable man would make;

(iv)   knowledge of circumstances which would indicate the facts to an honest and reasonable man; and

(v)   knowledge of circumstances which would put an honest and reasonable man on inquiry.

Gibson J held: 'the court will treat a person as having constructive knowledge of the facts if he wilfully shuts his eyes to the relevant facts which would be obvious if he opened his eyes.' The court accepted knowledge as (i) and constructive knowledge as (ii) and (iii). The tests in (ii) and (iii) require 'wilfully' and wilfully and recklessly'. These terms indicate conscious acts of neglect. The supposition being that sufficient awareness of the surrounding circumstances led the person to ignore the obvious or not to inquire further, whereas (iv) and (v) are cases of carelessness where the honest and reasonable man would have reacted differently, the distinction being drawn between wilful ignorance of the true facts and ignorance caused by carelessness.

It will be interesting to see the approach taken by the court when determining what standard will be applied to the test for knowledge under PCCL 2001. Although it is likely that, given the introduction of the Regulations (see below) and Guidance Notes (see below), the court may not have a great deal of sympathy for ignorance caused by carelessness.

However, it may well be that the exact definition of knowledge will become a moot point for academics, given the combined test of 'suspicion or knowledge'.

Whether the test for suspicion is subjective or objective has yet to be decided by the Cayman Islands courts. At the reading of the law, the then Cayman Islands' Attorney-General, in replying to a question as to what would suffice for suspicion, said:

'That is a straight forward question and there is a straight forward answer to it: The burden of proof lies where it always has in criminal matters, with the prosecution. The burden is to the criminal standard as well ... Who decides whether or not a person suspects, or should have suspected? The answer to that is that the court decides, the jury, the judge decides that.'

Cayman Islands *Hansard*, col 694, 20 September 1996.

The inherent problem with this reasoning is that the jury (or judge) is imparted with the duty of determining whether the person suspects or should have suspected. With the benefit of hindsight, possession of all the facts surrounding the predicate offence and a transactional history in a clear and concise format, the question as to whether suspicion arose, in the mind of the defendant, may be answered differently than if the jury (or judge) only had the same information available to the defendant when the transactions were conducted.

The further concern is that the threshold of liability for the service provider appears lower than that of the criminal whose proceeds he or she is involved with. This concern was addressed by the Foreign and Commonwealth Office as follows:

'It is true that the threshold of liability for the service provider appears lower than that of the criminal whose proceeds s/he is involved with. However it is worth running over what the prosecution would have to prove to convict the service provider in order to put this into its proper perspective:

(i)   the predicate offence;

(ii)   a link between the money and the predicate offence;

(iii)   proof that the service provider him/herself was, beyond reasonable doubt, suspicious about the transaction and failed to report it. It is therefore a defence for the service provider if he honestly believed that the transaction was not suspicious. The prosecution cannot use the reasonable man test to challenge this or indeed an admission by the service provider that he was too incompetent to recognize the transaction as suspicious.'

Taken from a letter from P T R Moody of the Economics Relations Department of the Foreign and Commonwealth Office, 24 May 1996

If this proposition is followed, the test will be subjective. Where the bar is set in relation to the *mens rea* will likely be determined throughout the later part of 2002, when the first prosecutions for offences under PCCL 2001 are brought before the Grand Court of the Cayman Islands.

The other tests expounded by the Foreign and Commonwealth Office are proof of the predicate offence and a link between the predicate offence and the money. The difficulty in establishing the predicate offence was discussed at above and appears to have been overcome with the recent legislation. The link between the predicate offence and the money will be a test of fact to be established by the prosecution.

Two specific defences are provided for the offence of assisting. In proceedings against a person for an offence under PCCL 2001, s 22, it is a defence to prove that they did not know or suspect that they were facilitating the retention of the proceeds of criminal conduct (PCCL 2001, s 22(4)). Such a defence would require proving lack of knowledge or suspicion to the civil standard of 'on the balance of probabilities'. This defence appears to be of little practical value for two reasons. First, it is exceedingly difficult for the defence to prove a negative (lack of knowledge or suspicion). Secondly, the prosecution is required to prove the knowledge or suspicion beyond reasonable doubt. Therefore, it must be mutually exclusive for the defendant to be able to also prove the converse lack of knowledge or suspicion on the balance of probabilities. If the prosecution cannot prove the case beyond reasonable doubt, the defendant is acquitted. If they can prove the case beyond reasonable doubt, the defendant cannot simultaneously prove the lack of the requisite *mens rea* on the balance of probabilities.

The second defence is a disclosure to the Reporting Authority of a suspicion or belief that any funds or investments are derived from or used in connection with criminal conduct, or a disclosure to the Reporting Authority of any matter on which such a suspicion is based (PCCL 2001, s 22(3)). The Reporting Authority's role has now been assumed by the Financial Reporting Unit (FRU), which is accountable to the Attorney-General's office. This unit is also responsible for investigating offences under PCCL 2001. The FRU was admitted to the Egmont Group of Financial Intelligence Units in June of 2001. Since the introduction of PCCL 2001, the FRU has co-operated on an 'all crimes' basis, exchanging information with other jurisdictions in the fight against international crime. It has co-operated with the Bahamas, Brazil, Canada, Germany, Hong Kong, Mexico, Peru, Russia, South Africa, the UK and the US.

If disclosure is made before a person performs any act in contravention of PCCL 2001, s 22, or the disclosure is made after they do the act, but is made on their own initiative and as soon as it is reasonable for them to make it, they do not commit an offence under this section (PCCL 2001, s 22(3)(b)).

The defence is extended to include where a defendant intended to disclose to the Reporting Authority a suspicion, belief or matter in relation to the arrangement (PCCL 2001, s 22(4)(c)(i)) and there is reasonable excuse his or failure to make disclosure (PCCL 2001, s 22(4)(c)(i)).

In order to ensure that a person making a disclosure does not suffer either criminal or civil penalty, PCCL 2001, s 22(3)(a) states:

'The disclosure shall not be treated as a breach of any restriction upon the disclosure of information by any enactment or otherwise and shall not give rise to any civil liability.'

A person who is guilty of the offence of assisting is liable on summary conviction to a fine of CI $5,000 and to imprisonment for two years. For conviction on indictment, they are liable to a fine and to imprisonment for 14 years.

Acquisition, possession or use of property representing proceeds of criminal conduct

PCCL 2001, s 23 sets out this offence as follows:

> 'Whoever, knowing that any property is, or in whole or in part directly or indirectly represents, another person's proceeds of criminal conduct, acquires or uses that property or has possession of it, is guilty of an offence.'

The requisite *mens rea* differs from that under the 'assisting' offence by the removal of suspicion and limiting the threshold to knowledge.

Further, s 23 contains similar provisions to those under the 'assisting' offence regarding the defence of making a report to the Reporting Authority. The defence that the defendant can prove that they did not know that the proceeds were from criminal conduct is removed. However, a further defence is introduced, being that the person charged, acquired or used the property or had possession of it for adequate consideration (PCCL 2001, s 23(2)). Inadequate consideration is defined as where the value of the consideration is significantly less than the value of the property. This will be a test for the judge or jury both as to the value of the property and what is a significant reduction in value. It should further be noted that the provision of services or goods which are of assistance in the criminal conduct shall not be treated as consideration for the purposes of this section (PCCL 2001, s 23(4)).

Concealing or transferring proceeds of criminal conduct

PCCL 2001, s 24(1) states:

> 'Whoever—
>
> (a) conceals or disguises property which is, or in the whole or in part directly or indirectly represents, his proceeds of criminal conduct; or
>
> (b) converts or transfers that property or removes it from the jurisdiction
>
> for the purpose of avoiding prosecution for an offence or of avoiding the making or enforcement of a confiscation order is guilty of an offence.'

This section relates to the situation where it is the same party that commits the predicate offence that is concealing or transferring the proceeds of their criminal conduct.

PCCL 2001, s 24(2) states:

'Whoever, knowing or having reasonable grounds to suspect that any property is, or in whole or in part directly or indirectly represents, another person's proceeds of criminal conduct—

(a)   conceals or disguises that property; or

(b)   converts or transfers that property or removes it from it from the jurisdiction,

with intent to assist any person to avoid prosecution for an offence or to avoid the making of a confiscation order is guilty of an offence.'

There is little substantive difference in the *actus reus* between this section and the assisting offence in PCCL 2001, s 22. The *mens rea* is changed from knowledge or suspicion to knowledge or having reasonable grounds to suspect. This change in terminology appears to be more of a drafting anomaly than creating a tangible difference. However, it is unfortunate the drafting of the legislation is not consistent, as the possibility for semantic arguments is created.

The major change from PCCL 2001, s 22 is that there is no defence incorporated into the section. It would therefore appear that even if a suspicious transaction report is made, a person may still be charged under PCCL 2001, s 24. Section 22 specifically includes the terms 'whether by concealment' and 'removal from the jurisdiction'. Terms that are almost identical to the s 24 offence. A person who discloses a suspicion or belief that funds are from criminal conduct would expect to be able to use the s 22 defence to any charge in relation to an act subsequently carried out. Instead, the result may well be a charge under s 24, with no defence available.

Failure to disclose knowledge or suspicion of money laundering

PCCL 2001 has introduced the offence of failure to disclose knowledge or suspicion of money laundering. This is set out in s 27(1):

'A person is guilty of an offence if—

(a)   he knows or suspects that another person is engaged in money laundering;

(b)   the information, or other matter, on which that knowledge or suspicion is based came to his attention in the course of his trade, profession, business, or employment; and

(c)   he does not disclose the information or other matter to the Reporting Authority as soon as is reasonably practicable after it comes to his attention.'

Professional legal advisors are exempted from this disclosure requirement if the information or other matter came to them in privileged circumstances. 'Money laundering' for the purposes of this section means doing any act which constitutes an offence under PCCL 2001, s 22, 23 or 24 or, in the case of an act done otherwise than in the Cayman Islands, would constitute such an offence if done in the Cayman Islands. This section has significantly increased the obligations of professionals (such as auditors). As at the time of writing, there have been no prosecutions under this section.

A defence is available where the person charged had a reasonable excuse for not disclosing the information or other matter in question (PCCL 2001, s 27(3)). What will constitute a 'reasonable excuse' is unknown at this stage.

Whoever is guilty of an offence under this section is liable: summary conviction, to a fine of CI $50,000; or, on conviction on indictment, to a fine and to imprisonment for two years.

Tipping-off

To ensure that an investigation is not prejudiced by advance notice to any person being investigated, PCCL 2001 has incorporated the offence of 'tipping-off' (s 25).1 PCCL 2001, s 25 encompasses both disclosing information to a person who the person disclosing the information knows or has reasonable grounds for suspecting that an investigation may be conducted into under the offences of PCCL 2001, or that a disclosure has been made to the Reporting Authority. Such a disclosure must be likely to prejudice the investigation.

The Money Laundering Regulations 2000

The Money Laundering Regulations 2000 have been brought into place to ensure compliance with worldwide 'know your client' and general compliance standards. The Regulations have introduced offences to which financial services providers may be subjected even if they do not have any clients that are dealing with the proceeds of criminal conduct. These offences will apply simply because the procedures as set out in the Regulations are not followed.

The Money Laundering Regulations 2000 were designed to supplement the offences that have been created under PCCL 1996. They are specifically designed to cover areas including the following.

Identification procedures

The Money Laundering Regulations 2000 introduce the requirement that financial services providers obtain satisfactory evidence of a prospective client's identity. Evidence is defined as being satisfactory if it is reasonably capable of establishing that the applicant is the person who they claim to be. This evidence should be obtained by the financial services provider as soon as is reasonably practicable.

Record-keeping procedures

This dictates that, in addition to maintaining identification records, the financial services provider must keep a record containing details relevant to all transactions carried out by the client. Records must be maintained for at least five years after the business relationship has been completed or, in relation to transactions, five years after the date of the transaction.

Training and awareness

Pursuant to the Money Laundering Regulations 2000, the financial services provider is required to ensure that appropriate measures are taken from time to time for the purposes of making employees aware of their duties regarding client identification, record keeping and internal reporting procedures. Employees must also be aware of the enactments relating to money laundering. The financial services provider must further provide the employees with training in the recognition of suspicious transactions.

Internal reporting procedures

Procedures must be in place to ensure that the financial services provider's employees are aware of the process for internal reporting of suspicious transactions and the line of internal reporting. These internal reporting procedures and such other procedures of internal control and communication must be appropriate for the purposes of identifying and preventing money laundering.

The Money Laundering Regulations 2000 have been purposefully drafted in a very wide and broad manner and have further introduced or made it an offence if they are contravened. Where an offence is committed by the financial service provider with the consent, connivance of, or is attributable to any neglect on the part of an officer of the financial service provider, that person as well as the financial service provider will be guilty of the offence and proceeded against and punished accordingly. On conviction on indictment for breach of the Regulations, a person may be liable to imprisonment not exceeding a term of two years or a fine or both, or on summary conviction to fine not exceeding CI $5,000. Financial service providers have until 31 December 2002 to ensure they are meeting the due diligence requirements under the Regulations.

The Guidance Notes

The Cayman Islands Monetary Authority (CIMA) issued Guidance Notes on the Prevention and Detection of Money Laundering in the Cayman Islands (the Guidance Notes) on 1 June 2001. CIMA states in the introduction to the Guidance Notes that they go beyond the requirements of the Money Laundering Regulations 2000. Therefore, whilst the financial service provider may not be liable for prosecution for a breach of the Guidance Notes, CIMA has indicated that it expects all institutions conducting relevant financial business to pay due regard to them. If it appears to CIMA that the financial service provider is not paying due regard to the Guidance Notes, it will seek an explanation and may conclude that the financial service provider is carrying on business in a manner that may give rise to sanctions under the applicable legislation. Further, the Guidance Notes, whilst not having statutory force, may be taken into account by the courts in determining whether a party has complied with the Money Laundering Regulations 2000.

CIMA itself has seen significant increases both in its ambit of responsibility and in its number of staff. It has responsibility for the regulation of financial institutions in accordance with current legislation and is also now charged with monitoring compliance with the Money Laundering Regulations 2000. Pursuant to these obligations, CIMA has been conducting on-site inspections of financial institutions to determine the degree of compliance with Regulations. The Monetary Authority Law (2002 Revision) empowers CIMA to have access to financial institutions' information for its own regulatory purposes. Recent amendments to this law have expanded CIMA's capability to co-operate with overseas regulators and sets out procedures for responding to requests for assistance. The legislation includes provisions to prevent 'fishing expeditions' and to safeguard the legitimate interests of the Cayman Islands.

Appendix 2.4

Guernsey

Stephen Hellman – Barrister, Furnival Chambers, London

Mark Dunster – Partner, Carey Langlois, Guernsey

Money laundering legislation

The anti-money laundering regime in Guernsey comprises the following laws, regulations and Guidance Notes.

Primary legislation

—The Money Laundering (Disclosure of Information) (Guernsey) Law 1995

This came into force on 6 July 1995. It applies only to Guernsey and the smaller islands of Herm and Jethou.

—The Criminal Justice (Proceeds of Crime) Bailiwick of Guernsey Law 1999

(CJ(PC)BGL 1999, generally known as the All Crimes Law), came into force on 1 January 2000. CJ(PC) BGL 1999 in part superseded two earlier pieces of legislation which dealt with specific types of offence. These were the Company Securities (Insider Dealing) (Bailiwick of Guernsey) Law 1989 and the Criminal Justice (Fraud Investigation) (Bailiwick of Guernsey) Law 1991 (the Serious Fraud Law). Although it is not proposed to deal with them here, these laws remain in force and are from time to time used by the prosecuting authorities. In particular, the Serious Fraud Law is used to obtain production orders.

—The Criminal Justice (International Co-operation) (Bailiwick of Guernsey) Law 2001

This came into force on 1 July 2001. It is included here because it contains provisions for obtaining material from the Bailiwick for use in criminal investigations and proceedings overseas.

Secondary legislation

—The Criminal Justice (Proceeds of Crime) (Bailiwick of Guernsey) (Enforcement of Overseas Confiscation Orders) Ordinance 1999

This came into force on 1 January 2000.

—The Drug Trafficking (Bailiwick of Guernsey) Law (Enforcement of External Forfeiture Orders) Ordinance 2000

This came into force on 1 January 2001.

—The Royal Court (International Co-operation) Rules 2002

These came into force on 18 February 2002.

—The Criminal Justice (Proceeds of Crime) (Enforcement of Overseas Confiscation Orders) (Amendment) Ordinance 2002

This came into force on 31 May 2002.

—The Criminal Justice (Proceeds of Crime) (Bailiwick of Guernsey) Regulations 2002

(The CJ(PC)BG Regulations 2002). They were issued by the States Advisory and Finance Committee under CJ(PC)BGL 1999 and came into force on 14 August 2002. They replace the Criminal Justice (Proceeds of Crime) (Bailiwick of Guernsey) Regulations 1999, which came into force on 1 January 2000, and which were amended by the Criminal Justice (Proceeds of Crime) (Bailiwick of Guernsey) (Amendment) Regulations 2002, which came into force on 28 June 2002.

Tertiary provisions

—Codes of Practice for corporate service providers, trust service providers and company directors

These Codes of Practice were issued by the Commission under the Regulation of Fiduciaries, Administration Businesses and Company Directors, etc (Bailiwick of Guernsey) Law 2000 (the Fiduciary Law). They were made on 20 March 2001 and came into effect on 1 April 2001.

—Guidance Notes on the prevention of money laundering and countering the financing of terrorism

(The Guidance Notes 2002) They were issued by the GFSC on 22 August 2002. They replace the Guidance Notes on the Prevention of Money Laundering issued by the Commission on 1 January 2000, which were amended on 31 May 2000 and 4 October 2001. These were a revision of the Guidance Notes on the Prevention of Money Laundering issued by the Guernsey Joint Money Laundering Steering Group in March 1997. They were in turn based on similar Guidance Notes issued by the equivalent Steering Group in the UK and replaced the Money Laundering Avoidance Guidance Notes issued by the Commission in July 1991. The Guidance Notes 2002 are known colloquially as 'the Rainbow Guide' on account of the brightly coloured, looseleaf binder in which they were issued.

Offences in relation to money laundering and terrorist funds

This section deals with the offences in relation to money laundering and terrorist funds created by the above laws; the provisions regulating financial services businesses contained in the CJ(PC)BGL Regulations 2002, Guidance Notes 2002 and Codes of Practice; and with civil remedies.

Money laundering offences are contained in CJ(PC)BG 1999, DT(BG)L 2000 and T&CL 2002.

The mental element necessary to commit an offence in relation to money laundering or terrorist funds under any of the above laws is typically either 'having reasonable grounds to suspect' or 'knowing or suspecting'. 'Having reasonable grounds to suspect' is an objective test. A person will be guilty of an offence having this element if they ought to have suspected but did not. 'Knowing or suspecting' is a subjective test. To be guilty of an offence having this element, a person must actually have known or suspected. They will not be guilty of an offence if they ought to have known or suspected but did not. 'Suspicion' and its cognates are not defined in any of the statutes.

—The Criminal Justice (Proceeds of Crime) Bailiwick of Guernsey Law 1999

CJ(PC)BGL 1999 contains three offences in connection with the proceeds of criminal conduct:

1   Concealing or transferring the proceeds of criminal conduct (CJ(PC)BGL 1999, s 38). A person is guilty of this offence if they:

    (i)   conceal or disguise any property which is, or in whole or in part directly or indirectly represents, their own or another's proceeds of criminal conduct; or

    (ii)   convert or transfer that property or remove it from the Bailiwick,

for the purpose of avoiding the prosecution of themselves or another for criminal conduct or the making or enforcement in their case, or the case of another, of a confiscation order.

2   *Assisting another person to retain the proceeds of criminal conduct* (CJ(PC)BGL 1999, s 39). A person is guilty of this offence if they enter into or are otherwise concerned in an arrangement whereby:

    (i)   the retention or control by or on behalf of another ('A') of A's proceeds of criminal conduct is facilitated (whether by concealment, removal from the Bailiwick, transfer to nominees or otherwise); or

(ii)   A's proceeds of criminal conduct:

–   are used to secure that funds are placed at A's disposal; or

–   are used for A's benefit to acquire property by way of investment,

knowing or suspecting that A is or has been engaged in criminal conduct or
has benefited from criminal conduct. It is a defence for a person to prove that
they did not know or suspect that the arrangement was of this kind.

3   *Acquisition, possession or use of the proceeds of criminal conduct*
(CJ(PC)BGL 1999, s 40). A person is guilty of an offence if, knowing that
any property is, or in whole or in part directly or indirectly represents,
another's proceeds of criminal conduct, they acquire or use that property
or have possession of it. It is a defence that they did so for adequate
consideration.

A person whose conduct would otherwise constitute an offence
under CJ(PC)BGL 1999, s 39 or 40 will not commit an offence if they disclose
their suspicion that the property in question is the proceeds of criminal conduct
to a police officer. This is provided that the disclosure is made before they do the
act concerned and the act is done with the consent of the police officer; or that
the disclosure is made after they do the act, but is made on their own initiative
and as soon as it is reasonable for them to make it. A person who is in
employment at the relevant time may instead make the disclosure to the
appropriate person under their employer's internal reporting procedures. The
employer is required to have in place such procedures under the CJ(PC)BG
Regulations 2002 and Guidance Notes 2002.

It is a defence to a charge under CJ(PC)BGL 1999, s 39 or 40 for a person to
prove that they intended to make a material disclosure to a police officer or
under their employer's internal reporting procedures but that there is a reasonable excuse for their failure to do so.

'Criminal conduct' means any conduct, other than drug trafficking (which is
covered by DT(BG)L 2000), which constitutes a criminal offence under the
laws of the Bailiwick and is triable on indictment or which would constitute
such an offence if it were to take place in the Bailiwick. It is therefore irrelevant
whether the conduct is criminal in the jurisdiction in which it was committed.

Certain categories of criminal conduct call for brief comment.

Fiscal offences. It is a common law offence to cheat the Revenue. The States of
Guernsey, which is the legislature for the island, levies income taxes and import
duties for Guernsey and Alderney. Thus it cannot be said that in the Bailiwick
there is no Revenue to cheat. Tax-related offences are therefore not a special
category of offence. The Guidance Notes 2002 state expressly that the proceeds
of a tax-related offence may be the subject of money laundering offences
under CJ(PC)BGL 1999.

Exchange control offences. There are no general exchange control regulations in the Bailiwick. However, the Control of Borrowing (Bailiwick of Guernsey) Ordinance 1959, as amended, in effect imposes exchange controls with respect to borrowing by companies. Moreover, exchange control offences in other jurisdictions will tend to involve conduct, such as false accounting, which is indictable in the Bailiwick.

Bribery. This is an offence at common law. Where a person in a position to perform a public duty takes a bribe to act corruptly in discharging their duty, it is an offence in both parties. The offer of a bribe is an attempt to bribe and is also an offence.

If a person is charged with an offence in connection with the proceeds of criminal conduct, it is thought that the predicate offence must be proved to the criminal standard, ie beyond a reasonable doubt.

A person guilty of one of the above offences is liable on summary conviction to imprisonment for a term not exceeding 12 months, a fine, or both; or on conviction on indictment to imprisonment for a term not exceeding 14 years, an unlimited fine, or both.

No prosecution shall be instituted for any of the above offences without the consent of HM Procureur (the Guernsey equivalent of the Attorney General).

—The Criminal Justice (Proceeds of Crime) (Bailiwick of Guernsey) Regulations 2002

CJ(PC)BGL 1999 requires the Committee to make regulations with respect to financial services businesses so as to forestall and prevent money laundering. Thus CJ(PC)BGL 1999 is of general application, but the CJ(PC)BG Regulations 2002 issued under it relate only to financial services businesses.

'Financial services businesses' are defined in the CJ(PC)BG Regulations 2002 to include businesses providing a wide range of financial and credit services. However, the CJ(PC)BG Regulations 2002 do not cover these services where they are provided by lawyers, accountants and actuaries and are incidental to the provision of legal, accounting or actuarial services.

A service is incidental if it is carried out by a lawyer, accountant or actuary without separate remuneration while providing legal, accounting or actuarial services and is subordinate to the purposes for which such legal, accounting or actuarial services are provided. Moreover, legal, accounting or actuarial services do not become financial services merely because they are provided to financial services businesses.

The CJ(PC)BG Regulations 2002 provide, in effect, that no person shall carry on a financial services business in Guernsey unless they comply with the following measures:

- establish and maintain identification, record keeping and internal reporting procedures in relation to the business;

- ensure that employees whose duties relate to financial services business are aware of the above procedures and the relevant laws; and

- provide key staff, ie all those who deal with customers/clients or their transactions, with comprehensive training in the relevant laws, their personal obligations under the laws, and the anti-money laundering and anti-financing of terrorism policies and procedures in place in the business ('vigilance policy').

It is an offence to contravene the CJ(PC)BG Regulations 2002. The penalty on conviction on indictment is imprisonment for up to two years or an unlimited fine, or both. The penalty on summary conviction is a fine.

—The Guidance Notes 2002

The Guidance Notes 2002 have been issued to assist financial services businesses to comply with the requirements of the relevant laws. Although technically the Guidance Notes 2002 are for guidance only, they are expressed to be a statement of the standard expected by the Commission of all financial services businesses in Guernsey. In practical terms, therefore, they are mandatory, and are universally regarded as such. The courts may take account of the Guidance Notes 2002 in any proceedings brought under the relevant laws or in determining whether a person has complied with the requirements of the CJ(PC)BG Regulations 2002.

Identification procedures: The Guidance Notes 2002 (as amended in January 2004) 'flesh out the bare bones' of the CJ(PC)BG Regulations 2002, particularly with respect to identification procedures. These apply to the following activities:

- the forming of a business relationship;

- a one-off transaction, or two or more one-off transactions which appear to be linked, where the total amount payable by or to the applicant for business is £10,000 or more; and

- any one-off transaction where the person handling the transaction on behalf of the financial services business knows or suspects that the applicant is engaged in money laundering or the financing of terrorism or that the transaction is carried out on behalf of another who is so engaged.

Identification procedures have two components: verification ('know-your-customer') and recognition of suspicious activities/transactions.

Verification: A financial services business should establish to its reasonable satisfaction that every person whose identity needs to be verified actually exists. This means the parties who will own or control the product, account or service provided by the business. They would include, for example, beneficial owners, settlors, controlling shareholders, directors and major beneficiaries. However, the standard of due diligence will depend on the exact nature of the relationship. Guidance is given as to the application of this principle to individuals, partnerships, companies (including corporate trustees), other institutions and intermediaries. There are a small number of exempt cases. The Guidance Notes 2002 do not specify what, in any particular case, will be sufficient evidence to complete verification.

Where verification cannot be completed (and where there are no reasonable grounds for suspicion) any business relationship with, or one-off transaction for, the applicant for business should be suspended and any funds held to the applicant's order returned. Funds should never be paid to a third party, but only to the source from which they came. If failure to complete verification itself raises suspicion, a report should be made and guidance sought from the Financial Intelligence Service ('FIS') (see below) as to how to proceed.

CJ(PC)BGL 1999 does not have retroactive effect. However, a suspicion raised prior to the introduction of CJ(PC)BGL 1999 should be reported if it remains in the mind of an existing member of the financial services business' staff after the commencement of CJ(PC)BGL 1999. The previous edition of the Guidance Notes stated that this does not mean that pre-existing customer files should be systematically reviewed to ensure that a suspicion should not have been raised previously or to identify previous suspicious transactions. However this statement has been deleted from the 2002 edition.

Recognition of suspicious customers/transactions: A suspicious transaction will often be one which is inconsistent with a customer's known legitimate business or activities, or with the normal business for that type of financial services product. It is, therefore, important that the financial services business knows enough about the customer's business to recognise that a transaction or a series of transactions is unusual.

Keeping of records

Financial services businesses should:

- retain each customer verification document, ie each document obtained or created by the financial services business during a customer verification process, in its original form, for at least six years after the day on which a business relationship or one-off transaction ceases or, where customer activity is dormant, six years from the last transaction; and

- retain each customer document that is not a customer verification document in its original form, or a complete copy of the original, certified by a manager, partner or director or the financial services business, for at least six years after the day on which all activities taking place in the course of the dealings in question were completed.

Where a financial services business knows that an investigation is proceeding in respect of its customer, or where requested by the FIS, it should not, without the prior approval of the FIS, destroy any relevant records, even though six years may have elapsed.

—Internal reporting procedures

Each financial services business is required to appoint a reporting officer. This means a senior manager, partner or director who has responsibility for vigilance policy and for dealing with reports of suspicious transactions. The reporting officer should be a senior member of staff with sufficient authority to ensure compliance with the Guidance Notes 2002.

Responsibility for maintaining vigilance policy may be delegated to one or more prevention officer(s). They should have the necessary authority to guarantee to the reporting officer compliance with the Guidance Notes 2002.

Financial services businesses should ensure that key staff know to whom their suspicions of criminal conduct should be reported; and that there is a clear procedure for reporting such suspicions without delay to the reporting officer. It is for the reporting officer to investigate the report. If, following that investigation, the reporting officer remains suspicious, they should promptly submit a report to the FIS.

—Training

The effectiveness of a vigilance policy is stated to be directly related to the level of awareness engendered in key staff. The duty of vigilance must become part of the living culture of the financial services business.

—Systems

Financial services businesses must put in place systems which enable them to carry out these duties. They should ensure that internal auditing and compliance departments regularly monitor the implementation and operation of such systems.

Financial services businesses should be aware of 'politically exposed persons' (or 'potentate') risk, the term given to the risk associated with providing financial and business services to government ministers or officials from countries with widely known problems of bribery, corruption and financial irregularity within their governments and society. This risk is said to be even more acute where such countries do not have anti-money laundering standards, or where these do not meet international financial transparency standards.

It is recommended that financial services businesses conduct detailed due diligence at the outset of the relationship and on an ongoing basis where they know or suspect that the business relationship is with a 'politically exposed person'. Financial services businesses should also develop and maintain 'enhanced scrutiny' to address potentate risk. Guidance is given as to what this might involve.

The CJ(PC)BG Regulations 2002 provide that in determining whether a person has complied with them, a court may take account not only of the Guidance Notes 2002 but of any other guidance issued, adopted or approved by the Commission (CJ(PC)BG Regulations 2002, reg 1). Under this provision, the Commission issued written guidance in November 2001 that henceforth best practice for banks on introduced business was as set out in the paper on 'Customer Due Diligence for Banks', published in October 2001 by the Basle Committee on Banking Supervision (the Basle Guidelines). This will make it much harder for banks to rely on due diligence undertaken by reliable introducers instead of undertaking it themselves. The Guidance Notes 2002 have not been amended from the previous edition of the Guidance Notes to include the provisions in the Basle Guidelines relating to introducers although they have been amended to take account of the provisions in the Basle Guidelines relating to correspondent bank accounts.

—The Codes of Practice

The Codes of Practice state that providers of trust and corporate services and company directors should comply with the CJ(PC)BG Regulations 2002 and Guidance Notes 2002.

Disclosure/tipping-off

As discussed earlier, in certain circumstances disclosure can provide a defence to offences in relation to money laundering and terrorist funds. This section is concerned with the effect of disclosure on civil liability; tipping off and other disclosure offences; account monitoring orders; disclosure reports; production orders and warrants; and requests by prosecuting authorities in other jurisdictions for material from the Bailiwick for use in criminal investigations and proceedings overseas.

Impact of disclosure on civil liability

The effect of the legislation against money laundering and terrorist funds is that a person who makes a disclosure to the authorities concerning what they know, believe or suspect to be the proceeds of criminal conduct or terrorist funds will not be regarded as having breached any civil or criminal prohibition against the disclosure of such information. It is implicit in the legislation that such disclosure must be made in good faith. *Quaere* whether the knowledge or suspicion on which it is based must be reasonable.

In addition, CJ(PC)BGL 1999 provides that if the disclosure is made by a person before he or she does an act to which the disclosure relates and the act is done with the consent of a police officer, the person doing the act shall incur no liability of any kind to any person by reason of such act. For example, the person doing the act would incur no liability by reason of that act as a constructive trustee. In practice, the authorities will often consent to an act in terms designed to avoid conferring a blanket immunity from civil liability. For example, they might consent to a bank continuing to operate an account 'in accordance with good financial services business practice'. This begs the question whether the bank would be acting in accordance with good financial services business practice if it did continue to operate the account.

Disclosure offences

—The Criminal Justice (Proceeds of Crime) Bailiwick of Guernsey Law 1999

CJ(PC)BGL 1999 contains two disclosure offences.

1   *Tipping-off* (see CJ(PC)BGL 1999, s 41) A person is guilty of this offence if they know or suspect that:

    (i)   a police officer is acting, or is proposing to act, in connection with an investigation which is being, or is about to be, conducted into money laundering; or

    (ii)   that a disclosure under CJ(PC)BGL 1999, s 39 or 40 has been made to a police officer or internally pursuant to an employer's internal reporting procedures,

and they disclose to any other person information or any other matter which is likely to prejudice that investigation or any investigation which might be conducted following the disclosure.

2   *Prejudicing an investigation.* Where, under CJ(PC)BGL 1999 (s 47):

    (i)   a production order has been made or has been applied for and has not been refused; or

    (ii)   a warrant has been issued,a person is guilty of an offence if, knowing or suspecting that the investigation is taking place, they make any disclosure which is likely to prejudice the investigation.

It is a defence to a charge of tipping off or prejudicing an investigation for a person to prove that they did not know or suspect that the disclosure was likely to be prejudicial to such investigation. It is also a defence to a charge of prejudicing an investigation for a person to prove that they had lawful authority or reasonable excuse for making the disclosure.

None of this makes it an offence for a professional legal adviser to disclose information in circumstances covered by legal professional privilege. Information disclosed with a view to furthering a criminal purpose is not covered by legal professional privilege.

'Money Laundering' means doing any act:

1   which constitutes an offence under CJ(PC)BGL 1999, ss 38, 39 or 40; or

2   in the case of an act done outside the Bailiwick, which would constitute such an offence if done in the Bailiwick.

A person guilty of either offence is liable on summary conviction to imprisonment for a term not exceeding 12 months, a fine, or both; and on conviction on indictment to imprisonment for a term not exceeding five years, an unlimited fine, or both.

—Account monitoring orders

Under T&CL 2002 the Bailiff or, in the case of Alderney and Sark, the appropriate judicial officer, may on an application by a police officer make an account monitoring order for the purposes of a terrorist investigation if satisfied that the tracing of terrorist property is desirable for the purposes of the investigation and will enhance its effectiveness (Sch 7, para 1). This is an order that the financial services business specified in the application must provide specified information relating to specified accounts for a specified period of up to 90 days to a police officer.

Disclosure reports

If the reporting officer of a financial services business decides that a disclosure should be made, a report should be sent to the FIS. A standard form is provided for this purpose in an appendix to the Guidance Notes 2002. In cases of urgency, initial notification to the FIS should be made by telephone. A financial services business should maintain a register of all reports made to the FIS.

The FIS aims to acknowledge promptly receipt of a report. To the extent permitted by law, financial services businesses should comply with any instructions issued by the FIS. In most cases, the FIS will give the financial services business written consent to continue operating the financial services product for the client. In exceptional cases, such as where the arrest of the client is imminent with consequential restraint of assets, such consent may not be given. The report will not be disclosed outside the FIS. The FIS may seek further information from the reporting financial services business and elsewhere.

Disclosures are treated similarly to disclosures made to the National Crime and Intelligence Service (NCIS) in the UK. Discreet inquiries are made to confirm the basis for suspicion, but the client is never approached. The information disclosed is assessed and, if appropriate, disseminated within or without the Bailiwick within the framework of CJ(PC)BGL 1999. In the event of a prosecution, the source of the information is protected. Production orders would be used to produce such material for the court. The Guidance Notes 2002 state that maintaining the integrity of the confidential relationship between law enforcement agencies and financial services businesses is regarded by the former as of paramount concern.

The Guidance Notes 2002 state that wherever possible the FIS will deliver feedback directly to financial services businesses that make suspicious transaction reports. Previous editions of the Guidance Notes provided a more detailed framework for this feedback.

In addition to reporting to the FIS, and at the same time, where a disclosure has been made under the Money Laundering (Disclosure of Information) Laws for Guernsey 1995, Alderney 1998 or Sark 2001, or CJ(PC)BGL 1999, the Commission expects financial services businesses also to report suspicions to it in the following circumstances: where the financial services business' systems failed to detect the transaction and the matter has been brought to its attention in another way, for example, by the FIS; the transaction may present a significant reputational risk to Guernsey and/or the financial services business; it is suspected that a member of the financial services business' staff was involved; or a member of the financial services business' staff has been dismissed for a serious breach of money laundering controls.

Disclosure by the authorities of disclosed material

Information which is the subject of a disclosure to the police under CJ(PC)BGL 1999 may not be disclosed by the police or anyone receiving the information from them, save as permitted by statute.

CJ(PC)BGL (s 43) deals with disclosure for purposes within the Bailiwick. Disclosure is permitted for purposes of the investigation of crime, or for criminal proceedings, within the Bailiwick. Disclosure is also permitted for other purposes in the Bailiwick to HM Procureur, the Commission, a police officer or any other person authorised by HM Procureur to obtain that information.

CJ(PC)BGL 1999 (s 44) deals with disclosure for purposes outside the Bailiwick. Disclosure is permitted with the consent of HM Procureur for the purposes of the investigation of crime, or for criminal proceedings, outside the Bailiwick. HM Procureur may give consent generally or specifically, and unconditionally or subject to conditions.

Under the Criminal Justice (Fraud Investigation) (Bailiwick of Guernsey) Law 1991, information obtained by or with the authority of HM Procureur may be disclosed in the interests of justice to any person or body for the purposes of any investigation or prosecution of an offence in the Bailiwick or elsewhere.

If so requested, HM Procureur will generally give the party making the disclosure under CJ(PC)BGL 1999 or producing the information or material under the Criminal Justice (Fraud Investigation) (Bailiwick of Guernsey) Law 1991 prior notice of a decision to disclose such information or material to investigating or prosecuting authorities outside the jurisdiction. This will give the party thus notified the opportunity to challenge the decision by way of judicial review. That a decision of this kind is amenable to judicial review in the Bailiwick was established by the 1999 decision of the Guernsey Court of Appeal in the case *of Bassington Ltd v HM Procureur* (26 Guernsey Law Journal para 86).

DT(BG)L 2000 does not contain any provisions analogous to CJ(PC)BGL 1999, s 43. However, it does contain provisions pursuant to the 1988 UN Convention Against Illicit Traffic in Narcotic Drugs and Psychotropic Substances for obtaining local evidence for use overseas in connection with criminal investigations and proceedings with respect to drug trafficking. The Criminal Justice (International Co-operation) (Bailiwick of Guernsey) Law 2001 makes analogous provisions with respect to criminal investigations and prosecutions generally. The provisions in both statutes are of general application and are therefore applicable to investigations and prosecutions in connection with money laundering.

On receipt of a request from an appropriate authority in the requesting state, HM Procureur may commence proceedings in the Guernsey courts to receive the evidence to which the request relates. This is provided that the offence has been committed under the laws of the requesting state, or that there are reasonable grounds for supposing as much, and that a criminal investigation or proceedings has been commenced in the requesting state in connection with that offence.

The most important circumstances in which information or documents supplied by a person pursuant to a request under the Terrorism (United Nations Measures) (Channel Islands) Order 2001 (SI 2001/3363) may be disclosed by the authorities are as follows.

They may be disclosed to the Crown on behalf of the UK government, to the States of Jersey, or the government of the Isle of Man or any British Overseas Territories listed in the Schedule to the Terrorism (United Nations Measures) (Channel Islands) Order 2001. They may also be disclosed to the UN or the government of any other country for the purpose of monitoring or securing compliance with the Order. They may further be disclosed in connection with proceedings for an offence under the Order in Jersey or under equivalent legislation in the UK, the Isle of Man or any British Overseas Territory listed in the Schedule to the Order.

Appendix 2.5

Hong Kong

Rosaline Cheung – Partner, Johnson Stokes & Master, Hong Kong

Alvin Hui – Solicitor, Johnson Stokes & Master, Hong Kong

Primary legislation

Anti-money laundering legislation

The two principal pieces of anti-money laundering legislation in Hong Kong are contained in the Drug Trafficking (Recovery of Proceeds) Ordinance (DTRPO) (Cap 405 of the Laws of Hong Kong) and the Organised and Serious Crimes Ordinance (OSCO) (Cap 455 of the Laws of Hong Kong). The two Ordinances contain similar provisions against money laundering and for the tracing, confiscation and recovery of illegal proceeds, except that DTRPO relates to drug trafficking whereas OSCO relates to organised and serious crime.

Money laundering

—The money laundering offence

Under DTRPO and OSCO (DTRPO, s 25 and OSCO, s 25), it is an offence to deal with any property knowing or having reasonable grounds to believe that such property in whole or in part, directly or indirectly represents the proceeds of drug trafficking or of an indictable offence.

In Hong Kong, crimes are defined by statute as being triable either summarily or on indictment. Generally, indictable offences are more serious offences, and include evasion of Hong Kong tax (Cap 112), murder, kidnapping, drug trafficking, assault, theft, robbery, obtaining property by deception, false accounting, firearms offences, manslaughter, bribery and smuggling.

It is irrelevant where the drug trafficking or indictable offence took place. Drug trafficking is defined to include drug trafficking anywhere in the world (DTRPO, s 2(1)), and an indictable offence includes a reference to conduct which would constitute an indictable offence if it had occurred in Hong Kong (OSCO, s 25(4)), regardless of whether the drug trafficking or conduct is illegal in the jurisdiction where it is committed. Accordingly, money laundering can be of proceeds of drug trafficking or of an indictable offence committed either in Hong Kong or elsewhere. The purpose is to deter people from using Hong Kong to launder proceeds of crime.

—Actus reus

The *actus reus* of a money laundering offence is 'dealing in property'. Dealing is defined widely to include:

(i)   receiving, acquiring, concealing, disguising, disposing of or converting the property;

(ii)   bringing the property into or removing it from Hong Kong; and

(iii) using the property to borrow money, or as security (DTRPO, s 2(1) and OSCO, s 2(1)).

A person 'deals' in terms of a money laundering offence whether the property represents the proceeds of his or her own crime or someone else's crime (*Lok Kar-win v HKSAR [1999] 4 HKC 796, CFA*).

There is no requirement to prove the actual drug trafficking or indictable offence (*HKSAR v Li Ching [1997] 14 HKC 108, HKCA*), nor that the property was the actual proceeds of the crime. In the case of *HKSAR v Wong Ping Shui Adam [2001] 1 HKLRD 346, CFA*, it was held that the *actus reus* of the offence was 'dealing in property' and there were no words qualifying or restricting such property. It was not open to the interpretation that the property must be confined to property which must have been or could only have been the proceeds of an indictable offence. The wrongdoing intended was the conspiracy to put into effect a criminal enterprise, and the argument that the proceeds had to be those of an indictable offence was not sustainable in law. Accordingly, a person commits a money laundering offence under DTRPO or OSCO once he or she 'deals with property' with the requisite *mens rea*.

—Mens rea

The *mens rea* of a money laundering offence consists of two parts. A person must either 'know' or 'have reasonable grounds to believe' that the property he or she is dealing with represents proceeds of drug trafficking or of an indictable offence.

The term 'know' includes evidence of the person's involvement with the commission of the crime, or by admission that they knew that the property was proceeds of a crime (*Seng Yuet-fong v HKSAR [1999] 2 HKC 833, CFA* (a case under the former DTRPO, s 25)). Hong Kong cases have not dealt with the issue of whether this includes constructive knowledge (for example, 'turning a blind eye'), but if a person was reckless or ignored such conduct, from the Hong Kong case cited below, they will probably be caught within the second limb of 'having reasonable grounds to believe'.

The term 'reasonable grounds to believe' involves both objective and subjective elements. The objective element requires proof that a common-sensed, right-thinking member of the public would consider that there were grounds sufficient to lead a person to believe that the property in whole or in part represented any person's proceeds of a crime. The subjective element requires proof that those grounds were known to the defendant (*HKSAR v Shing Siu-ming [1999] 2 HKC 818, HKCA*; and *Seng Yuet-fong v HKSAR [1999] 2 HKC 833, CFA* (both cases under the former DTRPO, s 25)). In the case of *Seng Yuet Fong v HKSAR [1999] 2 HKC 833, CFA*, on an application for leave to appeal against conviction, the applicant was the accountant of a third party who allegedly received an income of HK $6,000 per month as a salesman. Without explanation, large sums of money belonging to the third party were repeatedly deposited into accounts of the applicant, which were subsequently withdrawn by her and passed on to the third party. The third party was eventually convicted of drug trafficking and the applicant, having reasonable grounds for believing that the third party was a drug trafficker, was convicted of money laundering. The application for leave to appeal against conviction was dismissed by the Hong Kong Court of Final Appeal.

—Defences

In proceedings against a person for committing a money laundering offence, it is a defence to prove on a balance of probabilities that:

1   he or she intended to disclose to an authorised officer, as soon as it was reasonable for him or her to do so, any knowledge or suspicion of any property which directly or indirectly represented proceeds of or was used in connection with (or intended to be used in connection with) drug trafficking or an indictable offence; and

2   he or she had a reasonable excuse for failing to do so.

1   an authorised officer includes any police officer, any member of the Customs & Excise Service or any officer of the JFIU;

2   DTRPO, s 25(2) and OSCO, s 29(2).

If any person had, in fact, disclosed such knowledge or suspicion to an authorised person (whether before or after he or she did the act in contravention of the money laundering offence), he or she shall not be considered to have committed an offence if:

1   disclosure was made before he or she did that act and did the act with the consent of the authorised officer; or

2   disclosure was made on his or her own initiative and as soon as it was reasonable for him or her to do so after doing that act.

A person must report any knowledge or suspicion of money laundering activities to an authorised person as soon as it is reasonable for them to do so. This is discussed in further detail below.

—Penalty

A person who is convicted of a money laundering offence is liable to 14 years' imprisonment and to a fine of HK $5 million upon indictment, and to three years' imprisonment and a fine of HK $500,000 on summary conviction (DTRPO, s 25(3) and OSCO, s 25(3)).

In determining the length of a prison sentence, Hong Kong courts may consider the following factors:

1   the seriousness of the crime or predicate offence which gave rise to the proceeds, in particular, organised crime may attract a more severe penalty;

2   the amount of illegal proceeds involved;

3   whether there was any planned or organised money laundering;

4   the period of time the offender dealt with the property and whether it was an isolated incident or a continuous activity;

5   the offender's conduct when dealing with the property and the role he or she played in the money laundering process; and

6   whether the offender received any benefit from dealing with the property.

Reporting of suspicious money laundering transactions

—Statutory obligation to report

Both DTRPO and OSCO were amended in 1995 (The Drug Trafficking (Recovery of Proceeds) (Amendment) Ordinance 1995 and the Organised and Serious Crimes (Amendment) Ordinance 1995) to tighten money laundering provisions by imposing a statutory duty on all persons, including banks, solicitors and accountants, to report suspicious transactions relating to money laundering. The disclosure obligation applies to all persons. The Ordinance does not contain any geographical restriction on the disclosure obligation but, presumably, only persons subject to Hong Kong jurisdiction will be subject to Hong Kong law.

According to DTRPO (s 25A) and OSCO (s 25A), any person who knows or suspects that any property in whole or part directly or indirectly represents the proceeds of drug trafficking or of an indictable offence or was or is intended to be used in that connection, must report such knowledge or suspicion to an authorised officer as soon as it is reasonable for them to do so.

What constitutes suspicion of a money laundering transaction has not been clearly defined in Hong Kong but, generally, suspicion must arise from some factual foundation which, upon consideration, gives rise to an apprehension that a person might possibly have laundered illegal proceeds (*R v Heaney [1992] 2 VR 522*). Mere speculation is insufficient.

An authorised officer includes any police officer, any member of the Customs & Excise Department and the JFIU. A suspicious transaction report may be made to the JFIU by mail, fax or telephone in accordance with the instructions contained on its website – www.info.gov.hk/police/jfiu/. Following receipt of a suspicious transaction report, the JFIU will conduct preliminary research to determine whether the report merits further investigation and, where appropriate, allocate the matter to trained financial investigation officers in the police and the Customs & Excise Department for further investigation. This may involve seeking supplementary information from the person making disclosure and from other sources. Discreet inquiries are also made to confirm the basis for suspicion.

The JFIU will send the person making the suspicious transaction report a letter acknowledging receipt of the report. In case of suspicious transactions involving a bank account, if there is no immediate need for action against the relevant account, consent will usually be given by the JFIU within a few days of receipt of the report allowing the person filing the report to continue to operate the account (DTRPO, s 25A and OSCO, s 25A(2)) in accordance with normal banking practices. Until such consent is obtained, further transactions in respect of the account should be avoided.

On request, the JFIU, the police or the Customs & Excise Department to whom the suspicious transaction report has been made may, but are not obliged to, provide to the person making the report a status report on the relevant investigation.

For an employee, he or she may report any knowledge or suspicion of a money laundering transaction to the person designated by his or her employer (DTRPO, s 25A(4) and OSCO, s 25A(4)) and he or she would not be prosecuted for the offence under DTRPO or OSCO, notwithstanding that his or her employer or the person designated by his or her employer fails to, or determines not to, report the transaction to the relevant authorities.

Failure to report any such knowledge or suspicion is an offence, carrying a maximum penalty of three months' imprisonment and a fine, currently HK $50,000 (DTRPO, s 25A(7) and OSCO, s 25A(7)).

—Statutory protection for disclosure

Under Hong Kong law, banks are under a duty of confidentiality to customers (*Tournier v National Provincial and Union Bank of England [1924] 1 KB 461, CA*). It is an implied term of the contract between a bank and its customer that the bank will not divulge to any third party either the state of the customer's account or any of his or her transactions with the bank, or any information relating to the customer acquired through the keeping of his or her account unless:

1   disclosure is under compulsion of Hong Kong law;

2   disclosure is made with the express or implied consent of the customer;

3   there is a duty to the public to disclose; or

4   the interests of the bank require disclosure.

Further, personal data in Hong Kong is protected by the Personal Data (Privacy) Ordinance (Cap 486 of the Laws of Hong Kong), which prohibits the use of personal information (including the transfer or disclosure of such information) for any purpose other than the purpose for which it was collected, unless with the consent of the person in question. Personal information includes any information about a living individual from which it is reasonably practicable to ascertain the identity of the person in question.

In order to encourage the reporting of suspicious financial activity and to ensure a person is not penalised for making such a report, statutory protection is afforded to any person who has disclosed information pursuant to a report of known or suspected money laundering transactions. Such disclosure shall not be treated as a breach of any contract or of any enactment or rule of conduct restricting disclosure of information (including the banker's duty of confidentiality to customers and the prohibition contained in the Personal Data (Privacy) Ordinance (Cap 486 of the Laws of Hong Kong) against disclosure and shall not render the person making the disclosure liable in damages for any loss arising out of disclosure (DTRPO, s 25A(3) and OSCO, s 25A(3)).

Tipping-off

Under DTRPO and OSCO, a person commits an offence if knowing or suspecting that a report of a suspicious money laundering transaction has been made, he or she discloses to any other person any matter which is likely to prejudice an investigation into money laundering activities. The offence carries a maximum penalty of three years' imprisonment and a fine of HK $500,000 (DTRPO, s 25A(5) and OSCO, s 25A(5)).

It is a defence to prove that such person did not know or suspect such a disclosure was likely to be prejudicial to the investigation, or that he or she had lawful authority or reasonable excuse for doing so (DTRPO, s 25A(6) and OSCO, s 25A(6)).

Appendix 2.6

Isle of Man

Peter Clucas, Manx Advocate – Director and MLRO, Cains Advocates Ltd, Douglas

Geoff Kermeen, Manx Advocate – Associate, Cains Advocates Ltd, Douglas

Primary legislation

The Isle of Man's current armoury of statutory anti-money laundering measures provide for:

1   the criminalisation of money laundering in respect of the proceeds of drug trafficking under the Drug Trafficking Act 1996 (DTA 1996) which consolidated and repealed DTOA 1987;

2   a prohibition on providing financial assistance for terrorism under the Prevention of Terrorism Act 1990 (PTA 1990); and

3   the criminalisation of assisting others to benefit from the proceeds of serious criminal conduct under the Criminal Justice Act 1990, as amended (CJA 1990).

The Isle of Man's primary legislation aimed at meeting the direct threat of money laundering is contained within PTA 1990, CJA 1990 and DTA 1996 (together, the 'Anti-Money Laundering Acts').

The Anti-Money Laundering Acts (PTA 1990, CJA 1990 and DTA 1996) do not restrict their contents to anti-money laundering measures as they also include provisions, not all addressed herein, aimed at effectively protecting the Isle of Man generally against the ever increasing threat posed by terrorism, drug trafficking and serious criminal conduct, especially organised crime and international fraud. However, in relation to their approach to criminalising assistance given to money launderers, the Anti-Money Laundering Acts adopt a common approach. The Isle of Man legislature has not chosen to provide any generic definition of money laundering within its primary legislation. The absence of such a definition reflects the reality that any such definition would undoubtedly be too restrictive if introduced by way of general application. Instead, the Anti-Money Laundering Acts specify circumstances, often of wide application (for example, in relation to the definition of criminal conduct within CJA 1990, s 17A(7)), and then impose criminal sanctions to combat money laundering in relation to those circumstances.

For money laundering (ie the process whereby criminals attempt to conceal the true nature, origin and ownership of the proceeds of their criminal activities) to be effective, it requires the introduction of the proceeds of criminal activities into the financial system, especially by way of deposit taking institutions. Accordingly, the Anti-Money Laundering Acts (PTA 1990, CJA 1990 and DTA

1996), whilst of general application, are principally targeted at those organisations and their personnel within the Isle of Man that provide financial and corporate services to the international marketplaces and are thereby potential targets for money launderers.

The Anti-Money Laundering Acts (PTA 1990, CJA 1990 and DTA 1996) introduce into the Isle of Man's criminal law effective measures to combat this threat. They achieve this through the establishment of five basic offences, which may be summarised as:

1   facilitating the retention or control of the proceeds of specific criminal activities;

2   acquiring, possessing or using the proceeds of specific criminal activities, either directly or to secure funds or acquire investments;

3   concealing or transferring out of the Isle of Man property representing the proceeds of specific criminal activities for the purpose of assisting a person to avoid either prosecution or the making of a confiscation order;

4   failing to disclose to the relevant authorities knowledge or suspicion that property is the proceeds of specific criminal activities; and

5   disclosing to a person information that is likely to be prejudicial to an investigation into money laundering, knowing or suspecting that the investigation is or is about to be conducted.

These basic offences are, by and large, common throughout the Anti-Money Laundering Acts (PTA 1990, CJA 1990 and DTA 1996) and, as identified at above, are similar in both their terms and effect to the basic offences that exist under the UK's corresponding anti-money laundering legislation.

Consideration of the terms and effect of the basic offences may be addressed by reference to their provision within CJA 1990 and, in particular, within CJA 1990, ss17A–17J; these sections were introduced into CJA 1990 by the Criminal Justice (Money Laundering Offences) Act 1998.

CJA 1990, s 17A: assisting another to retain the benefit of criminal conduct

CJA 1990, s 17A(1) provides that:

'(1) Subject to subsection (3), if a person enters into or is otherwise concerned in an arrangement whereby—

(a)   the retention or control by or on behalf of another ("A") of A's proceeds of criminal conduct is facilitated (whether by concealment, removal from the jurisdiction, transfer to nominees or otherwise); or

(b)   A's proceeds of criminal conduct—

(i)   are used to secure that funds are placed at A's disposal; or

169

(ii)   are used for A's benefit to acquire property by way of investment,

knowing or suspecting that A is a person who is or has been engaged in criminal conduct or has benefited from criminal conduct, he is guilty of an offence ...'

'Criminal conduct' for the purposes of CJA 1990 is defined (CJA 1990, s 17A(7)) as any conduct which (a) constitutes an offence to which CJA 1990, Pt I applies or, (b) would constitute such an offence if it occurred in the Isle of Man. Thus it is important to establish what constitutes an offence to which CJA 1990, Pt I applies. The answer is found in CJA 1990, s 1(9)(c), which states that:

'(c)   references to an offence to which this Part applies are references to an offence which—

(i)   is a prescribed offence; or

(ii)   if not a prescribed offence, is an offence triable on information (whether or not it is exclusively so triable), other than a drug trafficking offence;'

No offences have, as yet, been prescribed under CJA 1990, s 1(9)(c)(i). Accordingly, at present, the phrase 'an offence to which Part I of CJA 1990 applies' is restricted to any offence which may be triable in the Isle of Man on information (ie in front of a judge and jury) whether or not such mode of trial is exclusive for the offence in question. The extension of the definition of criminal conduct also to include conduct which would constitute an offence triable on information in the Isle of Man if it had occurred in the Isle of Man gives the anti-money laundering measures within CJA 1990 an extra-territorial dimension. Clearly, such a measure is intended to cover situations where the factual constituents of the criminal conduct in question occur outside the Isle of Man. Crucially, this part of the definition of criminal conduct contained within CJA 1990 (s 17A(7)) does not require dual criminality. Therefore, if it is conduct outside the Isle of Man which is in issue, technically it does not matter whether or not such conduct constitutes a criminal offence under the laws of the jurisdiction in which it took place, provided that it would constitute an offence triable on information if it had occurred in the Isle of Man.

—Fiscal offences

Whilst it is not usually difficult to establish whether or not an offence is sufficiently serious to fall within the meaning of criminal conduct as set out in CJA 1990, s 17A(7), a degree of uncertainty was initially expressed as to whether the legislation was intended to capture fiscal offences. There are no provisions within CJA 1990 that carve out an exception for fiscal crimes. Accordingly, the likelihood is that any conduct, wherever transacted, in relation to a fiscal or revenue offence that is sufficiently serious to be capable of trial on information in the Isle of Man is caught by the Act. As far as particular fiscal offences are concerned, offences under the Isle of Man's VAT legislation are triable either summarily or on information and are clearly within the scope of

CJA 1990. Offences under the Income Tax Acts are triable only summarily and fall outside the scope of this legislation at present. However, this is not to say that tax evasion cannot fall within the ambit of CJA 1990. In the UK, there are common law offences of defrauding and/or cheating the public revenue which are triable either summarily or on information. Whilst it is by no means clear whether these offences have Manx equivalents (there as yet being no decision of the Manx courts directly on point), if there were such a common law offence in the Isle of Man of cheating the public revenue, it would certainly be triable on information. In addition, there are offences under the Theft Act 1981, such as false accounting, which may be relevant in the context of tax evasion schemes and clearly do fall within its scope. It seems clear, especially in the light of comments made in the Edwards Report, that the provisions of CJA 1990 are intended to be applied to tax evasion. If the Manx courts were to find any ambiguity in the question whether or not the statutory provisions extend to fiscal offences, regard need only be had (under *Pepper v Hart* principles) to the parliamentary debates concerning the passage of these provisions at Bill stages in both the UK and the Isle of Man legislatures to confirm their wide-reaching intent.

For the purposes of CJA 1990, s 17A, references to any person's 'proceeds of criminal conduct' include reference to any property which is, in whole or in part, directly or indirectly represented in his or her hands as proceeds of criminal conduct. The fact that this definition is only expressed to apply to CJA 1990, s 17A is surprising and appears to be a curious oversight. However, whilst the position will not be resolved until the Manx courts are seized with a case on point, they will probably interpret the phrase similarly in relation to all the anti-money laundering provisions contained in CJA 1990, with a view to maintaining a consistent approach to the legislation.

The maximum penalty for the offence created under CJA 1990, s 17A is, on summary conviction, a term of imprisonment not exceeding six months or a fine not exceeding £5,000, or both; or on conviction on information, a term of imprisonment not exceeding 14 years or an unspecified fine, or both.

Certain defences to CJA 1990, s 17A exist. First, CJA 1990, s 17A(3) provides that:

'(3)   Where a person discloses to a constable a suspicion or belief that any funds or investments are derived from or used in connection with criminal conduct or discloses to a constable any matter on which such a suspicion or belief is based—

    (a)   the disclosure shall not be treated as a breach of any restriction upon the disclosure of information imposed by statute or otherwise; and

    (b)   if he does any act in contravention of subsection (1) and the disclosure relates to the arrangement concerned, he does not commit an offence under this section if—

        (i)   the disclosure is made before he does the act concerned and the act is done with the consent of the constable; or

(ii)   the disclosure is made after he does the act, but is made on his initiative and as soon as it is reasonable for him to make it.'

Whilst CJA 1990 provides that this defence arises upon making disclosure to a constable, which is defined under Manx law as including an Isle of Man Customs & Excise officer, in practice, such disclosures are made to the Isle of Man's Financial Crime Unit (FCU), a unit of the Island's police force with central responsibility for combating financial crime within the Isle of Man.

The second defence is contained within CJA 1990, s 17A(4). This provides that:

'(4)   In proceedings against a person for an offence under this section, it is a defence to prove—

(a)   that he did not know or suspect that the arrangement related to any person's proceeds of criminal conduct; or

(b)   that he did not know or suspect that by the arrangement—

(i)   the retention or control by or on behalf of A of any property was facilitated; or

(ii)   any property was used, as mentioned in subsection (1); or

(c)   that—

(i)   he intended to disclose to a constable such a suspicion, belief or matter as is mentioned in subsection (3) in relation to the arrangement; but

(ii)   there is reasonable excuse for his failure to make disclosure in accordance with subsection (3)(b).'

CJA 1990, s 17B: acquisition, possession or use of proceeds of criminal conduct

The principal offence created by CJA 1990, s 17B states that:

'(1)   A person is guilty of an offence if, knowing that any property is, or in whole or in part directly or indirectly represents, another person's proceeds of criminal conduct, he acquires or uses that property or has possession of it.'

An interesting feature of this offence is that only a *mens rea* of knowledge will suffice to secure a conviction. This should be compared with the offences created under CJA 1990, s 17A that require the alleged guilty party only to have had a threshold *mens rea* of suspicion of criminal conduct. The precise meanings of 'knowledge' and 'suspicion' within the context of these provisions have not as yet received judicial comment in the Isle of Man. It is reasonable to assume though that the Manx courts will look to and apply the meanings that have been ascribed to such terms in comparable circumstances by the Commonwealth courts.

Both the previous defences identified in CJA 1990, s 17A are repeated for the purposes of CJA 1990, s 17B. Thus where a person discloses their suspicion or belief of money laundering to a constable in good faith before doing an act prohibited by CJA 1990, s 17B(1), or as soon as is reasonably practicable afterwards, they may have a defence to a charge under the section (s 17B(5). Where a person has done any act prohibited under s 17B(1) and has made no disclosure, prima facie they will not be entitled to the benefit of the disclosure defence. However, in certain circumstances they may be able to obtain a defence by asserting that they intended to make such a disclosure but that there was a reasonable excuse for failing to do so, either before doing the act or as soon as reasonably practicable thereafter (s 17B(7)). However, this defence is by no means as certain as the disclosure defence as it is for the person accused to prove on the balance of probabilities that there was a reasonable excuse for failing to make the disclosure.

It is a further defence to a charge of committing a CJA 1990, s 17B(1) offence for the person charged to have acquired or used the property or had possession of it for adequate consideration (s 17B(2)). Adequate consideration for the purposes of the subsection is addressed by the Act (CJA 1990, s 17B(3) and (4)).

The maximum penalties for commission of an offence under CJA 1990, s 17B are in identical terms to those prescribed for breaches of CJA 1990, s 17A.

CJA 1990, s 17C: concealing or transferring proceeds of criminal conduct

CJA 1990, s 17C creates two separate criminal offences. In common with the offences created under CJA 1990, s 17A and CJA 1990, s 17B, CJA 1990, s 17C(2) is directed against a person that may be found to have assisted or facilitated the principal criminal in the laundering of his or her criminal proceeds. The offence under s 17C(2) is expressed in terms that:

'(2) A person is guilty of an offence if, knowing or having reasonable grounds to suspect that any property is, or in whole or in part directly or indirectly represents, another person's proceeds of criminal conduct, he—

(a)   conceals or disguises that property; or

(b)   converts or transfers that property or removes it from the jurisdiction,

for the purpose of assisting any person to avoid prosecution for an offence to which this Part applies or the making or enforcement in his case of a confiscation order.'

It should be noted that the *mens rea* for this offence includes reasonable grounds to suspect that any property is another person's proceeds of criminal conduct. This would appear to be setting a different, and more objective, standard of suspicion to that expressed within the constituent part of the offences under CJA 1990, s 17A, considered at above. The inclusion of the word 'suspicion' within the *mens rea* of a criminal offence is novel in Manx law. A concept of 'belief' is well established as a state of mind falling short of knowledge; for example, a person may be guilty of dishonestly handling stolen goods if he or she handles them knowing or believing the goods to be stolen. Suspicion, however, does not require as much information as is required to satisfy a test based on belief. Although suspicion appears in other contexts within Manx law (for example, police powers of arrest may be exercised on reasonable grounds of suspicion), there is no accepted definition of suspicion within the context of any Manx criminal offence. Notwithstanding this, inclusion of the phrase 'reasonable grounds to suspect' as one of the requisite states of minds within CJA 1990, s 17C(2) strongly suggests that a distinction is being made between an objective level of suspicion under that section and a more subjective concept of suspicion under s 17A.

Furthermore, in order to achieve a conviction under CJA 1990, s 17C(2), the prosecution will not only have to demonstrate to the criminal standard that the accused had the requisite *mens rea* as discussed at above, but will also need to prove that the accused was acting in furtherance of one or other of the two prescribed purposes. These are set out as assisting any person to avoid either (i) prosecution for an offence to which CJA 1990, Pt I applies or (ii) the making or enforcement of a confiscation order (as for confiscation orders, see below).

CJA 1990, s 17C(1) creates an offence similar to that under CJA 1990, s 17C(2) but, in contrast, is directed at the principal launderer and his or her own proceeds of criminal conduct rather than at the person that may be assisting them in the laundering process.

Again, the maximum penalties for commission of an offence under CJA 1990, s 17C are in identical terms to those prescribed for breaches of CJA 1990, s 17A.

CJA 1990, s 17D: tipping-off

There are a number of provisions within CJA 1990, s 17D that relate to tipping off. In essence, the offence of tipping off arises where a money laundering disclosure has been made to the FCU or an investigation into money laundering is underway or imminent and disclosure is made to any person of information that is likely to prejudice that investigation or any future investigation. The full terms of the offence are set out in CJA 1990, s 17D(1)–(3):

'(1) A person is guilty of an offence if—

(a) he knows or suspects that a constable is acting, or is proposing to act, in connection with an investigation which is being, or is about to be, conducted into money laundering; and

(b) he discloses to any other person information or any other matter which is likely to prejudice that investigation, or proposed investigation.

(2) A person is guilty of an offence if—

    (a)   he knows or suspects that a disclosure ("the disclosure") has been made to a constable under section 17A or 17B; and

    (b)   he discloses to any other person information or any other matter which is likely to prejudice any investigation which might be conducted following the disclosure.

(3)   A person is guilty of an offence if—

    (a)   he knows or suspects that a disclosure of a kind mentioned in section 17A(5) or 17B(8) ("the disclosure") has been made; and

    (b)   he discloses to any person information or any other matter that is likely to prejudice any investigation that might be conducted following the disclosure.'

CJA 1990, s 17D makes provision for two statutory defences to a charge of tipping off or, more precisely, one exception and one defence to the offence. The exception to the offence relates to legal professional privilege. Accordingly it is only available to professional legal advisors. CJA 1990, s 17D(4) confirms that the tipping off offence will not be committed when the disclosure of information or any other matter is made by a professional legal adviser to (or to a representative of) a client of the legal adviser in connection with the provision by that lawyer of legal advice to the client or to any person in contemplation of or in connection with legal proceedings and for the purpose of those proceedings. The parameters of this legal privilege defence are unclear and may turn on whether or not legal proceedings exist at the time the advice to the client or other party is given. In any event, the exception is not available where the advice is given with a view to furthering a criminal purpose (17D(5)) which would include the purposes of avoiding prosecution or the making of a confiscation order under CJA 1990.

CJA 1990, s 17D(6) provides that it is a defence to a tipping off offence to prove that the person accused had no knowledge that the disclosure was likely to prejudice a money laundering investigation. This defence places at least the factual burden of proof on the accused and, notwithstanding that this burden is likely to require proof on the balance of probabilities, English authorities have questioned the compatibility of such reverse burden clauses (which would also include CJA 1990, s 17A(4)) with the presumption of innocence that is protected by the European Convention on Human Rights, art 6(2). Relevant decisions of the English courts in this respect are likely to be highly persuasive on this point, especially when the Isle of Man's Human Rights Act 2001 comes into full force.

The maximum penalties for commission of a tipping off offence under CJA 1990, s 17D are again identical to the penalties considered above. Accordingly, tipping off is potentially a very serious offence and highlights how the anti-money laundering legislation places an onerous duty upon financial institutions to fulfil their role in combating serious crime. Unfortunately, the restrictions on disclosure that s 17D places upon institutions with knowledge or suspicion of money laundering can occasionally conflict with the duties owed to their clients under private law. This aspect of the legislation is giving rise to increasing applications for guidance to the Isle of Man courts.

CJA 1990, s 17J: failure to disclose knowledge or suspicion of money launder-ing

The last of the basic offences created under CJA 1990 is that of failing to disclose to a constable (in practice, the FCU), as soon as reasonably practicable, information or other matters which gives rise to knowledge or suspicion that another person is engaged in laundering the proceeds of criminal conduct. The offence is only committed if the information or other matter comes to the attention of the accused in the course of their trade, profession, business or employment and, beyond this, CJA 1990, s 17J does not impose obligations upon the public at large.

In relation to CJA 1990, s 17J, the 'laundering of the proceeds of criminal conduct' is defined as doing anything that will constitute an offence under CJA 1990, ss 17A, 17B or 17C, or in the case of anything done outside the Isle of Man (s 17J(7)) or anything that would constitute any such offences if done within the Isle of Man. Accordingly, this offence imposes a mandatory require-ment to disclose to the FCU any suspicion of money laundering arising within a commercial setting. Disclosures are at the heart of the money laundering legislation and clearly were designed to be at the forefront of the Island's fight against laundering. Not only is the disclosure mechanism the means by which the law enforcement authorities gather intelligence for the enforcement of the Isle of Man's own laws, it serves as a source of information that, subject to certain safeguards, can be shared with law enforcement agencies located within other jurisdictions.

Given that, in practice, the information that gives rise to a suspicion that another person is engaged in the laundering of proceeds of criminal conduct usually comes to light within the course of some trade, profession or business, special arrangements have been made for employees of such businesses. In the context of CJA 1990, ss 17A, 17B and 17J, any disclosure requirement thereunder, which would normally be required to be made to the FCU, may be satisfied by an employee if made to the employer or, where the employer has established a procedure for making disclosure by employees, to the employer's appropriate person (eg, CJA 1990, s 17J(5)).

Again, special provision is made for a defence of reasonable non-disclosure and for legal professional privilege in the context of mandatory disclosures. Legal professional privilege is considered under CJA 1990, s 17J(9)–(10), which provides that:

'(9) For the purposes of this section, any information or other matter comes to a professional legal adviser in privileged circumstances if it is communicated, or given, to him—

(a) by, or by a representative of, a client of his in connection with the giving by the adviser of legal advice to the client;

(b) by, or by a representative of, a person seeking legal advice from the adviser; or

(c) by any person—

    (i) in contemplation of, or in connection with, legal proceedings; and

    (ii) for the purpose of those proceedings.

(10) No information or other matter shall be treated as coming to a professional legal adviser in privileged circumstances if it is communicated or given with a view to furthering any criminal purpose.'

Again, the maximum penalties for failing to disclose under CJA 1990, s 17J are identical to those described above.

Tipping-off

The rise in the number of disclosures has led to practical difficulties in the context of tipping off. As discussed at above, the legislation provides that once a disclosure has been made, any person with knowledge or suspicion of that fact is guilty of an offence if they disclose information which is likely to prejudice any investigation which might be conducted following the disclosure. This has created some concerns for banks and other financial institutions, especially where the ground for suspicion leading to the disclosure is serious fraud, carrying with it a concomitant risk of constructive trusteeship. Banks faced with such a situation have expressed concern that they may not be able to investigate the provenance of a customer's funds in such circumstances without running the risk of tipping off the customer that a suspicion transaction disclosure may have been made to the FCU. A not dissimilar issue arose for consideration by the Manx High Court in *Re Petition of Alliance & Leicester International Limited 4 May 2001, unreported, HC),* in which the Manx High Court considered the English Court of Appeal authority in *Bank of Scotland v A Ltd [2001] EWCA Civ 52, [2001] All ER 58, CA* and held that 'it is open to a bank to seek directions from the Court if it has a reasonable apprehension that it might be held as a constructive trustee'. Whilst the Manx High Court would appear from this case to be reasonably receptive to genuine cases where financial institutions face a dilemma due to fears of tipping off, the court still expects a party to consult with the FCU in the first instance, and only where a reasonable and workable solution cannot be reached with the FCU should an application be made to the court.

Inchoate offences

It is a general principle of Manx criminal law that a person need not be wholly involved in the commission of a complete offence to incur criminal liability. A person may be guilty of an offence if he or she has:

1   attempted to commit it;

2   conspired with another person(s) to commit it; or

3   incited another person(s) to commit it.

In addition, a person may be guilty as a secondary party to a criminal offence if he or she aids, abets, counsels or otherwise procures a commission of the principal offence.

There is no reason why these principles should not apply to the money laundering offences, though the main offences themselves are so widely drawn it seems improbable that prosecutors will ever need to resort to them.

Secondary legislation

The Anti-Money Laundering Code 1998

Following the amendment of CJA 1990 on 16 June 1998 by the Criminal Justice (Money Laundering Offences) Act 1998, CJA 1990, s 17F came into force and empowered the Isle of Man Government's Department of Home Affairs to make:

'(1)   ... such codes as it considers appropriate for the purposes of preventing and detecting money laundering (whether in respect of the benefits or proceeds of criminal conduct, drug trafficking within the meaning of the DTA 1996 or otherwise) and, but without prejudice to the generality of that power, a Code may:–

      (a)   provide practical guidance with respect to the requirements of any provision of this Part or any other statutory provision relating to the benefits or proceeds of criminal conduct or drug trafficking within the meaning of the Drug Trafficking Act 1996;

      (b)   require any person carrying on any trade or business specified in the code to institute and operate such systems, procedures, record-keeping, controls and training as may be specified in the code;

      (c)   require persons carrying on, employed in or otherwise concerned in any trade or business specified in the code to comply with such systems, procedures, record-keeping, controls and training as are required to be instituted and operated under para. (b);

      ...

(2)   A code under this section may incorporate by reference any relevant regulations, codes, directions and guidance made or issued by the Financial Supervision Commission or the Insurance and Pensions Authority.'

The Isle of Man government brought the Anti Money Laundering Code 1998 into force on 1 December 1998 and, by doing so, fully established a comprehensive and effective arsenal of laws and regulations to combat money laundering. Indeed, it is in relation to the scope and application of the Code that the Isle of Man regulations surpass those previously and currently in place in the UK – ie, the UK's Money Laundering Regulations 1993, SI 1993/1933.

As stated at above, the Anti-Money Laundering Code 1998 is not of general application. The explanatory note to the Code states that:

'... the provisions of the Code impose requirements on the businesses mentioned in the Schedule to establish anti money laundering procedures, training and record keeping. Failure to comply with the Code will be a criminal offence.'

The businesses mentioned in the Schedule to the Anti Money Laundering Code 1998 are collectively defined as 'relevant businesses'. The list of relevant businesses encompasses a very wide range of activities, each susceptible to being targeted by money launderers. The full list of relevant businesses is as follows:

1   Banking business within the meaning of the Banking Act 1998.

2   Investment business within the meaning of the Investment Business Act 1991.

3   Insurance business within the meaning of the Insurance Act 1986.

4   Business carried on by a building society within the meaning of the Industrial and Building Societies Act 1982, s 7.

5   Business carried on by a society registered as a credit union within the meaning of the Credit Unions Act 1993.

6   Business carried on by a society (other than a building society or credit union) registered under the Industrial and Building Societies Act 1982.

7   Any activity carried on for the purpose of raising money authorised to be borrowed under the Isle of Man Loans Act 1974.

8   Any activity carried on for the purpose of raising money by a local authority.

9   The business of a bureau de change.

10   The business of an estate agent with the meaning of the Estate Agents Act 1975.

11   The business of a bookmaker within the meaning of the Gaming, Betting and Lotteries Act 1988.

12   Any activity permitted to be carried on by a licence holder under a casino licence granted under the Casino Act 1986.

13   The business of the Post Office in respect of any activity undertaken on behalf of the National Savings Bank.

14   Any activity involving money transmission services or cheque encashment facilities.

15   Any activity in which money belonging to a client is held or managed by:

    (i)   an advocate;

    (ii)   a registered legal practitioner within the meaning of the Legal Practitioners Registration Act 1986; or

    (iii) an accountant or a person who, in the course of business, provides accountancy services.

16   The business of:

    (i)   promoting or forming bodies corporate;

    (ii)   acting as company secretary of bodies corporate; or

    (iii) providing registered offices for bodies corporate.

17   The business of acting as a trustee in return for payment, or providing or taking steps to provide persons to act as trustees in return for payment; and in this paragraph, trustee includes a person who is registered as the legal owner of any interest in a share in a body corporate as nominee for another.

The Anti Money Laundering Code 1998, para 3 sets out general requirements (the 'General Requirements') in relation to any person carrying on a relevant business (referred to within the Code as 'a relevant person'). The General Requirements provide that in conducting relevant business, a relevant person must not form a business relationship with a client or customer unless that relevant person maintains:

    (i)   procedures for the production by a client of satisfactory evidence of his identity;

    (ii)   record keeping procedures;

    (iii) procedures to provide for disclosures to be made by employees;

    (iv)   internal controls and communication procedures appropriate for forestalling and preventing money laundering;

    (v)   has in place appropriate measures to provide training to its employees regarding its procedures above and the provision of the money laundering requirements; and

    (vi)   provides general training to its employees in relation to suspicious transactions.

In relation to the General Requirements, money laundering is not defined, but 'money laundering requirements' is explained to mean DTA 1996, ss 45–49, CJA 1990, ss 17A–17D and PTA 1990, s 9 (Anti-Money Laundering Code

1998, para 2). In the circumstances, it would appear sensible to interpret money laundering when used within the Anti Money Laundering Code 1998 as a reference to the activities that are the subject of offences within the aforesaid primary legislation.

A breach of the Anti-Money Laundering Code 1998 constitutes a criminal offence (Anti-Money Laundering Code 1998, para 3(2)). The maximum penalties for such a breach were increased during 2001. They are, currently, on summary conviction, a fine not exceeding £5,000 or imprisonment for six months, or both; and on conviction on information, imprisonment not exceeding two years or a fine, or both.

Where the offence is committed by a relevant person which is a body corporate and it is proved to have been committed with the consent or connivance of, or to be attributable to neglect on the part of, a director, manager, secretary or similar officer of the body corporate, then that officer is also guilty of the offence and could be punished accordingly. Similar provisions deeming guilt in relation to a member in the case of a body corporate managed by its members or a partner in the case of a partnership is also included (Anti-Money Laundering Code 1998, para 3(5)–(7)).

In relation to any criminal proceedings against a person for an alleged breach of the General Requirements under the Anti Money Laundering Code 1998, a court is directed that it may take account of any relevant guidance that is applicable to that person (Anti Money Laundering Code 1998, para 3(3), SD 702/99). This could be guidance issued by either the FSC or the Insurance and Pensions Authority (IPA), or otherwise by a body that regulates or represents a trade or profession within the Isle of Man. It is a defence to a charge under the Code for a person to show that they took all reasonable steps and exercised all due diligence to avoid committing the offence although, as a defence, this would appear to be couched in terms that will be difficult to satisfy in reality (Anti-Money Laundering Code 1998, para 3(4)).

—Identification procedures under the Anti-Money Laundering Code 1998

The Anti-Money Laundering Code 1998, para 4(1) creates the fundamental requirement that all relevant businesses must establish and maintain identification procedures. These procedures must, as soon as reasonably practicable after contact is first made between a relevant person and their client (referred to within the Code as the 'Applicant for Business'), require the production by the Applicant for Business of 'satisfactory evidence' of his or her identity. It is through the establishment and maintenance of such procedures that relevant businesses in the Isle of Man operate an effective 'Know Your Customer' (KYC) regime. Business activities that are not identified within the Schedule to the Code are not required to operate any KYC checks at present. Further, certain professions named within the Code, such as lawyers and accountants, are only required to apply the Code (and hence the identification procedures) to certain parts of their business. For example, lawyers engaged in litigation or accountants conducting audit work are not subject to the Code unless, as an incident of such work, they hold or manage client's money. Of course, it is generally easier for any relevant business to obtain satisfactory KYC evidence at the outset of a new client relationship. Accordingly, in all circumstances, it may be prudent to give consideration to whether evidence of identity should be obtained from a new client whether or not client's money is actually being held or managed at the outset of the new relationship.

The Anti-Money Laundering Code 1998, when initially established, created a degree of uncertainty in relation to whether or not it was necessary to apply the identification procedures to clients of a relevant business where the business relationship had been entered into prior to the commencement of the Code. The matter was determined by an amendment to the Code, which introduced an additional para 2A to the Code. Paragraph 2A of the Code confirms that the Code does not require a relevant person to maintain procedures for the identification of any client where the business relationship with that client was formed before 1 December 1998. Indeed para 2A has the further effect of deeming such clients as having an established business relationship which is defined by para 2(2) of the Code as a business relationship formed by any relevant person with a client who has produced satisfactory evidence of his or her identity under the Code procedures. Accordingly, the amendment introduced at para 2A not only exempts relevant businesses from having to carry out KYC procedures in relation to their pre-December 1998 clients, it also deems that satisfactory KYC is in existence (whether or not that may be the case). How long this concession in relation to longstanding clients will be maintained is a matter that is already under debate within the Isle of Man. However, if there is to be any withdrawal from the current position, it will require a further amendment to the Code.

The Anti-Money Laundering Code 1998 does not attempt to prescribe what procedure amounts to satisfactory identification for the purposes of para 4 of the Code. Such matters are dealt with under guidance issued by the various regulators or governing professional/trade bodies that have responsibility for the relevant businesses. An overview of the guidance that has been issued to date by various Isle of Man bodies in respect of the Code is given below.

—Exemptions under the Anti-Money Laundering Code 1998

The Anti-Money Laundering Code 1998 has created certain exemptions under which a relevant business is not required to carry out KYC identification procedures on a client. The categories of exemption are directed towards clients who constitute a low risk of money laundering and reflect a presumption that the client is already regulated and/or subjected to approved anti-money laundering requirements. The categories of exemptions identified in the Code are as follows:

1   Any Applicant for Business that is a regulated person. A regulated person is defined as a person carrying on banking, investment or insurance business or providing corporate administration services in or from the Isle of Man in respect of which any necessary licence or authorisation has been issued by an Isle of Man licensing authority (Anti-Money Laundering Code 1998, paras 4(2)(a) and 2(2)).

2   Any authorised credit or financial institution in the European Economic Area which is covered by the EC Money Laundering Directive (Council Directive 91/308/EEC) (Anti-Money Laundering Code 1998, para 4(2)(b)).

3   Any authorised credit or financial institution in a country which is a member of FATF and which has anti-money laundering requirements which have been approved by FATF Anti-Money Laundering Code, para 4(2)(b)).

4   Any advocate (which means an advocate licensed to practice at the Manx Bar), registered legal practitioner within the meaning of the Legal Practitioners Registration Act 1986 (under which non-Manx lawyers may be registered to practice in the Isle of Man) or any accountant, provided that the relevant person is satisfied that the rules of the professional bodies of such Applicants for Business embody requirements equivalent to the Code (4(2)(d)). The requirement for equivalence with the Code clearly narrows this category of exemption as in order for the exemption to apply, the relevant professional body must have addressed equivalence with the Code within its professional rules.

5   Any Applicant for Business that acts in the course of a business in relation to which a regulatory authority outside the Isle of Man exercises regulatory functions and the Applicant for Business is based or incorporated in or is formed under the laws of:

(i)   Jersey or Guernsey; or

(ii)   a country outside the Isle of Man which is a member of FATF and which has anti money laundering requirements approved by FATF (Anti-Money Laundering Code 1998, para 4(3)).

In relation to each category of exemption above, the relevant business must have reasonable grounds for believing that the Applicant for Business is entitled to claim exemption.

A further category of exemption is established by the Anti-Money Laundering Code 1998, para 5, which relates to the nature of the business to be transacted and is defined under the Code as exempt one-off transactions. An exempt one-off transaction is defined as a one-off transaction (which may in fact be a series of linked transactions) where the amount (or in the case of linked transactions the aggregate) amount is less than e15,000 (Anti-Money Laundering Code 1998, para 2(2)). A further specific exemption is applied to one-off transactions involving bookmakers or casinos, for which the threshold is reduced to 3,000 euros. Other than satisfying any of the general exemptions set out, all other one-off transactions must satisfy the KYC requirements discussed above.

—Verification of KYC under the Anti Money Laundering Code 1998

A further identification procedure that is required to be carried out in respect of an Applicant for Business is the establishment and maintenance of a procedure by the relevant business which requires satisfactory verification of any evidence of identity that an Applicant for Business may have produced as soon as is reasonably practicable after a transaction is undertaken with or by that client which is significantly different from the normal pattern of previous business (Anti Money Laundering Code 1998, para 4(4)). What is expected by verification is, again, undefined by the Anti Money Laundering Code 1998 and left for relevant guidance. However, it is evident that this requirement of the Code imposes upon a relevant business a need to identify and understand the nature and scope of the business that it is accepting and to monitor the business relationship over time. Otherwise, it is difficult to see how a relevant business would be able to identify normal patterns of previous business and distinguish these from any transactions that are significantly different. This provision, which carries with it a requirement for ongoing vigilance on the part of the relevant business, is the key to understanding the full scope of KYC due diligence. Whilst the Code expresses basic requirements in terms of obtaining and, if necessary, verifying a client's identity, the true breadth of the procedures requires a relevant business not only to know its customer (ie KYC), but also to know its customer's business (ie KYCB). Where a relevant business obtains evidence to verify its client, it must maintain a record of that information in the Isle of Man (Anti Money Laundering Code 1998, para 7).

—Introduced business under the Anti Money Laundering Code 1998

As stated above, the Isle of Man financial services sector is now well developed and conducts its business across international borders on an increasing scale. Much of this business is conducted through intermediaries whose role is, in effect, to introduce new clients to relevant businesses within the Island. The Anti Money Laundering Code 1998, para 6 specifically addresses situations where a client is introduced to the relevant person by a third party (the 'Introducer'). In such circumstances, the basic identity procedures (ie the KYC and KYCB requirements) still apply, as do the exemptions described above. However, where business has been introduced by a third party, the Code recognises that, subject to the status of the Introducer, further exemptions or modifications to the normal identification procedures may be permitted. Accordingly, no identification procedures need be applied where there are reasonable grounds for believing that the Introducer itself falls within the exemptions set out at para 4(2) of the Code or where the client and the relevant person are bodies corporate within the same group (As defined by the Anti Money Laundering Code 1998, para 6(2)(b)). Furthermore, the introduced client is not required to produce evidence of his or her identity to the relevant person if the Introducer satisfies the exemption at para 4(3) and has entered into written terms of business with the relevant person, under which the Introducer has confirmed that he or she will:

1   verify the identity of all Applicants for Business introduced to the relevant persons sufficient to comply with anti-money laundering requirements;

2   maintain a record of the evidence of verification of identity and records of all transactions for at least five years;

3   supply to the relevant person forthwith upon request evidence of the verification of identity of any particular client; and

4   inform the relevant person specifically of each case where the Introducer is not required, or has not been able, to verify the identity of the applicant.

—Failure to provide information under the Anti-Money Laundering Code 1998

The Anti-Money Laundering Code 1998 is prescriptive in so far as the relevant person should not enter into a business relationship with a new client if he or she fails to obtain evidence (or verification) of the new client's identity. This prohibition is extended to similar failings in relation to new clients conducting one-off transactions and in relation to the procedures relating to introduced business. The Code does not prescribe any time limit during which any dealings pursuant to a new business relationship can be conducted but, rather, states that the relevant business' procedures comply with the Code if they require that whenever KYC (or KYCB) information is not obtained or produced the business relationship or transaction should end. It is unlikely that the Code intends to prohibit any dealings whatsoever between a relevant person and their new client pending compliance with the Code's identification procedures, given that such a prohibition would be a significant deterrent to commerce. Rather, it is left to relevant businesses and any relevant guidance to determine at what stage the business relationship should be terminated.

—Record keeping under the Anti Money Laundering Code 1998

Records of transactions: The Anti Money Laundering Code 1998, para 8 imposes a requirement upon relevant persons to maintain a record of all transactions carried out by or on behalf of any client whose identity is required to be verified. The obligation to verify a client's identity was discussed at above and arises out of the identification of transactions significantly different from the normal pattern of business. When a significantly different transaction is identified, para 9 of the Code requires that the relevant person must maintain a record of all transactions that may assist any investigating authority to compile an audit trail of suspected money laundering (for example, by identifying the source and recipients of payments). The relevant person will need to consider carefully how best to comply with the obligations both to verify the identity of the client and to record all future transactions, given that the identification of a transaction significantly different to previous business may require a suspicious transaction disclosure to be made to the FCU. If so, the relevant person will need to ensure that subsequent actions do not constitute a tipping off offence.

Retention of records: A relevant person is obliged to maintain records obtained by the identification and other procedures for at least five years from the date when the business relationship was formally ended or if the business relationship was not formally ended, when the last transaction was carried out (Anti-Money Laundering Code 1998, para 9(1)). However, where a report has been made to a constable or the person knows or believes that a matter is under investigation, the relevant person must retain all relevant records for so long as the constable requires (Anti-Money Laundering Code 1998, para 9(2)). There-fore, in these circumstances, the records relating to identification procedures and copies of the records sufficient to trace the nature and details of the transactions performed by and for the client must also be retained.

Register of money laundering inquiries: A relevant person must maintain a register of all inquiries made of it by law enforcement or other agencies acting under powers provided by the money laundering requirements (Anti-Money Laundering Code 1998, para 11). Such register must be kept separate from other records and must contain as a minimum the date and nature of the inquiry, the name and agency of the inquiring officer, the powers being exercised and details of the accounts or transactions involved.

—Reporting procedures under the Anti-Money Laundering Code 1998

A relevant person is also obliged to establish written disclosure procedures which, in relation to its relevant business (Anti-Money Laundering Code 1998, para 11(1)):

1   enable all persons involved in its management, and all appropriate employees to know to whom they should disclose any knowledge or suspicion of money laundering activity;

2   ensure that there is a clear reporting chain under which those suspicions will be passed to the appropriate person;

3   identify the appropriate person to whom a disclosure is to be made of any information or other matter which comes to the attention of the person handling the business and which in that person's opinion gives rise to a knowledge or suspicion that another person is engaged in money launder-ing;

4   require the appropriate person to consider any report in the light of all other relevant information available to him or her for the purpose of determining whether or not it gives rise to a suspicion of money launder-ing;

5   ensure that the appropriate person has reasonable access to any other information which may be of assistance to him or her and which is available to the relevant business; and

6   require that the information or other matter contained in the report be disclosed promptly to a constable where the appropriate person knows or suspects that another is engaged in money laundering.

The relevant person is further obliged to maintain a register of all disclosures that are made to a constable pursuant to these procedures (Anti-Money Laun-dering Code 1998, para 11(2)). This register must contain details of the date when the disclosure was made, the person who made the disclosure, the constable to whom it was made and information sufficient to identify the relevant papers.

—Education and training obligations under the Anti-Money Laundering Code 1998

The Anti-Money Laundering Code 1998, paras 13–15 provide that the relevant person must provide education and training for all persons involved in the relevant person's management and business and all appropriate employees to ensure that they are aware of:

1   the relevant provisions of the Anti-Money Laundering Acts and the Code (PTA 1990, CJA 1990 and DTA 1996);

2   their personal obligations under the money laundering requirements;

3   the disclosure procedures established under the Code; and

4   their personal liability for failing to report information or suspicions in accordance with the disclosure procedures.

The training and education provided should be appropriate to any particular category of staff and include the relevant business's policies and procedures to prevent money laundering, its customer identification, recording keeping and other procedures and the recognition and handling of suspicious transactions and money laundering techniques in general. Furthermore, refresher training at regular intervals to remind staff of their responsibilities and to make them aware of any changes in money laundering requirements should also be given.

Guidance issued by Isle of Man authorities

Guidance Notes in relation to anti-money laundering measures have been in existence in the Isle of Man in relation to investment and banking business since at least 1992, when issued as part of the regulatory and compliance codes issued under the banking and investment business Acts.

However, with the establishment of the Anti Money Laundering Code 1998, regulators and some professional bodies in the Isle of Man have issued bespoke Guidance Notes addressing the specific requirements of the Code. All banking, investment (including mutual funds) and corporate administration activities carried on by way of business in and from the Isle of Man require a licence issued by the FSC. In relation to its licence holders, the FSC has issued Anti-Money Laundering Guidance Notes for banks, investment businesses and corporate service providers, in December 2001 (available at www.fsc.gov.im). The guidance issued in relation to insurance and pension business in the Isle of Man has been addressed by its regulatory authority, the IPA, which has issued its Practice Notes on the Prevention of Money Laundering (September 2001). Industry Guidance Notes for accountants follow the Practice Notes issued by the Institute (which invariably means that the guidance is issued with primary regard to the UK's Money Laundering Regulations 1993 (SI 1993/1933) rather that the Code). Manx qualified lawyers (advocates) are regulated by the Isle of Man Law Society, which has incorporated compliance with the Code into its Practice Rules and issues a specimen Policy and Procedures Manual for compliance with the Code.

The guidance issued by these regulatory bodies provides detailed and practical guidance on how relevant persons should establish and maintain the procedures specified within the Anti-Money Laundering Code 1998, and are cross-referenced to the Code requirements. Notwithstanding that the guidance contains much prescriptive detail of how the Code procedures should be implemented, Guidance Notes do not carry the direct force of law and a failure to comply with a Guidance Note is not a criminal offence. However, guidance issued by the various regulators and professional bodies is reinforced by para 3(3) of the Code which, as stated above, provides that in relation to an alleged breach of the Code (which, of course, carries criminal sanction), a court is directed to have reference to any relevant guidance. Furthermore, regulatory authorities in the Isle of Man, in particular the FSC and IPA, require their licence holders to have proper regard to any relevant anti-money laundering guidance incidental to their status as regulated businesses.

It is not practical to cover each set of Guidance Notes in issue in the Isle of Man nor, indeed, to address every aspect of guidance contained therein. Whilst solely directed at its own licence holders, the guidance issued by the FSC is recognised as being the most comprehensive although, in general, there is little divergence of approach between the guidance that has been issued by any of the regulators or professional bodies. Given this common approach, it is useful to consider in more detail the general guidance that exists in relation to compliance with the requirements of the Anti-Money Laundering Code 1998 in the Isle of Man.

New business relationships and identity

In general, the guidance stresses that before a new business relationship is established, all relevant persons must satisfy themselves as to the identity of the client and, in the absence of satisfactory evidence, the business relationship should not proceed any further.

In relation to obtaining satisfactory evidence of identity, the guidance generally requires that documentary evidence should be obtained, usually in the form of a passport or a national identity card (carrying a photograph of the individual), failing which two formal documents carrying appropriate reference numbers may be used to establish the client's full name and nationality. In addition, further documented information concerning natural persons is recommended in order to establish the correct permanent address, date and place of birth, occupation, the purpose of the business relationship, the anticipated level of business, the source of funds, the source of wealth and the identity of any person who will be responsible for issuing instructions. Where the relevant person is unable to inspect original documents that have been submitted, copy documents must be certified as being true copies and the guidance requires the certifier to be a suitable person, such as a notary public or a consular official, who should confirm their identity and position on the copy documentation.

When it is necessary to verify the identity of a client, the generally recommended methods to be adopted include obtaining a reference from a 'respected professional' who knows the client, checking any official public registers, referring to credit reference agencies and requesting sight of a recent and original utility bill or a statement from a recognised bank. Alternatively, the FSC suggest that eligible financial institutions (namely, other licensed or authorised institutions within the Isle of Man) in certain circumstances may be prepared to verify the name, signatures and date of birth of a client.

In relation to corporate clients, the above methods of evidencing and verifying the identity of natural persons are expected to be applied to the key officers and/or owners of the body corporate. For example, it is generally recommended that the relevant person obtains a list of all directors and obtains evidence of the identity of at least two directors, one of whom should be an executive director. Furthermore, in appropriate cases, similar documentary evidence will need to be obtained from each of the beneficial owners of the body corporate and, in the case of an applicant for financial services, evidence of the account signatories should also be obtained. The FSC's Guidance Notes emphasise that 'The Isle of Man Government considers it vitally important for the international standing and economic wellbeing of the Island that it conforms to established international norms for combating money-laundering'. In recognition of such aspirations, the guidance then expressly refers to Recommendation 11 of the FATF 40 Recommendations and highlights the importance for anti-money laundering purposes of ensuring that the true customer's identity is known (ie the identity of the beneficial owner and/or the underlying principal).

In all cases where the Applicant for Business is a body corporate, it is generally a requirement that the relevant business obtains a Certificate of Incorporation or equivalent, as well as details of the registered office and place of business (if different). In order to meet the Anti-Money Laundering Code 1998's ongoing monitoring requirements, a relevant person may also need to obtain details of the applicant's business, the reason for the business, an indication of the expected turnover or level of transactions, the source of any funds to be introduced, the source of the applicant's wealth and a copy of the latest available accounts. The guidance issued by the FSC in relation to applicants that are bodies corporate also suggests that copies of board resolutions or other corporate authorities relevant to the new business relationship should be obtained.

In general, guidance issued for the identification of new clients that are trustees or otherwise acting in a fiduciary position require as a minimum that the identification steps described above are taken in respect of the trustee, the settler of the trust (and any person providing the funds settled or to be settled), the protector, if any, and any person with power to appoint or remove the trustees. Furthermore, evidence as to the source and origin of the assets subject to the trust arrangement should also be obtained.

Ongoing monitoring of business relationships

The guidance in relation to monitoring ongoing business relationships suggests that relevant persons consider what procedures are required to monitor the conduct and activities of the business relationship to ensure that it is consistent with the nature of business and estimate of turnover stated when the relationship was established. The procedures must be sufficient for relevant persons to be vigilant for any significant changes or inconsistencies in the pattern of transactions or client behaviour: possible areas to be monitored include the transaction type, frequency, size, geographic origin/destination, account signatories and, in the case of corporate administration services, the client company's activities.

Controls and communications

The principle guidance in relation to control systems is the requirement that relevant persons establish a written internal procedure manual so that, in the event of suspicious transactions being discovered, the relevant person's employees are aware of, and follow, the correct procedures. Key to this is the appointment of a suitably qualified and experienced officer within the relevant entity who is to have responsibility for establishing and maintaining the procedures manual and for overseeing the disclosure of suspicious transactions. This person, previously referred to as the appropriate person, but more commonly called the Money Laundering Reporting Officer (MLRO) should be a senior member of the relevant person's organisation whose responsibilities will be to determine whether or not external disclosure of any matter is required to be given to the FCU.

Record keeping

The guidance identifies the various records that the Anti-Money Laundering Code 1998 requires a relevant person to maintain. Generally, all relevant persons will be required to maintain records of the documentation obtained in relation to identifying their clients and monitoring transactions. In respect of monitoring transactions, the guidance emphasises that the purpose of retaining the documentation is to ensure that a satisfactory audit trail can be established for anti-money laundering purposes. This envisages that ultimately such documents may be required as evidence in criminal proceedings relating to money laundering. This purpose should not be overlooked by the relevant person and, where possible, documentary evidence should be obtained and recorded as best evidence. Relevant persons are also required to maintain registers containing details of any inquiries from law enforcement or other authorities and of all money laundering disclosures that it has made. The Guidance Notes add little to the Code in this respect, except that the FSC's guidance stresses that it expects its licence holders to be in a position to retrieve relevant information without undue delay in response to production orders, warrants etc.

Training

All relevant persons must establish a programme for training and the guidance reflects that the Anti Money Laundering Code 1998 does not specify the exact nature of training to be given, but leaves it to the relevant body to tailor its training programme to suits its own needs, depending on its size, resources and the type of business it undertakes.

Training should, however, be structured and directed as appropriate to the particular categories of staff. It should also include a programme for refresher training to be given at regular intervals. A training register, which demonstrates that the appropriate training has been provided to all participants, must also be maintained.

Appendix 2.7

Jersey

Martin Paul – Advocate, Bedell Cristin, St Helier

Legislative and regulatory structure

Primary legislation

Jersey's main provisions against money laundering, as considered in this chapter, are contained in the following laws:

1   the Drug Trafficking Offences (Jersey) Law 1988, as amended ('DTO(J)L 1988');

2   the Terrorism (Jersey) Law 2002 ('T(J)L 2002'); and

3   the Proceeds of Crime (Jersey) Law 1999 ('PC(J)L 1999').

Secondary legislation

Secondary legislation has been introduced which is specifically targeted at financial services businesses, namely the Money Laundering (Jersey) Order 1999. The Order requires all financial services businesses to establish procedures and training for the purpose of forestalling and preventing money laundering, with failure to establish and maintain such procedures and training being an offence.

Guidance

The final part of Jersey's anti-money laundering regime consists of guidance issued by the Jersey Financial Services Commission: the Anti-Money Laundering Guidance Notes for the Finance Sector (the Guidance Notes). The Guidance Notes were introduced at the same time as PC(J)L 1999, and have since been supplemented by a number of Anti-Money Laundering Guidance Updates issued by the Commission.

The Guidance Notes provide a practical interpretation of all of Jersey's anti-money laundering legislation, set out what currently represents 'best practice' and are intended to assist financial services businesses in complying with their obligations. The Guidance Notes do not have the force of law, but may be taken into account where a court has to determine whether a financial services business has complied with the Money Laundering (Jersey) Order 1999. In addition, the Commission has made it clear that it is prepared to use its regulatory powers to address failures to follow the Guidance Notes. Accordingly, for practical purposes, one may consider the Guidance Notes to be mandatory.

Primary legislation

The basic money laundering offences

In overview, Jersey's primary legislation establishes five basic offences, which may be summarised as follows:

1   assisting another to retain the proceeds of crime;

2   acquisition, possession or use of the proceeds of crime;

3   tipping-off;

4   concealing or transferring the proceeds of crime to avoid prosecution or a confiscation order; and

5   failing to disclose knowledge or suspicion of money laundering.

The first three basic offences are, in essence, common to each of DTO(J)L 1988, T(J)L 2002 and PC(J)L 1999. The fourth offence, concealing or transferring the proceeds of crime to avoid prosecution or a confiscation order, is common to PC(J)L 1999 and DTO(J)L 1988. The fifth offence, failing to disclose knowledge or suspicion of money laundering, is common to DTO(J)L 1988 and T(J)L 2002. The terms and effect of each of the above offences are set out below, principally in relation to PC(J)L 1999, but also in relation to DTO(J)L 1988 and T(J)L 2002.

Assisting another to retain the proceeds of crime

—The offence

PC(J)L 1999, art 32 provides that:

'(1)   Subject to paragraph (3), if a person enters into or is otherwise concerned in an arrangement whereby—

   (a)   the retention or control by or on behalf of another (in this Article referred to as "A") of A's proceeds of criminal conduct is facilitated (whether by concealment, removal from the jurisdiction, transfer to nominees or otherwise); or

   (b)   A's proceeds of criminal conduct—

      (i)   are used to secure that funds are placed at A's disposal; or

      (ii)   are used for A's benefit to acquire property by way of investment,

knowing or suspecting that A is a person who is or has been engaged in criminal conduct or has benefited from criminal conduct, he is guilty of an offence.'

'Criminal conduct' for the purposes of PC(J)L 1999 is defined as:

(a) conduct which constitutes an offence in Jersey for which a person is liable on conviction to imprisonment for a term of one or more years (criminal conduct, as defined, does not include offences involving drug trafficking or terrorism, as such offences are dealt with under DTO(J)L 1988 and T(J)L 2002 respectively); or

(b) conduct which if it occurs or has occurred outside Jersey (whether or not the person is also liable to any other penalty) would have constituted an offence under (a) if occurring in Jersey.

Offences for which a person is liable on conviction to imprisonment for a term of one or more years include all Jersey customary law offences and the more serious statutory offences.

In relation to conduct which takes place outside Jersey, whether such conduct constitutes an offence under the laws of the jurisdiction in which it took place is not relevant – there is no requirement for 'dual criminality' – rather, it is simply necessary to show that such conduct, if it had been committed in Jersey, could have resulted in a term of imprisonment of one year or more.

The question of whether fiscal offences constitute 'criminal conduct' for the purposes of PC(J)L 1999 has received particular attention. There is no exception or 'special category' for tax-related offences, the question being whether a fiscal offence constitutes an offence in Jersey for which a person is liable on conviction to imprisonment for a term of one or more years. The penalty under the Income Tax (Jersey) Law 1961 for fraudulently or negligently making incorrect statements in connection with a tax return is a fine, rather than imprisonment (Income Tax (Jersey) Law 1961, art 137). Thus tax evasion per se does not constitute criminal conduct for the purposes of PC(J)L 1999. However, a tax-related offence may (and often will) involve other offences, such as forgery, false accounting or the customary law offence of fraud 9As to which, see *Foster v A-G 1992 JLR 6*), which *can* lead to imprisonment for a term of one or more years. Accordingly, the commission of tax-related offences can constitute criminal conduct for the purposes of PC(J)L 1999, and the proceeds of a tax-related offence may be the subject of money laundering offences under that law.

In PC(J)L 1999, art 32, references to any person's 'proceeds of criminal conduct' include any property that in whole or in part, directly or indirectly, represented in his hands the proceeds of criminal conduct, that is property obtained by such person as a result of or in connection with criminal conduct. It has rightly been suggested that identifying the proceeds of criminal conduct may present a particular challenge for the prosecution in the case of fiscal offences.

—Knowledge or suspicion?

PC(J)L 1999, art 32 requires a *mens rea* of knowledge or suspicion. Neither is defined in PC(J)L 1999 and, to date, the Jersey courts have not been required to comment on the precise meaning of such terms in this context. To date there have been no prosecutions under PC(J)L 1999 in respect of the basic money laundering offences. The first prosecution (*A-G v Culkin [2001] Jersey Unreported 2001/255*) under DTO(J)L 1998, art 17A (Which is almost identical to PC(J)L 1999, art 33: see below), which requires knowledge to be proved involved a guilty plea. Given the similarity of PC(J)L 1999 to the UK Criminal Justice Act 1988, the Jersey courts are likely to be influenced by any decisions of the English courts as to the interpretation to be given to such terms. It has been commented that 'except where there is oral or documentary evidence (such as notes on a bank file) to support the allegation of suspicion or where there is a covert contemporaneous police investigation, it may be easy for defendants to put forward a credible argument tat they were innocent facilitators.' (Levi 'Incriminating Disclosures. An Evaluation of Money Laundering in England and Wales' (1995) 2 European Journal of Crime 206).Such comments may equally apply in the context of PC(J)L 1999.

—Penalties

This offence is punishable by up to 14 years' imprisonment or a fine, or both.

—Defences

PC(J)L 1999, art 32 provides for certain defences. First, art 32(3) provides that:

'(3)   Where a person discloses to a police officer a suspicion or belief that any property is derived from or used in connection with criminal conduct, or discloses to a police officer any matter on which such a suspicion or belief is based—

(a)   the disclosure shall not be treated as a breach of any restriction upon disclosure imposed by any statute or contract or otherwise, and shall not involve the person making it in liability of any kind; and

(b)   if he does any act in contravention of paragraph (1) and the disclosure relates to the arrangement concerned, he does not commit an offence under this Article if—

(i)   the disclosure is made before he does the act concerned and the act is done with the consent of a police officer; or

(ii)   the disclosure is made after he does the act, but is made on his initiative and as soon as it is reasonable for him to make it.'

Secondly, PC(J)L 1999, art 32(4) provides that:

'(4)   In proceedings against a person for an offence under this Article, it is a defence to prove—

(a)   that he did not know or suspect that the arrangement related to any person's proceeds of criminal conduct; or

(b)   that he did not know or suspect that by the arrangement the

> retention or control by or on behalf of A of any property was facilitated or (as the case may be) that by the arrangement any property was used as mentioned in paragraph (1); or

> (c)   that—

> > (i)   he intended to disclose to a police officer such a suspicion, belief or matter as is mentioned in paragraph (3) in relation to the arrangement; and

> > (ii)   there is reasonable excuse for his failure to make the disclosure in accordance with sub-paragraph (b) of paragraph (3).'

In practice, all such disclosures are made to the States of Jersey Police and Customs Joint Financial Crimes Unit, a joint police and customs unit with responsibility for combating financial crime within Jersey. In the case of employees, these defences have effect in relation to disclosures, and intended disclosures, to the 'appropriate person' within the organisation (for example, the Money Laundering Reporting Officer (MLRO)) in accordance with the procedures established by the employer for the making of such disclosures.

Thus disclosure to the police (or by an employee to the MLRO) and acting with the consent of, in practice, the Joint Financial Crimes Unit, and, in certain circumstances, the fact that one intended to make such disclosure, may provide a defence to a charge under PC(J)L 1999, art 32(1). In the case of art 32(4), the burden is on the accused to show on the balance of probabilities that there was a reasonable excuse for failing to make the disclosure.

A final point to note relates to the provision of PC(J)L 1999, art 32(3)(a), ensuring that any disclosure made will not be treated as a breach of any duty of confidentiality, and will not involve the person making it in liability of any kind. These provisions should not be regarded as providing a general immunity from criminal or civil actions in relation to any conduct of the person making the disclosure following the making of it, but rather should properly be regarded as providing specific protection from liability arising directly from the making of such disclosure. Further, it is suggested that, in order to benefit from this protection from liability, the making of the report must be reasonably justifiable.

Acquisition, possession or use of the proceeds of crime

—The offence

PC(J)L 1999, art 33 provides that:

> '(1)   A person is guilty of an offence if, knowing that any property is or in whole or in part directly or indirectly represents another person's proceeds of criminal conduct, he acquires or uses that property or has possession of it.'

—Knowledge or suspicion?

This offence requires knowledge, rather than knowledge or suspicion.

—Penalties

This offence is punishable by up to 14 years' imprisonment or a fine, or both.

—Defences

Both the defences available under PC(J)L 1999, art 32(3) and (4) are, with minor amendments, repeated for the purposes of PC(J)L 1999, art 33. Thus, as with art 32, disclosure to the police and, in certain circumstances, the fact that one intended to make such disclosure, may provide a defence to a charge under art 33(1). Again, protection for those making disclosures is provided in identical terms to PC(J)L 1999, arts 32(3)(a).

In addition, it is also a defence to a charge of committing an offence under PC(J)L 1999, art 33(1) for the person charged to have acquired or used the property or had possession of it for adequate consideration. Inadequate consideration is defined for the purposes of art 33 as where the value of any payment made is 'significantly less' than the value of the property acquired, used or possessed.

Finally, PC(J)L 1999, art 33(10) provides that no person shall be guilty of an offence under art 33 in respect of anything done by them in the course of acting in connection with the enforcement, or intended enforcement, of any provision of PC(J)L 1999 or of any enactment relating to criminal conduct or the proceeds of such conduct. Thus law enforcement officers are given protection.

Tipping-off

—The offence

PC(J)L 1999, art 35 provides that, broadly, a person will commit an offence if they disclose to any other person information or any other matter which is likely to prejudice any investigation into money laundering when they know or suspect that:

1   a disclosure has been made to the police;

2   an investigation into money laundering is being or is proposed to be conducted; or

3   a disclosure has been made to the money laundering reporting officer at their place of employment.

The exact provisions of PC(J)L 1999, art 35 are as follows:

   '(1)   A person is guilty of an offence if—

> (a)   he knows or suspects that the Attorney General or any police officer is acting or is proposing to act in connection with an investigation that is being or is about to be conducted into money laundering (other than drug money laundering, as defined in paragraph (7) of Article 18A of the Drug Trafficking Offences (Jersey) Law 1988); and
>
> (b)   he discloses to any other person information or any other matter that is likely to prejudice that investigation or proposed investigation.
>
> (2)   A person is guilty of an offence if—
>
> (a)   he knows or suspects that a disclosure ("the disclosure") has been made to a police officer under Article 32 or 33; and
>
> (b)   he discloses to any other person information or any other matter that is likely to prejudice any investigation that might be conducted following the disclosure.
>
> (3)   A person is guilty of an offence if—
>
> (a)   he knows or suspects that a disclosure of a kind mentioned in paragraph (5) of Article 32 or paragraph (8) of Article 33 ("the disclosure") has been made; and
>
> (b)   he discloses to any person information or any other matter that is likely to prejudice any investigation that might be conducted following the disclosure.'

PC(J)L 1999, art 35 can pose particular problems for financial services businesses. This is especially so in the context of civil proceedings, where a freezing order or an order for disclosure has been made, in which case financial services businesses can face particular difficulties caused by the tension between their duties to a client under private law, their obligations arising from the civil proceedings and their obligations under art 35.

—'Money laundering'

This offence refers to 'money laundering'. This is defined as conduct that is an offence under PC(J)L 1999, arts 32, 33 or 34 (or the equivalent offences under the provisions of DTO(J)L 1988 and T(J)L 2002) or conduct outside Jersey which would be such an offence if carried on in Jersey.

—Penalties

This offence is punishable by up to five years' imprisonment or a fine, or both.

—Defences

PC(J)L 1999, art 35(4) provides for a legal professional privilege exception to the tipping off offence as follows:

'(4)   Nothing in paragraph (1), paragraph (2) or paragraph (3) makes it an offence for a professional legal adviser to disclose any information or other matter—

(a)   to or to a representative of a client of his in connection with the giving by the adviser of legal advice to the client; or

(b)   to any person—

(i)   in contemplation of or in connection with legal proceedings; and

(ii)   for the purpose of those proceedings.

(5)   Paragraph (4) does not apply in relation to any information or other matter that is disclosed with a view to furthering a criminal purpose.'

This defence is only available to professional legal advisers and, as set out in PC(J)L 1999, art 35(4) above, is not available where disclosure is with a view to furthering a criminal purpose.

In addition, PC(J)L 1999, art 35(6) provides that it is a defence for a person to prove that they did not know or suspect that the disclosure was likely to prejudice a money laundering investigation.

Finally, PC(J)L 1999, art 35(8) mirrors the protection given to law enforcement officers by PC(J)L 1999, art 33(10) in providing that no person shall be guilty of an offence under art 35 in respect of anything done by them in the course of acting in connection with the enforcement, or intended enforcement, of any provision of PC(J)L 1999 or of any other enactment relating to offences constituting criminal conduct.

Concealing or transferring proceeds to avoid prosecution or a confiscation order

—The offences

PC(J)L 1999, art 34 provides for two separate, but related, offences, as follows:

'(1)   A person is guilty of an offence if he—

(a)   conceals or disguises any property that is or in whole or in part represents his proceeds of criminal conduct; or

(b)   converts or transfers that property or removes it from the jurisdiction, for the purpose of avoiding prosecution for an offence specified in the First Schedule or the making or enforcement in his case of a confiscation order.

(2)   A person is guilty of an offence if, knowing or having reasonable grounds to suspect that any property is or in whole or in part directly or indirectly represents another's proceeds of criminal conduct, he—

(a)   conceals or disguises that property; or

(b)   converts or transfers that property or removes it from the jurisdiction,

for the purpose of assisting any person to avoid prosecution for an offence specified in the First Schedule or the making or enforcement in his case of a confiscation order.

(3)   In paragraphs (1) and (2), the references to concealing or disguising any property include references to concealing or disguising its nature, source, location, disposition, movement or ownership or any rights with respect to it.'

Clearly, PC(J)L 1999, art 34(1) is aimed at the principal launderer of his or her own proceeds of criminal conduct, whereas art 34(2) is aimed at any person assisting them in that laundering process.

—Knowledge or suspicion?

The offence under PC(J)L 1999, art 34(2) requires for conviction that the person knows or has 'reasonable grounds' to suspect that the property represents another's proceeds of criminal conduct. This appears to set a more objective standard of suspicion than that within PC(J)L 1999, art 32.

In addition, it is worth noting that for a conviction, it must be proved that the accused was acting for one of the two specified purposes, being avoiding prosecution for an offence for which a person is liable on conviction to imprisonment for a term of one or more years (other than a drug trafficking or terrorism offence, which are dealt with under DTO(J)L 1988 and T(J)L 2002 respectively) or the making or enforcement of a confiscation order.

—Penalties

This offence is punishable by up to 14 years' imprisonment or a fine, or both.

—Defences

There are no statutory defences to a charge under PC(J)L 1999, art 34.

Failure to disclose knowledge or suspicion of money laundering

—The offence

The last of Jersey's basic money laundering offences is that of failing to disclose knowledge or suspicion of, respectively, drug money laundering (under DTO(J)L 1988) and providing financial assistance for terrorism (under T(J)L 2002).

DTO(J)L 1988, art 18A provides that:

'(1) A person shall be guilty of an offence if—

    (a) he knows, or suspects, that another person is engaged in drug money laundering;

    (b) the information, or other matter, on which that knowledge or suspicion is based came to his attention in the course of his trade, profession, business or employment; and

    (c) he does not disclose the information or other matter to a police officer as soon as is reasonably practicable after it comes to his attention.'

Whereas disclosure under PC(J)L 1999 gives rise to a defence from prosecution, DTO(J)L 1988, art 18A creates a mandatory requirement to disclose to the police any suspicion of drug money laundering arising within a commercial setting.

The offence is only committed if the information or other matter comes to the attention of the accused in the course of their trade, profession, business or employment and, beyond this, DTO(J)L 1988, art 18A does not impose obligations upon the public at large. Disclosure to a police officer means, in practice, disclosure to the Joint Financial Crimes Unit. In addition, employees may satisfy their reporting obligation by disclosure to the appropriate person (the MLRO) in accordance with the procedures established by their employer for the making of such disclosures, instead of to the Joint Financial Crimes Unit.

As elsewhere, provisions of DTO(J)L 1988, art 18A provide that any disclosure shall not be treated as a breach of any restriction imposed by statute, contract or otherwise, but the additional provision that such disclosure will not involve the person making it in liability of any kind (PC(J)L 1999, art 32(3) and elsewhere) is missing.

—Penalties

This offence is punishable by up to five years' imprisonment or a fine, or both.

—Defences

DTO(J)L 1988, art 18A(3) provides a defence of reasonable non-disclosure, as follows:

'(3) It is a defence to a charge of committing an offence under this Article that the person charged had a reasonable excuse for not disclosing the information or other matter in question.'

As with PC(J)L 1999, art 35, special provision is made under DTO(J)L 1988, art 18A in respect of legal professional privilege, as follows:

'(2) Paragraph (1) does not make it an offence for a professional legal adviser to fail to disclose any information or other matter which has come to him in privileged circumstances.

...

(9)   For the purposes of this Article, any information or other matter comes to a professional legal adviser in privileged circumstances if it is communicated, or given, to him—

(a)   by, or by a representative of, a client of his in connexion with the giving by the adviser of legal advice to the client;

(b)   by, or by a representative of, a person seeking legal advice from the adviser; or

(c)   by any person—

(i)   in contemplation of, or in connexion with, legal proceedings; and

(ii)   for the purpose of those proceedings.

(10) No information or other matter shall be treated as coming to a professional legal adviser in privileged circumstances if it is communicated or given with a view to furthering any criminal purpose.'

This exception, and the caveat thereto, are similar terms to that under PC(J)L 1999, art 35.

Secondary legislation

The Money Laundering (Jersey) Order 1999

PC(J)L 1999, art 37 provides that the Finance and Economics Committee of the States of Jersey should, by Order, prescribe procedures designed to forestall and prevent money laundering. Consequently, at the same time as the introduction of PC(J)L 1999, the Money Laundering (Jersey) Order 1999 was introduced, which is the Jersey equivalent of the UK Money Laundering Regulations 1993 (SI 1993/1933).

The definition of 'money laundering' in PC(J)L 19991 applies to the Money Laundering (Jersey) Order 1999 and, as a consequence, the Order is relevant to all types of money laundering (whether the proceeds of terrorism, drug trafficking or serious crime generally), notwithstanding that it is made pursuant to PC(J)L 1999 and there is no provision within either DTO(J)L 1988 or T(J)L 2002 for such an Order.

Application

Although relevant to all types of money laundering, the Money Laundering (Jersey) Order 1999, unlike the primary legislation, which is of general application, only applies to financial services businesses.

—'Financial services businesses'

The definition of 'financial services businesses' to which the Money Laundering (Jersey) Order 1999 applies is set out in the PC(J)L 1999, Second Schedule, as follows:

'Financial services business

1. Any deposit-taking business, as defined in Article 1(1) of the Banking Business (Jersey) Law 1991.

2. Any insurance business to which Article 4 of the Insurance Business (Jersey) Law 1996 applies.

3. The business of being a functionary of a collective investment fund, as defined in Article 1(1) of the Collective Investment Funds (Jersey) Law 1988.

4. Any investment business, as defined in Article 1(1) of the Investment Business (Jersey) Law 1998.

5. The business of providing trusteeship services (not being services as a trustee of an occupational pension scheme).

6. The business of company formation.

7. The business of company administration.

8. The business of a bureau de change.

9. The business of providing cheque cashing services.

10. The business of transmitting or receiving funds by wire or other electronic means.

11. The business of engaging in any of the following activities within the meaning of the Annex to the Second Banking Co-ordination Directive (No. 89/646/EEC) (not being a business specified in any of paragraphs 1 to 10 (inclusive))—

    (a) the acceptance of deposits and other repayable funds from the public;

    (b) lending;

    (c) financial leasing;

    (d) money transmission services;

    (e) the issuing and administering means of payment (such as credit cards, travellers' cheques and bankers' drafts);

    (f) guarantees and commitments;

    (g) trading for one's own account or for the account of customers in –

         (i) money market instruments (such as cheques, bills and CDs);

(ii)   foreign exchange;

(iii)   financial futures and options;

(iv)   exchange and interest rate instruments; or

(v)   transferable securities;

(h)   participation in securities issues and the provision of services related to such issues;

(i)   advice to undertakings on capital structure, industrial strategy and related questions and advice and services relating to mergers and the purchase of undertakings;

(j)   money broking;

(k)   portfolio management and advice;

(l)   the safekeeping and administration of securities;

(m)   credit reference services; and

(n)   safe custody services.'

It is worth noting that this definition extends beyond those businesses which are subject to regulation by the Jersey Financial Services Commission, such as, for example, bureaux de change. In addition, where businesses conduct both 'financial services business' and other business, the requirements of the Money Laundering (Jersey) Order 1999 will have to be followed in respect of the financial services business aspects of their business only. Accordingly, lawyers and accountants, for example, are subject to the Order only to the extent that their business activities constitute 'financial services business': for example, where providing safe custody services.

Duty to comply with procedures

The Money Laundering (Jersey) Order 1999, art 2 prohibits the formation of a business relationship, or the carrying out of a transaction, in the course of any financial services business carried on in Jersey, unless the prescribed money laundering prevention procedures are maintained and appropriate training is provided to employees as required by the Order.

The precise terms of Money Laundering (Jersey) Order 1999, art 2 are as follows:

'(1)   No person shall, in the course of any financial services business carried on by him in the Island, form a business relationship, or carry out a one-off transaction, with or for another person unless—

(a)   the person carrying on the financial services business maintains the following procedures in relation to his business—

      (i)   identification procedures in accordance with Articles 3 and 5;

      (ii)   record-keeping procedures in accordance with Article 8;

      (iii) internal reporting procedures in accordance with Article 9; and

      (iv) such other procedures of internal control and communication as may be appropriate for the purposes of forestalling and preventing money laundering;

  (b)   he takes appropriate measures from time to time for the purposes of making employees whose duties relate to the provision of financial services aware of—

      (i)   the procedures under sub-paragraph (a) that are maintained by him and relate to the business; and

      (ii)   the enactments relating to money laundering; and

  (c)   he provides those employees from time to time with training in the recognition and handling of transactions carried out by or on behalf of any person who is or appears to be engaged in money laundering.'

PC(J)L 1999, art 37 provides that any breach of any requirement of the Money Laundering (Jersey) Order 1999 by a person to which it applies shall be an offence, punishable by up to two years' imprisonment or an unlimited fine, or both, irrespective of whether money laundering has taken place. However, this strict position is mitigated somewhat by the provisions of art 37(10), which provides that it is a defence for a person to prove that they took all reasonable steps and exercised due diligence to avoid committing the offence of breaching a requirement of the Order.

Where an offence is committed by a body corporate, and is proved to have been committed with the consent or connivance of, or to be attributable to the neglect on the part of, a director, manager, secretary or other similar officer of the body corporate or any person who was purporting to act in any such capacity, that person, as well as the body corporate, shall be guilty of the offence and liable to be punished accordingly.

In deciding whether a person has complied with the requirement to maintain these procedures, the court may take into account any relevant guidelines issued or endorsed by the Jersey Financial Services Commission: in practice, the Anti-Money Laundering Guidance Notes for the Finance Sector issued by the Commission.

The procedures set out in the Money Laundering (Jersey) Order 1999

The provisions of the Money Laundering (Jersey) Order 1999 in relation to the procedures required to be put in place by the Money Laundering (Jersey)

Order 1999, art 2 are each considered in turn below. As noted above, the current provisions will be subject to review as and when the provisions of the position paper are implemented (as to which, see below).

The Money Laundering (Jersey) Order 1999, to some degree, sets out requirements expressed in broad terms, requiring that procedures are 'reasonable' or will produce 'satisfactory' results. The Guidance Notes then provide detailed guidance which may be taken into account when considering what measures are 'reasonable' or 'satisfactory' in a variety of circumstances. This detailed guidance is considered separately below.

The first, and perhaps the foundation, of the anti-money laundering deterrence procedures are the identification procedures.

—Identification procedures

The core requirement: Financial services businesses are required, in accordance with the Money Laundering (Jersey) Order 1999, art 3(1), to establish and maintain procedures which, in the relevant circumstances (ie any of Cases 1–4 below), require:

> '... as soon as is reasonably practicable after contact is first made between the financial services business and an applicant for business concerning any particular business relationship or one-off transaction—
>
> (a)   the production by the applicant for business of satisfactory evidence of his identity; or
>
> (b)   the taking of such measures, specified in the procedures, as will produce satisfactory evidence of his identity.'

An 'applicant for business' is defined for the purposes of the Money Laundering (Jersey) Order 1999 as any person seeking to form a business relationship, or to carry out a one-off transaction, with a person who is carrying on financial services business in Jersey.

In turn, a 'business relationship' is defined to mean any arrangement between two or more persons, the purpose of which is to facilitate the carrying on of transactions between the persons concerned on a frequent, habitual or regular basis and where the total amount of any payment to be made in the course of that arrangement is not known or capable of being ascertained at the time the arrangement is made. In contrast, a 'one-off transaction' is defined as any transaction that is not carried out in the course of an established business relationship formed by a person acting in the course of any financial services business.

Circumstances in which verification is required: The four main circumstances in which such verification of identity must be undertaken are as follows:

• *Case 1*: where the parties form or resolve to form a business relationship between them.

- *Case 2*: in respect of any one-off transaction, where the person dealing with the matter knows or suspects that the applicant is engaged in money laundering or that the transaction is carried out on behalf of another person engaged in money laundering.

- *Case 3*: where, in respect of any one-off transaction, payment is to be made by or to the applicant for business of £10,000 or more.

Thus the identity of occasional customers who have not formed a 'business relationship' with the financial services business must still be verified in respect of higher value transactions.

- *Case 4*: where two or more one-off transactions appear to be linked and involve an aggregate of £10,000 or more.

The inclusion of Case 4 clearly intended to assist in the prevention of 'smurfing', whereby a series of smaller transactions, each individually below the usual threshold, are undertaken for the purposes of laundering money without alerting the financial services business. In any event, where transactions take place on a frequent, habitual or regular basis, a financial services business ought to verify identity on the basis of a business relationship having been established.

Satisfactory evidence of identity: As will be appreciated, the Money Laundering (Jersey) Order 1999, art 3 requires that 'satisfactory' evidence of identity be obtained. The Order provides very limited guidance as to the meaning of this, art 7(1) providing that:

'7.-(1) Evidence of identity is satisfactory if—

(a)   it is reasonably capable of establishing that the applicant is the person he claims to be; and

(b)   the person who obtains the evidence is satisfied, in accordance with the procedures maintained under this Order in relation to the financial services business concerned, that it does establish that fact.'

Detailed guidance as to what evidence of identity should be obtained or independently verified in a variety of circumstances is provided in the Guidance Notes, as to which see below.

The Money Laundering (Jersey) Order 1999, art 7(2) then goes on to give similarly limited guidance as to the time in which satisfactory evidence should be obtained, as follows:

'(2)   In determining, for the purposes of paragraph (1) of Article 3, the time in which satisfactory evidence of a person's identity has to be obtained in relation to any particular business relationship or one-off transaction, all the circumstances shall be taken into account, including in particular—

(a)   the nature of the business relationship or one-off transaction concerned;

(b)   the geographical locations of the parties;

(c)   whether it is practical to obtain the evidence before commitments are entered into between the parties or before money passes; and

(d)   in relation to Case 3 or Case 4, the earliest stage at which there are reasonable grounds for believing that the total amount payable by an applicant for business is not less than £10,000.'

The Money Laundering (Jersey) Order 1999, art 7(2) clearly anticipates that commitments may be entered into between the parties, or money may pass, prior to obtaining satisfactory evidence of identity. At the same time, art 3(1) states that identification procedures must require that where evidence is not obtained the business relationship or one-off transaction in question shall not proceed any further (other than in accordance with the directions of a police officer).

The Guidance Notes provide useful further guidance on the issue of timing of verification and progression of transactions.

Payments by post or electronic means: Special provision is made in the Money Laundering (Jersey) Order 1999 as to the identity verification requirements in the case of payments made by post etc. Where verification of identity is required in accordance with the Money Laundering (Jersey) Order 1999, art 3, where a payment is to be made by the applicant for business and it is reasonable in all the circumstances for the payment or details of it to be sent by post or electronically (or, in the case of details of the payment, by telephone), the fact that the payment is debited from an account in the applicant's name at certain specified institutions can constitute the required evidence of identity.

The institutions specified for the purposes of the Money Laundering (Jersey) Order 1999, art 4 are:

'(a)   an institution that is for the time being registered under the Banking Business (Jersey) Law 1991;

(b)   any other institution that is an authorised credit institution; and

(c)   an institution that—

(i)   holds the account …in the course of a business in relation to which an overseas regulatory authority exercises its regulatory functions as such an authority; and

(ii)   is based or incorporated in or formed under the law of a country or territory (other than a member State) in which there are in force provisions at least equivalent to those required by the [EC Money Laundering Directive1].' Council Directive 91/308/EEC.

'Authorised credit institution' for these purposes means an undertaking whose business is to receive deposits or other repayable funds from the public and to grant credits for its own account which is authorised to carry on such business by a competent authority of an EU member state or of any of the British Islands.

Thus receipt of funds from an account, for example, at a UK bank may be relied upon as satisfactory evidence of identity without the need for further verification.

These special provisions do not apply where there is knowledge or suspicion of money laundering (ie, in Case 2 above), and also do not apply where the payment is made for the purposes of opening a relevant account (a 'relevant account' being defined as an account from which a payment may be made (either directly or indirectly) to a person other than the applicant for business).

Transactions on behalf of others: The Money Laundering (Jersey) Order 1999, art 5 provides that where an applicant for business is or appears to be acting otherwise than as principal, financial services businesses must establish and maintain identification procedures which require 'reasonable measures' to be taken for the purpose of establishing the identity of any person on whose behalf the applicant for business is acting. (Money Laundering (Jersey) Order 1999, art 5(2)).

Again, the Money Laundering (Jersey) Order 1999 does not provide detailed guidance on what measures might be 'reasonable', but leaves detailed guidance to the Guidance Notes, art 5(3) stating simply:

'(3)   In determining for the purposes of paragraph (2) what measures are reasonable in any particular case, regard shall be had to all the circumstances of the case and, in particular, to best practice that is followed for the time being in the relevant field of business and is applicable to those circumstances.'

Written assurances from other financial services businesses: Special provision is made in the Money Laundering (Jersey) Order 1999 in respect of circumstances where the applicant for business, acting as agent, acts in the course of a business in relation to which he or she is subject to regulation in another jurisdiction and is based or incorporated in or formed under the law of a territory in which there are in force provisions at least equivalent to the EC Money Laundering Directive (Council Directive 91/308/EEC). In such cases, the Money Laundering (Jersey) Order 1999, art 5(4) provides that it is reasonable for the purposes of verifying identity for the financial services business to accept a written assurance from the agent that evidence of the identity of any principal on whose behalf the agent is acting will have been obtained and recorded under procedures maintained by the agent.

Exemptions: There are several exemptions set out in the Money Laundering (Jersey) Order 1999 where no steps need to be taken to obtain evidence of identity either under the Money Laundering (Jersey) Order 1999, art 3 or 5. It is worth noting that none of the exemptions apply to Case 2; that is where there is knowledge or suspicion of money laundering. The exemptions are as follows:

1   where there are reasonable grounds for believing that the applicant for business is a person who themselves must maintain identification procedures pursuant to the Money Laundering (Jersey) Order 1999;

2   where there are reasonable grounds for believing that the applicant for business is a person who is covered by the EC Money Laundering Directive;

3   where a one-off transaction is carried out following an introduction effected by a person who falls under 1 or 2 above or there are reasonable grounds for believing such person acts in the course of a business in relation to which they are subject to regulation in another jurisdiction which is at least equivalent to the EC Money Laundering Directive (Council Directive 91/308/EEC) and such person provides a written assurance that evidence of all third parties introduced by them will have been obtained and recorded and such person actually identifies the third party;

4   where the person who would otherwise be required to be identified, in relation to a one-off transaction, is the person to whom the proceeds of that transaction are payable but to whom no payment is made because all of those proceeds are directly reinvested on their behalf in another transaction, of which a record is kept and which can result only in another reinvestment made on that person's behalf or in a payment made directly to that person;

5   in relation to insurance business consisting of a policy of insurance taken out in connection with an occupational pension scheme where the policy contains no surrender clause and may not be used as collateral for a loan;

6   in relation to single premium insurance business where the premium does not exceed £1,750; or

7   in relation to insurance business in respect of which a periodic premium is payable and the total amount payable in any calendar year does not exceed £750.

Existing customers: The Money Laundering (Jersey) Order 1999 provides that the requirement to verify identity does not apply retrospectively to any business relationship formed before the Order came into force. Thus, for the time being, financial services businesses are not required to verify the identity of customers who were existing customers prior to 1 July 1999.

—Record keeping procedures

The Money Laundering (Jersey) Order 1999, art 8 sets out the record keeping requirements. Records must be kept by each financial services business of both identity and transactions.

In relation to identity, where evidence of client identity is required by the Money Laundering (Jersey) Order 1999, records must be kept indicating the nature of the evidence obtained and comprising a copy of such evidence, such information as would enable a copy of such evidence to be obtained, or which (where it is not reasonably practicable to comply with the foregoing) provides sufficient information to enable the details as to a person's identity contained in the relevant evidence to be re-obtained.

In relation to transactions, records must be kept containing details relating to all transactions carried out by the client or counterparty in the course of the financial services business.

Broadly speaking, the Money Laundering (Jersey) Order 1999 stipulates that all such evidence must be kept for at least five years from the date of the financial services business's last dealings with an applicant for business or in relation to a transaction.

—Internal reporting procedures

The Money Laundering (Jersey) Order 1999, art 8 sets out the requirements for the internal reporting procedures which must be maintained. The procedures must:

1   identify a person as the appropriate person (generally referred to as the money laundering reporting officer (MLRO)) to whom a report is to be made of any information or other matter that comes to the attention of any person handling financial services in the business and, in the opinion of the person handling that business, gives rise to a knowledge or suspicion that another person is engaged in money laundering;

2   require that any such report is considered by the appropriate person (or other designated person) in the light of all other relevant information for the purposes of determining whether or not the information or other matter contained in the report does give rise to such a knowledge or suspicion;

3   allow the person charged with considering the report to have reasonable access to other information that may be of assistance to them and which is available to the person responsible for maintaining the internal reporting procedures concerned; and

4   ensure that the information or other matter contained in the report is disclosed to a police officer (in practice, the Joint Financial Crimes Unit) where the person who has considered the report knows or suspects that another person is engaged in money laundering.

Thus although, as will be appreciated, PC(J)L 1999 (unlike DTO(J)L 1988 and T(J)L 2002), does not create an offence of failing to report knowledge or suspicion of money laundering, financial services businesses will be obliged to maintain procedures which require such knowledge or suspicion to be reported internally and, in turn, to the authorities, and failure to maintain such procedures will constitute an offence.

In addition, it is clear that proceeding to do business for an individual whom an employee suspects has been engaged in criminal conduct may well constitute one of the new money laundering offences and the failure to make a disclosure when suspicious removes the defence which may otherwise have been available.

Thus, notwithstanding there being no offence of failure to report under PC(J)L 1999, failure to disclose risks criminal liability both for the employee and the employer.

—Training procedures

As noted above, pursuant to the Money Laundering (Jersey) Order 1999, art 2(1)(b), financial services businesses will be required to take appropriate measures from time to time for the purposes of making all employees whose duties relate to the provision of financial services aware of the money laundering prevention procedures maintained by their business in compliance with the Money Laundering (Jersey) Order 1999 and any enactments relating to money laundering. Training in the recognition and handling of suspicious transactions must also be provided. No specific guidance is provided in the Order as to what such appropriate measures might be, or as to the extent of such training, which guidance is left to the Guidance Notes and is discussed below.

—'Other' procedures

Financial services businesses will be required to take 'such other procedures of internal control and communication as may be appropriate for the purposes of forestalling and preventing money laundering'. No specific guidance is given in the Money Laundering (Jersey) Order 1999 as to what procedures may be appropriate but, certainly, such other procedures as are recommended in the Guidance Notes ought to be followed.

One area on which guidance is given in the Guidance Notes, but which does not fall under any of the more specific procedures required to be put in place by the Money Laundering (Jersey) Order 1999, is in relation to the requirement to 'Know Your Customer'. In addition to dealing with identification procedures, the Guidance Notes emphasise that 'the need within financial sector businesses for the "know your customer" process is vital for the prevention of money laundering and underpins all other activities'. The Commission has made it quite clear that there is a regulatory expectation that all regulated persons will undertake broader due diligence on customers, including, for example, the nature of the customer's business and the activity that the customer expects to conduct.

Guidance from the Jersey Financial Services Commission

General

The Guidance Notes issued by the Jersey Financial Services Commission are based on similar Guidance Notes issued by the Joint Money Laundering Steering Group in the UK.

The Guidance Notes outline the requirements of Jersey's money laundering legislation, provide a practical interpretation of the Money Laundering (Jersey) Order 1999 and give examples of current 'best practice'.

The Guidance Notes apply to all persons carrying on financial services business in Jersey, as such business is defined in PC(J)L 1999, Sch 2 (as to which, see above).

As noted above, although the Guidance Notes do not have the force of law, they may be taken into account where a court has to determine whether a financial services business has complied with the Money Laundering (Jersey) Order 1999, and the Commission has made it clear that it is prepared to use its regulatory powers to address failures to follow the Guidance Notes and, as such, following the Guidance Notes is effectively mandatory.

Since the Guidance Notes came into effect on 1 July 1999, the Commission has published a number of Anti-Money Laundering Guidance Updates which have supplemented and varied the Guidance Notes in specific aspects.

As is the case with the Money Laundering (Jersey) Order 1999, implementation of the position paper will necessitate further revision to the Guidance Notes in due course.

The Guidance Notes begin with sections giving a general background to money laundering and a summary of the requirements of Jersey's legislation. Subsequent sections provide detailed guidance on each of the procedures required to be maintained by the Money Laundering (Jersey) Order 1999.

Identification procedures

The Guidance Notes provide detailed guidance on the identification procedures which are to be maintained by those conducting financial services business.

The guidance is lengthy, and slightly different requirements are set out for different types of business: for example, different sections deal with banking, insurance and trust and company administration. The general principles relating to each business type are the same, however, addressing, among other things, the following issues.

—What is identity?

The Guidance Notes first clarify what is meant by a person's identity, namely their name and all other names used, their current permanent address at which they can be located and their date of birth.

—Evidence of identity

The Guidance Notes then go on to set out what might reasonably be expected in terms of satisfactory evidence of identity, although emphasising that it is for each business to satisfy itself that it has satisfactorily established the identity of its customer.

In respect of individual applicants for business, the Guidance Notes suggest that, wherever practicable, sight of a certified true copy of a current valid passport or national identity card should be obtained. The Guidance Notes also suggest the steps which might be taken in order to verify a customer's current permanent address, such as obtaining sight of a recent utility bill or bank statement, making a credit reference agency search or checking a local telephone directory.

In respect of corporate applicants for business, the Guidance Notes suggest that the following should normally be obtained:

1   the original or certified copy of the Certificate of Incorporation and Memorandum and Articles of Association of the company, or equivalent documents;

2   evidence of the authority of those representing the company, such as a board resolution;

3   for established businesses, a copy of the latest report and accounts; and

4   a search at the Companies Registry or an inquiry via a business information service.

In addition, in the case of private companies, evidence of the identity of at least two of the directors, secretary or shareholders should usually be obtained in the same manner as for individual applicants for business.

The Guidance Notes go on to provide guidance on a variety of other types of applicants for business, including trustees, partnerships and unincorporated associations.

Although clear recommendations are made as to what documentation should be obtained, the Guidance Notes also acknowledge that there is a wide range of other documents that may constitute evidence of identity, or steps that may be taken in order to verify a client's identity.

—Timing of verification

On the issue of the time period in which evidence of identity should be obtained, and what stage a transaction may reach without evidence having been obtained, the Guidance Notes suggest that financial services businesses may start processing the business immediately, provided that appropriate steps are promptly taken to verify the identity of the applicant for business. The Guidance Notes state that every effort should be made to complete verification of identity before settlement takes place and, in any event, before documents of title have been dispatched, and that a financial services business should not transfer or pay monies out to a third party until the identity requirements have been satisfied.

In relation to retail investment products, the Guidance Notes suggest that a financial sector business should 'freeze' the rights attaching to any investment acquired by a client pending receipt of the required evidence of identity and that, in the absence of the required evidence, redemption proceeds should be retained and no documents of title issued or income paid out.

—Reliance on others

The Guidance Notes outline certain circumstances in which it is reasonable to rely on another person or institution to undertake the procedures or to confirm identity, for example:

1   where a customer is introduced by one part of a corporate group to another, an introduction certificate in respect of the customer may be provided by the introducing group member or, alternatively, a general group compliance undertaken may be relied upon;

2   where a customer is introduced by a regulated institution covered by the Money Laundering (Jersey) Order 1999, the EC Money Laundering Directive (Council Directive 91/308/EEC) or based in a country listed in the Guidance Notes as having equivalent anti-money laundering legislation, an introduction certificate in respect of the customer may be provided; and

3   banks may, in certain circumstances, rely in part on confirmations of identity provided by other banks.

The Guidance Notes also acknowledge that reliance may also be placed on written assurances in respect of principals on whose behalf an agent acts in accordance with the provisions of the Money Laundering (Jersey) Order 1999, art 5.

—'Know-your-customer'

The Guidance Notes emphasise that in addition to evidence of client identity, it is vital for the prevention of money laundering for those conducting financial services business to undertake wider 'know your customer' due diligence, and encourage those conducting financial services business not to simply obtain the 'bare minimum' requirements in terms of client identity, but to collect and record all other relevant information on the client.

In particular, the Guidance Notes suggest that when a business relationship is being established, the nature of the business that the client expects to conduct with the financial services business should be ascertained in order to show what might be expected as normal activity, and that a clear understanding of the business of the client is obtained.

215

Record keeping

The Guidance Notes emphasise the importance of financial services businesses retaining records concerning customer identification and transactions for use as evidence in any investigation into money laundering.

The Guidance Notes provide that records should be such that the requirements of legislation are fully met, that competent third parties will be able to assess observance of money laundering procedures, that any transaction can be reconstructed and that the financial services business can retrieve relevant information without undue delay.

The Guidance Notes give details of the sort of records which should be kept, particularly in relation to different types of transactions.

The Guidance Notes also note that production orders granted by the court will usually require that the information specified should be available within seven calendar days.

Specific guidance on wire transfers is given, which guidance has been revised in an Anti-Money Laundering Guidance Update in accordance with FATF Recommendation VII.

Recognition and reporting of suspicious transactions

The Guidance Notes include examples of what might constitute suspicious transactions and suggest questions that a financial institution might consider when determining whether an established customer's transaction might be suspicious.

The Guidance Notes explain the role of the MLRO and that the MLRO should complete a personal questionnaire registered with the Commission. The Guidance Notes state that the MLRO should be 'sufficiently senior to command the necessary authority' as the MLRO has 'a significant degree of responsibility'.

Guidance on internal reporting procedures is given: for example, that suspicious transaction reporting lines should be as short as possible, that all suspicions reported should be documented and retained and that those making reports should be reminded not to do anything which might prejudice inquiries.

Guidance is also provided on external reporting: that reports should be made to the Joint Financial Crimes Unit in the suggested standard format, as to the nature of information to be disclosed and on the question of termination of a business relationship following a disclosure.

The Commission has also noted that where suspicions are such as to suggest that regulatory issues arise, the Commission would expect to be notified by the financial institution concerned.

Education and training

The Guidance Notes emphasise that financial services business are required to raise employee awareness of money laundering and to ensure that employees are fully aware of their responsibilities, including prompt reporting of suspicious transactions, and understand the importance of know-your-customer requirements.

The Guidance Notes recommend different types of education and training for different types of personnel (management, compliance, front and back office, new employees) and also recommend refresher training.

Appendix 2.8

Singapore

Cheong-Ann Png – Herbert Smith, London

Khoon-Jin Tan – Herbert Smith, Singapore

Legislative framework

The Corruption, Drug Trafficking and Other Serious Crimes (Confiscation of Benefits) Act (Cap 65A) (CDSCA), came into force on 13 September 1999. CDSCA, *inter alia*, extends the predicate list of offences for money laundering to a wide range of serious crime, clarified the requirement to report suspicious transactions, increased the authorities' powers of confiscation and introduced various other provisions to enhance the power of the authorities to combat money laundering.

Money laundering offences under CDSCA in relation to criminal conduct

—Assisting another to retain the benefits of criminal conduct

A person may be prosecuted for money laundering where he enters into or is concerned in an arrangement, knowing or having reasonable grounds to believe that the arrangement:

1   facilitates the retention or control by or on behalf of another person of that person's benefits from criminal conduct (whether by concealment, removal from jurisdiction, transfer to nominees or otherwise); or

2   uses another person's benefits from criminal conduct to secure funds that are placed at that other person's disposal; or

3   uses another person's benefits from criminal conduct to acquire property in any way for that other person's benefit,

and knowing or having reasonable grounds to believe that that other person is a person who engages in or has engaged in criminal conduct or has benefited from criminal conduct (CDSCA, s 44(1)).

—Concealing or transferring benefits of criminal conduct

A person may also be guilty of a money laundering offence for concealing or transferring benefits from criminal conduct if he:

1   conceals or disguises any property which is or represents his benefits from criminal conduct, or converts or transfers that property or removes it from the jurisdiction (CDSCA, s 47(1)); or

2   knowing or having reasonable grounds to believe that any property is or represents another person's benefits from criminal conduct,

    (i)   conceals or disguises such property; or

    (ii) converts or transfers such property or removes it from the jursidiction,

    (iii) in order to assist any person to avoid prosecution for a local or foreign serious offence or for the making or enforcement of a confiscation order (CDSCA, s 47(2)), or

3   acquires property for inadequate consideration, knowing or having reasonable grounds to believe that such property is or represents another person's benefits from criminal conduct (CDSCA, s 47(3)).

—Definition of 'criminal conduct'

Under CDSCA, criminal conduct is broadly defined to include:

1   doing or being concerned with any act that constitutes a local or foreign serious offence, other than the money laundering offences described above; or

2   the entering into or being concerned in, an arrangement which:

    (i)   facilitates the retention or control by or on behalf of another person of that person's benefit from an act referred to in 1 above; or

    (iii) uses the benefits from an act referred to in 1 above to secure funds that are placed at that other persons' disposal or used for that other person's benefit to acquire property; or

3   the concealing or disguising by a person of any property that is or represents his benefits from an act referred to in 1 above; or

4   the conversion or transfer by a person of any property referred to in 3 above or the removal or such property from the jurisdicton (CDSCA, s 2(1)).

—Definition of 'serious offence'

Under CDSCA, a 'serious offence' is defined by reference to a list of 182 specified offences under the Penal Code and various other pieces of legislation, such as the Prevention of Corruption Act (Cap 241) (CDSCA, s 2(1). The key purpose of CDSCA is to ensure that an accused found guilty of an offence cannot be allowed to retain or enjoy any benefits arising from their breach of the law. However, it should be noted that not all offences are caught under CDSCA and that there are specific predicate offences). The principal money laundering offences found in CDSCA itself are also defined as 'serious offences'. As with drug trafficking, the definition is wide enough to include inchoate offences such as conspiracy to commit and aiding and abetting any of the above offences.

The mens rea for the offences of money laundering under CDSCA

Generally, the *mens rea* requirement of the principal money laundering offences is that the offender must 'know' or 'have reasonable grounds to believe' that a certain state of affairs exists.

—Definition of 'knowledge'

There is no definition of the two terms in either CDSCA or the Penal Code. It is therefore necessary to examine the manner in which the Singapore courts have approached this issue. In this regard, some guidance may be obtained from *Sim Yew Thong v Thomas Ng Loy Yam [2000] 2 CLAS News 165*, where Yong Pung How CJ said that: 'There is no definition of the term "knowledge" in the Penal Code. In my judgement, for the purposes of section 321 of the Penal Code, the term "knowledge" encompasses both recklessness (where an accused knows he is likely to cause a result) and negligence (when an accused has reason to believe that he is likely to cause a result).'

The principal decision on the definition of 'knowledge' may be found in *Public Prosecutor v Koo Pui Fong [1996] 2 SLR 266*, where the High Court of Singapore considered a particular provision relating to the presumption to be drawn against an accused under the Immigration Act (Cap 133). In that case, Yong Pung How CJ stated that:

'It would be reasonable to say that a person "knows" of a certain fact if he is aware that it exists or is almost certain that it exists or will exist or occur. Thus knowledge entails a high degree of certainty. All the respondent had to show was that it was more likely than not that she did not have guilty knowledge. Of course, we would never have the benefit of going into the mind of another person to ascertain his knowledge and in every case, knowledge is a fact that has to be inferred from the circumstances. This concept of wilful blindness does not introduce a new state of mind to that of knowing (see *R v Griffiths (1974) 60 Cr App R 14*). It is simply a reformulation of actual knowledge. It seems to me that it is wholly in keeping with common sense and the law to say that an accused knew of certain facts if he deliberately closed his eyes to the circumstances, his wilful blindness being evidence from which knowledge may be inferred.' ([1996] 2 SLR 266 at 272.)

In the *Koo* case (*Public Prosecutor v Koo Pui Fong [1996] 2 SLR 266*), the High Court held that an employer was presumed to have knowingly employed an illegal immigrant unless they could show on a balance of probabilities that they did not know that the employee was an illegal immigrant. Knowledge was a fact to be inferred from the circumstances. The concept of wilful blindness should not automatically be equated with knowledge as it did not introduce an alternative state of mind to that of knowing, although it formed part of the overall evidence from which knowledge could be inferred. A distinction was also made between this and the concept of constructive knowledge, which deals with a situation where a person fails to make such inquiries as a reasonable and prudent person would make. The High Court clarified that proving constructive knowledge was inadequate for the purpose of establishing knowledge under the Immigration Act.

The *Koo* case is instructive in providing guidance on the approach of the Singapore courts to the meaning of 'knowing'. A person is deemed to know when either they know the relevant facts or occurrences or they are almost certain of such facts or occurrences. It also includes the situation where the person deliberately ignores such facts or circumstances. It does not, however, extend to include constructive knowledge, where a person will not be deemed to have the relevant knowledge when they had failed to make such inquiries as a reasonable and prudent person would make.

—Definition of 'reasonable ground to believe'

In *Bridges Christopher v PP [1997] 1 SLR 406*, a case to determine, *inter alia*, whether the accused knew or had reasonable ground to believe that the information communicated to him was 'protected' information under the Official Secrets Act (Cap 213), Yong Pung How CJ held that 'a person has reasonable ground to believe a thing if he has sufficient cause to believe that thing, but not otherwise'. After an evaluation of the facts (from the perspective of both a reasonable person and the accused himself), Yong CJ held that an inference that the accused had reasonable ground to believe that the information was 'protected' information could not be drawn. On appeal, the Court of Appeal agreed with Yong CJ, reiterating this same test. The Court of Appeal also concluded that as the accused did not know as a matter of fact, that the information communicated to him was 'protected' information, his knowledge had to be inferred from the surrounding circumstances and the proven primary facts.

—Exception to the requirement of mens rea

The only exception to the *mens rea* requirement described above is when the offence is for the concealment or disguise of any property that is, or represents, the benefits of drug trafficking or from criminal conduct; or the conversion or transfer of any such property or its removal from the jurisdiction. No *mens rea* requirement is specifically provided in CDSCA. However, this does not necessarily mean that strict liability entails. In the *Bridges Christopher* case the Court of Appeal stated that 'it should be borne in mind that the well-established general rule is that *mens rea* is presumed to be a necessary ingredient of an offence in the absence of clear words to the contrary'. This principle was reiterated by Yong Pung How CJ in *PP v Ong Phee Hoon James [2000] 3 SLR 293*, a case involving the harbouring of illegal immigrants. Although there are no reported cases on this particular aspect of CDSCA, a certain standard of *mens rea* will most probably be ascribed to the offence (see WC Chan 'Criminal Law: *Mens rea*' (2000) Singapore Academy of Law J 122). However, it remains unclear as to what the appropriate requirement might be.

Burden of proof

CDSCA provides that any question of fact to be decided by a court in proceedings under CDSCA, save for those that the prosecution is required to prove, shall be decided on the balance of probabilities (CDSCA, s 51). Otherwise, as with other criminal offences in Singapore, the onus should be on the prosecution to prove beyond a reasonable doubt.

Application of CDSCA to body corporates and other forms of associations

Offences under CDSCA may be committed by a body corporate where it can be established that the relevant offence has been committed with the consent or connivance of, or is attributable to any neglect on the part of, any director, manager, secretary or other similar officer or any person purporting to act in such a capacity (CDSCA, s 59). This would mean that any compliance officer of a company charged with the responsibility of making any disclosure reports and who is, or is acting in, the capacity of a director, manager or a secretary may also cause the commission of the offences by the company if the commission was due to his failure to make any necessary disclosures. In this regard, any director or such officer who is found liable may be prosecuted together with the body corporate.

As it is traditionally difficult to establish the relevant *mens rea* element of criminal offences committed by body corporates, CDSCA further provides that it is sufficient to find the relevant mental element against a body corporate if the director, employee or agent of the body corporate by whom the alleged conduct was made had the requisite state of mind and was acting within the scope of their actual or apparent authority (CDSCA, s 52(1)).

The legislation went further, to state that any conduct engaged in or on behalf of a body corporate either by a director, employee or agent of the body corporate within the scope of his actual or apparent authority, or by any other person at the direction or with the consent or agreement of a director, employee or agent of the body corporate (provided that the giving of the direction, consent or agreement is within the scope of the actual or apparent authority of the director, employee or agent), shall be deemed to have been engaged in by the body corporate (CDSCA, s 52(2)). The same approach was also adopted under CDSCA to impute the mental state of persons who are either the employees or agents of persons other than body corporates, such as in the case of firms and partnerships (CDSCA, s 52(3) and (4)).

Defences in relation to the laundering of benefits of criminal conduct

For the offence of assisting another to retain the benefits of criminal conduct, it is also a defence for the accused to prove that he:

1   did not know and had no reasonable ground to believe that the arrangement related to any person's proceeds derived from criminal conduct;

2   did not know and had no reasonable ground to believe that, by the arrangement, the retention or control by or on behalf of the relevant

person of any property was facilitated, or that by the arrangement, any property was used in the manner contemplated by CDSCA, s 44(1) as described above;

3   intended to disclose to an authorised officer (See CDSCA, s 2(1)) in a manner described at para 28.32 below, such knowledge, belief or matter in relation to the arrangement and there is reasonable excuse for his failure to make disclosure; or

4   disclosed the knowledge, belief or matter to the appropriate person in a manner described below, in accordance with the procedure established by his employer for the making of such disclosures if he was employed at the time in question and had entered into or was otherwise concerned with the arrangement in the course of his employment (CDSCA, s 44(4). See paras 28.33 to 28.36 below for the discussion on disclosure requirements under CDSCA and related issues).

In addition, an accused shall not be guilty if he disclosed to an authorised officer his knowledge or belief that any property, funds or investments are derived from or used in connection with criminal conduct or any matter on which such knowledge or belief is based,

1   before he does the act concerned, being an act done with the consent of the authorised officer; or

2   the disclosure is made after the act but it is made on his own initiative and as soon as it is reasonable for him to make it (see CDSCA, s 44(3)).

There is no defence under CDSCA to the offence of concealing or transferring benefits of criminal conduct.

Penalties

Any person who is found guilty of any of the principal money laundering offences under CDSCA, ss 43, 44, 46 and 47 shall be subject either to a fine not exceeding S$200,000, to imprisonment not exceeding seven years, or to both (CDSCA, ss 43(5), 44(5), 46(6) and 47(6)).

Prosecutions

As with some of the other jurisdictions, prosecution of money laundering offences in Singapore has not been too extensive. Two successful prosecutions to date were *PP v Ong Choon Ho; PP v Yeo Kok Wei* and *PP v Andrew Yip.* In the *Ong Choon Ho* case, the defendants were bank officers who had conspired with a number of others to use a forged letter to authorise the transfer of S$600,000 from a customer's account to an accomplice's account and subsequently applied part of the funds to purchase shares for the purpose of disguising the source of the funds. The defendants were both found guilty, *inter alia,* under DTA and were each sentenced to 24 months' imprisonment. In the *Andrew Yip* case, the defendant remitted part of the S$4.52 million he had misappropriated from his bank accounts to a casino in Australia, where the funds were used in gambling.

In addition to cheating offences, the defendant was found guilty under DTA and was sentenced to 24 months' imprisonment.

Disclosure requirements

Duty to disclose knowledge or suspicion

With the exception of information or matter subject to legal privilege (CDSCA, s 39(4)), where a person knows or has reasonable grounds to suspect that any property: (a) in whole or in part, directly or not, represents the proceeds of; (b) was used in connection with; or (c) is intended to be used in connection with, drug trafficking or criminal conduct and the relevant information upon which the suspicion or knowledge is based, came to his attention in the course of their trade, profession, business or employment, he must disclose the knowledge or suspicion or the relevant information to an authorised officer as soon as is practicable (CDSCA, s 39(1)).

Any such disclosure shall not be treated as a breach of any legal, contractual or professional conduct-related restriction upon the disclosure. The person making the disclosure shall also not be liable for any loss arising out of the disclosure or any consequential act or omission (CDSCA, s 39(6)). Any contravention of the disclosure requirement is an offence for the purpose of CDSCA and the offender shall be liable on conviction to a fine not exceeding S$10,000 (CDSCA, s 39(2)).

It is a defence against a charge under this offence if the person charged had a reasonable excuse for the non-disclosure or they had disclosed the relevant information or matter to an appropriate person according to the procedure for the making of such disclosures established by their employer (CDSCA, s 39(5) and (7)).

There is, however, no definition for the expression 'reasonable ground to suspect' in CDSCA. There is also no reported case, as yet, which deals with an applicable definition for the term used in CDSCA. None the less, it is clear that the level of threshold for the expression 'reasonable ground to suspect' is lower than that of 'reasonable ground to believe'.

Tipping-off

There are two offences for tipping off in relation to an investigation or a possible investigation by an authorised officer under CDSCA. First, it is an offence for any person, who knows or has reasonable grounds to suspect that an investigation is or is about to be conducted under CDSCA, to disclose to another person any information or matter which is likely to prejudice the investigation (CDSCA, s 48(1)). Secondly, when a person knows or has reasonable grounds to suspect that a disclosure has been made to an authorised officer under CDSCA, it is an offence for that person to disclose to another person information or matter which is likely to prejudice any investigation which might be conducted after that disclosure has been made (CDSCA, s 48(2)).

However, unless the relevant information and matter is disclosed in furtherance of an illegal purpose (CDSCA, s 48(4)), it is not an offence for a Singapore lawyer to disclose the relevant information or matter: (a) to his client if it is in connection with his advice to the client and given in the course of and for the purpose of his professional employment; or (b) to any person for the purpose of legal proceedings, either in contemplation of or in connection with those proceedings (CDSCA, s 48(3)).

In addition to the tipping off offences, CDSCA also provides a broader offence which penalises a person for making any disclosure which is likely to prejudice an investigation into drug trafficking or criminal conduct, if that person knows or suspects that the investigation is taking place and if in relation to that investigation, either a production order has been made or applied for (but not rejected), or where a search warrant has been issued (CDSCA, s 49(1)).

Any person who is found guilty of the tipping off offences or of making such disclosure as is likely to prejudice an investigation into drug trafficking or criminal conduct shall be liable on conviction to a fine not exceeding S$30,000, to imprisonment for a term not exceeding three years, or to both (CDSCA, ss 48(1), (2) and 49(3)).

As is the case in some other jurisdictions such as the UK, persons under a duty to make disclosures for the purpose of CDSCA may find themselves in an unenviable position. Where a person engaged in a transaction has made a disclosure under CDSCA against its counter party, that person may face grave difficulties in deciding how he should proceed with the transaction. On the one hand, if the person chooses to suspend the transaction, he may incur civil liabilities with respect to his counter party should it be found subsequently that no money laundering was involved in the transaction. To avoid any such liabilities, the person may have to provide an explanation to his counter party. However, this may amount to the tipping off of that counter party. On the other hand, should the person choose to proceed with the transaction, he may be found to have been assisting his counter party in money laundering activities with the knowledge or suspicion that money laundering was taking place, since the person had made a disclosure report of such knowledge or suspicion. The person may also suffer civil liabilities for dishonest assistance or knowing receipt. There does not appear to be a ready answer in this regard, and it remains to be seen how the issue will be dealt with in the Singapore courts.

Appendix 2.9

United States of America

Dr Kern Alexander

Butterworths Senior Research Fellow in International Financial Regulation and Lecturer in Law, Institute of Advanced Legal Studies, University of London; Member, The Florida Bar, and Solicitor of the Supreme Court of England and Wales

Statutory framework of US anti-money laundering laws

The Money Laundering Control Act 1986

The Money Laundering Control Act 1986 (MLCA 1986) provides the original statutory basis for making the act of money laundering itself a criminal offence, aside from the predicate criminal offence that generated the illicit funds. The legislation is contained in the US Code, ss 1956 and 1957. MLCA 1986 creates four specific criminal offences, namely, the actual laundering of monetary instruments (18 USC, s 1956(a)(1)), an international transportation offence (18 USC, s 1956(a)(2)), the sting offence (18 USC, s 1956(a)(3)) and the receipt of property deriving from 'specified unlawful activity' (18 USC, s 1957). First, the laundering of *monetary instruments offence* occurs when a person knowingly conducts or attempts to conduct a financial transaction involving the proceeds of 'specified unlawful activity' with either:

1   the intent to promote the specified unlawful activity;

2   the knowledge that the transaction is designed to conceal or disguise the nature, location, source, ownership or control of the funds or to avoid a transaction reporting requirement; or

3   the intent to conduct tax fraud or evasion.

Specified unlawful activity is dealt with below and includes offences under US law such as drug trafficking, fraud, tax evasion, embezzlement, bribery, gambling, theft, kidnapping, racketeering, arson, counterfeiting, smuggling and murder.

Secondly, an international transportation offence (18 USC, s 1956(a)(2)) occurs when a person transports, transmits, (ie, electronic wire transfer or Internet commerce) or transfers funds or monetary instruments into or out of the US if one of two conditions apply – the person has:

1   the intent to promote 'specified unlawful activity'; or

2   the knowledge that the funds or monetary instruments represent the proceeds of some type of unlawful activity and that such transportation, transmission or transfer is intended in whole or in part:

(i) to conceal or disguise the nature, the location, the source, the ownership, or the control of the proceeds of a specified crime; or

(ii) to avoid a transaction reporting requirement under federal or state law.

Thirdly, the law enforcement 'sting' offence (18 USC, s 1956(a)(3)) is created that may form the basis of a criminal prosecution if the accused conducted, or attempted to conduct, a financial transaction that:

1   involved property represented by a federal law enforcement officer (acting in an undercover capacity) or other authorised person (ie state or local investigator, or informant acting with an investigator) to be the proceeds of specified unlawful activity or property used to conduct or facilitate specified unlawful activity; and

2   the person acted either:

(i) to promote the carrying on of specified unlawful activity;

(ii) to conceal or disguise the nature, location, source, ownership or control of property believed to be the proceeds of specified unlawful activity; or

(iii) to evade a transaction reporting requirement under federal or state law.

Fourthly, a financial transaction offence (18 USC, s 1957) is created for knowingly (individual or entity) engaging, or attempting to engage, in virtually any monetary transaction in property with a value of more than US $10,000 and is derived from 'specified unlawful activity'. A monetary transaction is defined as 'a deposit, withdrawal, transfer, or exchange, in or affecting interstate or foreign commerce, of funds ... by, through, or to a financial institution' (18 USC, s1957(f)(1)). The offence criminalises the *receipt* of criminally derived property (including funds), even in the absence of any intent to promote or conceal unlawful activity, provided the person knew that the property was derived from some type of criminal activity (18 USC, s1957(c)). This means that although the prosecutor is required to prove that the receipt of such property was in fact derived from specified unlawful activity, it is only necessary to show that the defendant knew, based on an objective standard, that the property they received was derived from some type of criminal activity (not necessarily specified unlawful activity) under US federal or state law.

In the case of trade or sale, a seller will not have committed the offence through the mere receipt of criminally derived property as payment for a sale, but would be liable for depositing or transferring the proceeds of such property through a financial institution. MLCA 1986, s 1957 aims at the receipt of laundered funds, and the recipient need not have exchanged or laundered the proceeds to have committed the offence. By enacting the section, Congress sought to deter ordinary commercial transactions with persons known to, or suspected to, have engaged in criminal activity, and therefore sought to make any subsequent transaction using criminal proceeds an offence in perpetuity, subject to the knowledge requirement. The Patriot Act 2001, Title III expands the definition of covered financial institution for purposes of the s 1957 financial transaction offence to include not only domestic US depository institutions, but also a commercial bank or trust company, a private banker, an agency or branch in the US of a foreign bank, a thrift institution, a securities broker-dealer, and in some circumstances foreign banks that receive or disburse US $10,000 or more for a US person (see 67 FR 60565 (26 September 2002), codified at 31 USC, s 5318(j)).

Specified unlawful activity (SUA) is defined in MLCA 1986, s 1956 to include a wide range of serious federal and state criminal offences, such as drug trafficking, fraud, tax evasion, embezzlement, bribery, gambling, theft, kidnapping, racketeering, arson, counterfeiting, smuggling and murder. The Patriot Act 2001, Title III has expanded the list of domestic predicate offences to include firearms violations, certain computer fraud offences and felony offences under the Foreign Agents Registration Act 1938. The US Congress has also designated certain foreign crimes as SUAs that occur outside US territory but which qualify as predicate offences for the financial transaction offence under s 1956 (For the list of these extraterritorial offences, see 18 USC, s 1956(c)(7)(B)(I)(iii), as amended by the Patriot Act 2001, Title III). These extraterritorial predicate offences include extortion, fraud against a foreign bank, kidnapping, narcotics, robbery, and violations of the Arms Export Control Act (18 USC, s 1956 (c)(7)(B)(I)(iii)). The Patriot Act 2001, s 315 expands the list of extraterritorial predicate offences to include bribing foreign officials in violation of the Foreign Corrupt Practices Act, violating US export controls (These violations fall under both Arms Export Control Act's Munitions List (22 USC, s 2778) and the Export Administration Act's Regulations (15 CFR, Pts 730–44) regarding export controls of goods and services that may be re-exported or re-sold from a third country to a targeted country, terrorist group or criminal organisation), providing material support or assistance to designated terrorist groups and committing acts of international terrorism (Patriot Act 2001, Title III, s 315).

MLCA 1986 defines the term 'financial transaction' broadly to cover all the transactions mentioned above and any type of wire transfer or transaction involving a financial institution. Moreover, the penalties for violating MLCA 1986 can be severe. An MLCA 1986, s 1956 violation can result in a custodial sentence of imprisonment for up to 20 years, plus substantial civil and criminal fines that may rise to US $500,000 per violation *or* twice the value of the property involved in the transaction, and criminal and/or civil forfeiture of the money or property related to the offence. MLCA 1986, s 1957 offences may result in up to ten years' imprisonment and/or a criminal fine. Section 1957 contains no civil penalty provisions. It should be noted that the court will determine the actual terms of imprisonment and fines for a criminal conviction by referring to the applicable US Sentencing Guidelines. The Guidelines require that the length of a prison sentence be within specified ranges, unless the court finds extenuating circumstances to depart upward or downward. The criteria used by the court in determining a particular sentence range for an MLCA 1986 offence will depend on the statutory provision violated, the amount of money laundered and defendant's criminal history.

—MLCA 1986 knowledge requirement

MLCA 1986's effectiveness as a prosecutorial and regulatory measure is enhanced by the expansive way in which 'knowledge' is defined and can be proved in order to obtain a conviction for the four substantive offences discussed above. The 'knowledge' element of these offences does not require that the accused knew that he or she was dealing with the proceeds of a *'specified unlawful activity'*. Proving knowledge for the three MLCA 1986, s 1956 offences requires that it be proved that the person 'knew the property involved in the transaction represented proceeds from some form, though not necessarily which form, of activity that constitutes a felony under State, Federal or foreign law', regardless of whether that criminal activity constitutes a 'specified unlawful activity' (18 USC, s 1956(c)(1)).

There are also important differences between MLCA 1986, ss 1956 and 1957 in the standard of knowledge that must be satisfied. For example, as 1956 offence requires a higher standard of knowledge to be proved that the defendant had a subjective intent or actual knowledge that a person intended to promote a criminal activity, or had knowledge that a person knew that the purpose of a transaction was to conceal the nature of the proceeds or to avoid a reporting requirement (MLCA 1986, s 1956(a)). In addition to subjective or actual knowledge, wilful blindness will satisfy the knowledge requirement for the three offences under s 1956, discussed above. By contrast, s 1957 does not require such a purposive intention or knowledge; rather, it requires merely that the prosecution show that the defendant has knowingly engaged in a monetary transaction with criminally derived property valued at more than US $10,000 (See J Popham and M Probus 'Structured Transactions in Money Laundering: Dealing with Tax Evaders, Smurfs, and other Enemies of the People' (1988) 15 AJ Crim L 83. See also J Arrastia 'Money Laundering – A US Perspective' in B A K Rider (ed) *Money Laundering Control* (1996) pp 243–45). This lesser burden of proof adopts an objective knowledge standard based on the reasonable person test, which makes prosecution under s 1957 much easier (see the discussion in Arrastia above).

—Constructive knowledge

Under US federal criminal law, the requirement of knowledge can also be satisfied by constructive knowledge through what is known as the doctrine of 'conscious avoidance' (also known as 'wilful blindness' or 'deliberate ignorance'). The doctrine seeks to prevent a person from wilfully and intentionally remaining ignorant of a fact that is material to his or her conduct in order to avoid criminal liability. For example, a defendant's constructive knowledge of a fact required to prove guilt may arise from proof that they intentionally avoided learning of the fact whilst aware of a high probability of its existence. US courts frequently apply this doctrine in money laundering cases where a party has deliberately avoided learning facts about the conduct of another party to the transaction, even though the circumstances of the case made it highly likely that the defendant party was aware that the other party was seeking to launder the proceeds of criminal activity.

—Corporate and business entity liability and compliance programmes

US courts apply the common law theory of respondeat superior to impose criminal liability on business entities for the acts or omissions of their officers and employees while acting within the course and scope of their responsibility. US courts have also developed the doctrine of *collective intent*, so that the intent or acts of individual employees can be attributed to the corporation or entity which employed them. Corporations are deemed to have the collective knowledge or intent of all of their employees. As discussed below, such collective intent has been attributed to financial institutions for the cumulative acts and knowledge of their employees with respect to violations of BSA 1970.

Because of these principles of corporate and entity liability under US law, Congress considered it necessary to enact statutory requirements that corporations and business entities covered by the money laundering laws maintain anti-money laundering compliance programmes. The Treasury Department administers and monitors compliance with these programmes. The programmes focus on internal risk management practices, procedures and controls that include, among other things, designation of compliance officers, maintenance of an ongoing employee training programme and implementing an independent audit function to test the adequacy of the compliance programmes.

In addition, the US courts encourage the adoption of compliance programmes through the US Sentencing Guidelines (The US Sentencing Commission has adopted 'Organisational Sentencing Guidelines that mandate specific penalties for corporations and other business entities convicted of federal crimes, based on the review of specific criteria'). Specifically, regarding corporate compliance with US anti-money laundering guidelines, a US court can vary the penalties imposed under the US Sentencing Guidelines based on the assessment of specified factors, including the effectiveness of corporate compliance programmes. Although the Guidelines are primarily applied to business entities convicted of criminal offences, prosecutors and judges may rely on the criteria set forth in the Guidelines (including entities' compliance programmes) to determine whether to charge an entity with a crime and, if so, what type of charge to institute. The Guidelines provide a variety of incentives to those companies who have implemented 'effective programs to prevent and detect violations of the law' (Official Commentaries 'United States Sentencing Guidelines' (2000)). The minimum requirements for such 'due diligence' includes, among other things, the following:

- establishing compliance standards and procedures for employees and other agents that can reasonably reduce the prospect of criminal conduct;

- due care not to delegate authority to individuals whom the organisation knows, or has reason to know, to have the propensity to engage in illegal activities; and

- to take all reasonable steps to respond appropriately to an offence after it has become known, and to adopt necessary modifications to compliance programmes.

Under the Guidelines, reporting violations of money laundering laws to the authorities before any governmental investigations would serve as a mitigating factor. The Guidelines also emphasise that senior management have the responsibility of scrutinising 'high-level personnel' allegedly involved in wrongdoing, and toleration of pervasive misconduct and obstruction of justice: see Official Commentaries, US Sentencing Guidelines (2000).

Extraterritoriality and US anti-money laundering laws

The statutory language of MLCA 1986, s 1957(d) provides that jurisdiction will apply only to an unlawful transaction that 'takes place in the United States or in the special maritime and territorial jurisdiction of the United States', or, alternatively, when the transaction occurs outside the US but the defendant is a US person (18 USC, s 1957(d)). There have been no US court cases to interpret the extraterritorial reach of the provision, but the Department of Justice has adopted a more expansive interpretation of s 1957's extraterritorial reach by defining the monetary transaction offence as being composed of not one act or event, but of a series of acts or events that have taken place before or after the actual deposit is made (US Department of Justice *Department of Justice Manual* Criminal Division, Ch 105: Money Laundering s 9–105.100A, s 9–2128.1 (1994–1 Supp) (the Department of Justice Manual)). According to this view, so long as one act or event of the broader illicit transaction took place within the US, then a foreign financial institution that received a deposit of more than US $10,000 in another country would be subject to extraterritorial subject matter jurisdiction under s 1957(d) if the deposit contained the proceeds of criminal activity that amounted to an unlawful specified activity (B Harmon 'United States Money Laundering Laws: International Implications' (1988) 9 NYL Sch J Int & Comp 1 at 19–20).

In addition, the Patriot Act 2001, s 317 grants US courts 'long-arm jurisdiction' over foreign persons who commit money laundering offences under US law. This extraterritorial jurisdiction also applies to foreign banks opening US bank accounts and to foreign persons who convert assets ordered confiscated by a US court.

—Conspiracy, aiding and abetting, and extraterritorial jurisdiction for money laundering violations

US courts have interpreted the federal aiding and abetting statute as creating equal criminal liability for any person who aids or abets another person in committing any federal crime. Similarly, the federal conspiracy statute creates an offence of conspiring to commit any federal offence, including the substantive offences found in MLCA 1986, ss 1956 and 1957. The conspiracy statute contains two distinct clauses that create two different conspiracy offences; it states in the relevant part:

'If two or more persons conspire either to commit any offence against the United States, or to defraud the United States, or any agency thereof in any manner or for any purpose, and one or more of such persons do any act to effect the object of the conspiracy, each shall be fined under this title or imprisoned not more than five years, or both.'

If the conspiracy involves a non-US party who conspires in a foreign territory to violate a US federal offence, the US courts may assume extraterritorial jurisdiction over the foreign conspirator (62 Stat 701, c 645 (25 June 1948) (original language of conspiracy statute); *Chua Han Mow v United States 730 F 2d 1308 at 1311 (9th Cir, 1984), cert den 470 US 1031 (1985)*; see also *United States v Cotten 471 F 2d 744 at 750 (9th Cir, 1972), cert den 411 US 936 (1973)*. The federal conspiracy statute has been codified at 18 USC, s 371 (1998)). Moreover, a non-US national who has agreed and participated in a scheme outside the US that violates the extraterritorial provisions of US criminal law will also be subject to the extraterritorial reach of the US conspiracy statute if the agreement and conduct entered into by the foreign party is 'intended to take effect' or has a direct effect in the US (Department of Justice Manual, para 33.32 n 2 above, s 9–2128.2 (1994–1 Supp), citing 18 USC, s 1871). For example, a foreign institution with no business presence in the US could incur liability under the substantive money laundering offences based on the US federal statutes criminalising conspiracies to commit crimes and aiding and abetting crimes against the US (See 18 USC, s 2 (1998); see also 18 USC, s 371 (1998)). The Second Circuit Court of Appeals ruled in *Melia v United States* (667 F 2d 300 (2nd Cir, 1981)) that the US could exercise jurisdiction over a party outside the US who conspired with persons within the US.

Regarding aiding and abetting, a US District Court ruled in *United States v Noriega 764 F Supp 1506 at 1516 (SD Fla, 1990)* that the federal aiding and abetting and conspiracy statutes could be applied extraterritorially to overseas conduct that was defined as criminal by the underlying substantive offence. The court in the *Noriega* case adopted the reasoning of the Eleventh Circuit Court of Appeals in *United States v Inco Bank & Trust Corpn 845 F 2d 919 at 923–24 (11th Cir, 1988)* (in this case, US conspirators had begun the conspiracy in the US and it continued to function in the US until the US conspirators took it to the Cayman Islands, where Inco Bank agreed to launder money on behalf of the US conspirators. The court held that although Inco Bank joined the conspiracy in the Cayman Islands and undertook no acts in US territory, it had knowingly become part of a conspiracy that would continue to operate in the US, and thus was liable as a co-conspirator), where it was recognised as a well-settled principle of US criminal law that the US government has the power to prosecute every member of a conspiracy regardless of their territorial location if any act or agreement of the conspiracy occurred in the US.

As a defence, a non-US person or institution could argue that they should not be subject to liability because they did not have the necessary *mens rea* to commit the offence under US law. A foreign defendant could assert that the US government had failed to provide adequate notice that the transaction (involving a money laundering offence under the extraterritorial provisions of US law) for which the foreign defendant was providing assistance, or was involved in a conspiracy, was an offence under US law. Indeed, because of this lack of notice, foreign defendants could argue that they did not possess the culpable intent or required knowledge necessary to be liable, either criminally or civilly, under US anti-money laundering law, and thus the extraterritorial application and enforcement would violate due process under the US Constitution. The imputation of criminal liability, however, will likely be justified if the foreign defendant has availed itself of the privileges of conducting any type of business in US territory and, therefore, would be presumed to be aware of the laws of the US. The more difficult issue, however, concerns the non-US person who has no business activity in US markets, but who may still be subject to extraterritorial third-party liability because it knowingly advised a transaction, lawful under the laws of its own country, but which violated the extraterritorial provisions of US anti-money laundering law or other financial sanction laws.

—US state anti-money laundering laws

US anti-money laundering laws do not supersede legislative and regulatory efforts by the states, Commonwealths and Territories of the US to prohibit money laundering and to impose regulatory requirements on the business and financial communities (18 USC, s 1956(d) expressly states that it does not supersede 'State or other law imposing criminal penalties or affording civil remedies in addition to those provided for in this section'). Indeed, MLCA 1986 expressly states that federal law will not be the exclusive remedy in combating money laundering, and that '[s]tate and other law' may impose additional criminal penalties and/or afford civil remedies against money laundering (18 USC, s 1956(d)). Most US states have responded by adopting anti-money laundering laws that contain many of the essential elements of the federal regime, while some have provided additional civil remedies, in particular, private rights of action to obtain damages and restitution against money launderers and those third parties who have facilitated or provided assistance to money launderers (see 13 LPRA, s 8076). Given space limitations, only the main elements of the state anti-money laundering laws of California and New York will be generally discussed here.

Knowledge standard

—Collective knowledge standard and corporate criminal liability

US courts have adopted the principle of corporate liability for corporations and financial institutions whose employees have committed acts or omissions, while performing within the scope of their responsibility, that violate federal law. Regarding corporate criminal liability, US courts have applied the *collective knowledge* theory that allows a corporation or financial institution to be charged with the knowledge of its employees acting within the scope of their responsibility. This was demonstrated in *US v Bank of New England 821 F 2d 844 (1st Cir, 1987), cert den 484 US 943 (1987)*, in which criminal charges were brought against a bank for failing to report the transactions of a client who presented several cheques to a bank teller for amounts each under US $10,000, but which totalled more than US $10,000, and the teller would in turn transfer a sum of cash for more than US $10,000. The bank was charged with 'wilfully' violating the reporting requirements, which meant that it was necessary to prove the defendant's knowledge of the reporting requirements and its specific intent to commit the crime. The First Circuit Court of Appeals held that the use of multiple cheques during a single transfer of currency was not the same as multiple currency transactions, so that the cashing of multiple cheques could be considered a single currency transfer in excess of US $10,000 from the bank to the client (*United States v Bank of New England 821 F 2d 844 at 849 (1st Cir, 1987)*).

Significantly, the court held the bank liable based on the *collective knowledge* theory (*United States v Bank of New England 821 F 2d 844 at 849 (1st Cir, 1987)*). The court reasoned that a collective knowledge instruction to the jury was entirely appropriate in order to impose corporate criminal liability on the bank because the acts of a corporation are simply the acts of its employees operating within the scope of their employment. Moreover, the principle of corporate criminal liability permitted the knowledge obtained by corporate employees to be imputed to the corporation. Corporations could not avoid liability by compartmentalising knowledge and subdividing the elements of specific duties and operations into smaller components in order to prevent any one employee from having complete knowledge of the offence in question. The aggregate of these component areas of knowledge constituted the corporation's overall knowledge of the particular operation. Accordingly, the court rejected the bank's argument that it was not liable because no one employee had sufficient knowledge to commit the offence, as it was irrelevant whether an employee involved in one component of the operation knew the specific activities of an employee involved in another aspect of the operation.

The *collective knowledge standard* is important because it can result in civil or criminal liability being imputed to the bank or financial institution for violations committed by employees, even when the bank had taken proper precautions and had acted reasonably in supervising the employee who committed the breach. Essentially, the collective knowledge doctrine treats the bank or corporation as if it possessed all the knowledge of all individuals affiliated with it (ie, directors, officers and employees). To demonstrate collective knowledge, prosecutors must prove that the business entity had knowledge of the violation by offering evidence that the aggregate knowledge of each individual employee and its related parties amounted to actual knowledge of the intended crime, or amounted to knowledge that would put a reasonable person on notice that a crime was being committed. Some observers have commented that the application of the collective knowledge theory to impute liability to the corporation in modern financial markets, where universal banking has become commonly accepted, will make it extremely difficult, if not impractical, for large, complex banking institutions to avoid liability for the acts or omissions of their many employees and will thus increase the cost of doing business and so result in curtailed financial services (S Salva Money Laundering and Financial Intermediaries (2000) pp 314–327). On the other hand, it is argued that the corporation itself is best positioned to incur the cost of regulatory compliance by being primarily responsible for implementing risk management practices that reduce the incidence of breach of money laundering standards.

—Wilful blindness

The stringent application of the collective knowledge theory to corporations and other business entities for violations of federal law may also result in corporate or entity liability based on the 'wilful blindness' theory. Under this theory, a court can attribute the requisite knowledge and intent to a corporation when its employees deliberately decline to investigate the facts behind a suspicious transaction. The First Circuit Court of Appeals has upheld the attribution of knowledge based on wilful blindness in a case involving an employee of a credit union who was told by state auditors that she needed to report certain transactions to the IRS, but who had failed to investigate and to report suspicious transactions (*United States v St Michael's Credit Union 880 F 2d 579 (1st Cir, 1989)*. The First Circuit upheld the conviction of the credit union for the knowing and wilful failure to file CTRs required by BSA 1970 based on the employee's conspicuous disregard of the reporting requirements. The court ruled that a wilful blindness instruction would be appropriate in circumstances where:

1   the defendant claimed a lack of knowledge;

2   the facts suggested a conscious course of deliberate ignorance by the employee; and

3   a juror could not understand the instruction, on the whole, as mandating the wilful blindness inference *United States v St Michael's Credit Union 880 F 2d 579 at 584 (1st Cir, 1989)*.

The determination of the first and third conditions are purely factual matters, while the second requires an interpretation of the facts of each case.

The purpose of the wilful blindness theory was to impose criminal liability on persons who had appreciated the likelihood of wrongdoing, but who nevertheless consciously refused to conduct a reasonable investigation given the facts of the case. Although some observers have recognised that this theory creates a high standard of knowledge for liability purposes (see S Savla Money Laundering and Financial Intermediaries (2000) p 332), the First Circuit Court of Appeals recognised that, even though the evidence was not overwhelming, the jury could infer that the relevant bookkeeper had read the CTRs, which she had been given by the state auditor (*United States v St Michael's Credit Union 880 F 2d 579 at 586 (1st Cir, 1989)*. Based on the fact that there were warnings on the back of the CTRs about the penalties for failure to file, the jury could reasonably infer that the relevant bookkeeper knew that the failure to file the reports was an offence.

Based on the above principles, it can be said that the courts have relied on two knowledge standards for determining whether liability will be attributed to the corporation or firm for assisting or facilitating offences in breach of BSA 1970. The first standard is known as the purposeful indifference or deliberate ignorance standard. This standard requires bankers to be proactive in identifying suspicious activities, which means that it is not enough that a customer tells the banker that a business or transaction is legitimate. The banker has the further obligation of conducting a due diligence inquiry to ascertain if the statements of the prospective customer appear to be true and correct. Secondly, the *wilful blindness standard* provides that if the bank ignores or avoids information which could have led to the discovery of criminal activity, it will be responsible for whatever information an investigation would have revealed. A bank, therefore, would attract criminal liability if it had consciously and/or deliberately avoided knowledge of facts which were essential proof of a criminal violation.

These knowledge standards for imposing liability have the result of requiring US financial institutions to 'know your customer' and to take reasonable steps to ensure that they do not facilitate transactions for money launderers. For example, liability will be imposed on the financial institution if its employee knows that a complete and truthful report has not been filed by a customer that has recently entered the US while transporting in excess of US $10,000 without reporting it to the US Customs Service. The potential that civil and criminal liability can be imputed to the financial institution on account of employee violation makes it crucial that risk management practices are adopted to ensure effective communication across and within functional areas of the financial institution.

Patriot Act 2001

On 26 October 2001, President Bush signed into law the 'Uniting and Strengthening America by Providing Appropriate Tools Required To Intercept and Obstruct Terrorism' (the Patriot Act 2001) (Pub L 107–56, 115 Stat 272 (26 October 2001). For Congressional debate, see Congressional Record, vol 147, S10990–02). The Patriot Act 2001, Title III, entitled the 'International Money Laundering Abatement and Anti-Terrorist Financing Act 2001' (Pub L 107–56, 115 Stat 272 (26 October 2001)), contains important provisions that, *inter alia*, extend the financial reporting requirements of BSA 1970 to foreign financial institutions if they maintain interbank payable through accounts or correspondent bank accounts with US financial institutions or other financial firms. Prior to the Patriot Act 2001, US banking law provided a narrow definition for the term 'financial institution' for purposes of BSA 1970 that excluded many financial firms from the requirements of reporting suspicious transactions. The Patriot Act 2001, s 321 amends this omission by defining the term 'financial institution' broadly to include credit unions, futures commission merchants, commodity trading advisers, securities brokers/dealers and commodity pool operators (Patriot Act 2001, s 321(a)–(c)). Moreover, Title III expands the list of predicate offences for the money laundering offence to include, among other things, acts of international terrorism.

Appendix 3

Supra-national

Appendix 3.1

The Forty Recommendations (2003)(FATF on Money Laundering)

Introduction

Money laundering methods and techniques change in response to developing counter-measures. In recent years, the Financial Action Task Force (FATF)[1] has noted increasingly sophisticated combinations of techniques, such as the increased use of legal persons to disguise the true ownership and control of illegal proceeds, and an increased use of professionals to provide advice and assistance in laundering criminal funds. These factors, combined with the experience gained through the FATF's Non-Cooperative Countries and Territories process, and a number of national and international initiatives, led the FATF to review and revise the Forty Recommendations into a new comprehensive framework for combating money laundering and terrorist financing. The FATF now calls upon all countries to take the necessary steps to bring their national systems for combating money laundering and terrorist financing into compliance with the new FATF Recommendations, and to effectively implement these measures.

The review process for revising the Forty Recommendations was an extensive one, open to FATF members, non-members, observers, financial and other affected sectors and interested parties. This consultation process provided a wide range of input, all of which was considered in the review process.

The revised Forty Recommendations now apply not only to money laundering but also to terrorist financing, and when combined with the Eight Special Recommendations on Terrorist Financing provide an enhanced, comprehensive and consistent framework of measures for combating money laundering and terrorist financing. The FATF recognises that countries have diverse legal and financial systems and so all cannot take identical measures to achieve the common objective, especially over matters of detail. The Recommendations therefore set minimum standards for action for countries to implement the detail according to their particular circumstances and constitutional frameworks. The Recommendations cover all the measures that national systems should have in place within their criminal justice and regulatory systems; the preventive measures to be taken by financial institutions and certain other businesses and professions; and international co-operation.

The original FATF Forty Recommendations were drawn up in 1990 as an initiative to combat the misuse of financial systems by persons laundering drug money. In 1996 the Recommendations were revised for the first time to reflect evolving money laundering typologies. The 1996 Forty Recommendations have been endorsed by more than 130 countries and are the international anti-money laundering standard.

In October 2001 the FATF expanded its mandate to deal with the issue of the financing of terrorism, and took the important step of creating the Eight Special Recommendations on Terrorist Financing. These Recommendations contain a set of measures aimed at combating the funding of terrorist acts and terrorist organisations, and are complementary to the Forty Recommendations[2].

A key element in the fight against money laundering and the financing of terrorism is the need for countries systems to be monitored and evaluated, with respect to these international standards. The mutual evaluations conducted by the FATF and FATF-style regional bodies, as well as the assessments conducted by the IMF and World Bank, are a vital mechanism for ensuring that the FATF Recommendations are effectively implemented by all countries.

Footnotes:

[1] The FATF is an inter-governmental body which sets standards, and develops and promotes policies to combat money laundering and terrorist financing. It currently has 33 members: 31 countries and governments and two international organisations; and more than 20 observers: five FATF-style regional bodies and more than 15 other international organisations or bodies. A list of all members and observers can be found on the FATF website at http://www.fatf-gafi.org/Members_en.htm

[2] The FATF Forty and Eight Special Recommendations have been recognised by the International Monetary Fund and the World Bank as the international standards for combating money laundering and the financing of terrorism.

The Forty Recommendations

A. LEGAL SYSTEMS

Scope of the criminal offence of money laundering

—Recommendation 1

Countries should criminalise money laundering on the basis of United Nations Convention against Illicit Traffic in Narcotic Drugs and Psychotropic Substances, 1988 (the Vienna Convention) and United Nations Convention against Transnational Organized Crime, 2000 (the Palermo Convention).

Countries should apply the crime of money laundering to all serious offences, with a view to including the widest range of predicate offences. Predicate offences may be described by reference to all offences, or to a threshold linked either to a category of serious offences or to the penalty of imprisonment applicable to the predicate offence (threshold approach), or to a list of predicate offences, or a combination of these approaches.

Where countries apply a threshold approach, predicate offences should at a minimum comprise all offences that fall within the category of serious offences under their national law or should include offences which are punishable by a maximum penalty of more than one year's imprisonment or for those countries that have a minimum threshold for offences in their legal system, predicate offences should comprise all offences, which are punished by a minimum penalty of more than six months imprisonment.

Whichever approach is adopted, each country should at a minimum include a range of offences within each of the designated categories of offences[3].

Predicate offences for money laundering should extend to conduct that occurred in another country, which constitutes an offence in that country, and which would have constituted a predicate offence had it occurred domestically. Countries may provide that the only prerequisite is that the conduct would have constituted a predicate offence had it occurred domestically.

Countries may provide that the offence of money laundering does not apply to persons who committed the predicate offence, where this is required by fundamental principles of their domestic law.

Footnotes:

[3] See the definition of "designated categories of offences" in the Glossary.

—Recommendation 2

Countries should ensure that:

(a) The intent and knowledge required to prove the offence of money laundering is consistent with the standards set forth in the Vienna and Palermo Conventions, including the concept that such mental state may be inferred from objective factual circumstances.

(b) Criminal liability, and, where that is not possible, civil or administrative liability, should apply to legal persons. This should not preclude parallel criminal, civil or administrative proceedings with respect to legal persons in countries in which such forms of liability are available. Legal persons should be subject to effective, proportionate and dissuasive sanctions. Such measures should be without prejudice to the criminal liability of individuals.

Provisional measures and confiscation

—Recommendation 3

Countries should adopt measures similar to those set forth in the Vienna and Palermo Conventions, including legislative measures, to enable their competent authorities to confiscate property laundered, proceeds from money laundering or predicate offences, instrumentalities used in or intended for use in the commission of these offences, or property of corresponding value, without prejudicing the rights of bona fide third parties.

Such measures should include the authority to: (a) identify, trace and evaluate property which is subject to confiscation; (b) carry out provisional measures, such as freezing and seizing, to prevent any dealing, transfer or disposal of such property; (c) take steps that will prevent or void actions that prejudice the State's ability to recover property that is subject to confiscation; and (d) take any appropriate investigative measures.

Countries may consider adopting measures that allow such proceeds or instrumentalities to be confiscated without requiring a criminal conviction, or which require an offender to demonstrate the lawful origin of the property alleged to be liable to confiscation, to the extent that such a requirement is consistent with the principles of their domestic law.

B. MEASURES TO BE TAKEN BY FINANCIAL INSTITUTIONS AND NON-FINANCIAL BUSINESSES AND PROFESSIONS TO PREVENT MONEY LAUNDERING AND TERRORIST FINANCING

—Recommendation 4

Countries should ensure that financial institution secrecy laws do not inhibit implementation of the FATF Recommendations.

Customer due diligence and record-keeping

—Recommendation 5

Financial institutions should not keep anonymous accounts or accounts in obviously fictitious names.

Financial institutions should undertake customer due diligence measures, including identifying and verifying the identity of their customers, when:

● establishing business relations;

● carrying out occasional transactions: (i) above the applicable designated threshold; or (ii) that are wire transfers in the circumstances covered by the Interpretative Note to Special Recommendation VII;

- there is a suspicion of money laundering or terrorist financing; or

- the financial institution has doubts about the veracity or adequacy of previously obtained customer identification data.

The customer due diligence (CDD) measures to be taken are as follows:

(a) Identifying the customer and verifying that customer's identity using reliable, independent source documents, data or information[4].

(b) Identifying the beneficial owner, and taking reasonable measures to verify the identity of the beneficial owner such that the financial institution is satisfied that it knows who the beneficial owner is. For legal persons and arrangements this should include financial institutions taking reasonable measures to understand the ownership and control structure of the customer.

(c) Obtaining information on the purpose and intended nature of the business relationship.

(d) Conducting ongoing due diligence on the business relationship and scrutiny of transactions undertaken throughout the course of that relationship to ensure that the transactions being conducted are consistent with the institution's knowledge of the customer, their business and risk profile, including, where necessary, the source of funds.

Financial institutions should apply each of the CDD measures under (a) to (d) above, but may determine the extent of such measures on a risk sensitive basis depending on the type of customer, business relationship or transaction. The measures that are taken should be consistent with any guidelines issued by competent authorities. For higher risk categories, financial institutions should perform enhanced due diligence. In certain circumstances, where there are low risks, countries may decide that financial institutions can apply reduced or simplified measures.

Financial institutions should verify the identity of the customer and beneficial owner before or during the course of establishing a business relationship or conducting transactions for occasional customers. Countries may permit financial institutions to complete the verification as soon as reasonably practicable following the establishment of the relationship, where the money laundering risks are effectively managed and where this is essential not to interrupt the normal conduct of business.

Where the financial institution is unable to comply with paragraphs (a) to (c) above, it should not open the account, commence business relations or perform the transaction; or should terminate the business relationship; and should consider making a suspicious transactions report in relation to the customer.

These requirements should apply to all new customers, though financial institutions should also apply this Recommendation to existing customers on the basis of materiality and risk, and should conduct due diligence on such existing relationships at appropriate times.

(**See Interpretative Notes:** Recommendation 5 **and** Recommendations 5, 12 and 16)

Footnotes:

[4] Reliable, independent source documents, data or information will hereafter be referred to as "identification data".

—Recommendation 6

Financial institutions should, in relation to politically exposed persons, in addition to performing normal due diligence measures:

(a)   Have appropriate risk management systems to determine whether the customer is a politically exposed person.

(b)   Obtain senior management approval for establishing business relationships with such customers.

(c)   Take reasonable measures to establish the source of wealth and source of funds.

(d)   Conduct enhanced ongoing monitoring of the business relationship.

(See Interpretative Note)

—Recommendation 7

Financial institutions should, in relation to cross-border correspondent banking and other similar relationships, in addition to performing normal due diligence measures:

(a)   Gather sufficient information about a respondent institution to understand fully the nature of the respondent's business and to determine from publicly available information the reputation of the institution and the quality of supervision, including whether it has been subject to a money laundering or terrorist financing investigation or regulatory action.

(b)   Assess the respondent institution's anti-money laundering and terrorist financing controls.

(c)   Obtain approval from senior management before establishing new correspondent relationships.

(d)   Document the respective responsibilities of each institution.

(e)   With respect to "payable-through accounts", be satisfied that the respondent bank has verified the identity of and performed on-going due diligence on the customers having direct access to accounts of the correspondent and that it is able to provide relevant customer identification data upon request to the correspondent bank.

—Recommendation 8

Financial institutions should pay special attention to any money laundering threats that may arise from new or developing technologies that might favour anonymity, and take measures, if needed, to prevent their use in money laundering schemes. In particular, financial institutions should have policies and procedures in place to address any specific risks associated with non-face to face business relationships or transactions.

—Recommendation 9

Countries may permit financial institutions to rely on intermediaries or other third parties to perform elements (a) – (c) of the CDD process or to introduce business, provided that the criteria set out below are met. Where such reliance is permitted, the ultimate responsibility for customer identification and verification remains with the financial institution relying on the third party.

The criteria that should be met are as follows:

(a)   A financial institution relying upon a third party should immediately obtain the necessary information concerning elements (a) – (c) of the CDD process. Financial institutions should take adequate steps to satisfy themselves that copies of identification data and other relevant documentation relating to the CDD requirements will be made available from the third party upon request without delay.

(b)   The financial institution should satisfy itself that the third party is regulated and supervised for, and has measures in place to comply with CDD requirements in line with Recommendations 5 and 10.

It is left to each country to determine in which countries the third party that meets the conditions can be based, having regard to information available on countries that do not or do not adequately apply the FATF Recommendations. (See Interpretative Note)

—Recommendation 10

Financial institutions should maintain, for at least five years, all necessary records on transactions, both domestic or international, to enable them to comply swiftly with information requests from the competent authorities. Such records must be sufficient to permit reconstruction of individual transactions (including the amounts and types of currency involved if any) so as to provide, if necessary, evidence for prosecution of criminal activity.

Financial institutions should keep records on the identification data obtained through the customer due diligence process (eg, copies or records of official identification documents like passports, identity cards, driving licenses or similar documents), account files and business correspondence for at least five years after the business relationship is ended.

The identification data and transaction records should be available to domestic competent authorities upon appropriate authority. (See Interpretative Note)

—Recommendation 11

Financial institutions should pay special attention to all complex, unusual large transactions, and all unusual patterns of transactions, which have no apparent economic or visible lawful purpose. The background and purpose of such transactions should, as far as possible, be examined, the findings established in writing, and be available to help competent authorities and auditors. (See Interpretative Note)

—Recommendation 12

The customer due diligence and record-keeping requirements set out in Recommendations 5, 6, and 8 to 11 apply to designated non-financial businesses and professions in the following situations:

(a) Casinos – when customers engage in financial transactions equal to or above the applicable designated threshold.

(b) Real estate agents – when they are involved in transactions for their client concerning the buying and selling of real estate.

(c) Dealers in precious metals and dealers in precious stones – when they engage in any cash transaction with a customer equal to or above the applicable designated threshold.

(d) Lawyers, notaries, other independent legal professionals and accountants when they prepare for or carry out transactions for their client concerning the following activities:

- buying and selling of real estate;

- managing of client money, securities or other assets;

- management of bank, savings or securities accounts;

- organisation of contributions for the creation, operation or management of companies;

- creation, operation or management of legal persons or arrangements, and buying and selling of business entities.

(e) Trust and company service providers when they prepare for or carry out transactions for a client concerning the activities listed in the definition in the Glossary.

(See Interpretative Note)

Reporting of suspicious transactions and compliance

—Recommendation 13

If a financial institution suspects or has reasonable grounds to suspect that funds are the proceeds of a criminal activity, or are related to terrorist financing, it should be required, directly by law or regulation, to report promptly its suspicions to the financial intelligence unit (FIU). (See Interpretative Note)

—Recommendation 14

Financial institutions, their directors, officers and employees should be:

(a) Protected by legal provisions from criminal and civil liability for breach of any restriction on disclosure of information imposed by contract or by any legislative, regulatory or administrative provision, if they report their suspicions in good faith to the FIU, even if they did not know precisely what the underlying criminal activity was, and regardless of whether illegal activity actually occurred.

(b) Prohibited by law from disclosing the fact that a suspicious transaction report (STR) or related information is being reported to the FIU.

(See Interpretative Note)

—Recommendation 15

Financial institutions should develop programmes against money laundering and terrorist financing. These programmes should include:

(a) The development of internal policies, procedures and controls, including appropriate compliance management arrangements, and adequate screening procedures to ensure high standards when hiring employees.

(b) An ongoing employee training programme.

(c) An audit function to test the system.

(See Interpretative Note)

—Recommendation 16

The requirements set out in Recommendations 13 to 15, and 21 apply to all designated non-financial businesses and professions, subject to the following qualifications:

(a) Lawyers, notaries, other independent legal professionals and accountants should be required to report suspicious transactions when, on behalf of or for a client, they engage in a financial transaction in relation to the activities described in Recommendation 12(d). Countries are strongly encouraged to extend the reporting requirement to the rest of the professional activities of accountants, including auditing.

(b) Dealers in precious metals and dealers in precious stones should be required to report suspicious transactions when they engage in any cash transaction with a customer equal to or above the applicable designated threshold.

(c)   Trust and company service providers should be required to report suspicious transactions for a client when, on behalf of or for a client, they engage in a transaction in relation to the activities referred to Recommendation 12(e).

Lawyers, notaries, other independent legal professionals, and accountants acting as independent legal professionals, are not required to report their suspicions if the relevant information was obtained in circumstances where they are subject to professional secrecy or legal professional privilege. (**See Interpretative Notes:** Recommendation 16 and Recommendations 5, 12, and 16)

Measures to be taken with respect to countries that do not or insufficiently comply with the FATF Recommendations

—Recommendation 21

Financial institutions should give special attention to business relationships and transactions with persons, including companies and financial institutions, from countries which do not or insufficiently apply the FATF Recommendations. Whenever these transactions have no apparent economic or visible lawful purpose, their background and purpose should, as far as possible, be examined, the findings established in writing, and be available to help competent authorities. Where such a country continues not to apply or insufficiently applies the FATF Recommendations, countries should be able to apply appropriate countermeasures.

—Recommendation 22

Financial institutions should ensure that the principles applicable to financial institutions, which are mentioned above are also applied to branches and majority owned subsidiaries located abroad, especially in countries which do not or insufficiently apply the FATF Recommendations, to the extent that local applicable laws and regulations permit. When local applicable laws and regulations prohibit this implementation, competent authorities in the country of the parent institution should be informed by the financial institutions that they cannot apply the FATF Recommendations.

Transparency of legal persons and arrangements

—Recommendation 33

Countries should take measures to prevent the unlawful use of legal persons by money launderers. Countries should ensure that there is adequate, accurate and timely information on the beneficial ownership and control of legal persons that can be obtained or accessed in a timely fashion by competent authorities. In particular, countries that have legal persons that are able to issue bearer shares should take appropriate measures to ensure that they are not misused for money laundering and be able to demonstrate the adequacy of those measures. Countries could consider measures to facilitate access to beneficial ownership and control information to financial institutions undertaking the requirements set out in Recommendation 5.

—Recommendation 34

Countries should take measures to prevent the unlawful use of legal arrangements by money launderers. In particular, countries should ensure that there is adequate, accurate and timely information on express trusts, including information on the settlor, trustee and beneficiaries, that can be obtained or accessed in a timely fashion by competent authorities. Countries could consider measures to facilitate access to beneficial ownership and control information to financial institutions undertaking the requirements set out in Recommendation 5.

GLOSSARY

In these Recommendations the following abbreviations and references are used:

"**Beneficial owner**" refers to the natural person(s) who ultimately owns or controls a customer and/or the person on whose behalf a transaction is being conducted. It also incorporates those persons who exercise ultimate effective control over a legal person or arrangement.

"**Core Principles**" refers to the Core Principles for Effective Banking Supervision issued by the Basel Committee on Banking Supervision, the Objectives and Principles for Securities Regulation issued by the International Organization of Securities Commissions, and the Insurance Supervisory Principles issued by the International Association of Insurance Supervisors.

"**Designated categories of offences**" means:

- participation in an organised criminal group and racketeering;
- terrorism, including terrorist financing;
- trafficking in human beings and migrant smuggling;
- sexual exploitation, including sexual exploitation of children;
- illicit trafficking in narcotic drugs and psychotropic substances;
- illicit arms trafficking;
- illicit trafficking in stolen and other goods;
- corruption and bribery;
- fraud;
- counterfeiting currency;
- counterfeiting and piracy of products;
- environmental crime;

- murder, grievous bodily injury;

- kidnapping, illegal restraint and hostage-taking;

- robbery or theft;

- smuggling;

- extortion;

- forgery;

- piracy; and

- insider trading and market manipulation.

When deciding on the range of offences to be covered as predicate offences under each of the categories listed above, each country may decide, in accordance with its domestic law, how it will define those offences and the nature of any particular elements of those offences that make them serious offences.

"Designated non-financial businesses and professions" means:

(a) Casinos (which also includes internet casinos).

(b) Real estate agents.

(c) Dealers in precious metals.

(d) Dealers in precious stones.

(e) Lawyers, notaries, other independent legal professionals and accountants – this refers to sole practitioners, partners or employed professionals within professional firms. It is not meant to refer to 'internal' professionals that are employees of other types of businesses, nor to professionals working for government agencies, who may already be subject to measures that would combat money laundering.

(f) Trust and Company Service Providers refers to all persons or businesses that are not covered elsewhere under these Recommendations, and which as a business, provide any of the following services to third parties:

- acting as a formation agent of legal persons;

- acting as (or arranging for another person to act as) a director or secretary of a company, a partner of a partnership, or a similar position in relation to other legal persons;

- providing a registered office; business address or accommodation, correspondence or administrative address for a company, a partnership or any other legal person or arrangement;

- acting as (or arranging for another person to act as) a trustee of an express trust;

- acting as (or arranging for another person to act as) a nominee shareholder for another person.

"**Designated threshold**" refers to the amount set out in the Interpretative Notes.

"**Financial institutions**" means any person or entity who conducts as a business one or more of the following activities or operations for or on behalf of a customer:

- (1) Acceptance of deposits and other repayable funds from the public[5]

- (2) Lending[6]

- (3) Financial leasing[7]

- (4) The transfer of money or value[8]

- (5) issuing and managing means of payment (eg, credit and debit cards, cheques, traveller's cheques, money orders and bankers' drafts, electronic money).

- (6) Financial guarantees and commitments.

- (7) Trading in:

  - (a) money market instruments (cheques, bills, CDs, derivatives etc.);

  - (b) foreign exchange;

  - (c) exchange, interest rate and index instruments;

  - (d) transferable securities;

  - (e) commodity futures trading.

- (8) Participation in securities issues and the provision of financial services related to such issues.

- (9) Individual and collective portfolio management.

- (10) Safekeeping and administration of cash or liquid securities on behalf of other persons.

- (11) Otherwise investing, administering or managing funds or money on behalf of other persons.

- (12) Underwriting and placement of life insurance and other investment related insurance[9]

- (13) Money and currency changing.

When a financial activity is carried out by a person or entity on an occasional or very limited basis (having regard to quantitative and absolute criteria) such that there is little risk of money laundering activity occurring, a country may decide that the application of anti-money laundering measures is not necessary, either fully or partially.

In strictly limited and justified circumstances, and based on a proven low risk of money laundering, a country may decide not to apply some or all of the Forty Recommendations to some of the financial activities stated above.

Footnotes:

[5] This also captures private banking.

[6] This includes *inter alia*: consumer credit; mortgage credit; factoring, with or without recourse; and finance of commercial transactions (including forfaiting).

[7] This does not extend to financial leasing arrangements in relation to consumer products.

[8] This applies to financial activity in both the formal or informal sector e.g. alternative remittance activity. See the Interpretative Note to Special Recommendation VI. It does not apply to any natural or legal person that provides financial institutions solely with message or other support systems for transmitting funds. See the Interpretative Note to Special Recommendation VII.

[9] This applies both to insurance undertakings and to insurance intermediaries (agents and brokers).

"**FIU**" means financial intelligence unit.

"**Legal arrangements**" refers to express trusts or other similar legal arrangements.

"**Legal persons**" refers to bodies corporate, foundations, anstalt, partnerships, or associations, or any similar bodies that can establish a permanent customer relationship with a financial institution or otherwise own property.

"**Payable-through accounts**" refers to correspondent accounts that are used directly by third parties to transact business on their own behalf.

"**Politically Exposed Persons**" (PEPs) are individuals who are or have been entrusted with prominent public functions in a foreign country, for example Heads of State or of government, senior politicians, senior government, judicial or military officials, senior executives of state owned corporations, important political party officials. Business relationships with family members or close associates of PEPs involve reputational risks similar to those with PEPs themselves. The definition is not intended to cover middle ranking or more junior individuals in the foregoing categories.

"**Shell bank**" means a bank incorporated in a jurisdiction in which it has no physical presence and which is unaffiliated with a regulated financial group.

"**STR**" refers to suspicious transaction reports.

"**Supervisors**" refers to the designated competent authorities responsible for ensuring compliance by financial institutions with requirements to combat money laundering and terrorist financing.

"**the FATF Recommendations**" refers to these Recommendations and to the FATF Special Recommendations on Terrorist Financing.

Interpretative Notes to the Forty Recommendations (2003)

Interpretative Notes – General

(1)   Reference in this document to "countries" should be taken to apply equally to "territories" or "jurisdictions".

(2)   Recommendations 5–16 and 21–22 state that financial institutions or designated non-financial businesses and professions should take certain actions. These references require countries to take measures that will oblige financial institutions or designated non-financial businesses and professions to comply with each Recommendation. The basic obligations under Recommendations 5, 10 and 13 should be set out in law or regulation, while more detailed elements in those Recommendations, as well as obligations under other Recommendations, could be required either by law or regulation or by other enforceable means issued by a competent authority.

(3)   Where reference is made to a financial institution being satisfied as to a matter, that institution must be able to justify its assessment to competent authorities.

(4)   To comply with Recommendations 12 and 16, countries do not need to issue laws or regulations that relate exclusively to lawyers, notaries, accountants and the other designated non-financial businesses and professions so long as these businesses or professions are included in laws or regulations covering the underlying activities.

(5)   The Interpretative Notes that apply to financial institutions are also relevant to designated non-financial businesses and professions, where applicable.

Interpretative Note to Recommendations 5, 12 and 16

The designated thresholds for transactions (under Recommendations 5 and 12) are as follows:

- Financial institutions (for occasional customers under Recommendation 5) – USD/EUR 15,000.

- Casinos, including internet casinos (under Recommendation 12) – USD/EUR 3000

- For dealers in precious metals and dealers in precious stones when engaged in any cash transaction (under Recommendations 12 and 16) – USD/EUR 15,000.

Financial transactions above a designated threshold include situations where the transaction is carried out in a single operation or in several operations that appear to be linked.

Interpretative Note to Recommendation 5 (Thresholds Interpretative Note)

Customer due diligence and tipping off

(1)   If, during the establishment or course of the customer relationship, or when conducting occasional transactions, a financial institution suspects that transactions relate to money laundering or terrorist financing, then the institution should:

(a)   Normally seek to identify and verify the identity of the customer and the beneficial owner, whether permanent or occasional, and irrespective of any exemption or any designated threshold that might otherwise apply.

(b)   Make a STR to the FIU in accordance with Recommendation 13.

(2)   Recommendation 14 prohibits financial institutions, their directors, officers and employees from disclosing the fact that an STR or related information is being reported to the FIU. A risk exists that customers could be unintentionally tipped off when the financial institution is seeking to perform its customer due diligence (CDD) obligations in these circumstances. The customer's awareness of a possible STR or investigation could compromise future efforts to investigate the suspected money laundering or terrorist financing operation.

(3)   Therefore, if financial institutions form a suspicion that transactions relate to money laundering or terrorist financing, they should take into account the risk of tipping off when performing the customer due diligence process. If the institution reasonably believes that performing the CDD process will tip-off the customer or potential customer, it may choose not to pursue that process, and should file an STR. Institutions should ensure that their employees are aware of and sensitive to these issues when conducting CDD.

CDD for legal persons and arrangements

(4)   When performing elements (a) and (b) of the CDD process in relation to legal persons or arrangements, financial institutions should:

(a)   Verify that any person purporting to act on behalf of the customer is so authorised, and identify that person.

(b)   Identify the customer and verify its identity – the types of measures that would be normally needed to satisfactorily perform this function would require obtaining proof of incorporation or similar evidence of the legal status of the legal person or arrangement, as well as information concerning the customer's name, the names of trustees, legal form, address, directors, and provisions regulating the power to bind the legal person or arrangement.

(c)   Identify the beneficial owners, including forming an understanding of the ownership and control structure, and take reasonable measures to verify the identity of such persons. The types of measures that would be normally needed to satisfactorily perform this function would require identifying the natural persons with a controlling interest and identifying the natural persons who comprise the mind and management of the legal person or arrangement. Where the customer or the owner of the controlling interest is a public company that is subject to regulatory disclosure requirements, it is not necessary to seek to identify and verify the identity of any shareholder of that company.

The relevant information or data may be obtained from a public register, from the customer or from other reliable sources.

Reliance on identification and verification already performed

(5)   The CDD measures set out in Recommendation 5 do not imply that financial institutions have to repeatedly identify and verify the identity of each customer every time that a customer conducts a transaction. An institution is entitled to rely on the identification and verification steps that it has already undertaken unless it has doubts about the veracity of that information. Examples of situations that might lead an institution to have such doubts could be where there is a suspicion of money laundering in relation to that customer, or where there is a material change in the way that the customer's account is operated which is not consistent with the customer's business profile.

Timing of verification

(6)   Examples of the types of circumstances where it would be permissible for verification to be completed after the establishment of the business relationship, because it would be essential not to interrupt the normal conduct of business include:

- Non face-to-face business.

- Securities transactions. In the securities industry, companies and intermediaries may be required to perform transactions very rapidly, according to the market conditions at the time the customer is contacting them, and the performance of the transaction may be required before verification of identity is completed.

- Life insurance business. In relation to life insurance business, countries may permit the identification and verification of the beneficiary under the policy to take place after having established the business relationship with the policyholder. However, in all such cases, identification and verification should occur at or before the time of payout or the time where the beneficiary intends to exercise vested rights under the policy.

(7)   Financial institutions will also need to adopt risk management procedures with respect to the conditions under which a customer may utilise the business relationship prior to verification. These procedures should include a set of measures such as a limitation of the number, types and/or amount of transactions that can be performed and the monitoring of large or complex transactions being carried out outside of expected norms for that type of relationship. Financial institutions should refer to the Basel CDD paper (section 2.2.6.) (Guidance Paper on Customer Due Diligence for Banks issued by the Basel Committee on Banking Supervision in October 2001) for specific guidance on examples of risk management measures for non-face to face business.

Requirement to identify existing customers

(8)   The principles set out in the Basel CDD paper concerning the identification of existing customers should serve as guidance when applying customer due diligence processes to institutions engaged in banking activity, and could apply to other financial institutions where relevant.

Simplified or reduced CDD measures

(9)   The general rule is that customers must be subject to the full range of CDD measures, including the requirement to identify the beneficial owner. Nevertheless there are circumstances where the risk of money laundering or terrorist financing is lower, where information on the identity of the customer and the beneficial owner of a customer is publicly available, or where adequate checks and controls exist elsewhere in national systems. In such circumstances it could be reasonable for a country to allow its financial institutions to apply simplified or reduced CDD measures when identifying and verifying the identity of the customer and the beneficial owner.

(10)   Examples of customers where simplified or reduced CDD measures could apply are:

• Financial institutions – where they are subject to requirements to combat money laundering and terrorist financing consistent with the FATF Recommendations and are supervised for compliance with those controls.

• Public companies that are subject to regulatory disclosure requirements.

• Government administrations or enterprises.

(11)   Simplified or reduced CDD measures could also apply to the beneficial owners of pooled accounts held by designated non financial businesses or professions provided that those businesses or professions are subject to requirements to combat money laundering and terrorist financing consistent with the FATF Recommendations and are subject to effective systems for monitoring and ensuring their compliance with those requirements.

Banks should also refer to the Basel CDD paper (section 2.2.4.), which provides specific guidance concerning situations where an account holding institution may rely on a customer that is a professional financial intermediary to perform the customer due diligence on his or its own customers (i.e. the beneficial owners of the bank account). Where relevant, the CDD Paper could also provide guidance in relation to similar accounts held by other types of financial institutions.

(12) Simplified CDD or reduced measures could also be acceptable for various types of products or transactions such as (examples only):

- Life insurance policies where the annual premium is no more than USD/EUR 1000 or a single premium of no more than USD/EUR 2500.

- Insurance policies for pension schemes if there is no surrender clause and the policy cannot be used as collateral.

- A pension, superannuation or similar scheme that provides retirement benefits to employees, where contributions are made by way of deduction from wages and the scheme rules do not permit the assignment of a member's interest undcr the scheme.

(13) Countries could also decide whether financial institutions could apply these simplified measures only to customers in its own jurisdiction or allow them to do for customers from any other jurisdiction that the original country is satisfied is in compliance with and has effectively implemented the FATF Recommendations.

Simplified CDD measures are not acceptable whenever there is suspicion of money laundering or terrorist financing or specific higher risk scenarios apply.

Interpretative Note to Recommendation 6

Countries are encouraged to extend the requirements of Recommendation 6 to individuals who hold prominent public functions in their own country.

Interpretative Note to Recommendation 9

This Recommendation does not apply to outsourcing or agency relationships.

This Recommendation also does not apply to relationships, accounts or transactions between financial institutions for their clients. Those relationships are addressed by Recommendations 5 and 7.

Interpretative Note to Recommendation 10 and 11

In relation to insurance business, the word "transactions" should be understood to refer to the insurance product itself, the premium payment and the benefits.

Interpretative Note to Recommendation 13

(1)   The reference to criminal activity in Recommendation 13 refers to:

    (a)   all criminal acts that would constitute a predicate offence for money laundering in the jurisdiction; or

    (b)   at a minimum to those offences that would constitute a predicate offence as required by Recommendation 1.

Countries are strongly encouraged to adopt alternative (a). All suspicious transactions, including attempted transactions, should be reported regardless of the amount of the transaction.

(2)   In implementing Recommendation 13, suspicious transactions should be reported by financial institutions regardless of whether they are also thought to involve tax matters. Countries should take into account that, in order to deter financial institutions from reporting a suspicious transaction, money launderers may seek to state inter alia that their transactions relate to tax matters.

Interpretative Note to Recommendation 14 (tipping off)

Where lawyers, notaries, other independent legal professionals and accountants acting as independent legal professionals seek to dissuade a client from engaging in illegal activity, this does not amount to tipping off.

Interpretative Note to Recommendation 15

The type and extent of measures to be taken for each of the requirements set out in the Recommendation should be appropriate having regard to the risk of money laundering and terrorist financing and the size of the business.

For financial institutions, compliance management arrangements should include the appointment of a compliance officer at the management level.

Interpretative Note to Recommendation 16 (Thresholds Interpretative Note)

(1)   It is for each jurisdiction to determine the matters that would fall under legal professional privilege or professional secrecy. This would normally cover information lawyers, notaries or other independent legal professionals receive from or obtain through one of their clients: (a) in the course of ascertaining the legal position of their client, or (b) in performing their task of defending or representing that client in, or concerning judicial, administrative, arbitration or mediation proceedings. Where accountants are subject to the same obligations of secrecy or privilege, then they are also not required to report suspicious transactions.

(2) Countries may allow lawyers, notaries, other independent legal professionals and accountants to send their STR to their appropriate self-regulatory organisations, provided that there are appropriate forms of co-operation between these organisations and the FIU.

Interpretative Note to Recommendation 19

(1) To facilitate detection and monitoring of cash transactions, without impeding in any way the freedom of capital movements, countries could consider the feasibility of subjecting all cross-border transfers, above a given threshold, to verification, administrative monitoring, declaration or record keeping requirements.

(2) If a country discovers an unusual international shipment of currency, monetary instruments, precious metals, or gems, etc., it should consider notifying, as appropriate, the Customs Service or other competent authorities of the countries from which the shipment originated and/or to which it is destined, and should co-operate with a view toward establishing the source, destination, and purpose of such shipment and toward the taking of appropriate action.

Interpretative Note to Recommendation 23

Recommendation 23 should not be read as to require the introduction of a system of regular review of licensing of controlling interests in financial institutions merely for anti-money laundering purposes, but as to stress the desirability of suitability review for controlling shareholders in financial institutions (banks and non-banks in particular) from a FATF point of view. Hence, where shareholder suitability (or "fit and proper") tests exist, the attention of supervisors should be drawn to their relevance for anti-money laundering purposes.

Interpretative Note to Recommendation 25

When considering the feedback that should be provided, countries should have regard to the FATF Best Practice Guidelines on Providing Feedback to Reporting Financial Institutions and Other Persons.

Interpretative Note to Recommendation 26

Where a country has created an FIU, it should consider applying for membership in the Egmont Group. Countries should have regard to the Egmont Group Statement of Purpose, and its Principles for Information Exchange Between Financial Intelligence Units for Money Laundering Cases. These documents set out important guidance concerning the role and functions of FIUs, and the mechanisms for exchanging information between FIU.

Interpretative Note to Recommendation 27

Countries should consider taking measures, including legislative ones, at the national level, to allow their competent authorities investigating money laundering cases to postpone or waive the arrest of suspected persons and/or the seizure of the money for the purpose of identifying persons involved in such activities or for evidence gathering. Without such measures the use of procedures such as controlled deliveries and undercover operations are precluded.

Interpretative Note to Recommendation 38

Countries should consider:

(a)   Establishing an asset forfeiture fund in its respective country into which all or a portion of confiscated property will be deposited for law enforcement, health, education, or other appropriate purposes.

(b)   Taking such measures as may be necessary to enable it to share among or between other countries confiscated property, in particular, when confiscation is directly or indirectly a result of co-ordinated law enforcement actions.

Interpretative Note to Recommendation 40

(1)   For the purposes of this Recommendation:

- "Counterparts" refers to authorities that exercise similar responsibilities and functions.

- "Competent authority" refers to all administrative and law enforcement authorities concerned with combating money laundering and terrorist financing, including the FIU and supervisors.

(2)   Depending on the type of competent authority involved and the nature and purpose of the co-operation, different channels can be appropriate for the exchange of information. Examples of mechanisms or channels that are used to exchange information include: bilateral or multilateral agreements or arrangements, memoranda of understanding, exchanges on the basis of reciprocity, or through appropriate international or regional organisations. However, this Recommendation is not intended to cover co-operation in relation to mutual legal assistance or extradition.

(3)   The reference to indirect exchange of information with foreign authorities other than counterparts covers the situation where the requested information passes from the foreign authority through one or more domestic or foreign authorities before being received by the requesting authority. The competent authority that requests the information should always make it clear for what purpose and on whose behalf the request is made.

(4)   FIUs should be able to make inquiries on behalf of foreign counterparts where this could be relevant to an analysis of financial transactions. At a minimum, inquiries should include:

- Searching its own databases, which would include information related to suspicious transaction reports.

- Searching other databases to which it may have direct or indirect access, including law enforcement databases, public databases, administrative databases and commercially available databases.

Where permitted to do so, FIUs should also contact other competent authorities and financial institutions in order to obtain relevant information.

Appendix 3.2

Non-Cooperative Countries and Territories (NCCTs)

The following list of non-cooperative countries and territories is current as of 27 February 2004 and was last changed on 27 February 2004:

(1) Cook Islands

(2) Guatemala

(3) Indonesia

(4) Myanmar

(5) Nauru

(6) Nigeria

(7) Philippines

Background and description of the initiative

The FATF is engaged in a major initiative to identify non-cooperative countries and territories (NCCTs) in the fight against money laundering. Specifically, this has meant the development of a process to seek out critical weaknesses in anti-money laundering systems which serve as obstacles to international co-operation in this area. The goal of this process is to reduce the vulnerability of the financial system to money laundering by ensuring that all financial centres adopt and implement measures for the prevention, detection and punishment of money laundering according to internationally recognised standards.

On 14 February 2000, the FATF published an initial report on NCCTs. The report sets out twenty-five criteria, which help to identify relevant detrimental rules and practices and which are consistent with the FATF Forty Recommendations. It describes a process whereby jurisdictions having such rules and practices can be identified and encourages these jurisdictions to implement international standards in this area.

The next step in the NCCT initiative was the publication in June 2000 of the first Review identifying specific NCCTs. The report named 15 jurisdictions (Bahamas, Cayman Islands, Cook Islands, Dominica, Israel, Lebanon, Liechtenstein, Marshall Islands, Nauru, Niue, Panama, Philippines, Russia, St. Kitts and Nevis, and St. Vincent and the Grenadines) as having critical deficiencies in their anti-money laundering systems or a demonstrated unwillingness to co-operate in anti-money laundering efforts.

Since the June 2000 Review, many of the jurisdictions identified made significant and rapid progress in remedying their deficiencies. In June 2001, the FATF updated the list of NCCTs with the publication of its second NCCT Review.

Four countries left the list (Bahamas, Cayman Islands, Liechtenstein, and Panama); however six other jurisdictions were added (Egypt, Guatemala, Hungary, Indonesia, Myanmar, and Nigeria). At the subsequent FATF Plenary meeting in September 2001, two additional countries were added to the list (Grenada and Ukraine). Decisions were also made at this Plenary meeting as to the timing of counter-measures that may be applied to jurisdictions failing to make adequate progress in remedying identified deficiencies.

In June 2002, the FATF removed four more countries from the NCCT list: Hungary, Israel, Lebanon, and St. Kitts and Nevis. The FATF also published its third NCCT Review. In October 2002, the FATF again removed four countries from the NCCT list: Dominica, Marshall Islands, Niue and Russia.

Because of Ukraine's failure to enact comprehensive anti-money laundering legislation, on 20 December 2002 the FATF recommended the application of counter-measures to Ukraine. However, due to significant legal reforms after that time, in February 2003 the FATF withdrew the application of counter-meaures, although Ukraine remains on the NCCTs list. Also in February 2003, the FATF removed Grenada from the NCCTs list.

In June 2003, the FATF removed St. Vincent and the Grenadines from the NCCT list and published the fourth NCCT Review.

On 3 November 2003, FATF members began applying additional counter-measures to Myanmar due to its failure to address major deficiencies.

In February 2004, the FATF removed Egypt and Ukraine from the NCCTs list because of the substantial implementation of anti-money laundering reforms in those countries.

The FATF remains committed to the NCCT process and welcomes the continued progress by many of the countries on the list in addressing identified deficiencies. FATF members will continue to provide assistance and support where appropriate. The FATF will also continue to review the situation of listed countries as a priority matter at each FATF Plenary meeting and similarly will closely monitor developments in countries that are removed from the list.

Appendix 3.3

The Wolfsberg Principles

Preamble: The following guidelines are understood to be appropriate for private banking relationships. Guidelines for other market segments may differ. It is recognised that the establishment of policies and procedures to adhere to these guidelines is the responsibility of management.

1. Client Acceptance: General Guidelines

1.1 General

Bank policy will be to prevent the use of its worldwide operations for criminal purposes. The bank will endeavour to accept only those clients whose source of wealth and funds can be reasonably established to be legitimate. The primary responsibility for this lies with the private banker who sponsors the client for acceptance. Mere fulfilment of internal review procedure does not relieve the private banker of this basic responsibility.

1.2 Identification

The bank will take reasonable measures to establish the identity of its clients and beneficial owners and will only accept clients when this process has been completed.

1.3 Client Identification

Natural persons: identity will be established to the bank's satisfaction by reference to official identity papers or such other evidence as may be appropriate under the circumstances.

Corporations, partnerships, foundations: the bank will receive documentary evidence of the due organisation and existence.

Trusts: the bank will receive appropriate evidence of formation and existence along with identity of trustees.

Identification documents must be current at the time of opening.

1.4 Beneficial Owner Identification

Beneficial ownership must be established for all accounts. Due diligence must be done on all principal beneficial owners identified in accordance with the following principles:

Natural persons: when the account is in the name of an individual, the private banker must establish whether the client is acting on his/her own behalf. If doubt exists, the bank will establish the capacity in which, and on whose behalf, the account holder is acting.

Legal entities: where the client is a company, such as a PIC, the private banker will understand the structure of the company sufficiently to determine the provider of funds, principal owner(s) of the shares and those who have control over the funds (eg, the directors) and those with the power to give direction to the directors of the company. With regard to other shareholders the private banker will make a reasonable judgement as to the need for further due diligence. This principle applies regardless of whether the share capital is in registered or bearer form.

Trusts: where the client is a trustee, the private banker will understand the structure of the trust sufficiently to determine the provider of funds (eg' settlor), those who have control over the funds (eg, trustees), and any persons or entities who have the power to remove the trustees. The private banker will make a reasonable judgement as to the need for further due diligence.

Unincorporated associations: the above principles apply to unincorporated associations.

1.5   Accounts held in the name of money managers and similar intermediaries

The private banker will perform due diligence on the intermediary and establish that the intermediary has a due diligence process for its clients, or a regulatory obligation to conduct such due diligence, that is satisfactory to the bank.

1.6   Powers of attorney/ authorised signers

Where the power of a holder of a power of attorney or another authorised signer is appointed by a client, it is generally sufficient to do due diligence on the client.

1.7   Practices for walk-in clients and electronic banking relationships

A bank will determine whether walk-in clients or relationships initiated through electronic channels require a higher degree of due diligence prior to account opening.

1.8   Due diligence

It is essential to collect and record information covering the following categories:

—   Purpose and reasons for opening the account;

— Anticipated account activity;

— Source of wealth (description of the economic activity which has generated the net worth);

— Estimated net worth;

— Source of funds (description of the origin and the means of transfer for monies that are accepted for the account opening); and

— references or other sources to corroborate reputation information where available.

Unless other measures reasonably suffice to do the due diligence on a client (eg favourable and reliable references), a client will be met prior to account opening.

1.9   Oversight responsibility

There will be a requirement that all new clients and new accounts be approved by at least one person other than the private banker.

2   Client Acceptance: Situations Requiring Additional Diligence / Attention

2.1   Numbered or alternate name accounts

Numbered or alternate name accounts will only be accepted if the bank has established the identity of the client and the beneficial owner.

2.2   High-risk countries

The bank will apply heightened scrutiny to clients and beneficial owners resident in and funds sourced from countries identified by credible sources as having inadequate anti-money laundering standards or representing high-risk for crime and corruption.

2.3   Offshore jurisdictions

Risks associated with entities organised in offshore jurisdictions are covered by due diligence procedures laid out in these guidelines.

2.4   High-risk activities

Clients and beneficial owners whose source of wealth emanates from activities known to be susceptible to money laundering will be subject to heightened scrutiny.

2.5 Public officials

Individuals who have or have had positions of public trust (such as government officials, senior executives of government corporations, politicians, important political party officials etc) and their families and close associates require heightened scrutiny.

3 Updating Client Files

The private banker is responsible for updating the client file on a defined basis and/or when there are major changes. The private banker's supervisor or an independent control person will review relevant portions of client files on a regular basis to ensure consistency and completeness. The frequency of the reviews depends on the size, complexity and risk posed by the relationship.

4 Practices when Identifying Unusual or Suspicious Activities

4.1 Definition of unusual or suspicious activities

The bank will have a written policy on the identification of and follow-up on unusual or suspicious activities. This policy will include a definition of what is considered to be suspicious or unusual and give examples thereof. Unusual or suspicious activities may include:

— Account transactions or other activities which are not consistent with the due diligence file;

— Cash transactions over a certain amount; and

— Pass-through/in-and-out-transactions.

4.2 Identification of unusual or suspicious activities

Unusual or suspicious activities can be identified through:

— Monitoring of transactions;

— Client contacts (meetings, discussions, in-country visits, etc);

— Third party information (eg, newspapers, Reuters, internet); and

— Private banker's/internal knowledge of the client's environment (eg, political situation in his/her country)

4.3 Follow-up on unusual or suspicious activities

The private banker, management and/or the control function will carry out an analysis of the background of any unusual or suspicious activities. If there is no plausible explanation a decision will be made involving the control function:

— To continue the business relationship with increased monitoring;

— To cancel the business relationship; or

— To report the business relationship to the authorities.

The report to the authorities is made by the control function and senior management may need to be notified (eg, Senior Compliance Officer, CEO, Chief Auditor, General Counsel). As required by local laws and regulations, the assets may be blocked and transactions may be subject to approval by the control function.

5 Monitoring

A sufficient monitoring programme must be in place. The primary responsibility for monitoring account activities lies with the private banker. The private banker will be familiar with significant transactions and increased activity in the account and will be especially aware of unusual or suspicious activities (see 4.1). The bank will decide to what extent fulfilment of these responsibilities will need to be supported through the use of automated systems or other means.

6 Control Responsibilities

A written control policy will be in place establishing standard control procedures to be undertaken by the various 'control layers' (private banker, independent operations unit, compliance, internal audit). The control policy will cover issues of timing, degree of control, areas to be controlled, responsibilities and follow-up, etc).

7 Reporting

There will be regular management reporting established on money laundering issues (eg number of reports to authorities, monitoring tools, changes in applicable laws and regulations, the number and scope of training sessions provided to employees).

8 Education, Training and Information

The bank will establish a training programme on the identification and prevention of money laundering for employees who have client contact and for compliance personnel. Regular training (eg annually) will also include how to identify and follow-up on unusual or suspicious activities. In addition, employees will be informed about any major changes in anti-money laundering procedures. The bank will establish record retention requirements for all anti-money laundering related documents. The documents must be kept for a minimum of five years.

9 Record Retention Requirements

The bank will establish record retention requirements for all anti-money laundering related documents. The documents must be kept for a minimum of five years.

10 Exceptions and Deviations

The bank will establish an exception and deviation procedure that requires risk assessment and approval by an independent unit.

11 Anti-money Laundering Organisation

The bank will establish an adequately staffed and independent department responsible for the prevention of money laundering (eg, compliance, independent control unit, legal).

Copyright Wolfsberg Group of Banks

Appendix 3.4

Guidance on Enhanced Scrutiny for Transactions that may Involve the Proceeds of Foreign Official Corruption

THE DEPARTMENT OF THE TREASURY

THE BOARD OF GOVERNORS OF THE FEDERAL RESERVE SYSTEM

THE OFFICE OF THE COMPTROLLER OF THE CURRENCY

THE FEDERAL DEPOSIT INSURANCE CORPORATION

THE OFFICE OF THRIFT SUPERVISION

AND THE DEPARTMENT OF STATE

January 2001

I. Introduction

Action Item 2.1.1 of the National Money Laundering Strategy for 2000 calls for "[t]he Departments of the Treasury and Justice, and the federal bank regulators, [to] work closely with the financial services industry to develop guidance for financial institutions to conduct enhanced scrutiny of those customers and their transactions that pose a heightened risk of money laundering and other financial crimes." The expert-level working group convened to develop this Guidance, which was chaired by the Deputy Secretary of the Treasury and counted among its members representatives of each of the federal financial institutions supervisory agencies, concluded that there are several areas of potentially high-risk activity for which enhanced scrutiny may be appropriate. Initially, the working group has developed guidance for one type of high-risk activity – namely, transactions involving senior foreign political figures, their immediate family or their close associates that may involve the proceeds of foreign official corruption. This "Guidance on Enhanced Scrutiny for Transactions that May Involve the Proceeds of Foreign Official Corruption" is being issued by the Department of the Treasury, the Board of Governors of the Federal Reserve System, the Office of the Comptroller of the Currency, the Federal Deposit Insurance Corporation, the Office of Thrift Supervision, and the Department of State.

The working group determined to focus initially on transactions by senior foreign political figures and their close associates that may involve the proceeds of foreign official corruption for several reasons. First, while all significant corruption adversely affects individual segments in an economy, high-level corruption can be particularly damaging to a nation's economy and development. This sort of corruption can undermine local efforts to establish and strengthen market-based economic systems; interfere with the international community's efforts to support and promote economic development; discour-

268

age foreign private investment; and foster a climate conducive to financial crime and other forms of lawlessness. The impact of this form of corruption is felt disproportionately by developing nations. And this form of corruption directly impedes the achievement of a core United States diplomatic and international economic policy objective – namely, the promotion of democratic institutions and economic development around the world. It is thus squarely in the United States' interest to combat this form of corruption. Depriving corrupt officials access to well-established international financial markets, including the United States financial system, can contribute significantly to achieve this goal.

Second, a financial institution that engages in a financial transaction, knowing that the property involved in the transaction represents the proceeds of foreign official corruption, may be involved in the crime of money laundering under United States law, if the proceeds involved in the transactions were generated by a "specified unlawful activity," and if the other statutory elements are met. See 18 U.S.C. 1956 & 1957.

Third, regardless of whether the funds involved in the transaction constitute "proceeds" for the purposes of U.S. criminal money laundering laws, business relationships with persons who have high-ranking public positions in foreign governments, or other closely related persons or entities, can, under certain circumstances, expose financial institutions to significant risk, especially if the person involved comes from a country in which corruption and the illicit use of public office to obtain personal wealth may be widespread. This risk is even more acute if the person involved comes from a country whose counter-money laundering regime does not meet international financial transparency standards. Financial institutions that engage, directly or indirectly, in business relationships with senior political figures or closely related persons from such countries thus may be subjecting themselves to significant legal risks, reputational damage, or both.

To assist financial institutions in ensuring that they do not unwittingly hide or move the proceeds of foreign official corruption, this document provides guidance to financial institutions in applying enhanced scrutiny to transactions by senior foreign political figures and closely related persons and entities. This Guidance is intended to help financial institutions more effectively detect and deter transactions that involve the proceeds of foreign corruption, and thus better protect themselves from being used as a conduit for such transactions. This Guidance contains suggested procedures for account opening and maintenance for persons known to be senior foreign political figures, their immediate family or their close associates. It also contains a list of questionable or suspicious activities that, when present, often will warrant enhanced scrutiny of transactions involving such persons.

Banks should apply this Guidance to their private banking activities and accounts, and also may wish to apply this Guidance in connection with high dollar-value accounts or transactions in other relevant areas of their operations. Similarly, other financial institutions should apply this Guidance, as applicable, in connection with high dollar-value accounts or transactions in relevant parts of their operations. (Where this document refers to "accounts" and "business relationships," it should be read and understood in this fashion.)

This Guidance is intended to build upon financial institutions' existing due diligence and anti-money laundering programs, policies, procedures and controls, and to assist financial institutions in the continuing design and development of comprehensive due diligence programs to identify and manage particular risks that may exist. Sound risk management policies and procedures vary among financial institutions and, therefore, the application of this Guidance also may vary among institutions.

This Guidance is not a rule or regulation and should not be interpreted as such. It is advice that financial institutions are encouraged to employ in conjunction with policies, practices and procedures that are in place to enable financial institutions to comply with applicable laws and regulations and to minimise reputational risks. The Federal financial institutions supervisory agencies will continue to monitor whether financial institutions have appropriate controls to identify and deter money laundering, but will not examine, review or audit financial institutions solely for compliance with this Guidance. If, however, deficiencies emerge at a financial institution that would have been minimised or eliminated if the advice contained in this Guidance had been followed, the relevant financial institution supervisor, depending on the severity of the identified deficiencies, may require that the advice contained in this Guidance be integrated into the risk management policies and procedures of the affected institution.

This Guidance is intended to be consistent with applicable civil and criminal laws as well as the regulations of the particular financial institution's supervisory or regulatory agency and the Department of the Treasury. It does not replace, supersede or supplant any financial institution's legal obligations, nor does compliance with this Guidance create a "safe harbor" against action by the United States, any federal agency, or the federal financial institutions supervisory agencies.

II. Enhanced Scrutiny Guidance

A. General

As described further herein, financial institutions are encouraged to develop and maintain "enhanced scrutiny" practices and procedures designed to detect and deter transactions that may involve the proceeds of official corruption by senior foreign political figures, their immediate family, or their close associates. These practices and procedures should be viewed as an application of institutions' due diligence and anti-money laundering policies and procedures and should ensure that institutions report such activity as suspicious in accordance with applicable suspicious activity reporting requirements. In order to ensure that practical steps are taken to provide this enhanced scrutiny, it is prudent practice for a financial institution to review its practices in this area as part of its overall internal and external audit.

The manner in which a financial institution may elect to apply the advice contained in this Guidance will vary depending on the extent of the risk determined to exist by each institution as a general matter, given its normal business operations, and in each case as it is presented. Each financial institution should exercise reasonable judgment in designing and implementing policies and procedures regarding senior foreign political figures, their immediate family and their close associates, and for determining any necessary actions to be undertaken by the institution regarding their transactions.

This Guidance should not be read or understood as discouraging or prohibiting financial institutions from doing business with any legitimate customer, including a senior foreign political figure, or his or her immediate family or close associates. To the contrary, this Guidance is designed solely to assist financial institutions in determining whether a transaction by a senior foreign political figure, his or her immediate family or his or her close associates merits enhanced scrutiny so that the institution, through the application of such scrutiny, is better able to identify and avoid transactions involving the proceeds of foreign corruption and, as necessary and appropriate, to file suspicious activity reports.

In undertaking the reasonable steps and reasonable efforts suggested in this Guidance concerning (1) whether a person or entity is a Covered Person (see Section II.B), (2) the establishment and maintenance of accounts for a Covered Person (see Section II.C), and (3) potentially questionable or suspicious activities involving a Covered Person's transactions (see Section II.D), a financial institution should not rely solely on information obtained from the Covered Person or his or her associates, but should attempt to obtain additional information from its organisation and from independent sources (see Section II.E.).

B.   Definition of Covered Person

For the purposes of this Guidance, a "Covered Person" is a person identified in the course of normal account opening, maintenance or compliance procedures to be a "senior foreign political figure," any member of a senior foreign political figure's "immediate family," and any "close associate" of a senior foreign political figure.

A "senior foreign political figure" is a senior official in the executive, legislative, administrative, military or judicial branches of a foreign government (whether elected or not), a senior official of a major foreign political party, or a senior executive of a foreign government-owned corporation. In addition, a "senior foreign political figure" includes any corporation, business or other entity that has been formed by, or for the benefit of, a senior foreign political figure.

The "immediate family" of a senior foreign political figure typically includes the figure's parents, siblings, spouse, children and in-laws.

A "close associate" of a senior foreign political figure is a person who is widely and publicly known to maintain an unusually close relationship with the senior foreign political figure, and includes a person who is in a position to conduct substantial domestic and international financial transactions on behalf of the senior foreign political figure.

When, during its normal account opening, maintenance or compliance procedures, a financial institution learns of information indicating that a particular individual may be a senior foreign political figure, a member of a senior foreign political figure's immediate family, or a close associate of a senior foreign political figure, it should exercise reasonable diligence in seeking to determine whether the individual is, in fact, a Covered Person. We recognize that, in some instances, it is not possible even through the exercise of reasonable diligence to determine whether a particular individual is a Covered Person.

C. Account Establishment and Maintenance Procedures For Covered Persons

In conjunction with financial institutions' policies, practices and procedures that are in place to enable financial institutions to comply with applicable laws and regulations, financial institutions are encouraged to employ the following practices when establishing and maintaining a business relationship with a Covered Person:

Ascertain the Identity of the Account Holder and the Account's Beneficial Owner

If, in the course of normal account opening, maintenance or compliance procedures with regard to private banking or other applicable accounts, a financial institution learns of information indicating that the beneficial owner of the account may be a Covered Person, the institution should undertake reasonable efforts to determine whether, in fact, a Covered Person holds or will hold a beneficial interest in the account. If, after making a reasonable effort to make this determination, substantial doubt persists as to whether a Covered Person holds a beneficial interest in the account, the financial institution may wish not to open the account if the institution is unable to determine the capacity in which, and on whose behalf, the proposed account-holder is acting.

If a financial institution is requested to open an account for a Covered Person who comes from a "secrecy jurisdiction," the financial institution should require the Covered Person to provide the information that the institution typically collects to identify the client and his/her source of funds or wealth at the outset of the relationship and to waive any secrecy protections provided by local law so that the institution is able to obtain the information that the institution typically collects when opening an account for a United States resident. For the purposes of this Guidance, a secrecy jurisdiction is a country or territory that, among other things, does not participate in international counter-money laundering information sharing arrangements or, either by law or practice, permits account holders to forbid financial institutions from cooperating with international efforts to obtain account information as part of an official investigation.

Each financial institution should undertake reasonable efforts to determine whether a legitimate reason exists for any request by a Covered Person to associate any form of secrecy with an account, such as titling the account in the name of another person (which could include a family member), personal investment company, trust, shell corporation or other such entity.

Obtain Adequate Documentation Regarding the Covered Person

Concurrent with establishing a business relationship with a Covered Person, the financial institution should obtain from the Person (or others working on his or her behalf) documentation adequate to identify the Covered Person. Concurrent with establishing a business relationship with a Covered Person, the financial institution should take reasonable steps to assess the Covered Person's business reputation.

Understand the Covered Person's Anticipated Account Activity

Concurrent with establishing an account for a Covered Person, the financial institution should document the purpose for opening the account and the anticipated account activity. The institution should take reasonable steps to determine whether the Covered Person has any legitimate business or investment activity in the United States that would make having an account in the United States a natural occurrence.

Determine the Covered Person's Source of Wealth and Funds

Each financial institution asked to establish an account for a Covered Person should undertake reasonable efforts to determine the source of the Covered Person's wealth, including the economic activities that generated the Covered Person's wealth and the source of the particular funds involved in establishing the relationship. Among other things, the institution should take reasonable steps to determine the official salary and compensation of the Covered Persons as well as the individual's known legitimate sources of wealth apart from his or her official position.

Apply Additional Oversight to the Covered Person's Account

The decision to accept or reject establishing an account for a Covered Person should directly involve a more senior level of management than is typically involved in decisions regarding account opening.

All material decisions taken in the course of establishing an account for a Covered Person should be recorded.

An institution that has determined, in the course of its normal account opening, maintenance or compliance procedures, that it has established a business relationship with a Covered Person should undertake an annual review (or more frequently as events dictate) of each such Covered Person's account to determine whether to continue doing that business, including consideration of pertinent account activity and documentation.

D. Questionable or Suspicious Activities That Often Will Warrant Enhanced Scrutiny of Transactions Involving Covered Persons

When conducting transactions for or on behalf of Covered Persons, financial institutions should be alert to features of transactions that are indicative of transactions that may involve the proceeds of foreign official corruption. The following non-exhaustive list of potentially questionable or suspicious activities is designed to illustrate the sort of transactions involving Covered Persons that often will warrant enhanced scrutiny, but does not replace, supersede or supplant financial institutions' legal obligations regarding potentially suspicious transactions generally. The list should be evaluated by each financial institution along with other information the institution may have concerning the Covered Person, the nature of the transaction itself, and other parties involved in the transaction, in evaluating a particular transaction. The occurrence of one or more of the items on the list in a transaction involving a Covered Person often will warrant some form of enhanced scrutiny of the transaction, but does not necessarily mean, in itself, that a transaction is suspicious.

Institutions should pay particular attention to:

- A request by a Covered Person to establish a relationship with, or route a transaction through, a financial institution that is unaccustomed to doing business with foreign persons and that has not sought out business of that type;

- A request by a Covered Person to associate any form of secrecy with a transaction, such as booking the transaction in the name of another person or a business entity whose beneficial owner is not disclosed or readily apparent;

- The routing of transactions involving a Covered Person into or through a secrecy jurisdiction or through jurisdictions or financial institutions that have inadequate customer identification practices and/or allow third parties to carry out transactions on behalf of others without identifying themselves to the institution;

- The routing of transactions involving a Covered Person through several jurisdictions and/or financial institutions prior to or following entry into an institution in the United States without any apparent purpose other than to disguise the nature, source, ownership or control of the funds;

- The use by a Covered Person of accounts at a nation's central bank or other government-owned bank, or of government accounts, as the source of funds in a transaction;

- The rapid increase or decrease in the funds or asset value in an account of a Covered Person that is not attributable to fluctuations in the market value of investment instruments held in the account;

- Frequent or excessive use of funds transfers or wire transfers either in or out of an account of a Covered Person;

- Wire transfers to or for the benefit of a Covered Person where the beneficial owner or originator information is not provided with the wire transfer, when inclusion of such information would be expected;

- Large currency or bearer instrument transactions either in or out of an account of a Covered Person;

- The deposit or withdrawal from a Covered Person's account of multiple monetary instruments just below the reporting threshold on or around the same day, particularly if the instruments are sequentially numbered;

- High-value deposits or withdrawals, particularly irregular ones, not commensurate with the type of account or what is known and documented regarding the legitimate wealth or business of the Covered Person;

- A pattern that after a deposit or wire transfer is received by a Covered Person's account, the funds are shortly thereafter wired in the same amount to another financial institution, especially if the transfer is to an account at an offshore financial institution or one in a "secrecy jurisdiction;"

- The frequent minimal balance or zeroing out of an account of a Covered Person for purposes other than maximising the value of the funds held in the account (e.g., by placing the funds in an overnight investment and having the funds then return to the account); and

- An inquiry by or on behalf of a Covered Person regarding exceptions to the reporting requirements of the Bank Secrecy Act (eg, Currency Transaction Reports and Suspicious Activity Reports) or other rules requiring the reporting of suspicious transactions.

E.   Sources of Information

In addition to a financial institution's existing information sources, several sources of information exist that may assist financial institutions in determining whether to conduct business with an individual who may be a Covered Person, and in determining whether such a Person may be engaging in transactions that may involve proceeds derived from official corruption. While there is no requirement to do so, a financial institution may wish to consult some or all of the following sources:

- The annual National Money Laundering Strategy issued jointly by the Department of the Treasury and the Department of Justice (www.treas.gov/press/releases/reports.htm);

- Advisories and other publications issued by the Financial Crimes Enforcement Network (FinCEN) of the Department of the Treasury (www.treas.gov/fincen);

- Evaluations of particular nations in the International Narcotics Control Strategy Report, prepared annually by the State Department (http://www.state.gov/www/global/narcotics_law/narcotics.html);

- The World Factbook published annually by the Central Intelligence Agency (www.cia.gov/cia/publications/factbook/index.html);

- The Department of State's annual Country Reports on Human Rights Practices (www.state.gov/www/global/human_rights/drl_reports.html);

- Reports issued by the General Accounting Office on international money laundering issues (www.gao.gov);

- Publications and other materials posted on web-sites of United States Government Departments and Agencies (www.firstgov.gov);

- Reports issued by Congressional Committees of hearings and investigations concerning international money laundering (www.house.gov; www.senate.gov);

- Reports of the Financial Action Task Force (FATF) on Money Laundering concerning countries and territories that are non-cooperative in the international effort to combat money laundering, as well as the FATF's annual reports and FATF's annual "Report on Money Laundering Typologies" (www.oecd.org/fatf);

- Reports on corruption and money laundering issued by International Financial Institutions (eg, the World Bank (www.worldbank.org), the International Monetary Fund (www.imf.org));

- Reports on crime and corruption prepared by various components of the United Nations and other multinational institutions and organisations, such as the Organisation for Economic Development and Cooperation (www.oecd.org), the Organisation of American States (www.oas.org), the Council of Europe (www.coe.fr), the G-7 and the G-8;

- Reports prepared by non-government organisations that identify corruption, fraud and abuse, such as the annual Corruption Perceptions Index of Transparency International (www.transparency.de);

- Information published on the World Wide Web by foreign countries; and

- Publicly available sources such as newspapers, magazines and other articles from information service providers available in hard-copy or from on-line services.

In addition to these published sources of information, if a financial institution is unsure whether an individual holds a position within the government of a particular country, it is encouraged to contact the United States Department of State at www.state.gov, which may be able to provide that information.

Copyright HMSO

Appendix 4

Know-Your-Customer

Appendix 4.1

Position Paper: Overriding Principles for a Revised Know-Your-Customer Framework

Guernsey Financial Services Commission

Isle of Man Financial Supervision Commission

Jersey Financial Services Commission

Status and overview of this paper

1. In December 2000, Commissions in the Bailiwicks of Guernsey and Jersey and in the Isle of Man ("Island Regulators")[1] issued a joint consultation paper entitled: Overriding principles for a revised know your customer framework ("the joint consultation paper"), addressing issues where recommendations were made in respect of the Islands' anti-money laundering regimes.

[1] Guernsey Financial Services Commission, Isle of Man Financial Supervision Commission, Jersey Financial Services Commission

2. Recommendations made largely concerned the account opening process and therefore the matters discussed in this Position Paper ("Paper") (and in the joint consultation paper) have highlighted verification of identity issues. This Paper does not address the important role of continuing account monitoring and ongoing due diligence over the life of a client relationship. The absence of discussion on such matters should not be read to mean that Island Regulators do not consider such matters to be important. On the contrary they are considered to be extremely important and will be subject to enhanced guidance when each Island's various Guidance Notes are amended. However such matters are not examined in detail in this Paper.

3. Having carefully considered the responses to the joint consultation paper, Island Regulators have reached the conclusions set out in this Paper. They now intend to start the process of drafting proposed amendments to anti-money laundering laws and Guidance Notes in each jurisdiction. In this respect, each jurisdiction will consult its industry further on the drafting of amendments to the Guidance Notes which will be required so as to implement the conclusions set out in this Paper.

4. For the avoidance of doubt, this Paper does not amend the Guidance Notes or "all crimes" anti-money laundering legislation nor should it be considered to be formal guidance issued by Island Regulators. However, Island Regulators expect financial services businesses ("FSBs")[2] to move towards implementing the changes to anti-money laundering practices detailed in this Paper. Island Regulators will address any difficulties in this process on a case-by-case basis. As noted above, detailed Guidance Notes will be drafted with the assistance of finance sector anti-money laundering steering groups.

[2] In the Channel Islands, financial services businesses (FSBs) are all persons subject to all crimes anti-money laundering legislation. In the Isle of Man this term refers to licence applicants and licence holders of the Commission.

5. The Isle of Man Insurance and Pensions Authority, although not party to the joint consultation paper, is fully supportive of the highest standards in the international fight against money laundering. In this respect it will be consulting independently with its market on proposals for further changes to its Guidance Notes.

Background

6. Island Regulators issued the joint consultation paper in response to: a) positive evaluations conducted in 1999 by the Offshore Group of Banking Supervisors (OGBS) and in 2000 by the Financial Action Task Force ("FATF") as part of its review of non-cooperative countries and territories; and b) a commitment to remove opportunities for arbitrage between the Crown Dependencies in areas related to financial crime and money laundering.

7. Approximately 60 responses were received in each jurisdiction. This included a response from the Isle of Man IPA which was not party to the original document, but which did circulate copies to life insurance licence holders in the Isle of Man for comment.

8. Briefly, the overriding principles proposed were:

(a)   a requirement to know and verify the identity of all customers and, if different, the principals behind those customers;

(b)   a requirement to hold copy documentary evidence used to verify identity of customers, and, where different, the principals behind those customers;

(c)   a restriction on those who might be relied upon to introduce business where an accepting person[3] is able to rely on verification of identity conducted by another person;

(d)   a common list of jurisdictions considered to have equivalent anti-money laundering legislation (*"equivalent jurisdictions"*[4]);

(e)   implementation of a "progressive programme" to verify the identity of current customers which were taken on before the introduction of all crimes anti-money laundering legislation in each jurisdiction; and

(f)   re-examination of the identification exemption for relationships opened using the "postal concession"[5]

[3] Accepting person refers to a person that has been requested to establish a relationship with an applicant for business. Person includes natural persons and any bodies of persons corporate or unincorporate.

[4] Italicised words used in this Paper are defined at appendix 1.

[5] In summary, products opened by post, telephone, or electronic transfer which do not offer third party transmission facilities (and which cannot be transferred to an account offering such transmission facilities), where funds originate from a specified institution.

9. Generally, the pan-Island approach was welcomed by respondents to the joint consultation paper, as was the proposal to produce a joint list of *equivalent jurisdictions*. A number of common concerns were also identified in consultation responses.

(a)   Many were critical of the "paper chase" that would result from the requirement to hold copy documentation for all customers (and principals where different) at each location offering products, and questioned the value of obtaining such documentation from other parties, particularly where it might now be out of date (eg passports).

(b)   Many thought that accepting persons should be entitled to continue to rely upon an undertaking to provide identification documentation on demand, on the basis that such undertakings would be provided only by regulated persons in *equivalent jurisdictions.* They also considered that receipt of identification documentation at the start of a business relationship placed an effective obligation on the accepting institution to re-verify identity, and evidenced mistrust of anti-money laundering procedures adopted in FATF countries and in the Crown Dependencies.

(c)   Many were also concerned that the Islands should not move ahead of anti-money laundering procedures in place in FATF countries (identifying an adverse economic impact in doing so). Reference was often made to Luxembourg, the Republic of Ireland, Switzerland and the United Kingdom ("UK").

(d)   The proposal to require accepting persons to verify the identity of principals of applicants for business[6] (including trust beneficiaries) and to hold copy documentation for such principals attracted some support but many practical and legal difficulties were highlighted, eg obtaining such information from "secrecy" jurisdictions (and in all probability any jurisdiction with confidentiality and data protection requirements), and constructive trust issues. Others questioned the value in verifying the identity of discretionary beneficiaries (particularly where they were members of the settlor's family).

(e)   A number thought that proposals in respect of "pooled" and client accounts would inevitably lead to their undesirable use as a means of circumventing the general requirement to hold copies of identification documentation.

(f)   Responses to the proposal for a "progressive programme" were polarised. A number of respondents remarked that they had already started a programme to verify the identity of customers pre-dating each jurisdiction's "all crimes" anti-money laundering legislation (indeed some had already completed such a process), but most opposed the proposal. Those opposing the proposal did so because:

    (i)   few other jurisdictions had applied identification requirements to accounts pre-dating anti-money laundering legislation (and some had introduced "grand-fathering" provisions to specifically exclude existing accounts from verification);

    (ii)   they believed that the absence of such documentation presented little risk to their business and would amount to no more than a "box-ticking" exercise;

    (iii)   difficulties were anticipated in dealing with long established customers, and those who were not prepared to provide the documentation requested;

    (iv)   they were uncertain as to the procedures to be followed where the identity of existing customers could not be verified; and

    (v)   they considered the cost and resourcing implications of the proposals to be unreasonable.

(g)   Those in the Channel Islands commenting on the re-examination of the "postal concession" were reluctant to remove the concession whilst it was still available in the UK and Republic of Ireland. Those in the Isle of Man highlighted the inequity of the concession's availability in the Channel Islands and UK, but not in the Isle of Man.

[6] A person or persons seeking to form a business relationship, or to carry out a one-off transaction, with a person who is carrying on any financial services business.

10. As discussed above, many respondents commented on the need to be able to compete on equal terms with other jurisdictions. As a result, Island Regulators have considered (and will continue to consider) the deliberations of the FATF, Basel Committee on Banking Supervision/OGBS Working Group on Cross-Border Banking ("the Cross Border Group"), the UK Joint Money Laundering Steering Group, the European Union's ("EU") revised anti-money laundering directive, and the IAIS anti-money laundering guidance notes for insurance supervisors and insurance entities, and believe that proposals set out in this Paper are broadly in line with international standards and discussions, whilst recognising that efforts will also be required in other jurisdictions if Island businesses are to be able to compete on equal terms.

The FATF is currently engaged in a review of its 40 Recommendations. It will issue options papers later in 2002 and expects to conclude its review in 2003. Island Regulators do not expect this review to fundamentally alter the customer identification principles set out in this Paper. Other matters arising from the

FATF's review will be taken into account in the drafting of amendments to anti-money laundering laws and Guidance Notes in each jurisdiction.

The requirements of the United States' USA PATRIOT Act of 2001 (eg the requirement that US banks be in a position to identify underlying customers of banks for which they act as correspondent) serve to emphasise the need for the Islands to continue to develop anti-money laundering systems that meet global requirements.

11. Since February 2001, Island Regulators have held a series of joint meetings to consider the above and to prepare a position paper reflecting current thinking.

Revised overriding principles

Headings in italic type below follow those used in the joint consultation paper.

12. Knowing client identity

In the joint consultation paper, respondents were asked to comment on:

(a)   the proposal that, in addition to being required to know the identity of all (underlying) customers, accepting persons should be in possession of a copy of identification documentation;

(b)   the proposal that certain persons described in the joint consultation paper should be considered to be the underlying principals for a number of common business relationships; and

(c)   what percentage should be considered to be appropriate for the de minimis provisions for companies.

13. Clarification was requested on the definition of identity of natural persons. In the case of natural persons, Island Regulators consider identity to comprise name (and any former names), residential address, date of birth, place of birth, and nationality. The essential elements of customer identification are currently under review by the Cross Border Group.

14. As a general principle, Island Regulators consider that the identity of an applicant for business and any underlying principals should be established and verified before a relationship is established, and certified copies (or originals for utility bills and the like) of all relevant documentation pertaining to identity should be held by an accepting person ("documentary evidence"). Some exceptions to this principle will be considered and addressed at the time that the Guidance Notes are updated, for example:

*   one-off transactions (where the amount of the transaction or series of linked transactions does not exceed an agreed monetary amount)[7]; and

*   policies of insurance with no surrender value (however, strict guidance will be required for cancelled policies where premiums are returned).

Exceptions to this general principle are under review at the current time by the FATF. Island Regulators will wish to ensure that applicants for business are not able to benefit from such exceptions where a relationship is intentionally structured so as to avoid identification requirements.

[7] The Guernsey Financial Services Commission discourages its registered insurance intermediaries from taking advantage of the exemption for small one-off transactions where such transactions involve single premium transactions for life policies.

15. Know your customer/ customer due diligence

Respondents to the joint consultation paper also requested clarification on requirements in relation to establishing source of wealth and source of funds. Island Regulators believe that an accepting person will wish to establish a profile for an applicant for business to enable it to satisfy its obligations under "all crimes" anti-money laundering legislation. This is commonly referred to as "know your customer" or "customer due diligence".

An accepting person should always understand why an applicant for business has requested a particular product or service, that person's expected activity, and the source of funds for the transaction in question. Where the type of product or service being offered makes it appropriate to do so, or where the product or service is not consistent with information held on the applicant, an accepting person should also establish the source of wealth of the person applying for the product or service. The information required to establish a profile, and the means by which it is obtained, will depend, inter alia, on product and applicant for business.

16. Who should be considered a principal?

As a general principle, Island Regulators consider that an accepting person should identify the beneficial owners of, those who have control of, and those with a beneficial interest in any relationship established (referred to in this Paper as "principals").

Where this Paper proposes a concession which limits application of this important principle, then an accepting person should always carefully assess whether an applicant for business has structured itself so as to avoid the identification of underlying principals. Where it considers that an intended relationship has been so structured, then it must not apply a concession.

Each concession will be available only in controlled circumstances.

Often, an accepting person will need to place reliance on another person to name the underlying principals behind a relationship, for example, the directors of a private company to name the shareholders of that company, and a trustee to name the settlor and beneficiaries for a trust. In considering whether or not to enter into a relationship, and as part of its ongoing assessment of that relationship, an accepting person should be satisfied that all principals have been named.

Notwithstanding the need to monitor activity on a relationship which falls outside a regular pattern, and the need to hold evidence of identity of principals, an accepting person is not expected to seek information (as a matter of course) to enable it to assess whether or not the recipient of a payment or transfer of assets has a right to it (unless it already has some legal requirement to do so).

17. Specifically, the following should be considered principals for the purposes of verifying identity:

(a) *Deposits placed by banks with other banks in a "fiduciary" capacity (most commonly with Swiss banks) and pooled client accounts opened by professional intermediaries*[8].

Professional intermediaries frequently hold funds on behalf of their clients in "client accounts" opened with other financial services businesses. Similarly banks (typically branches or subsidiaries of Swiss banks) receive deposits placed on a fiduciary basis held in pooled accounts. Where such accounts are held in general "omnibus" accounts, holding the funds of many clients, and where the intermediary (or, where a bank is placing a fiduciary deposit, the bank) is both regulated and operating in the Bailiwick of Guernsey, Isle of Man, Bailiwick of Jersey, or an *equivalent jurisdiction*, an accepting person is not required to look through this arrangement, ie it is not required to obtain documentary evidence of identity for the underlying clients, so long as it has assessed and is satisfied with the customer due diligence procedures in place at the professional intermediary (or bank). An accepting person may treat the professional intermediary (or bank) (i.e. the bank placing the deposit on a fiduciary basis) as the principal to be identified.

Pooled accounts must not be abused. The primary motive for the use of pooled accounts must not be for the circumvention of know your customer or customer verification disciplines. In addition, trust companies should ensure that any such use is compatible with relevant trust deeds, and applicable legislation and Codes of Practice.

Where a professional intermediary is not regulated, is not operating in the Bailiwick of Guernsey, Isle of Man, Bailiwick of Jersey or an *equivalent jurisdiction*, or is assessed as having inadequate due diligence procedures in place, then the accepting person is required to verify the identity of the underlying clients for whom the professional intermediary is acting.

(b) *Non-pooled client accounts opened by professional intermediaries*

When an accepting person has knowledge or reason to believe that a client account opened by a professional intermediary is on behalf of a single client (including a joint account), then that client is the principal to be identified. Where a client is not a natural person, then guidance set out in c) to l) below should also be followed.

(c)   *The establishment of a trust relationship by a trustee*

When establishing a trust relationship, the trustee should identify the settlor(s) (including any person settling assets into the trust), any protector(s)[9], and the beneficiary(ies) since they are to be regarded as principals. Beneficiaries should be identified as far as possible when defined. It is recognised that it may not be possible to identify the beneficiaries of trusts precisely at the outset. Practical issues are likely to arise from the identification of potential beneficiaries and these, together with the issue of the timing of the verification of identity, will be addressed following further consultation in the redrafting of the Guidance Notes.

No payments or transfers of assets may be made by the trustee to (or on behalf of) any beneficiary unless the identity of that beneficiary has been verified.

(d)   *Trustee as applicant for business*

When entering into a business relationship with a trustee, an accepting person should identify the trustee, the settlor(s) of the trust (including any person settling assets into the trust), any protector(s), and the beneficiary(ies) since they are to be regarded as principals.

Beneficiaries should be identified as far as possible when defined. It is recognised that it may not be possible to identify the beneficiaries of trusts precisely at the outset. Practical issues are likely to arise from the identification of potential beneficiaries and these, together with the issue of the timing of the verification of identity, will be addressed following further consultation in the redrafting of the Guidance Notes.

Verification of identity of beneficiaries should be carried out by an accepting person before any distribution from the property of the trust to (or on behalf of) any of the beneficiaries disclosed by the trustee[10]. No payments or transfers of assets may be made by the accepting person to (or on behalf of) any beneficiary disclosed by the trustee unless the identity of that beneficiary has been verified.

The verification of identity of other principals should be carried out at the time that the business relationship is established.

(e)   *Companies not listed on a recognised stock exchange*

The principal requirement for such companies is to look behind the corporate entity to identify the ultimate beneficial owners and those who have direct or indirect control over the business and the company's assets. What constitutes control for this purpose will depend on the nature of the company, and may rest in those who are mandated to manage funds, accounts or investments without requiring further authorisation, and who would be in a position to over-ride internal procedures and control mechanisms.

In accordance with the above, the company itself, beneficial owner(s) owning 10% or more of the company, and any other person with control over the company's assets (which will often include directors and account signatories) should be considered to be principals to be identified. Where the owner is another corporate entity or trust, the objective is to undertake reasonable measures to look behind that company or vehicle and verify the identity of the principals as set out in this Paper.

(f)   *Companies listed on a recognised stock exchange*

Where a company is listed on a recognised stock exchange or is a subsidiary of such a company ("recognised" to be defined in the Guidance Notes), then the company itself may be considered to be the principal to be identified. An accepting person should, however, consider whether there is effective control of a listed company by an individual or small group of individuals. If this is the case then those controllers should also be considered to be principals.

(g)   *Partnerships (including limited partnerships)*

Along with the partnership itself, those partners with a beneficial interest in the partnership of greater than 10%, and those persons exercising control or significant influence over the partnership's assets (such as the senior/managing partner and account signatories) should be treated as principals to be identified.

(h)   *Investment funds*

Where an open- or closed-ended investment company, unit trust, or limited partnership is an applicant for business, then, so long as the fund itself (or its manager, trustee, general partner, or administrator if responsible for the fund's customer due diligence) is regulated11, operates in the Bailiwick of Guernsey, Isle of Man, Bailiwick of Jersey, or from an *equivalent jurisdiction*[12], and the accepting person has assessed and is satisfied with the customer due diligence procedures in place, then the accepting person should consider the following to be principals:

- the fund itself;

- its directors or any controlling board where it is a company;

- its trustee where it is a unit trust;

- its managing (general) partner where it is a limited partnership; and

- any other person who has control over the relationship, eg fund administrator or manager.

Where a fund does not meet these particular criteria, then in addition to the above, investors (unit holders, shareholders, or limited partners) should also be considered to be principals in line with (d) above if a unit trust, (e) or (f) above if a company, and (g) if a limited partnership.

For managers, trustees, or general partners of an investment fund, the fund's principals should be considered to be the fund's investors (i.e. shareholders, unitholders or limited partners). Until such time as legislation is amended to provide managers, trustees, and general partners with the power to determine beneficial ownership of shares, units, or partnership interests (where this differs to legal ownership), managers, trustees, and general partners should exercise best efforts to do so.

In this context, exchange based trading for investment funds has grown recently and this has resulted in securities depositaries becoming increasingly significant. In these instances, fund investors' holdings may be registered in the nominee company of an exchange trading system, clearing house or securities depository. In general these systems provide mechanisms for supplying information on registered ownership, which may differ from beneficial ownership. As noted in the preceding paragraph, until such time as legislation is amended to provide managers, trustees, and general partners with the power to determine beneficial ownership of shares, units, or partnership interests (where this differs to legal ownership), managers, trustees, and general partners should exercise best efforts to do so.

(i) *Clubs, societies, charities, church bodies, associations, institutes and other similar bodies*

Along with the organisation itself (through its constitutional or other documents of organisation or establishment), principals should be considered to be those persons exercising control or significant influence over the organisation's assets. This will often include members of the governing body or committee plus executives and account signatories.

(j) *Central government and local authorities*

Along with the government or authority itself, principals should be considered to be those persons exercising control or significant influence over the organisation's assets.

(k) *Retirement benefit schemes*

Where an occupational pension scheme, employee benefit trust or share option plan is an applicant for business, then so long as the scheme itself (or its manager, trustee, or administrator if responsible for the scheme's customer due diligence) is regulated, operates in the Bailiwick of Guernsey, Isle of Man, Bailiwick of Jersey, or from an *equivalent jurisdiction*[13], and the accepting person has assessed and is satisfied with the customer due diligence procedures in place, then an accepting person should consider the "sponsoring" employer, the trustee, and any other person who has control over the relationship, eg administrator or scheme manager as principals to be identified.

Where a scheme does not meet these particular criteria, or where it is a private or personal pension scheme, a retirement annuity trust scheme, or a SSAS, then each scheme member should also be considered to be a principal.

For persons managing or acting as trustee to occupational schemes, eg group personal pension schemes, the "sponsoring" employer should be considered as the principal to be identified so long as the accepting person has assessed and is satisfied with the procedures in place at the "sponsoring employer" to ensure that only bona fide employees are permitted entry to the scheme. For non- occupational schemes, the manager or trustee should verify the identity of each member itself.

(l)   Mutuals, friendly societies, co-operatives and provident societies

Where these entities are the applicant for business then, along with the organisation itself (through its constitutional or other documents of organisation or establishment), principals should be considered to be those persons exercising control or significant influence over the organisation's assets. This will often include board members plus executives and account signatories.

[8] Including regulated lawyers, stockbrokers, and trust companies.

[9] Any person able to exercise significant influence over the trustee.

[10] It is the responsibility of the trustee to: (i) advise that payment is to an individual for which certified copy documentation is already held by the accepting person; or (ii) to provide such documentation at the time that a distribution is requested.

[11] Subject to prudential supervision by a regulatory authority discharging functions corresponding with those of Island Regulators. Prudential supervision involves monitoring the adequacy of management, financial resources, and internal systems and controls.

[12] Where an investment company is established under laws outside of the Bailiwick of Guernsey, Isle of Man, Bailiwick of Jersey, or an *equivalent jurisdiction*, then the fund may be considered to be operating in the jurisdiction in which its manager, trustee, or general partner is domiciled.

[13] Where a scheme is established under laws outside of the Bailiwick of Guernsey, Isle of Man, Bailiwick of Jersey, or an *equivalent jurisdiction*, then the scheme may be considered to be operating in the jurisdiction in which its manager or trustee is domiciled.

18. Reliable/eligible introductions

In the joint consultation paper, respondents were asked to comment on whether only regulated financial services businesses operating in *equivalent jurisdictions* and certain group companies should be relied upon to have verified the identity of an applicant for business and/or underlying principals, and on whether accepting persons should also hold copy identification documentation.

Interpretation of the term "reliable/eligible introductions" caused some confusion amongst respondents, since what is understood by the term varies between the three jurisdictions. Island Regulators consider that difficulties that have arisen from these differences are best addressed by:

- clarifying what is meant by an introduction;

- setting out who may be relied upon to have verified the identity of principals for business relationships (now to be known as an *acceptable or group introduce*r); and

- requiring an accepting person to obtain original or certified copies of all relevant documentary evidence for all applicants for business and under-lying principals.[14]

[14] Documents should always be obtained to avoid the possibility that they may not be available on request. For example, an acceptable introducer might no longer operate in the same jurisdiction as the accepting person, might no longer trade, or have destroyed evidence of identity on the basis that its relationship with the applicant for business has been terminated (and the time required to retain the documents under statutory record-keeping requirements has expired).

19. Introductions should be considered in their widest sense, covering both referred business and business where the applicant is acting other than on its own behalf (eg as agent, nominee, or trustee).

20. Who can be relied upon to have verified identity?

Island Regulators consider that it is acceptable to rely upon another party to have verified the identity of an applicant for business and/or principals only in certain controlled circumstances. Even in these circumstances, ultimate respon-sibility for obtaining satisfactory evidence of identity continues to rest with the accepting person. Reliance may be placed on:

(a)   an acceptable introducer; and

(b)   a group introducer.

Where an introducer is not an *acceptable or group introduce*r, then reliance cannot be placed on it to have verified identity. Such an introducer may act only as a *suitable certifier* (where it meets the required criteria) or as a conduit for the passing of relevant documentary evidence, which itself must have been certified as a true copy of an original document by a *suitable certifie*r. In such cases the document used by the applicant for business to evidence identity must always be current at the time of making the application.

21. What is relevant documentary evidence?

Where reliance has been placed on an *acceptable or group introducer* to have verified the identity of an applicant for business (or underlying principals), that party may provide either:

(a)   a copy of documentary evidence held on its file which it had used (historically) to verify the identity of its applicant for business or underly-ing principals. This may have been obtained some time previously and might now have expired (but was current at the time that identity was verified). Such a copy document may be accepted as long as no aspect of the client's identity on that verification document has changed in any way and is still correct and applicable; or

(b)   originals or copies of documents obtained specifically in relation to that particular application for business.

All copy documentary evidence passed to the accepting person should be certified by the *acceptable or group introducer* as being a true copy of either an original or copy document held on its file.

Copy documentary evidence may be provided and/or stored on an electronic medium so long as it is always immediately available on that medium to the accepting person. Where evidence is held on a central group server, then it need not be certified as being a true copy of either an original or copy document held.

22. Where an accepting person is not satisfied that documentary evidence provided to it meets the requirements of "all crimes" anti-money laundering legislation (and guidance issued thereunder), then it should itself verify the identity of the applicant for business or underlying principals. Where documentation provided by an *acceptable or group introducer* is in line with requirements in the accepting person's jurisdiction but where the accepting person's standards exceed these requirements, an accepting person may still wish to verify identity itself. This will be a matter of judgement for the accepting person.

23. Equivalent jurisdictions

In the joint consultation paper, respondents were asked to comment on the proposed method for selecting jurisdictions deemed to host regulated persons operating under equivalent "all crimes" anti-money laundering legislation[15]. Whilst operating within agreed parameters, earlier proposals envisaged allowing each jurisdiction to draw up its own list of *equivalent jurisdictions*. As a result of responses to the joint consultation paper however, Island Regulators have agreed instead to a harmonised list of *equivalent jurisdictions* initially drawn from FATF or EU membership.

[15] The joint consultation paper proposed that this selection should be restricted to FATF Members, jurisdictions covered by the EU's anti-money laundering directive, and the Crown Dependencies.

24. Thus, Guernsey has reinstated Gibraltar to its list of *quivalent/jurisdictions* in Appendix C to the Guidance Notes. The Isle of Man Financial Supervision Commission has recognised Canada and Japan and removed Turkey from its list of jurisdictions in Appendix D of the Guidance Notes. Jersey has removed Turkey from its list in Appendix D to the Guidance Notes.

25. No Commission is prepared, at this time, to recognise the equivalence of Argentina, Aruba, Austria, Brazil, Mexico, or the Netherlands Antilles (all of which are FATF members or included within the membership of a FATF member).

26. *Business relationships existing at the date of the introduction of "all crimes" legislation*

In the joint consultation paper, respondents were asked to comment on proposals for a programme to review customer files pre-dating "all crimes" anti-money laundering legislation.

27. Why establish such a programme?

As discussed above, many respondents to the joint consultation paper considered that proposals to review relationships in existence at the time of the introduction of "all crimes" anti-money laundering legislation were of limited value in the fight against economic crime. Island Regulators believe, however, that there are a number of compelling reasons for establishing such a programme:

(a) Knowing and verifying the identity of applicants for business or, where different, principals is an essential part of any effective know your customer regime, and assists in identifying and managing risk, avoiding breaches of United Nations and other sanctions, in reporting suspicious transactions, and in identifying any potential links with terrorist funding.

(b) The Islands were criticised by OGBS and FATF in separate reports for failing to have measures in place to verify identity of all customers, irrespective of the date of the commencement of the business relationship.

(c) Since these reports, FATF has again stated that failure to verify identity of all clients does provide potential for established accounts to be misused.

(d) Identification is a vital part of the audit trail for law enforcement when conducting investigations, which can falter because the identity of an applicant was not verified previously.

28. Basis for the programme

Having taken account of comments received on the joint consultation paper, Island Regulators consider that all FSBs should undertake a "progressive programme". The programme should focus primarily on the extent of evidence of customer identity already held for relationships pre-dating "all crimes" anti-money laundering legislation, and whether that documentary evidence is sufficient to satisfactorily verify the identity of that customer (and underlying principals as defined in this Paper). Where evidence of identity held is deemed to be deficient by an FSB, then it should take steps to obtain documentary evidence sufficient to verify identity.

The programme should also be extended to include not only those relationships in existence at the time of the introduction of "all crimes" anti-money laundering legislation but also those relationships established after the introduction of "all crimes" anti-money laundering legislation, where the identity of underlying principals (as previously defined in this Paper) is not held on file (or has not been verified).

29. The programme should be based on risk prioritisation, and all higher risk relationships for which a deficiency in verification documentation exists should be addressed and completed as a matter of priority[16].

[16] Appendix 2 provides guidance on determining the risk profile of customers.

30. Other relationships should be reviewed for any deficiency in verification documentation following the occurrence of a "trigger" event[17]. This should run concurrently with a review of higher risk relationships. If the FATF introduce a deadline by which time a full progressive review should be achieved in its member states, then Island Regulators will implement FATF's requirements.

[17] Appendix 2 provides guidance on what might be appropriate trigger events. Events occurring within two years of the establishment of a relationship need not be considered to be "trigger events".

31. In carrying out the programme, FSBs may also identify gaps in their customer due diligence/know your customer information. Where this occurs, FSBs should take steps to obtain further information as considered appropriate to ensure that records remain up to date and relevant.

32. Scope of programme

The following relationships may be excluded from the scope of the progressive programme:

(a)   small exempted one-off transactions as defined in the relevant law of each jurisdiction;

(b)   FSBs falling within the following definitions where the FSB is the customer itself and acting on its own behalf with no underlying principal:

    (i)   Guernsey: a person regulated by the Commission or who has applied for a licence under the Regulation of Fiduciaries, Administration Businesses and Company Directors, etc (Bailiwick of Guernsey) Law, 2000 or is an authorised FSB subject to anti-money laundering measures in an equivalent jurisdiction;

    (ii)   Isle of Man: where the FSB is regulated by the Commission and is a person in Appendix M(b) or where the FSB is an insurance company authorised under the Insurance Act 1986; or

    (iii)   Jersey: a regulated FSB which is bound by the Money Laundering (Jersey) Order 1999 or is in an equivalent jurisdiction;

(c) relationships properly established on the basis of any "postal concession" available in the three jurisdictions under legislation or Guidance Notes issued by Commissions at that time; and

(d) all insurance policies where there is no surrender value.

33. Where an FSB has previously relied upon another person to have verified identity for introductions then it should re-verify identity itself, except where that person is an *acceptable or group introducer*, where it should obtain suitably certified copy documentation from that third party (or suitably certified documents directly from its customer where this is not possible).

34. Verification of address for the purposes of the progressive programme

FSBs should be satisfied that the address they hold is the current residential address of the applicant for business. Any subsequent notification of a change of address is deemed acceptable if it is supported by a written confirmation from the applicant for business where the applicant for business's signature on that letter can be verified. In any event monies or assets should not be paid to the applicant for business without the current address being independently verified by one of the methods set out in appendix 3 or in paragraph 35.

35. Where an FSB has sent regular correspondence to the address that they hold for a customer and has reasonable grounds for supposing that it has been received (eg mail has not been returned "gone away" or "return to sender"), then an FSB may consider that this provides a suitable basis for verification of a customer's address.

36. Where historical correspondence is relied upon to provide a suitable basis for verification, "care of" addresses,"hold all mail", and any obvious or suspected non-residential addresses are not acceptable.

37. Verification of identity (except address) for the purposes of the progressive programme

Where it is necessary to verify the identity of a customer (excluding address), this should be done in accordance with the existing Guidance Notes.

38. Inability to verify identity

It is recognised that FSBs may, in some circumstances, be unable to obtain satisfactory documentary evidence of identity, despite several attempts and having exercised best efforts. FSBs are expected to ascertain as far as possible why they are having difficulty in obtaining this information. Solutions should be sought to remove any obstacles identified.

39. Where there is evidence of deliberate obstruction or a lack of co-operation by a customer or, where different, the underlying principal, FSBs should request an explanation from the customer or underlying principal. Where a customer's behaviour or explanation for failing to provide documentation leads an FSB to

form a suspicion that the motive for the customer's refusal to co-operate is that he is dealing with the proceeds of crime or financing terrorism, an FSB should make a disclosure to law enforcement as usual. Where there is no suspicion, an FSB may still wish to reassess its business relationship, terminating it if appropriate. If such a relationship is continued then Island Regulators consider that it should be subject to enhanced monitoring of transactions.

40. In cases where there is no evidence of deliberate obstruction/non-co-operation by the customer or, where different, the underlying principal, but an FSB has been unable to satisfactorily verify identity, Island Regulators consider that all such relationships should also be subject to enhanced monitoring of transactions.

41. Supervisory overview

When undertaking a "progressive programme", FSBs will not be routinely required to submit any initial risk assessment or project plan to their regulator, but should be ready to do so if requested (eg at the time of a compliance or on-site visit).

42. Progress with the "progressive programme" will be considered as part of regular supervisory visits to FSBs.

43. Exemptions for certain postal, telephonic and electronic business

In the joint consultation paper, comment was invited on whether FSBs should continue to benefit from exemptions for certain postal, telephonic and elec-tronic business in the Channel Islands and in the Isle of Man in respect of insurance business, and whether the exemption should be available in the Isle of Man in respect of non-insurance business.

44. This class of business relationship is set out in:

(a)   Paragraphs 54 to 56 of the Guernsey Guidance Notes;

(b)   Section 3.07 of the Isle of Man Guidance Notes; or

(c)   Sections 4.86 – 4.90, 5.93 – 5.101, 6.59 – 6.64 and 7.52 – 7.60 of the Jersey Guidance Notes.

45. Channel Islands' regulators will consider what the UK and Republic of Ireland have done about their equivalent concessions before removing the concession. In the UK, HM Treasury has announced its intention to review the application of Regulation 8 (postal concession) when the 2nd Money Launder-ing Directive is implemented in that jurisdiction.

46. The Isle of Man Financial Supervision Commission has resolved that there will be no "postal concession" for non-insurance business.

Appendix 1 – glossary of terms

Equivalent jurisdiction   An Appendix C jurisdiction in the Bailiwick of Guernsey, an Appendix D jurisdiction in the Isle of Man, and an Appendix D jurisdiction in the Bailiwick of Jersey.

Group introducer   A group introducer refers business to an accepting person, or acts as an agent, nominee, or trustee. It is part of the same group as the accepting person, and is subject to consolidated supervision by a regulator in the Bailiwick of Guernsey, Isle of Man, Bailiwick of Jersey or an *equivalent jurisdiction*.

Acceptable introducer   An acceptable introducer refers business to an accepting person, or acts as an agent, nominee, or trustee. It operates in the Bailiwick of Guernsey, Isle of Man, Bailiwick of Jersey or an *equivalent jurisdiction*, is regulated, and will have been assessed by an accepting person as having satisfactory customer due diligence procedures in place. It certifies that the documentary evidence provided to an accepting person is a true copy of either an original or copy document held on its file.

Suitable certifier   A suitable certifier will be:

- an embassy, consulate or high commission of the country of issue of documentary evidence of identity;

- a member of the judiciary, a senior civil servant, or a serving police or customs officer;

- a lawyer or notary public;

- an actuary;

- an accountant holding a recognised professional qualification; or

- a director, officer, or manager of a regulated financial services business operating in an *equivalent jurisdiction.*

A suitable certifier will certify that he or she has seen original documentation, and that the copy document provided (which he or she certifies) is a complete and accurate copy of that original. The certifier will also sign and date the copy document, printing his or her name clearly in capitals underneath and indicate his or her position or capacity.

Appendix 2– risk profiling and trigger events.

Risk profiling (paragraph 29)

Each FSB will be best placed to decide the risk profile of its own customer base. However, the following risk criteria (which are not set out in any particular order of importance nor should they be considered exhaustive), should be considered in isolation or in combination:

(a)   turnover;

(b)   geographical origin of customer;

(c)   geographical sphere of customer's activities;

(d)   nature of activity (eg whether trading or identified as "sensitive" by an Island regulator);

(e)   frequency of activity;

(f)   type and complexity of account/business relationship;

(g)   value of account/ business relationship;

(h)   customer type, eg potentates/politically exposed persons;

(i)   whether hold mail arrangements are in place;

(j)   whether an account/business relationship is dormant;

(k)   whether there is any form of delegated authority in place (eg power of attorney, "mixed" boards, and representative offices);

(l)   company issuing bearer shares;

(m)   cash withdrawals/placement activity in or outside the jurisdiction; and

(n)   suspicion or knowledge of money laundering or other crime.

Trigger events (paragraph 30)

Occurrences that might be considered to be trigger events include:

(a)   a significant transaction (relative to a relationship);

(b)   a material change in the operation of a business relationship;

(c)   a transaction which is out of keeping with previous activity;

(d)   a new product or account being established within an existing relationship;

(e)   a change in an existing relationship which increases a risk profile (as above);

(f)   the early redemption of a fixed term investment or insurance product;

(g)   the assignment or transfer of ownership of any product;

(h)   a non-regular "top-up" of an existing insurance product;

(i)   the addition of or a change to a principal in any relationship;

(j)   the roll-over of any fixed term product (taking into account the length of the roll-over period); and

(k)   an insurance claim.

The above should not be considered an exhaustive list.

Appendix 3– verification of address

FSBs regulated by the Isle of Man Financial Supervision Commission can follow existing guidance on address verification (Section 3.02(c) of the Isle of Man Financial Supervision Commission's Guidance Notes). In Guernsey and Jersey, FSBs should consider:

(a)   checking a register of electors;

(b)   making a credit reference agency search;

(c)   checking a local telephone directory;

(d)   requesting sight of a recent rates, property tax or utility bill. Care must be taken that the document is an original and not a copy;

(e)   an account statement from a recognised bank or recognised bank credit card. The statement should be the most recent available and an original, not a copy. Statements featuring a "care of" or accommodation address are not acceptable. Non-bank cards, such as store cards, are not acceptable;

(f)   using one of the address validation/verification services on offer;

(g)   making a record of a personal visit to the home of an applicant for business; or

(h)   obtaining the most recent original mortgage statement from a recognised lender.

Appendix 4.2

Money Laundering Regulations – Identification Procedures

Individuals

Current valid full passport/National Identity Card

Full driving licence

Pension book/child benefit book

HM Forces ID Card

Young persons NI card (under 18 only)

Pensioner's travel pass

Bank/building society passbook

Bank or recognised credit or debit card

Credit reference agency search

Gas, electricity, telephone bill

Mortgage statement

Council tax demand, Inland Revenue coding

Bank/building Society/credit card statement

Young persons medical card (under 18 only)

Home visit to applicants address*

Check of local telephone directory*

Check of voter's roll

Tenancy agreement

Council/housing association rent book

TV/vehicle licence reminder

*Suitable for proof of address only

Corporate Customers

Registered number/address

Obtain a certified copy of the Certificate of Incorporation or the Certificate to Trade

Carry out a company search

Ask for latest reports and accounts (audited where applicable)

Ask for brochures and other publicity material

If appropriate, take steps to verify the identity of one or more of the Directors and the major shareholders

Evidence that any individual representing the company has the necessary authority to do so

Identify those persons who ultimately own and control the company

Make a credit reference agency search or take a bankers reference

(The above are also applicable to proprietors of an unincorprated business.)

Appendix 4.3

Verification of Address

FSBs regulated by the Isle of Man Financial Supervision Commission can follow existing guidance on address verification (Section 3.02(c) of the Isle of Man Financial Supervision Commission's Guidance Notes). In Guernsey and Jersey, FSBs should consider:

(a) checking a register of electors;

(b) making a credit reference agency search;

(c) checking a local telephone directory;

(d) requesting sight of a recent rates, property tax or utility bill. Care must be taken that the document is an original and not a copy;

(e) an account statement from a recognised bank or recognised bank credit card. The statement should be the most recent available and an original, not a copy. Statements featuring a "care of" or accommodation address are not acceptable. Non-bank cards, such as store cards, are not acceptable;

(f) using one of the address validation/verification services on offer;

(g) making a record of a personal visit to the home of an applicant for business; or

(h) obtaining the most recent original mortgage statement from a recognised lender.

Appendix 4.4

Client Identification Checklist – in accordance with Money Laundering Regulations and the JMLSG Guidance Notes

Type of Customer	Documents Required

Private Limited Companies
Guidance
For a complex corporate structure where there are intermediate companies, the same information is needed for all companies through to the beneficial owner.
Where an incorporated company acts as the Company Secretary, then please provide their authorised signatory list and verification of identity* of all those individuals.
Personal identity and address must be separately evidenced (ie if a current UK photo-card driving licence is provided as a personal identity document, the another form of documentary evidence must be provided as evidence of the individual's address).
For non-UK resident individuals, a separate proof of identity and address is also required. All documents should be the country's equivalent of the requested UK documents.
PO box addresses cannot be accepted.
	1) list of director(s); beneficial owner(s); and shareholder(s);
	
	2) verification of identity* of the beneficial owner(s) of the company;
	
	3) verification of identity* of any other person with principal control over the company's assets: including the Finance director and the Managing Director;
	
	4) verification of identity* of all signatories to the account; and
	
	5) verification of identity of all shareholders:
	
	  – in case of a private person as a shareholder: verification of identity
	
	  – in case of a legal person as a shareholder:
	
	    ● certified copy of the company's registration certificate;
	    ● list of all shareholders and verification of identity*;
	    ● list of directors;
	    ● list of any other person with principal control over the company's assets and verification of identity*
	
	Where shareholding is Bearer, confirmation that these individuals do not have principal control over the company.
	
	Verification of identity comprises two separate documents, one from each of the following (ie, one personal identity document and one documentary evidence of address:
	
	— **Personal identity documents**
	
	Current signed passport.
	
	Residence permit issued by the Home Office to EU nationals on the sight of own country passport.
	
	Current UK photo-card driving licence.
	
	Current full UK driving licence (old version).
	
	Inland Revenue tax notification.
	
	Firearms certificate.
	
	— **Documentary evidence of address**
	
	Recent utility bill (not mobile).
	
	Local authority tax bill (current year).
	
	Current UK photo-card driving licence (if not used for category above).
	
	Current full UK driving licence (old version).
	
	Bank, building society or credit union statement or passbook containing current address.
	
	Most recent mortgage statement form a recognised lender.
	
	Local council rent card or tenancy agreement.

The Guidance Notes state that all copies of documentation must be certified as a 'True Copy and Original seen'. Only certain individuals can certify copies ie, the Company Secretary, the company's lawyers, accountants or a notary.

Type of Customer	Documents Required
UK Trusts, Offshore Trusts Nominees and Fiduciaries Guidance it is imperative to provide the verification of the identity of the provider of funds ie, the settlor, the controller of funds ie, the trustees, and any controllers who have the power to remove trustees. If a protector has been appointed to take over the control of the trust from the trustees he must be identified.	1) name of the provider of funds ie, the settlor; 2) name of the controllers of the funds ie, trustees and any controllers who have power to remove the trustee or any underlying principals; 3) name of the beneficiary/ies, and verification of identity; 4) name of the protector if one exists, and verification of identity; 5) certified copy of the trust deed; 6) written confirmation by the trustees that there are no anonymous principals; 7) establishment of the nature of trust and source of funds.
	Verification of identity (see previous table) is required for 1–4 above.

Type of Institution/Customer	Documents or Checks Required
UK Resident Private Individuals (authorised to place deposits only) Guidance The verification of identity and address must be separately checked (ie, if a current UK photo-card driving licence is accepted as a personal identity document, then another form of evidence must be obtained for the individual's address). You must have sight of the original document and must sign the copy documents to certify that you have seen the originals. If sight of the originals is not possible, then the Company Secretary or a notary must certify a copy of the original a true copy. For Non-UK resident individuals, a separate proof of identity and address is required as above. The documents used for identity must be authenticated by you or by another employee who can read that language. PO box addresses cannot be accepted.	**Documentary evidence – personal identity documents** Current signed passport. residence permit issued by the Home Office to EU nationals on sight of own country passport. Current UK photo-card driving licence. Current full UK driving licence (old style provisional licences are not acceptable). Inland revenue tax notification. Documentary evidence of address. Record of home visit. Search from an electoral register. Recent utility bill (not mobile telephone bill). Local authority tax bill (current year). Current UK photo-card driving licence. Current full UK driving licence (old style provisional licences are not acceptable)-if not used for verifying identity. Bank, building society or credit union statement or passbook containing current address. Most recent mortgage statement from recognised lender. Local council rent card or tenancy agreement.

Type of Institution/Customer	Documentation/Checks Required
Non-UK Resident Private Individuals	**Documentary evidence – personal identity documents**
Guidance	Current signed passport
Wherever possible sight of an original document must be noted, and a photocopy taken. Copies of documents provided must be certified as true copies of the original.	National identity card
Extra care must be taken in respect of applications for business from jurisdictions that are not recognised as having equivalent anti-money laundering legislation.	Other comparable document showing the individual's nationality, date of birth and date and place of issue
	Documentary evidence of address
	Documents similar to those listed for UK resident individuals are acceptable. Additional comfort can be obtained by receiving confirmation from a bank or other credit institution where there is an existing relationship.
	Confirmation from an accountant or a lawyer

Appendix 5

Report Forms

Appendix 5.1

Internal Report to Money Laundering Report Officer

Client name _____ **Reference** _____	
Report by _____	
Individual/Legal Entity Details: Eg full name, address, business details (eg Company number, tax reference, VAT registration number)	
Details of Transaction:	
Reason for Disclosure:	
Signed _____ **Date** _____	
For use by MLRO only **Report received (Date)** _____ **Report sent to NCIS (Date)** _____ **Our Ref** _____ **NCIS Ref** _____	
Reason(s) NCIS not notified (if applicable):	
Signed _____ **Date** _____	

Appendix 5.2

NCIS Disclosure Reports

Standard disclosure report form

NCIS
NATIONAL CRIMINAL INTELLIGENCE SERVICE

PO Box 8000
London
SE11 5EN
Tel: 020 7238 8282
Fax: 020 7238 8286

SOURCE REGISTRATION DOCUMENT

IMPORTANT - THE DETAILS IN THIS FORM MUST BE PROVIDED WITH YOUR FIRST DISCLOSURE TO NCIS OR FOLLOWING ANY SUBSEQUENT CHANGE TO THOSE DETAILS.

Institution Name:

Institution Type:

Regulator:

Regulator ID:

Contact Details (1): Forename:

Surname:

Position:

Address:

Telephone Details:

Facsimile Details:

E-mail Address:

Contact Details (2): Forename:
(where applicable)

Surname:

Position:

Address:

Telephone Details:

Facsimile Details:

E-mail Address:

Version 1 Febuary 23rd 2004 Appendix 2

NCIS
NATIONAL CRIMINAL INTELLIGENCE SERVICE

PO Box 8000
London
SE11 5EN
Tel: 020 7238 8282
Fax: 020 7238 8286/3441

DISCLOSURE REPORT DETAILS: STANDARD REPORT:

Reporting Institution:

Your Ref:

Disclosure Reason:

PoCA 2002: ○   Terrorism Act 2000: ○

Branch/ Office:

Consent Required: ☐

Disclosure Date: [ ] - [ ] - [ ]   Type: New ○   OR Update ○

D D   M M M   Y Y Y Y

Existing Disclosure ID/s: (where applicable)

Please use whichever sheets you feel are necessary and indicate below how many of each you are submitting.

REPORT SUMMARY:

Number of 'Subject Details' sheet appended relating to a Main Subject: [ ]

Number of 'Additional Details' sheets appended relating to Main Subject: [ ]

Number of 'Subjects Details' sheets appended relating to Associated Subject/s: [ ]

Number of 'Additional Details' sheets' appended relating to Associated Subject/s: [ ]

Number of 'Transaction Detail' sheet/s appended: [ ]

Number of 'Reason For Disclosure Sheets' appended: [ ]

Once completed please collate your sheets in the above mentioned order and then sequentially number your sheets at the bottom of each page. This will ensure that the information is processed in the correct sequence.

Total number of pages submitted including this Header: [ ]

Page 1 of [ ]

Appendix 5: Report forms

■ **SUBJECT DETAILS:**   Version 1 Febuary 23rd 2004 Appendix 3   ■

Subject Type: Main Subject: ○   **OR**   Associated Subject: ○ (number ☐ of ☐)

Individual's Details:

Subject Status: Suspect : ○   **OR**   Victim: ○

Surname:

Forename 1:

Forename 2:

Occupation:

DoB: ☐ - ☐ - ☐   **Gender:** Male ○   Female ○
      D D   M M M   Y Y Y Y

Title: Mr ○   Mrs ○   Miss ○   Ms ○   Other

Reason for Association of this subject to the Main Subject (for use only with Associated Subject details)

OR

Legal Entity's Details

Subject Status: Suspect : ○   **OR**   Victim: ○

Legal Entity Name:

Legal Entity No: **VAT No:**

Country of Reg:

Type of Business:

Reason for Association of this subject to the Main Subject (for use only with Associated Subject details)

Page ☐ of ☐

306

■   <u>ADDITIONAL DETAILS:</u>   Version 1 Febuary 23rd 2004 Appendix 4   ■

Do these details refer to the Main Subject: ◯   OR   to an Associated Subject ◯

(Please indicate the Associate's number where applicable)

Subject Name:

Premise No/Name: Current: ☐   Type:

Street:

City/Town:

County: Post Code:

Country:

Premise No/Name: Current: ☐   Type:

Street:

City/Town:

County: Post Code:

Country:

Premise No/Name: Current: ☐   Type:

Street:

City/Town:

County: Post Code:

Country:

Information Type: **Unique Information Identifier:**

Extra Information / Description

Information Type: **Unique Information Identifier:**

Extra Information / Description

■   Page ☐ of ☐   ■

307

Appendix 5: Report forms

■ **TRANSACTION DETAILS: (Complete if applicable)** ■

MAIN SUBJECT ACCOUNT SUMMARY   Version 1 Febuary 23rd 2004 Appendix 5

Institution Name:

Account Name:

Sort Code: Account No /Identifier:

Business Relationship Commenced: (DD-MMM-YYYY)   Acct Bal:

Business Relationship Finished: (DD-MMM-YYYY)   Bal Date: (DD-MMM-YYYY)

Turnover Period: Credit Turnover:

            Debit Turnover:

TRANSACTION/S

Activity Type: Activity Date: (DD-MMM-YYYY)

Amount: Currency: Credit: ○ or Debit: ○

Other party name: Account No/ Identifier:

Institution Name or Sort Code:

Activity Type: Activity Date: (DD-MMM-YYYY)

Amount: Currency: Credit: ○ or Debit: ○

Other party name: Account No/ Identifier:

Institution Name or Sort Code:

Activity Type: Activity Date: (DD-MMM-YYYY)

Amount: Currency: Credit: ○ or Debit: ○

Other party name: Account No/ Identifier:

Institution Name or Sort Code:

Activity Type: Activity Date: (DD-MMM-YYYY)

Amount: Currency: Credit: ○ or Debit: ○

Other party name: Account No/ Identifier:

Institution Name or Sort Code:

Page ☐ of ☐

308

■   **REASON FOR DISCLOSURE:**   Version 1 Febuary 23rd 2004 Appendix 6   ■

Main Subject Name:
(cross reference purposes)

Report Activity Assessment
(Please use only where you know or suspect what the offence behind the reported activity may be)

Drugs: ☐   Missing Trader, Inter Community (VAT) ☐   Immigration: ☐   Tobacco/Alcohol Excise Fraud: ☐
                     Fraud

Personal Tax Fraud: ☐   Corporate Tax Fraud: ☐   Other Offences:

Reason for Disclosure:

■   Page ☐ of ☐   ■

Limited intelligence value report form

NCIS
NATIONAL CRIMINAL INTELLIGENCE SERVICE

PO Box 8000
London
SE11 5EN
Tel: 020 7238 8282
Fax: 020 7238 8286/3441

PROCEEDS OF CRIME ACT 2002 - LIMITED INTELLIGENCE VALUE REPORT

Reporting Institution

Your Ref:

Branch/ Office:

Disclosure Date:

[ ] - [ ] - [ ]

D D - M M M - Y Y Y Y

SUBJECT DETAILS:

Individual's Details: Main Subject Status: Suspect : ○   OR   Victim: ○

Surname:

Forename:

DoB: [ ] - [ ] - [ ]   Gender: Male ○   Female ○

D D   M M M   Y Y Y Y

Title: Mr ○   Mrs ○   Miss ○   Ms ○   Other [ ]

Legal Entity Details:

Legal Entity Name:

Legal entity No: [ ]   VAT No: [ ]

REASON FOR DISCLOSURE:

Appendix 6

P v P Case Report

This case was heard in the Family Division of the High Court of Justice before Dame Elizabeth Butler-Sloss, P. The hearing dates of the case were 15 – 17 July 2003.

The neutral citation for the case is listed as EWHC Fain 2260.

The parties involved were represented by the following people:

1.   Applicant – Mr Nicholas Mostyn QC and Mr Christopher Pocock (instructed by Manches).

2.   Respondent – Miss Florence Baron QC and Miss Deborah Bangay (instructed by Mishcon De Reya).

3.   National Criminal Intelligence Service – Mr Andrew Mitchell QC.

4.   Inland Revenue – Mr Andrew Tidbury and Mr Kennedy Talbot.

5.   Law Society – Mr Nicholas Elliott QC.

6.   Bar Council – Mr Phillip Moor QC appeared for the Bar Council

Approved Judgment

I direct that pursuant to CPR PD 39A para 6.1 no official shorthand note shall be taken of this Judgment and that copies of this version as handed down may be treated as authentic – *Dame Elizabeth Butler-Sloss.*

This judgment is being handed down in private on 8 October 2003 It consists of 24 pages and has been signed and dated by the judge. The judge hereby gives leave for it to be reported.

Dame Elizabeth Butler-Sloss:

1.   An application was made to me on the 15 July 2003 by Mr Mostyn QC, on behalf of the wife to seek the ruling of the court as to the effect of the Proceeds of Crime Act 2002 ('PoCA') on his client's application for ancillary relief in divorce proceedings. Counsel and solicitors acting for the wife sought urgent directions from the court in respect of their obligations under the PoCA. Exceptionally they did so without giving notice to the respondent (the husband), his solicitors or counsel. The

genesis of these extraordinary events is apparent from the history of the wife's correspondence with the National Criminal Intelligence Service (NCIS) to which I shall refer later.

The family background

2. The husband and wife were married in April 1979. He s now 50 years old, and she is 52 years old. In January 2002, the wife filed her divorce petition, This court has not been asked to make any findings as to the parties' assets, but it is suggested by the wife that they are substantial and may exceed £19 million. The wife made her application for financial relief, and a Financial Dispute Resolution appointment was listed for July 18 2003 before a High Court judge.

3. The accountants' forensic reports were first made available in October 2002. The husband's accountant's reply to the wife's additional questions was supplied on the 2 May 2003. It was not until a conference was held with leading and junior counsel for the wife on the 16 June that the wife's legal advisers became sufficiently concerned about the husband's financial position to consider that issues under Part 7 of the PoCA might arise. In particular, her legal team was concerned about the possibility of committing an offence under section 328 of the Act. Based on the financial information they had seen and the advice of their forensic accountant, the wife and her legal team became suspicious that part of the matrimonial assets might be 'criminal property' within the meaning of the Act. The wife's solicitors and counsel were worried that, in acting for the wife in the litigation and/or settlement of a financial dispute, they might fall foul of the section 328 prohibition and might become concerned in an arrangement which might facilitate 'the acquisition, retention, use or control of criminal property' by the wife. Accordingly, they sought to protect themselves and their client by invoking the protection offered by section 328(2)(a) and on 18 June 2003 the wife's solicitors wrote to the NCIS making disclosure of the following information:

    (a) that the wife and the husband were involved in ancillary relief proceedings listed for trial in December 2003;

    (b) certain identifying information about the husband's business interests;

    (c) that the wife and her solicitors had suspicions that the assets might comprise criminal property;

    (d) that the wife would be seeking a substantial sum from the husband in the ancillary relief proceedings; and

    (e) that the disclosure was being made on behalf of the wife, her solicitors and counsel.

4. The solicitors' letter stated that an answer would be expected within 7 days as to whether the solicitors 'should continue to take steps in the proceedings'. Further, the letter sought advice as to whether in light of the

'tipping-off' rules, the letter could be disclosed to the husband's solicitors. The NCIS did not respond in writing to that letter. A number of telephone calls were made by the wife's solicitors to the duty officer at NCIS, whose advice (which NCIS now accepts was misleading) was that the decision to continue to act was purely a 'business decision' for the solicitors. The officer advised that a report was only required if money were actually about to change hands. He also thought, however, that if the money were not to pass through the solicitors' hands that a report might not be necessary at all. This advice was wrong. Crucially, the NCIS officer also advised that the wife's solicitors were not permitted to tell either the other s de, or their own client, that the disclosure report had been made, as it would contravene the tipping off provisions and/or the prohibition against prejudicing an investigation.

5. Having been instructed not to disclose the fact of their report to either the husband or the wife, nor to the husband's solicitors, the wife's solicitors felt that they were left in an extremely difficult position. Further attempts to seek clarification from the NCIS proved unsuccessful. Letters were sent on 25 June and 9 July, but by 15 July a response had not been received.

6. On 15 July I first heard this application on an urgent *ex parte* basis. Mr Mostyn, on behalf of himself and the wife's solicitors, submitted that they had been placed in an untenable position. It was impossible, he said, to reconcile the NCIS' instructions to them not to disclose the fact of the report, with their professional obligations to the court, his client, and the respondent. He could not see how they could proceed with the Financial Dispute Resolution on 18 July whilst prevented from disclosing the full facts to either of the parties, the opposing solicitors or the court.

7. Given the complexity of the issues and the proximity of the FDR appointment, I saw no alternative but to vacate the listed FDR date. I also adjourned the *ex parte* application until 17 July so as to afford the NCIS, the Inland Revenue, the Law Society and the Bar Council the opportunity to be heard. In light of the extremely unusual nature of the case, I ordered that neither the husband nor his legal representatives were to be given a copy of any order other than my order to vacate the date of the FDR.

8. As it happened, on receipt of the order to vacate the FDR, the husband's representatives obtained from the Mechanical Recording Department, as they were quite entitled to do in the absence of any specific order of the Court, a copy of the transcript of the 15 July hearing and immediately made an urgent application before me on 16 July to attend the 17 July hearing. I gave them permission to do so, on the condition that they were not to tell their client. That order was of a type rarely made in this court, and whilst clearly necessary at the time in the extremely unusual circumstances of this case, I hope that it will seldom be necessary in the future. In the result, the order endured for not more than 24 hours and I am satisfied that the temporary interference with the husband's Article 6 rights of the ECHR was necessary and proportionate in all the circumstances.

9.   The wife's solicitors finally received a letter from NCIS, dated 15 July and received on16 July, clarifying their response to the request for consent to act. In the letter the NCIS advised that:

'On this occasion NCIS consents to you proceeding with the transaction specified in [the] Disclosure Report [of 9 July].

This is an "appropriate consent" within section 335 of the Proceeds of Crime Act 2002, with the result that if you do proceed with that transaction you will not be committing an offence under section 327, 328 or 329 of that Act ...'

10.   On 17 July I heard submissions from the wife, the husband, the NCIS, the Inland Revenue, the Law Society and the Bar Council. I am particularly grateful to Mr Mitchell QC on behalf of NCIS, whose submissions have been most helpful in illuminating the workings of the Act. By agreement, I received further written submissions from all the parties, other than the Inland Revenue who supported the final submissions of NCIS.

The Proceeds of Crime Act 2002

11.   The PoCA came into force on the 24 February 2003. Part 7 is headed 'Money Laundering'; Part 8 is headed 'Investigations', Within Part 7 and 8, there are three key aspects of relevance to the present case: (i) acting in relation to an arrangement; (ii) tipping-off; and (iii) prejudicing an investigation.

(i)   *Section 328 – An Arrangement*

12.   Section 328 makes it an offence to enter into or become concerned in a relevant arrangement. Section 328 reads as follows:

'328 Arrangements

(1)   A person commits an offence if he enters into or becomes concerned in an arrangement which he knows or suspects facilitates (by whatever means) the acquisition, retention, use or control of criminal property by or on behalf of another person.

(2)   But a person does not commit such an offence if—

    (a)   he makes an authorised disclosure under section 338 and (if the disclosure is made before he does the act mentioned in subsection (1)) he has the appropriate consent;

    (b)   he intended to make such a disclosure but had a reasonable excuse for not doing so;

    (c)   the act he does is done in carrying out a function he has relating to the enforcement of any provision of this Act or of any other enactment relating to criminal conduct or benefit from criminal conduct.'

13.　'Criminal property' is defined in section 340(3):

'(3) Property is criminal property if—

(a)　it constitutes a person's benefit from criminal conduct or it represents such a benefit (in whole or part and whether directly or indirectly), and

(b)　the alleged offender knows or suspects that it constitutes or represents such a benefit.'

14.　'Criminal conduct' is defined in section 340(2):

'(2) Criminal conduct is conduct which—

(a)　constitutes an offence in any part of the United Kingdom, or

(b)　would constitute an offence in any part of the United Kingdom if it occurred there.'

15.　Consequently, a person is protected from potential liability under s 328(1) if before acting he makes an 'authorised disclosure' and obtains the 'appropriate consent', as defined in sections 338 and 335 respectively. Section 335 reads, *inter alia,* as follows:

'335 Appropriate consent

(1)　The appropriate consent is—

(a)　the consent of a nominated officer to do a prohibited act if an authorised disclosure is made to the nominated officer;

(b)　the consent of a constable to do a prohibited act if an authorised disclosure is made to a constable;

(c)　the consent of a customs officer to do a prohibited act if an authorised disclosure is made to a customs officer.

(2)　A person must be treated as having the appropriate consent if—

(a)　he makes an authorised disclosure to a constable or a customs officer, and

(b)　the condition in subsection (3) or the condition in subsection (4) is satisfied.

(3)　The condition is that before the end of the notice period he does not receive notice from a constable or customs officer that consent to the doing of the act is refused.

(4)　The condition is that—

(a)　before the end of the notice period he receives notice from a constable or customs officer that consent to the doing of the act is refused, and

(b)　the moratorium period has expired.

    (5)   The notice period is the period of seven working days starting with the first working day after the person makes the disclosure.

    (6)   The moratorium period is the period of 31 days starting with the day on which the person receives notice that consent to the doing of the act is refused.

    ...

    (9)   A nominated officer is a person nominated to receive disclosures under section 338.'

16.   Section 338 provides for 'authorised disclosures' which may be made to a constable, a customs officer or a nominated officer (authorised by the Director General of NCIS) and made in the form and manner prescribed in section 339. The disclosure is authorised only upon the satisfaction of one or other or the two conditions set out in section 338:

'(2) The first condition is that the disclosure is made before the alleged offender does the prohibited act.

    (3)   The second condition is that-

        (a)   the disclosure is made after the alleged offender does the prohibited act,

        (b)   there is good reason for his failure to make the disclosure before he did the act, and

        (c)   the disclosure is made on his own initiative and as soon as it is practicable for him to make it.'

17.   Failure to comply with the requirements of Part 7 is a criminal offence and the penalties are set out in section 334. As I understand, the Secretary of State for the Home Office has not yet provided regulations under the provisions of section 339.

(ii)   *Section 333 Tipping-off*

18.   Under section 333 of the Act,

'(1) A person commits an offence if—

        (a)   he knows or suspects that a disclosure falling within section 337 or 338 has been made, and

        (b)   he makes a disclosure which is likely to prejudice any investigation which might be conducted following the disclosure referred to in paragraph (a).'

19.   An important exception, however, is contained in sub-sections (2) and (3) which state:

'(2) But a person does not commit an offence under subsection (1) if—

    (a)   he did not know or suspect that the disclosure was likely to be prejudicial as mentioned in subsection (1);

    (b)   the disclosure is made in carrying out a function he has relating to the enforcement of any provision of this Act or of any other enactment relating to criminal conduct or benefit from criminal conduct;

    (c)   he is a professional legal adviser and the disclosure falls within subsection (3).

(3)   A disclosure falls within this subsection if it is a disclosure—

    (a)   to (or to a representative of) a client of the professional legal adviser in connection with the giving by the adviser of legal advice to the client, or

    (b)   to any person in connection with legal proceedings or contemplated legal proceedings.

(4)   But a disclosure does not fall within subsection (3) if it is made with the intention of furthering a criminal purpose.'

20.   The act of informing the client or any other person that a disclosure has been made to NCIS would itself appear to be a 'disclosure' within the meaning of section 333(1).

(iii)   *Section 342 – Prejudicing an investigation*

21.   In addition to the 'tipping-off' offences, section 342 of the Act makes it an offence to prejudice an investigation. It states:

'342 Offences of prejudicing investigation

(1)   This section applies if a person knows or suspects that an appropriate officer or (in Scotland) a proper person is acting (or proposing to act) in connection with a confiscation investigation, a civil recovery investigation or a money laundering investigation which is being or is about to be conducted.

(2)   The person commits an offence if—

    (a)   he makes a disclosure which is likely to prejudice the investigation, or

    (b)   he falsifies, conceals, destroys or otherwise disposes of, or causes or permits the falsification, concealment, destruction or disposal of, documents which are relevant to the investigation.'

22.   As in section 333, section 342 contains the legal professional exemption:

'(3)   A person does not commit an offence under subsection (2)(a) if—

(a)   he does not know or suspect that the disclosure is likely to prejudice the investigation,

(b)   the disclosure is made in the exercise of a function under this Act or any other enactment relating to criminal conduct or benefit from criminal conduct or in compliance with a requirement imposed under or by virtue of this Act, or

(c)   he is a professional legal adviser and the disclosure falls within subsection (4).

(4)   A disclosure falls within this subsection if it is a disclosure—

    (a)   to (or to a representative of) a client of the professional legal adviser in connection with the giving by the adviser of legal advice to the client, or

    (b)   to any person in connection with legal proceedings or contemplated legal proceedings.

(5)   But a disclosure does not fall within subsection (4) if it is made with the intention of furthering a criminal purpose.'

23.   The act of informing the client or any other person that a disclosure is about to be made to NCIS would appear to be a 'disclosure' within the meaning of section 342(2).

The Issues

24.   From the above provisions two main issues arise in the context of family proceedings and the application by the wife in the present proceedings:

    (a)   whether and in what circumstances it is permitted to act in relation to an arrangement; and

    (b)   whether and in what circumstances a legal adviser, having made an authorised disclosure, is permitted to tell others of the fact that s/he has done so.

25.   It is not appropriate for this judgment to range more widely since the issues which may arise in the future would be more appropriately considered within the factual matrix giving rise to those problems.

The Submissions

NCIS

26.   Mr Mitchell QC, on behalf of NCIS, recognised that the advice given by the desk officer to the wife's solicitors was wrong and misleading. This arose from a misunderstanding of the questions asked. The solicitors were correct to bring the matter to the attention of the NCIS when they did. At that stage the NCIS should have advised the solicitor whether consent was appropriate and was wrong to have advised the solicitor that it was not an

appropriate case to seek consent. The NCIS did later give advice as to consent by a letter of the I5 July and consent was given so that the legal adviser would be able to conclude a financial settlement with disclosure made. It was not necessary, in order for there to be a disclosure, that funds actually passed through solicitors' client's account. The test for the legal adviser would be whether s/he had become concerned in an arrangement.

27. In a later written submission in response to the submissions of the husband and the wife, Mr Mitchell pointed out that the requirement under section 328 was to disclose 'suspicion' not 'belief. The purpose of the legislation was to stop the movement of criminal property and the obliga-tion on a legal adviser was to make sure that s/he did not become involved at any stage with such an arrangement and to make the appropriate disclosure. There was no legal professional privilege protection in sec-tion 328. In written submissions he said:

'It is and remains the view of the NCIS that: any common law obligation to make full and frank disclosure during the statutory waiting period of 7 days and then the subsequently triggered 31 days is overridden by the statute. There is plainly room for an exception to this where the lawyer seeks the permission of the NCIS or makes application to the Court in the absence of agreement. No obligation to be full and frank about the affairs and circumstances of a person in private law proceedings can override the statutory waiting period which permits for inquiries and then investigation, There can be no matrimonial exception to this position.'

28. He pointed out that when the Money Laundering Regulations came into force, probably in January 2004, then the legal advisers would be regu-lated and obligations under section 330 would arise, albeit with the legal professional privilege exception.

29. In relation to tipping-off, he said that no offence was committed by a legal adviser who informed his client or the other side of a future intention to disclose a suspicion. But he questioned whether there would ever be any legitimate purpose for a solicitor to make such a disclosure. To inform the client or the other side of the actual intention to disclose his suspicions would have the effect of warning the client and would be tantamount to becoming concerned in an arrangement, since if such a suspicion was well founded the client was bound to try and avoid detection. To inform the client before or after making a disclosure might also come within the provisions of section 342 by prejudicing an investigation.

30. Mr Mitchell submitted that the intention of 'furthering a criminal pur-pose' in sections 333(4) and 342(5) need not belong to the discloser. He referred me to the decision of *R v Central Criminal Court, ex parte Francis & Francis 11989] AC 346*, in which the House of Lords was considering section 27 of the Drug Trafficking Offences Act 1986. The police had obtained an *ex parte* order for the production of files from a firm of solicitors relating to financial transactions of one of their clients. The police believed that the client had been provided with money to purchase property by an alleged drug trafficker. The solicitors relied on

the exemption in section 27(4)(ii) that the material to which the order related included 'items subject to legal privilege'. The definition of 'items subject to legal privilege' was to be found in section 10(1) of the Police and Criminal Evidence Act 1984 which states:

'10 Meaning of "items subject to legal privilege" '

(1) Subject to subsection (2) below, in this Act "items subject to legal privilege" means—

(a) communications between a professional legal adviser and his client or any person representing his client made in connection with the giving of legal advice to the client;

(b) communications between a professional legal adviser and his client or any person representing his client or between such an adviser or his client or any such representative and any other person made in connection with or in contemplation of legal proceedings and for the purposes of such proceedings; and

(c) items enclosed with or referred to in such communications and made—

(i) in connection with the giving of legal advice; or

(ii) in connection with or in contemplation of legal proceedings and for the purposes of such proceedings,

when they are in the possession of a person who is entitled to possession of them.

31. It will be seen that this definition was subject to section 10(2) which stated:

'Items held with the intention of furthering a criminal purpose are not items subject to legal privilege.'

32. The House of Lords took the view that on a purposive construction of section 10(2), the relevant 'intention' did not have to belong to the particular person holding the items; rather, if the intention of furthering a criminal purpose were held by anyone, the items would lose their privilege. A drug trafficker with criminal intent could not protect himself by placing his documents in the hands of a solicitor. Privilege belonged to the client, not the solicitor, and a criminal intent disentitled the client to privilege. This was simply the statutory form of the established principle in common law since *R v Cox and Railton 14 QBD 153*, that legal privilege did not attach where the advice sought was being obtained for the purpose of committing a crime. The alternative construction of section 10(2) could only lead to, in the words of Lord Goff of Chieveley (at 391), 'absurd consequences'.

33. Mr Mitchell submitted that, by analogy, *Francis* would apply to the passing of information by a legal adviser, who might therefore not be protected under the legal professional exemption. He submitted that the

statute overrode the private law right of full and frank disclosure. The purpose of the PoCA was to place an obligation on anyone who became suspicious about money laundering, to report their concerns if received in pursuit of a regulated business and or, whoever was concerned, not to enter into an arrangement in relation to criminal property.

The Wife

34. Mr Mostyn believed that it was clearly necessary for the wife's legal advisers to make the disclosure under section 328 since they had a strong suspicion that part of the husband's assets might have been derived from untaxed income. They had been placed in a very difficult position by the advice given by NCIS and the requirements of the NCIS after the disclosure had been made. NCIS had never withdrawn its requirement that they should not tell the other side about the disclosure. They therefore felt it necessary to seek directions from the court.

35. In a later written submission Mr Mostyn expressed his concern about the 'clash' between the requirements under sections 333 and 342 not to 'tip-off' nor to 'prejudice an investigation' and the clear obligation in ancillary relief' applications to make full and frank disclosure. The protection afforded by section 333(2)(c) and (3)(a) or section 342(3)(c) and (4)(a) would be ineffective in the light of Mr Mitchell's submission that to disclose to the client or to the other party would bring counsel and/or solicitors within section 333(4) or section 342(5) that is to say a disclosure made with the intention of furthering a criminal purpose.

The Husband

36. Miss Baron QC, on behalf of the husband, made it clear that the husband's legal team was, of course, equally bound by the provisions of the PoCA. They did not, however, consider that there was anything to report to NCIS. They could well understand why the wife's legal team felt it necessary to make disclosure but had themselves carefully considered the facts available to them and were satisfied that disclosure under the PoCA was not necessary.

37. Miss Baron pointed out that, since the NCIS had not responded to the letter of the 18 June from the wife's solicitors, there was no necessity to write a further letter on the 25 June, the 7 day period having elapsed. The further disclosure of the 9 July was unnecessary since no new issue had arisen and time did not run again. She also submitted that section 333 stood alone and was not tied to or part of the time periods imposed by the PoCA.

38. In a later written submission on behalf of the husband, it was argued that, contrary to the submission of Mr Mitchell, the PoCA made considerable changes to the pre-existing legislation although it borrowed heavily from parts of it. In particular there was now, in general, no distinction between drug trafficking offences and other offences, There were two significant

changes made by the PoCA which affected the role and duties of professionals. Firstly the definition of 'criminal conduct' was far wider than before and secondly there was now a positive duty to report criminal conduct in cases involving no attempt to conceal or launder the proceeds of crime.

The Law Society and the Bar Council

39.   The provisions of Part 7 and section 342 of PoCA have become of increasing concern to the legal profession practising civil litigation and, more particularly, in the field of family law. The Bar and solicitors dealing with financial relief disputes of clients with substantial assets or making ancillary relief claims in such cases have been unsure as to their obligations under the PoCA and the extent to which the provisions of the PoCA might be a barrier to the resolution of financial disputes. When the present application was made, the Law Society and the Bar Council made it clear that each wished to be heard on the wider aspects of the impact of PoCA on the legal profession.

40.   The Law Society and the Bar Council, in written submissions, welcomed the opportunity to intervene and pointed out that the present case was not exceptional. The issues raised by the application reflected wider problems faced by barristers and solicitors, particularly those handling matrimonial matters.

The Law Society

41.   The main concern of the Law Society related to the effect of section 328 which was drafted widely and appeared to cover non-transactional matters. One crucial problem in ancillary relief applications arising from divorce was the requirement of full disclosure of the assets of the spouses under the *Family Proceedings Rules 1991*, as amended. Tax evasion by one of the parties might well be disclosed or revealed in the family proceedings, often in cases in which the assets were not substantial. This information might become available at any stage of the proceedings and would come within section 328. The Law Society was most concerned that there should be no uncertainty as to the exact extent of a solicitor's duties in relation to potential money- laundering offences. It submitted that the ambit of section 328 was potentially wider than the NCIS had suggested and therefore the appropriate consent would be required in a greater number of cases than had been envisaged, The application of section 328 to disclosures made before the 'prohibited act' was causing practical difficulties but section 328 did apply to less specific activity and, in the view of the Law Society, it was necessary to make a request for consent in such cases to 'becoming concerned in an arrangement'.

42.   In a further written submission the Law Society referred to the ethical difficulties experienced by solicitors arising from sections 333, 'tipping-off' and section 342, 'prejudicing investigations', in acting for and communicating openly with clients, The Law Society suggested that it should

be an acceptable form of compliance with section 328 if, in the case of a wife applicant, there was one joint authorised disclosure by the barrister, solicitor and client. The proposals put forward by NCIS in its position statement represented a sensible and practical way forward in cases similar to the present application. In other more complicated cases, particularly those in which the solicitor may have to make an authorised disclosure to NCIS about his own client, the position of the solicitor was more uncertain and placed solicitors in the impossible position of withholding material matters from their clients. There was urgent need for guidance about circumstances where a solicitor could tell a client or third party about an authorised disclosure of which the client's activities were the subject.

43.   Mr Elliott QC, on behalf of the Law Society, stressed the concerns of individual solicitors around the country and the volume of inquiries made to the Law Society by solicitors seeking guidance in quite small cases. It was an every day problem.

The Bar Council

44.   Mr Moor QC on behalf of the Bar Council expressed similar concerns to those of the Law Society. The Bar Council had issued guidance to the barristers in respect of money laundering. In a written submission it pointed out that the inclusion of suspicion in section 342(1) broadened the scope of the offence and might include those representing clients. The suggestion in the NCIS written submission that 'the solicitor should not tell the other side that a report has been made unless not to do so would breach an obligation to make disclosure in the context of the particular financial settlement proceedings' was not realistic in the context of family law. All ancillary relief cases required full and frank disclosure. If there was anything relevant in the report to the NCIS it might well affect the value of the assets. It followed therefore that, when a report was made, the other side and the clients on both sides would have to be informed. One particular problem might arise on disclosures made at the door of the court.

The Inland Revenue

45.   In matrimonial financial proceedings the Inland Revenue is the most likely agency to be involved. In its submissions the Inland Revenue accepted that the wife's solicitors needed to make an authorised disclosure pursuant to section 338 and that the interpretation of the law as expressed by the NCIS to the wife's solicitors was not correct. The statute did not state that it is only when funds pass through the hands of solicitors that consent is required. The wording of sections 327, 328, 329 and 330 was much broader. Repeated consent was not required for the same facts. Where an authorised disclosure has been made and the facts have not

materially changed there is no need for further consent even if a further letter is written and no need for a further time delay for consent or refusal of consent.

46. The Inland Revenue was not however able to give the appropriate consent under section 335 which had to be given by NCIS. Equally the Inland Revenue was not in a position to sanction the disclosure by the wife's solicitors to the husband that an authorised disclosure had been made to NCIS. The Inland Revenue had no objection to consent being given to the wife's solicitors.

Conclusions

47. The Law Society, the Bar Council and family law practitioners in particular are understandably concerned about the implications for the legal profession of Part 7 and section 342 of the PoCA. Although Mr Mitchell pointed out that similar legislation has been in force for over 10 years, without entering into a careful comparison of the earlier legislation and the PoCA, I agree with Miss Baron that the PoCA appears to be broader in its ambit with the result that there is a greater potential effect on members of the legal profession engaged in particular in family financial applications.

(a) Whether and in what circumstances it is permitted to act in relation to an arrangement

48. There is a range of ways in which a legal professional might become 'concerned in' an arrangement. It was not submitted to me, nor do I believe it could be the case, that the offence under section 328 can only be committed at the point of execution of the arrangement. None of the parties before me disagreed with the submission of Mr Mitchell that the act of negotiating an arrangement would equally amount to being 'concerned in' the arrangement.

49. In my view, the duties under section 328 of a barrister or solicitor engaged in family litigation are straight-forward. There is nothing in that section to prevent a solicitor or barrister from taking instructions from a client. However, if having taken instructions the solicitor or barrister knows or suspects s/he or his/her client will become involved in an arrangement that might involve the acquisition, retention, use or control of criminal property, then an authorised disclosure should be made and the appropriate consent sought under section 335. Therefore, if it seems to the solicitor or barrister that there are grounds for suspicion that any arrangement being sought from the court or negotiated between the parties is contrary to the requirements of section 328(1), then authorisation should be sought. Whilst the provisions under sections 327 and 329 were not raised before me in this case, it would seem that the position as set out above would apply equally to both of those sections.

50. Issues of legal professional privilege do not seem to me to arise under sections 327, 328 or 329 and there is no professional privilege exemption in these sections.

51. The effect of section 335 is that a person may make a disclosure, generally but not necessarily, to NCIS seeking consent to continue taking steps in relation to an arrangement. The person must not take any further steps in relation to the arrangement, until the person either:

    (i) receives from NCIS notice of consent within 7 working days from the next working day after the disclosure is made ('the notice period' – section 335(5)), in which case the person may resume acting in relation to the arrangement (by virtue of section 335(3)); or

    (ii) hears nothing from NCIS within the notice period, in which case the person is treated as having deemed consent to resume acting in relation to the arrangement (by virtue of section 335(3)); or

    (iii) receives from NCIS notice of refusal of consent within the notice period, in which case the person must not act in relation to the arrangement for the duration of the moratorium period of 31 days starting with the day on which the person receives the refusal notice (by virtue of section 335(4)). Once the moratorium period has expired the person may resume acting in relation to the arrangement.

52. In practice then, the longest possible time for which a person could be prevented from taking steps in relation to an arrangement, after sending a notice to the NCIS, will be 31 days plus 7 working days.

53. The statutory purpose behind section 335(4) is clearly to allow the relevant investigating authority time to take any action it deems necessary in relation to the disclosure where it has decided that consent should be refused.

54. In most cases in the family courts, the criminal property will have been acquired by some form of tax evasion or possibly social security fraud and I would be surprised if there were to be refusal of consent within the notice period in the majority of cases.

55. The consent procedures in sections 335 and 338 apply to those persons who make the authorised disclosure. So, for example, if a solicitor makes an authorised joint disclosure on behalf of himself, Counsel and his client, then all three will be protected from prosecution. Indeed where the solicitor acts for the innocent party, it would be sensible as a matter of practice for solicitors to do so. If a solicitor is disclosing suspicions about his own client, it may, of course, be a different matter.

56. It is important for the legal profession to take into account, as Mr Mitchell reminded us, that the Act makes no distinction between degrees of criminal property. An illegally obtained sum of £10 is no less susceptible to the definition of 'criminal property' than a sum of £1 million. Parlia-

ment clearly intended this to be the case. Whatever may be the resource implications, the legal profession would appear to be bound by the provisions of the Act in all cases, however big or small. If this approach is scrupulously followed by the legal advisers, the result is likely to have a considerable and potentially adverse impact upon the NCIS and would create serious consequential delays in listing and hearing family cases, including child cases.

(b)   Whether and in what circumstances a legal adviser, having made an authorised disclosure, is permitted to tell others of the fact that s/he has done so.

57.   Of much greater concern to the legal profession are the implications of sections 333 and 342, which prevent a person from 'tipping-off', or prejudicing an investigation. Section 93D of the Criminal Justice Act 1988 (now repealed) contained a prohibition against tipping off in relation to criminal investigations of money laundering. In *Governor and Company of the Bank of Scotland v A Ltd [2001] EWCA Civ 52; 1 WLR 754*, the Court of Appeal considered the meaning of the legal professional exemption contained in section 93D(4) of the Criminal Justice Act 1988, a provision dealing with 'tipping off' in almost identical terms to section 333. In that case the Bank suspected that the moneys held in a client's account had been obtained by fraud. Lord Woolf CJ at paragraph 7 of the judgment of the court said:

'During argument there was discussion as to the extent of the defence provided by section 93D(4). Mr Crow helpfully drew our attention to the similarity between the language of section 93D(4) and the scope of legal professional privilege. Based on this assistance, we conclude that the subsection broadly protects a legal adviser when that adviser is engaged in activities which attract legal professional privilege.'

58.   That passage would appear to support the protection given to members of the legal profession in carrying out their duties to their clients, and that was the joint view of Mr Talbot and Mr Tidbury, for the Inland Revenue, who submitted in their skeleton argument that the natural meaning of section 333 was such as to permit a solicitor or barrister to carry out his duties to the court and to his client without fear of committing the tipping-off offence.

59.   There were no submissions made to me about the nature of the duties of a legal professional, whether solicitor or barrister, to the court, his client and his opponent, but the relevant principles are widely known and accepted. In general terms, of course, all legal professionals are bound by professional ethics which require openness and disclosure of relevant information to both the client and the opponent. (See generally, *Halsbury 's Laws of England,* Volume 44(1), 4th edition, paragraphs 148 – 149).

60.   In addition, there is an enhanced duty of full and frank disclosure upon legal professionals acting in family proceedings, and particularly in ancillary relief proceedings. (See *Jenkins v Livesey (formerly Jenkins) [1985] AC 424; Clibbery v Allen [2002] Fain 261).* In accordance with

this duty of full and frank disclosure in financial disputes between spouses, details of the size and description of family assets and actual or potential debts are crucial to the attempts of the legal advisers to settle these cases and to the FDR process, see *Family Proceedings Rules 1991* (as amended) rule 2.61 A-E. If financial irregularities are discovered and investigated, it may diminish the value of the assets, the subject of the ancillary relief proceedings. The purpose of the FDR would be frustrated if the judge or district judge did not have the true facts and the parties were unable to negotiate a genuine settlement in the absence of the requisite knowledge as to the true value of the assets. In general terms the professional duties in family proceedings do, in my view, appear to attract the protection of section 333(3) and 342(4) in order to permit a legal adviser to inform, for instance, the other side that a disclosure either will be, or has been, made to the NCIS.

61. I see the force of the contrary submission of Mr Mitchell that the full effect of the legislation may be impeded by the passing of information of those who may seek to take advantage of it. I am not however convinced that the words of the statute support the interpretation which Mr Mitchell suggested. In *Francis* the court was concerned with the attachment, and loss, of legal professional privilege to items held on a client's behalf. The decision of the House of Lords in that case reflected the historical position and genesis of section 10(2) by confirming that clients with a criminal purpose cannot hide behind privilege. However, the present case does not appear to me to be analogous. This case raises the issue of the right of a solicitor to make a disclosure to a client, or another, such as an opponent. The question of privilege does not arise.

62. Sections 333 and 342 specifically recognise a legal adviser's duty in ordinary circumstances to make the relevant disclosures, even where the result would be to tip off their client, where to do so would fall within the ambit of being in connection with the giving of legal advice or with legal proceedings actual or contemplated. A central element of advising and representing a client must be, in my view, the duty to keep one's client informed and not to withhold information from him/her. (See *Halsbury 's Law of England*, above). Since the function of the Act is to regulate the proceeds of criminal behaviour, it is clear that in every circumstance where a solicitor believes an authorised disclosure to the NCIS is necessary there will be at least a suspicion of criminal purpose. If, as the NCIS suggests, sections 333(4) and 342(5) bite every time a party who is suspected of holding a criminal purpose is given notice that a disclosure has been or will be made to the NCIS (ie, is 'tipped-off?'), then the legal professional exemptions in sections 333(3) and 342(4) would be rendered meaningless. Sections 333(4) and 342(5) must have some purpose and the interpretation suggested by the NCIS cannot in my view be correct. The exemption is lost if a disclosure to a client is made 'with the intention of furthering a criminal purpose'. The natural meaning of those words would seem to be clear. The approach which the House of Lords took to the construction of the word 'held' in *Francis* should not be transposed into this context in relation to the word 'made', nor would it he necessary

or proper to attempt to do so. Whereas the purpose of holding documents can be tainted by the intention of any number of people (including client and third parties), the intention of a legal adviser in choosing to make a disclosure would seem to belong to the adviser alone. The context and purpose of this particular section of the PoCA is distinguishable from that in *Francis,* not least because the PoCA has specifically underlined the duty of disclosure by legal advisers.

63. The speech of Lord Griffiths in *Francis* indeed recognises the distinction between loss of privilege on the one hand, and the right to discuss matters with a client on the other hand. In dealing with a submission that the solicitors could not consult their client about the appeal for fear of breaching the equivalent tipping off provisions, Lord Griffiths said (at 386):

'I have no doubt that ... if an order to give access to documentation is made under section 27, the solicitor-client relationship provides a reasonable excuse within the meaning of the section for the solicitor to take his client's instructions as to whether the order should be contested.'

64. In other words, even though the client's criminal intent disqualified him from claiming privilege, it did not disqualify' him from his entitlement to be consulted by his lawyer without falling foul of the tipping off rules.

65. Of course there may well be instances where a solicitor' s disclosure to a client is in breach of section 333(4) or section 342(5), because the solicitor makes the disclosure with an improper purpose. In such a case the legal professional exemption would, of course, be lost. I cannot, as I understood Mr Mostyn to suggest, give a blanket guarantee to all family practitioners that they will never lose the protection of the exemption. But unless the requisite improper intention is there, the solicitor should be free to communicate such information to his/her client or opponent as is necessary and appropriate in connection with the giving of legal advice or acting in connection with actual or contemplated legal proceedings.

66. I recognise that the conclusion I have reached may cause some difficulty to the investigating authorities. The time lines set out in sections 328, 335 and 338 are independent from the provisions of sections 333 and 342. Having complied with the obligations under section 328, there is nothing in the statute to require a solicitor to delay in informing his client. Either he is entitled to do so forthwith by virtue of the section 333(3) exemption, or if section 333(4) or 342(5) bites, he is not entitled to do so at all. There is no middle ground.

Good Practice

67. I am however concerned that the purpose of the Act be respected, and that as a matter of good practice (as opposed to statutory obligation) the investigation authorities should be permitted time to do their job without frustration. In most cases I cannot see why a delay of, at most, 7 working days before informing a client would generally cause particular difficulty

to the solicitor's obligations to his client or his opponent. Where appropriate consent is refused and a 31 day moratorium is imposed, best practice would suggest that the legal adviser and the NCIS (or other relevant investigating body) try to agree on the degree of information which can be disclosed during the moratorium period without harming the investigation, In the absence of agreement, or in other urgent circumstances where even a short delay in disclosure would be unacceptable (such as where a hearing or FDR is imminent, or orders for discovery require immediate compliance) the guidance of the court may be sought.

68. The Court of Appeal in *C v S and others [1999] 2 All ER 343* set out a procedure to be followed where compliance with an order for disclosure of information in civil proceedings might reveal money-laundering and cause the financial institution to be in breach of tipping off provisions under section 93D of the Criminal Justice Act 1988 (as amended). In *The Bank of Scotland v A Ltd* the Court of Appeal suggested a similar procedure whereby the bank in that case could have made an application to the court naming the Serious Fraud Office as respondent. The application could be held in private and there would be no question of serving the customer since he would not be a party. The procedures suggested by the Court of Appeal in those two cases might usefully be adapted to the family financial proceedings where a disclosure has been made. Since the purpose of such an application is to protect the legal advisers and, in some cases, the client, I cannot see how one can impose an obligation on the NCIS to be the applicant (although the NCIS would however also be entitled to approach the court if it wished to do so). In my view, it would be appropriate for the legal advisers to make the application without notice to the other side, making the NCIS the respondent to the application. It would be an application however within the ambit of the existing court proceedings and I do not see any difficulty at the moment in the court making any appropriate order, including, if in the High Court, declarations, In the present case I granted declarations since the situation was entirely new and I did so to clarify the situation. It would not seem to me to be necessary for the court generally to grant declarations, but rather to deal with the practical consequences of the authorised disclosure to the NCIS. The application would of course be heard in private and the court should direct that any mechanical recording of the proceedings should not be disclosed or transcribed without the leave of the judge.

69. I should like to remind legal advisers that it would not seem to be necessary to make repeated disclosures on the same facts, unless it is proposed to enter into a new arrangement or a variation of the same arrangement. Each time a further disclosure is made, time will start running again for 7 days or possibly 7 plus 31 days.

NCIS Position Statement

70. Mr Mitchell has provided to the court a position statement setting out the approach of the NCIS to the PoCA, which has now have posted on the NCIS' website (www.ncis.co.uk/legaldisclosures.asp). I have appended a copy of it to this judgment.

71. Subject to my expanded conclusions above, paragraphs 2 to 8 of the Position Statement are not substantially altered by my judgment in this case.

72. Paragraphs 9 and 10 purport to be expressed in different terms from each other, but the only possible reading of them is that the legal professional exemption under sections 333(3) and 342(4) is lost, by virtue of sections 333(4) and 342(5), whenever any person possesses a criminal purpose regardless of whether the disclosure to the client/opponent is made before or after the making of the authorised disclosure. For the reasons set out above, I do not accept the NCIS' interpretation and would recommend that in light of my judgment, paragraphs 9 and 10 of the guidance be amended.

73. Paragraphs 11 and 12 accord entirely with my views set out herein, and do not require amendment. Paragraphs 13 and 14 do not require my comments. I do however note that the view taken by the NCLS in the last sentence of paragraph 14 simply underlines the importance of a legal adviser making use of his professional exemption and disclosing the relevant information to his/her client so that the client is jointly protected from potential liability under the Act.

The Present Case

74. In the circumstances of this case, the wife's legal advisers were clearly right to make an authorised disclosure to NCIS. It was also entirely proper for the wife's legal team to approach the court for guidance. The coming into force of this Act in February has caused immense confusion and disruption in family proceedings, and no criticism should be made of the wife's representatives for seeking clarification of their statutory obligations, particularly in the light of the approach of the NCIS to the disclosure made by them. In fact, since there was no reply by the end of the 7 day period, the wife's legal advisers were free to continue to deal freely with the other side and to inform the other side that a disclosure had been made to NCIS. They would not have been exposed to the risk of prosecution for tipping off or prejudicing an investigation, as I have found, contrary to the submissions on behalf of the NCIS. But they could not have reasonably know this at the time. This position was reinforced by the consent given in the NCIS letter of the 15 July. The wife's solicitors were not however certain from the NCIS letter that they had that right. Mr Mitchell and Mr Tidbury told me that neither the NCIS nor the Inland Revenue had any objection to the husband being informed of the fact that the disclosure report had been made. Accordingly, I ordered that my previous order of 16 July preventing the husband's legal team from making the disclosure to their client should be set aside. I also granted the declarations sought by the wife's representatives, that:

    (1) the wife' s representatives can disclose to the husband and his representatives a copy of their report to the NCIS;

(2)   the wife's representatives can disclose to the wife a copy of their report to the NCIS;

(3)   The consent given by the NCIS to the wife's solicitors extends to Counsel and the wife herself; and

(4)   The consent given by the NCIS extends to implementation of any arrangement agreed.

75.   I indicated that I would hear the parties' submissions on costs after I handed down this judgment, should they wish me to do so.

APPENDIX

Proceeds of Crime Act 2002, Part 7.

Position of the National Criminal Intelligence Service in relation to disclosures by the legal profession

1.   In the view of the NCIS the following constitutes good practice on the part of a legal adviser who is advising a client in relation to a matter that might involve a suspicious financial arrangement.

2.   There is no need to seek the consent of the NCIS to act – that is to take instructions and learn what a case is about. The NCIS will not accept such requests for consent.

3.   Should a concern arise in relation to a prospective financial arrangement then the legal adviser should learn sufficient about the client and the source (or final destination) of any funds involved in the arrangement, including as necessary seeking information from the legal advisers, if any, on the other side.

4.   Should the legal adviser then have a suspicion at the stage that there is a step to be taken in the case that would involve the legal adviser or their client becoming involved in an arrangement which he knows or suspects facilitates by whatever means the acquisition, retention, use or control of criminal property by or on behalf of another person or there is the possibility of offences under s 327 or s 329 of Proceeds of Crime Act 2002, a written report setting out all relevant details including the grounds for any suspicion should be submitted to the NCIS.

5.   Where consent is to be sought to enter into an arrangement this should be explicitly stated and highlighted in the written report faxed to the NCIS Duty Desk.

6.   For there to be a disclosure there is no necessity at all for any funds to be contemplated as having to pass through the legal advisers client account or actually to pass through such an account. The test for the legal adviser would simply be whether he had become concerned in an arrangement.

7.   At that stage the NCIS will follow the procedure in accordance with s 335 either giving or with holding consent as the case may be. That is that they will give or refuse consent within 7 days; if after 7 days there has been no response from the NCIS consent to proceed on the basis of the information disclosed will be deemed to have occurred. If the NCIS refuse to give consent then there would follow a 31-day period from the date of the refusal during which the legal adviser could not proceed with the arrangement, without risking the commission of a money laundering offence.

8.   Once a disclosure has been made to the NCIS then the solicitor is free to continue with the arrangement (as reported to NCIS) if consent is given, or at the end of the moratorium period if consent is withheld.

9.   If a legal adviser takes the view that he should inform his client (or any other person) before making such a disclosure to the NCIS, then he must have regard to s 342. If the legal adviser at least suspects that an investigator, a customs officer, a police officer or in some cases the director of the assets recovery agency is acting or proposing to act in connection with a confiscation, money laundering or civil recovery investigation which is being or is about to be conducted the offence of prejudicing an investigation is made out, whether or not there has been a disclosure to the NCIS. The legal adviser needs to be alert to the defence contained in s 342(3) which permits disclosures to a client or to any person in connection with legal proceedings. This defence is not available where the disclosure is made with the intention of furthering a criminal purpose. The NCIS take the view that the legal adviser does not have to share or be a party to this intention (which may be held solely by the client) for the defence in s 342(3) not to be available (see *Regina v Central Criminal Court Ex Parte Francis & Francis [1989] AC 346*).

10.   The NCIS would wish the legal profession to note that subject to s 333(4), under s 333(3) PoCA there is no restriction on the legal adviser informing any person of the fact that they have made a report to the NCIS if such a disclosure is to a client or his representative in connection with the giving of legal advice to the client or the disclosure is made in connection with legal proceedings or contemplated legal proceedings.

11.   Where the legal adviser has made a disclosure to the NCIS, the NCIS would prefer as a matter of practise the legal adviser not to make any reference to that fact during the seven days following the disclosure or during the period of 31 days following a refusal to consent to an arrangement, unless not to do so would be in breach of a disclosure obligation imposed by the particular proceedings.

12.   In the event that the legal adviser considers that a requirement of the legal proceedings is to require disclosure of the fact of the disclosure to the NCIS, but there has been no consent from NCIS within seven days or the period is still running then the legal adviser should firstly inform the NCIS and try to seek agreement on the way ahead. In the absence of such agreement the legal adviser should consider making a without notice application to the Court for directions giving the NCIS an opportunity to

make representations. (*See C v S and others (Money Laundering: Discovery of Documents) [1999] 1 WLR 1551* and *Bank of Scotland v A Limited [2001] 1 WLR 752*).

13. Legal advisers must not assume that 'the other side' in proceedings has reported a suspicion to the NCIS and such enquiries should not be made of the NCIS.

14. Where the client of the legal adviser has joined in the disclosure that has been made the client would, from the point in time when a disclosure is made to the NCIS, not be regarded as having committed an offence under s 327 – 329. Where a legal adviser makes a disclosure without the knowledge of their client then plainly aid necessarily such protection for the client would not apply.

(NCIS website August 2003)

Appendix 7

Trustees and Money Laundering

Case studies

Appendix 7.1

Case study one

Consider the following facts and identify the criminal offences and by whom committed, if any.

Nice Profit Company Limited ('NPC') is a Hong Kong incorporated company, doing business in import export. It's entire issued share capital, HK$2.- is legally and beneficially owned by its two directors, Mr P and Mr Q, who are HK residents.

It commenced business in June 2003, having been incorporated by the owners' solicitors in April 2003. The service company of these solicitors acts as company secretary to NPC. The registered office is the principal place of business, an office owned by a BVI company ('PropCo') owned as to 50% each by the trustee of the P and Q family trusts; the trustee is the HK service company of the accountants of Mr P and Mr Q who are the auditors of NPC, which also acts as director of PropCo.

The rental paid for the office is at a rate more than three times the market rate, but PropCo has a lot of HK tax losses and the solicitors and accountants, who both advised in respect of the structuring of NPC, thought that this was a good way to minimise the profits of NPC.

The profits of NPC are also minimised by the payment of a 3% commission on all sales introduced to NPC by, ComCo, a sister company of PropCo with the same director. The commission arrangement was recommended by the two advisors and the agreement was drafted by the solicitors. ComCo, also a BVI company, has no staff or activity; the commission payments are paid to the client account of the accountants, as there has been some difficulty in opening a bank account for ComCo.

NPC gets nearly all the products its sells and exports manufactured in China by various third parties; it assists the directors of some of those third parties by paying the invoices less 'agreed charges of 5%' and then paying that amount to the BVI company owned by the directors whom it is assisting, companies set up by the same solicitors, the payment being to the solicitors' client account and against invoicing done by the solicitors' firms staff 'for services rendered'.

NPC sells nearly all of the products it buys from China around the region, mostly to companies in Indonesia, Korea or The Philippines. It generally assists the directors of the buyer companies to minimise their companies' taxes by over-invoicing and then paying out the surplus over the real price to the accounts of banks in Hong Kong or Singapore nominated by the buyers' directors; in the records of NPC these payments appear as 'finance charges on trade facilities arranged for and due by overseas customers'.

NPC elected to have a short first financial period, to 30 November 2003; this was done in the expectation that there would be losses and that NPC would then get the usual four year exemption from filing profits tax returns. The audit of the accounts of NPC has just been signed by the directors and accountants with a clean audit report.

Some of the items which NPC is able to source and sell are subject to quota restrictions in either the US, or the EU; in anticipation of finding buyers for these goods, at meetings in Hong Kong Mr Q made an arrangement with his brother in Dubai, Mr P with his brother in Mauritius, for the issue of Certificates of Origin from those countries whenever needed, 'costing a little more if the goods weren't shipped via there'; both relatives are Government officials in their respective countries of residence.

Case study two

Consider the following facts and identify and comment upon any reporting obligations which you may determine the facts suggest could require, upon whom they fall, and with whom liability for failure to report rests.

All Good Corporate Services Ltd is a Hong Kong company wholly owned by the partners of All, Good, Chan & Associates, a firm of Accountants practicing in Hong Kong. The directors are some of partners of the firm, as well as some of the employees.

The firm is affiliated to PD International and as such has access to the 'world-wide PD partnership'. The firm holds itself out as possessing 'multi-national, multi-disciplinary staff and expertise'. The firm routinely gives tax advice other than in respect of Hong Kong, sometimes having checked the same with overseas affiliated offices – if the client so requested and was paying for the same. One such affiliate is in the PRC.

All Good Corporate Services Ltd often receives referrals of work from the overseas affiliates of the firm, as well as receiving instructions on corporate structures, and the like, from the partners of the firm in Hong Kong. The standing instructions are to accept such referrals and instructions without needing to check further.

For the most part 'Corporate Services' conducts a corporate secretarial practice for clients – that is to say it sets up local and foreign companies, acts as the Company Secretary, either directly or through a wholly-owned 'nominee company', provides a registered office or a correspondence address to foreign companies, and provides administrative support.

The services do not include directors or employees of 'Corporate Services' acting as director of client companies. Where clients require directors of record, this work is given to retired partners of the firm who have no direct dealing with the clients and merely collect a fee and sign whatever is prepared and sent round to them for signature by 'Corporate Services'.

These former partners are all indemnified by the current partners in respect of all liabilities arising from their acting as directors of client companies.

One of the wholly-owned 'nominee companies' is AGC Nominees Ltd, a Hong Kong incorporated company, the directors of which are the same as those of All Good Corporate Services Ltd, plus some extra members of the firm's staff; it acts as nominee shareholder and trustee of trusts declared for the benefit of clients, generally to 'put a bit of distance' between the client and the underlying company managed by All Good Corporate Services Ltd.

Two of the directors of 'Nominees' are HK admitted solicitors who are employed by the 'Corporate Services'.

In June 2001 one of the partners of the firm, who is also a director of both 'Corporate Services' and 'Nominees' was approached by the partner of the affiliated firm in the PRC to set up a structure for the managing director of a formerly state-owned company there, now privatized and listed in Shanghai, which gentleman, Mr X, will be running the soon to be set-up in Hong Kong subsidiary of the listed company.

The partner from the PRC affiliate informed the HK partner that the Hong Kong company will be used to reinvoice goods of the parent to overseas buyers, 'trapping the profits in Hong Kong' and making it easier to 'manage the parent's cash flow and exchange control problems'. Whilst the structure to be set up for Mr X, was to be used to enable him, who will continue to reside in the PRC but just come to HK for board meetings, to benefit from a 'split contract type arrangement'.

Due to the 'market sensitive nature' of the transactions, the Hong Kong partner was asked to keep the identity of Mr X, the client, to himself. He did so, but later advised the firm's management committee of the fact of the structure having been set up.

That structure which was set up upon his instructions, consists of a 'blind trust' owning a BVI company. 'Nominees' is the trustee of said trust and 'Corporate Services' manages the BVI company, with one of the former partners acting as its sole director. Corporate Services also provides secretarial accounting and administration (consisting of the reinvoicing activity) to the subsidiary of the PRC company and the firm audit its accounts.

There is a contract between the said subsidiary and the said BVI company, written by one of the solicitor directors of 'Nominees', under which the services of Mr X are provided to the subsidiary for USD20,000.- per quarter, plus an annual profit share. There is no contract between Mr X and the BVI company.

The activity of the HK subsidiary gradually built up, and all of the profits from the reinvoicing, net of the quarterly fee to the BVI company and various professional charges for the company and the trust/BVI company structure, were retained in the subsidiary.

On 31 December, 2003 Mr X declared that the profit share due to the BVI company for the period from commencement to date would be USD1,500,000 – approximately 80% of the profits from the reinvoicing activity; the director of the BVI company duly signed the invoice for this amount when it was presented to him by 'Corporate Services' on 2 January, 2004 and at the same time he signed documentation for the same amount to be paid by the BVI company, as dividend, in favour of Nominees, its shareholder; against the instructions of the partner in charge Nominees immediately made a 'distribution' to the three adult children of Mr X who are now studying in the US as soon as the money was received by Nominees – having been transferred directly there from the HK company 'to save time and bank charges.

On 10 January, 2004 it was reported that Mr X had sadly died in a car accident.

Case study three

Consider the following facts and identify and comment upon any issues of possible criminal or civil liability, other than in respect of any breach of trust, which you may determine the facts suggest.

ABC Ltd is the sole trustee of a trust subject to BVI Law, T Family Trust. ABC Ltd is incorporated in Hong Kong and is managed and controlled by a board of directors all of whom are HK resident individuals. ABC Ltd carries on its business from offices in HK. The funds of T Family Trust are for the most part held in an account with LM Bank in Hong Kong, an account which is operated by various operated by staff of ABC Ltd; a small sum, being the initial settlement sum of HKD100.- is held in the file of T Family Trust maintained by ABC Ltd at its HK offices.

The settlor of T Family Trust, who provided the HKD100.- out of her own money, was at the time a member of staff of ABC Ltd, who is not a member of the T Family; she was later dismissed for stealing money from various clients' funds, but no report was made to the police and no money was recovered.

The named beneficiaries of T Family Trust are The International Red Cross HK Branch and The Community Chest of HK.

The balance of the trust funds were received by a series of transfers to ABC Ltd from a HK bank account of a BVI IBC of which Mr T is the sole director and bank account signatory; ABC Ltd provide a correspondence address and a corporate 'authorised signatory' to that company; the bearer share certificate was delivered by ABC Ltd to Mr T, a HK resident at the time, but now a resident of Australia, as he has been since November 2002. One of the directors of ABC Ltd knows that the BVI company was funded by transfers from Mr T's personal bank account in Hong Kong and that the bearer share certificate is kept in the safety deposit box which Mr T still has with that bank.

On several occasions since March 2003, at the request of Mr T, various invoices for 'services rendered' have been issued by the BVI IBC, signed by various persons allowed to represent the corporate authorised signatory, and addressed to a company in Australia and to the attention of Mr T. Mr T advised ABC Ltd that the payments were to reduce his tax exposure in Australia, by reducing the amount of his salary from the Australian company.

All of these invoices have been paid and the funds then immediately transferred to ABC Ltd, for the A/c of T Family Trust. Over the same period, again at the request of Mr T, various payments have been made out of the trust funds held at LM Bank to persons in the US, Australia and the UK. All of these payments were recorded in the records of T Family Trust as loans to Mr T and then, one week later, forgiven.

Some of the interest earned on the bank deposits of T Family Trust has been given to The Community Chest.

Case study four

Consider the following facts and identify and comment upon any issues of possible criminal or civil liability, or reporting obligations, which you may determine the facts suggest.

R, S & T, HK Representative Office, is the HK Representative Office of one of Switzerland's oldest private banks, which, in turn, is wholly owned by a large English bank, D Bank.

X, Y & Co are D Bank's Hong Kong solicitors.

The staff of the Rep.Office routinely instruct X, Y & Co to set up structures to hold the money of the banks new clients, whilst the solicitors routinely suggest to their clients that they should consider appointing the Swiss bank to manage their money and arrange appointments at the Rep Office.

Most of the structures advised upon by the solicitors end up being managed by D Bank Trustees Ltd., a BVI licensed trustee company with offices in various parts of the world, including with a Part XI registration in Hong Kong. A partner of X, Y & Co is a director of D Bank Trustees Ltd.

Mr K is a US citizen, resident in both Thailand and Hong Kong; he runs a large and successful company in Hong Kong dealing in Asian antiques and artifacts, LK Ltd. That company is BVI incorporated, but has a Part XI registration in HK. It is owned as to 50% by D Bank Trustees Ltd, operating via their HK branch, as nominee for the wife of Mr K, who is a Philippine citizen resident in Hong Kong – where she works for an airline as a flight attendant; and as to the other 50% by D Bank Trustees Ltd, operating via their Jersey branch, as trustee for Mr. L and his issue, he being a Swiss citizen and resident with a business there, 'Asia-Europe Exchange' importing Asian antiques and artifacts from LK Ltd. Administration to that business is provided by D Bank Trustees Ltd, Zug branch.

Asia-Europe Exchange makes merely nominal profits from its business, enough to cover Mr. L's costs.

Mrs. K approaches one of the staff of the Rep Office, Zinkie, and tells her that she is concerned that Mr. K might be about to leave her and so she wants to get a structure set up that will protect her and the K children if that happens – she wants to take the remainder of the 50% of the profits paid out over the years as dividends from LK Ltd to D Bank Trustees Ltd, HK branch, that were not paid directly to Mr K, which remainders have always been and are presently held on one month call deposits in D Bank's Singapore branch, and place them into a trust and then have the Swiss bank manage the money.

Zinkie sends Mrs. K along to X, Y & Co for confirmation of the 'trust structuring' advice she has given Mrs K, via the brochure of D Bank Trustees Ltd.

Co-incidentally, the HK wife of Mr L has just instructed the same firm to act for her in her intended divorce of Mr L. She has told the solicitor handling the matter that once the divorce is out of the way and she has got her share she intends to report Mr L to the Swiss authorities, because she is sure he has never told them about his 'hidden ownership' of LK Ltd and she thinks that he also imports entertainers and domestic helpers from Thailand into Europe under the Asia-Europe Exchange business, ladies who are officially employed by LK Ltd to do market research amongst customers – contracts of employment actually prepared by the firm upon instructions from Mr K.

Appendix 7.2

Extracts from 'Practical Implications of Money Laundering Regulations – Tax Evasion'

by John Nugent

Director PKF (Isle of Man) Limited

for the STEP Winter Conference 2003

Introduction

This paper deals with the potential implications of advance money laundering legislation for organisations that have, perhaps unconsciously, assisted in the evasion of taxes. Whilst this is only one aspect of money laundering legislation it is by no means a narrow issue and if the following analysis is correct its short and long-term effects could be substantial.

The implications of money laundering legislation for tax evasion are dealt with from the perspective of the offshore financial centres, but this is a reasonable perspective given that they have probably been the natural home for the bulk of pure tax evasion. However, the potential implications do not only attach to those latter day tax havens and their businesses, but may involve onshore clients and professional advisors who have had no involvement in any culpable activity. The problems highlighted therefore need to be taken seriously by a wide range of individuals and organisations in offshore and onshore locations.

Tax evasion

The UK tax authorities may consider tax evasion and tax avoidance to be equally unacceptable activities but the real difference between them can be highlighted by the way in which they are identified, and by the remedies that are then available to attack and counteract them. In the case of tax evasion, the tax authorities have the full force of their investigative armoury, supplemented by flows of information from voluntary tip-offs, exchanges of information with other departments, exchanges of information with other jurisdictions, money laundering disclosures and more recently the extraction of information from organisations which are suspected of harbouring certain species of tax evasion arrangements. The action they can then take to discourage tax evasion includes well publicised criminal prosecutions resulting in jail sentences. On the other hand, tax avoidance is identified by the careful scrutiny of tax returns and other tax records and by the systematic investigation of suspected wide-ranging avoidance techniques. Avoidance arrangements are then dealt with by means of technical challenges which the tax authorities hope will prove that the arrangements do not work and which will then lead to a financial settlement. Future tax avoidance is tackled by means of detailed anti-avoidance legislation.

Although both are economically unacceptable it is therefore clear that tax evasion is considered at some level to be more serious than tax avoidance. It is quite simply a criminal activity.

Tax evasion involves some blameworthy act or omission and is in reality equivalent to fraud. It is typified by a deliberate failure to report something to the tax authorities which the law requires should be reported; or by a distortion or falsification of information or documents knowing that such falsehoods may reduce a liability which would otherwise be due. In essence tax evasion therefore involves the concealment of the true facts of an arrangement.

In contrast tax avoidance can be considered as an attempt to reduce a tax liability in a manner which is contrary to the intentions of the authority who set out the law which enforces the system of taxation. Importantly though, it does not involve any element of concealment or alteration of the true facts of an arrangement. It does not involve fraud. Tax avoidance seeks to reduce a potential tax liability by the exploitation of opportunities which exist because of the structure of the taxing legislation, but to do so in a way that can be fully and properly disclosed to the taxing authorities. Indeed the only safe approach for an organisation which does not want to be involved with tax evasion is to focus on full and proper disclosure.

The Inland Revenue have traditionally only prosecuted in a small number of the investigations they carry out each year, but (during 2003) they have been told that they must boost their rate of prosecutions, at a time when they are increasing their focus on offshore tax evasion. Publicising such prosecutions is obviously part of their strategy and the selection of cases for prosecution will no doubt sometimes be influenced by the impact they will have on the public and professionals. From the Inland Revenue's point of view, a prosecution which results in an accountant in Jersey going to jail is an extremely worthwhile exercise in the fight against offshore tax evasion. Publicity of this nature has two major implications for the Inland Revenue:

— It hopefully leads to improving standards and some reduction in the willingness of professionals and offshore service providers to be involved in tax evasion or shoddy tax avoidance.

— At least up until the abandonment of the Hansard procedure it fed the system by ensuring co-operation during investigations and by driving out new voluntary disclosures.

It can therefore be envisaged that further offshore related prosecutions will follow, and that these may be as a result of one or more of the following key issues:

(a) The Inland Revenue will continue to come across cases which are so unacceptable as to warrant prosecution on their own merits. Unfortunately, the offshore world may have a plentiful supply of such cases.

(b) The *Charlton* and *Dimsey and Allen* cases were largely focused on the Channel Islands, and may well have had a greater impact there than in other offshore locations. It could therefore be that the Inland Revenue will want to specifically identify professionals and offshore service providers who are exposed to possible prosecution in relation to arrangements in other specifically targeted jurisdictions.

(c)   The prosecutions mentioned above were also in connection with relatively small scale offshore operations, and it may be convenient for the Inland Revenue to send a suitable message to larger organisations by a carefully selected prosecution. This would however have to be balanced against the risk of disturbing the growing willingness for these organisations to face up to and sort out any problems they have offshore.

(d)   Mass marketed offshore tax schemes are held in particularly low esteem and it may be that the Inland Revenue seek to undermine this approach to tax planning by finding examples that are so objectionable that they can categorise them as tax evasion and so institute criminal proceedings. There are already hints that a new approach to marketed tax schemes is emerging.

(e)   From a strategic point of view, the SCO may want to quickly demonstrate its new sources of information from NCIS or even the offshore jurisdictions themselves. They may therefore seek to identify potential prosecutions which have come through these new routes to be able to say: *look we have just put an offshore service provider in jail as a result of information we received from a money laundering report.*

(f)   Taking the points made above, they may seek to identify potential prosecution cases relating to offshore service providers involved in regular tax evasion or marketed schemes which they can classify as tax evasion, which have come to their attention through money laundering reports.

Ignoring tax evasion

Cynics have argued the case that tax evasion has not been reported because:

—   certain professionals have not fully appreciated either the scope of the relevant legislation or the extent of their responsibilities under it; or

—   the subjective test imposed by the legislation meant that even those who were fully aware of their obligations could effectively ignore situations where they could claim they did not have a suspicion.

Both of these perceived restrictions on the flow of information may be stripped away by PoCA because the new regime is forcing a new level of awareness on the regulated sector and because it makes it much harder to ignore certain situations.

Money laundering legislation does of course exist in offshore locations, but there is no indication that these regimes have provided much assistance in the identification of any widespread tax evasion. This may be because tax evasion is not covered by the local reporting requirements, it is not thought to be covered, any information regarding possible tax offences is not routinely passed to the UK, or the tests for when tax evasion must be reported are set so high that they can effectively be ignored.

There is no indication that on its own the offshore based 'triumvirate' of Regulation, KYC, and EoI is fundamentally undermining offshore tax evasion. That does however appear to be on the verge of changing, and the UK provides a perfect example of the way in which onshore legislation may work to greater effect than anything that can be imposed on the offshore world. Despite the intense pressure that offshore locations have been under to co-operate with the fight against tax evasion, the most dramatic change is likely to come from the type of legislation found in the PoCA. The reporting requirements introduced in this legislation cut through the apparent loopholes mentioned above by imposing an objective test on the UK 'regulated sector'. Importantly, it raises the stakes from a minimum of suspicion to 'reasonable grounds' for suspicion. This immediately puts those who worry that their poor vision may mean that they are missing something under pressure to get an eye test. It will now be necessary for those caught by PoCA to go beyond the point at which they do not have a suspicion of tax evasion to ensure that there are no circumstances surrounding the matter which are known or should be investigated which would give reasonable grounds for a suspicion.

The business proposition

So does this all mean that the evasion of UK taxes has been dealt a death blow and that such activities will be impossible in the future? It seems unlikely. Any student of human nature will sensibly answer that as long as there are taxes there will be some who will seek to evade those taxes, and onshore and offshore there will be those who are foolish or greedy enough to want to help them.

What does seem to be fatally wounded by objectively biased anti-money laundering legislation is 'institutionalised tax evasion'. This is in effect mass tax evasion facilitated by organisations who honestly do not know [or] turn a blind eye to [or] do not care about [or] actively encourage the fact that their clients and customers are evading taxes These organisations are normally based in offshore centres, although they may be owned by or have related entities in the onshore jurisdictions. Indeed those most immediately affected by the problems explored in this paper will be medium to large size organisations who have wide-ranging business interests beyond the entity containing the tax evasion arrangements.

It is interesting to consider why on earth such an industry could have grown up, especially when some of those involved in it seem otherwise to be reputable financial institutions. Its genesis would seem to rest on a relatively simple business proposition, which may be adopted consciously or unconsciously, but which runs broadly as follows.

—The original business proposition

1.   Large-scale offshore services are profitable;

2.   here are potentially substantial amounts of undeclared funds that can be held in offshore arrangements;

3.   The obtaining and servicing of such business requires a lower level of skill, care and attention (and hence investment) than legitimate tax avoidance;

4.   The customer or client has an interest in being discrete;

5.   Such arrangements do not seem to break local laws and in any case it may be someone else who is breaking a law; and

6.   There is no obligation to report or otherwise be concerned about someone else breaking someone else's law.

This may have allowed that ever useful 'blind eye' to be turned on tax evasion.

However, in some cases the basic business proposition was then subject to the following amendments.

—The first amendments

7.   There may be an obligation to report the breaking of someone else's laws but only if there is knowledge or suspicion; and

8.   Even if a money laundering report has to be made it may not go beyond the local jurisdiction.

The view seems to have been taken that this First Amendment did not necessarily reduce the attractions of the Business Proposition, but it then suffered a further potential set back:

—The second amendment

9.   The local jurisdiction may supply information, but only at some point in the future, and only on request, or in relation to clearly defined situations which can probably be avoided.

This may have made some people stop and think seriously about the type of business in their organisation and perhaps to even consider cleaning up certain aspects of that work, but the indications are that it has not yet led to an unravelling of the offshore tax evasion industry.

There now appear to be two key issues which will or should cause offshore organisations who have followed the business proposition to seriously rethink their positions:

•   Firstly, there is the apparent refocusing of attention by tax investigators on the facilitators of offshore tax evasion; and

•   Secondly, and timed almost perfectly to build on the first point is the potentially substantial amount of new intelligence that will flow to the tax authorities as a result of legislation like PoCA.

Offshore organisations

Organisations which provide offshore arrangements need urgently to review the services they provide, to ensure that they are not running the risk of attracting new tax evasion arrangements and to analyse their existing clients and customers to identify any existing tax evasion arrangements.

Offshore service providers who do not want the nature of their work to be misunderstood need to be careful about the way they present themselves. Their adverts, marketing literature and websites must not give any hint that they are prepared to deal with anything other than legitimate tax avoidance arrangements. Just as importantly, their staff must be properly briefed on the nature of the work that the organisation is prepared to deal with. To protect themselves, their staff, and their customers and clients, they must adopt a culture that is set firmly against any involvement in tax evasion.

A thorough review of existing clients and customers is needed to identify cases which may represent tax evasion so that decisions can be made on the action needed to clean up those cases. It is vital that this review is undertaken by competent and suitably qualified in-house or external tax specialists. The aim here is to identify those situations which do or could involve tax evasion, or which are at risk of being classified as tax evasion by the tax authorities. At this stage the organisations must not rely on vague assurances given to them by their clients or customers, or by their clients' or customers' advisers, unless perhaps those advisers are themselves reputable taxation specialists.

The first difficulty that such organisations face is the identification of cases which involve evasion or which have aspects to them which could be classified as evasion. This involves trying to identify:

(a) Actual evasion where the situation is known or suspected by the offshore organisation.

(b) Hidden evasion where there is no current knowledge or suspicion but where there may be reasonable grounds for suspecting that evasion has taken place.

(c) Default evasion where cases were originally intended as legitimate tax avoidance exercises, but which have, because of subsequent events, turned into evasion.

(d) Assumed evasion involving arrangements which do work to legitimately avoid tax but which have some element to them (such as dummy settlors or bearer shares) which is indicative of tax evasion and which could lead to an attack by the tax authorities.

(e) Deemed evasion in which legitimate avoidance schemes may be found not to work and which because of the way they have been handled may be classed as evasion by the tax authorities.

Having identified the various categories of evasion or potential evasion, the organisation involved then needs to decide what action should be taken. This will again require specialist advice and will vary depending on the nature of the cases involved, but it is likely to have to meet the following key requirements:

(a)   Any approach which needs to be made to the tax authorities and any money laundering reports which are required will have to be dealt with as quickly as possible.

(b)   Any approach to the tax authorities must be handled extremely carefully, to ensure that the organisation itself is protected as far as possible and that any future negotiations with the Inland Revenue by any other party are not prejudiced.

(c)   Similarly any approach that is needed to any other party involved in the arrangements needs to be dealt with as quickly as possible, but again in a way which as far as possible protects the offshore organisation and does not prejudice future negotiations.

Those organisations who do find themselves burdened with some element of tax evasion or potential tax evasion have various options available to them depending on whether:

—   *a large proportion of their business is represented by tax evasion*;

—   *they find a substantial number of cases which could be tax evasion, but they also deal with a wide-range of legitimate commercial or tax avoidance arrangements*; or

—   *they have limited exposure to tax evasion risks.*

Depending on the extent of their infection with tax evasion these organisations could be considered as critically ill, seriously ill or poorly.

Critically Ill: Those organisations that find that a very substantial proportion of their business could be classed as tax evasion face serious and urgent problems. They have to realise that for the reasons outlined above, that business could in future come to the attention of the tax authorities, and unless they face up to that fact and take the appropriate action, they face uncontrolled assaults on their finances, reputation and wider business interests. Perhaps more worrying for individuals involved is the fact that the spectre of prosecution could well become a reality if it is felt that tax evasion monies have been actively sought or that the organisations welcomed such business when it arrived.

Although incomprehensible to most onshore professionals, the fact is that such organisations do exist. What may be even harder to comprehend is the fact that, whilst some of these organisations are well known local and grubby, some are parts of well known reputable international businesses. These offshore anomalies cannot be explained away only by the Business Proposition put forward above. It does not seem feasible that the serious minded onshore owners of such organisations would have allowed such a situation to develop. There must therefore be other factors involved in addition to the basic Business Proposition, and it seems likely that these may have included a lack of control of the offshore entities, a lack of parental understanding of the business, and the need for the offshore management to strive for easy profits. Add to these explanations the fact that certain offshore organisations seem to have bought themselves into trouble by acquiring offshore services providers to access the funds within the client base, and the growth and spread of these organisations starts to make some sense. *The fact is though that some onshore parents may not be fully aware of the deep seated problem that their seemingly successful offshore children have stored up.*

Organisations in this situation clearly need to handle matters extremely carefully, and will no doubt need a range of specialist help to try to protect themselves and their employees from the wrath of the authorities, their customers and clients, and the market place. It may well be that the problems are so extensive that, when faced with the task of trying to remodel and rebuild, the client base has to be pared so much, or that the risk and reward analysis of the owner swings so far in favour of the former, that it is not worth continuing with the business. Unfortunately, a sale of the business is unlikely to be viable. There may not be much worth selling, and in any case some understanding of the problems identified here are already starting to dawn on the consciousness of the offshore world, to the extent that the market for certain sorts of businesses may have already evaporated. There may therefore be no choice but to break up the business, but this itself has to be managed very carefully. It may be necessary to work closely with regulators to ensure that the wider interests of the organisation are not tainted by the infected business unit. Clients and customers will obviously have to be handled with kid gloves to get rid of problem cases and find new homes for good cases, without jeopardising their position further and again to seek to ensure that the process does not damage the reputation of the organisation.

Seriously Ill: For the sake of the offshore centres themselves it must be hoped that there are not too many organisations that are as infected with tax evasion as those described above, but there are likely to be some in most jurisdictions. More common will be organisations who it may be unfair to claim have engaged in institutionalised tax evasion, but who do have a reasonable weight of cases which are at risk of being classed as tax evasion. Once again these organisations need to take urgent and careful action. This is not only to identify and sort out old problems, but also to ensure no new tax evasion business is accepted and to protect the good quality businesses, because unlike the basket cases mentioned above, it *will* be possible to save these businesses. The business unit will to some extent contract, but with care it may be possible for it to be saved and rebuilt. The biggest problem faced by this category of organisation may well be managing the way they are perceived by the regulatory and tax authorities, by their introducers of business and by their good quality clients and customers.

Poorly: The final category of organisation that needs to be taking some action consists of businesses which identify a relatively small proportion of evasion or possible evasion. These will be able to sort themselves out and still have viable ongoing businesses, but it is vital that their lack of exposure does not lead to complacency. They must be vigorous in their determination to create a business which is based solely on good quality, legitimate arrangements which are not tainted by any risk of tax evasion. If they handle matters properly they will, together with those healthy organisations who are free from tax evasion, be thriving offshore service providers in future years.

Appendix 7.3

STEP Commentary on Trusts and AML Regimes

Introduction

The FATF 40 Recommendations are an international set of minimum standards for anti-money laundering measures. These standards are designed to be sufficiently broad to be applicable to all nation states. They are not written for the circumstances and constitutional frameworks of a particular nation state, but rather the recommendations will be interpreted and implemented by national Governments and regulators.

FATF recommendations are not specifically tailored for trust and estate practitioners, but rather all lawyers, bankers, accountants and service providers who are involved in the fight against crime. Nevertheless the special language and structure of trusts – for example the settlor, trustee and beneficiary – needs to be explained so that money laundering regulations are effective when implemented. Misunderstanding the trust instrument will lead to less effective and possibly more onerous regulation.

STEP has looked at the main areas of ambiguity arising out of the FATF's revised 2003 40 Recommendations and particularly recommendations 5 and 34. We have attempted to provide a commentary to the recommendations for trust and estate practice.

The comments below only deal with some narrow issues relating to anti-money laundering measures which are specific to trust situations. They are not meant to represent a review of the due diligence action needed by those involved with or providing advice or services to trusts. Nevertheless, this commentary is written to help those professionals involved in the creation and running of anti-money laundering regimes including:

- Regulators

- Legislators

- Crime prevention specialists

- Professional bodies

- Practitioners, including lawyers and accountants

- Bankers

This paper will only consider express trusts. It will not deal with constructive trusts or nominee arrangements nor with special kinds of commercial trusts such as pension funds. It will concern itself with the creation, administration and management of trusts, but will not consider tax compliance issues.

Key elements of the FATF 40 Recommendations

STEP commentary

FATF recommends

- 'Financial institutions should undertake customer due diligence measures, including identifying and verifying the identity of their customers'...[1]

- The identification and verification of the 'customer' and the 'beneficial
  owner':[2] including 'adequate, accurate and timely information on express
  trusts, including information on the settlor, trustee and beneficiaries'.[3]

- Financial institutions should take 'reasonable measures to understand the
  ownership and control structure of the customer'.[4]

- 'Ongoing due diligence on the business relationship and scrutiny of
  transactions.'[5]

[1]   FATF 40 Recommendations 2003, recommendations 5(a) and (b), p. 3

[2]   Ibid, recommendations 5(a) and (b), p. 3

[3]   Ibid, Recommendation 34, p. 9

[4]   Ibid, Recommendation 5(d), p.3

[5]   Ibid, Recommendation 5 (d), p.3

It is important that in the context of trusts that these phrases are understood so
that due diligence can be carried-out effectively: accordingly we will explore
the following areas:

1.   What is a trust?

2.   Who is the 'customer' in the context of a trust?

3.   Who is the 'beneficial owner' of a trust?

4.   What does 'identification' and 'verification' involve?

5.   What is the 'control structure' of a trust?

6.   What is 'ongoing due diligence'?

1.   What is a trust?

The OECD acknowledges that the trust is an 'important, useful, and legitimate
vehicle for the transfer and management of assets'.[6] Trusts are used to facilitate
control and management of assets held for the benefit of minors and individuals
who are incapacitated, for charitable purposes, for tax and estate planning and
for supporting corporate transactions such as securitisations and escrow fund
arrangements.

It is important to understand what a trust is, and what it is not. In the common law tradition, a trust is not a legal person but a relationship in which one person (the trustee) holds property which is not his own absolute property so that he is not free to deal with it as entirely as he thinks fit.

In some cases, the trustee will hold the trust assets on trust for some other person or persons who will be absolutely entitled to those assets as against the trustee. In other cases, the trustee may hold property for clearly defined interests, so that one person or class may be entitled to the income arising as of right, while another or others will be interested (subject to the prior interest) in the capital remaining. In each such case, it is meaningful to talk of the beneficiaries of the trust (at least collectively) as the beneficial owners of the trust assets.

In other cases, however, the trusts assets will be held by the trustee to apply in a particular way, either for the benefit of persons or to achieve purposes. In such cases, it may not be accurate to talk of a beneficial owner. There may be persons to whom duties are owed, who are objects of a discretion, but in many cases none of them can be described as having ownership of any identifiable part (or even proportion) of the trust assets.

It is also important to understand the relationship which subsists between the settlor and the trustees. (The settlor is the person, usually an individual, on whose instructions a trust is created who provides the assets to the trustees.) Once the settlor has transferred assets to the trustees, he has no further control or rights over the trust assets save to the extent that he has reserved those rights under the terms of the trust or they are conferred on him in accordance with powers contained in it. In particular, and contrary to views sometimes mistakenly expressed in civil law jurisdictions, the trustees should not be seen as the agents of the settlor.

Trusts have been thought to assist money laundering as they are felt to be 'opaque', and the possibility of abuse needs to be borne in mind by those involved. It should however be remembered that the creation of a complex trust generally requires the involvement of professionals. As such the identities of all the main parties – the settlor, the trustees and, where appropriate, the beneficiaries – must be known to a professional who is himself now likely to be subject to money laundering regulations and obliged to undertake identity checks.

[6.]   OECD Report, Behind the Corporate Veil, p. 25

2.   Who is the 'customer' in the context of trusts?

(a)   *The 'customer' at the creation of a trust*

In the context of trusts and estates, the initial 'customer' of the trustee and/or those advising on the establishment of the trust is the 'settlor'.

Occasionally the identity of the settlor may not be readily apparent. The trust may be created under a declaration of trust with funds provided by a corporate entity. In such circumstances, it will be necessary to determine the identity of the ultimate settlor, that is the person who in real or economic terms has provided the assets of the trust, and to verify the identity of that person.

(b) The 'customer' after the creation of the trust

It follows from the analysis given in Section 1, that – on the assumption that one is acting 'for the trust' (rather than for the settlor, the beneficiaries or another party) – once the trust has been established, it is the trustees who are the customer. The lack of separate legal personality for trusts may be a cause of confusion. Good practice suggests that details of the particular trust should be obtained in relevant cases rather than simply relying on the identity of the trustee as such; it is therefore suggested that one should establish not simply who the trustees are, but also as trustees of which particular trust they are acting.

For the reasons given in Section 1, where one is dealing with the trustees, there should be no requirement for a third party to establish the identity either of the beneficiaries (save where the beneficiaries are absolutely entitled to the trust property as against the trustees, so that it can be said to belong to them beneficially) or, strictly, that of the settlor.

However, as is explained below, this does not detract in any way from the trustees' pre-existing obligations in relation to the identity of their beneficiaries.

3. Who is the 'beneficial owner' of a trust?

The FATF refers to identifying and verifying the 'beneficial owner', defining this as:

> '**Beneficial owner**. refers to the natural person(s) who ultimately owns or controls a customer and/or the person on whose behalf a transaction is being conducted. It also incorporates those persons who exercise ultimate effective control over a legal person or arrangement.'

In dealing with trusts, for the reasons given in Section 1, the FATF definition of 'beneficial owner' is not particularly helpful. The extent to which there can be said to be a beneficial owner will depend upon the terms of the trust. However, the need to verify the trustees in their particular capacity in relation to a specific trust overlaps to some extent with the 'beneficial owner' question. For this reason it is useful to have sight of the trust deed at an early stage.

The 'beneficial owner' should be construed as the beneficiaries of the trust in cases where there are identifiable interests in its assets or income. Where there are discretions in the trustees' hands, the position is less straightforward. For practical reasons, not least because it is consistent with a trustee's duties to have as good a knowledge as possible of the identity of the objects of his discretions, it is considered that a trustee should make efforts to identify every potential beneficiary where this is possible. In these circumstances, however, it is suggested that the duty to identify beneficiaries is one best left with the trustees rather than those for whom the trustees are the customer.

Although it is understood that in many cases those dealing with the trustees will wish to understand as much as possible about the extent of the beneficial class, trustees (and their staff) will bear a responsibility for being fully aware of the terms of the trust deed and assessing the implications and weight to be attached to any letter of wishes. Third parties for whom the trustee(s) is or are customers should ensure that they are satisfied as to the probity, professionalism and competence of their clients, so as to be able to rely on them to be aware of the interests referred to. It is considered that only in exceptional circumstances should third parties need to make reference to letters of wishes to identify whose actually intended to benefit.

Often, for proper motives of flexibility and capacity over the life of the trust to provide for changing and unexpected circumstances, a trust deed will include a wide class of beneficiaries, many of whom may not be intended to benefit from the trust fund other than in remote circumstances. Instructions to verify every future contingent beneficiary might be unrealistic, unnecessary and unduly onerous and in some circumstances impossible. Furthermore, it is not uncommon for trusts to contain a power to add beneficiaries – which may be exercisable by the trustees, the settlor or a protector or other person.

Recommendation 5 allows financial institutions to determine the extent of the customer due diligence measures on a risk sensitive basis depending on the type of customer, business relationship or transaction in the following terms:

> 'Countries may permit financial institutions to complete the verification [of beneficial ownership] as soon as reasonably practicable following the establishment of the relationship, where the money laundering risks are effectively managed and where this is essential not to interrupt the normal conduct of business'.[7]

This approach is also consistent with the FATF Note on Recommendation 5[8] which states:

> 'Examples of the types of circumstances where it would be permissible for verification to be completed after the establishment of the business relationship, because it would be essential not to interrupt the normal conduct of business include:...
>
> - Life insurance business. In relation to life insurance business, countries may permit the identification and verification of the beneficiary under the policy to take place after having established the business relationship with the policyholder. However, in all such cases, **identification and verification should occur at or before the time of payout** or the time where the beneficiary intends to exercise vested rights under the policy.'

In this instance trusts it is considered that trust business merits the exercise of a similar discretion to life insurance business where it would not be practicable to verify the identity of future contingent beneficiaries.

It is therefore proposed that a similar approach should be adopted by trustees. In low risk cases and in order not to interrupt the normal conduct of business, those acting as trustees should be permitted to undertake the verification of beneficiaries *after* having established the business relationship. However, in all such cases, verification of beneficiaries should occur prior to a distribution of assets; as a matter of practice, the trustees' duties as trustees will require them to have verified the identity of the beneficiary as a precursor to making the distribution.

For example, in the case of a beneficiary in a discretionary trust who is not entitled to be considered for a distribution until he or she reaches the age of twenty-one and who is presently a minor, there would be no verification process required until a distribution was considered. Similarly, where there is a power to add beneficiaries it is patently absurd to seek to identify those who have not yet been added. Since the aim is to prevent criminals from having access to the trust assets, or to enable criminal property to be traced, the identification of those who are to benefit immediately prior to a distribution will effectively manage the money laundering concerns while avoiding the need to undertake (and keep updated) the identification of those who may never receive anything from the trust.

There may be circumstances in which a greater level of verification is demanded by good professional practice and this may require more extensive due diligence at the outset in particular cases, both on the part of the trustees themselves and of those dealing with them. This may be required, for example, where the money laundering risk is considered high even if a distribution is not in immediate prospect: for example, if the settlor or a beneficiary is from a jurisdiction on the Financial Action Tax Force (FATF) blacklist. In those circumstances, those dealing with the trustees will not need to identify the settlor or the beneficiaries so much as a part of the process of identifying the customer but as a means of understanding the nature of the relationship or transaction with which they are involved and as part of the general risk management process.

7.   FATF 40 Recommendations 2003, recommendation 5, p.5

8.   FATF 40 Recommendations 2003, recommendation 5, p.20

4.   What does 'identification' and 'verification' involve?

It is important to distinguish between identification and verification.

Identification is the process by which identity is established. This might include establishing the full name, date and place of birth, nationality and current permanent address. It is important to stress that not all beneficiaries will necessarily have an identity, since they may not yet be born.

Verification is the process whereby the identity is confirmed. It is essential to verify the identity of a recipient of trust assets in advance of receipt and verification should take place when there is a realistic prospect of a distribution of assets.

5.   What is the 'control structure' of a trust?

It is important to identify the persons who actually exercise the trust powers under the trust instrument. In a simple trust, control will rest with the trustees and therefore no additional checks will be needed beyond, if required, the identification and verification of the trustees.

In more complex trust arrangements, third parties (sometimes known as 'appointors' or 'protectors') may also have joint powers with the trustees or exercise certain powers exclusively.

An appointer is an individual who exercises a power to appoint property to be held on particular trusts or a person to hold a particular office.

A protector is 'a watchdog'. He or she (or sometimes a committee) usually has specific functions or powers under a trust, for example: (i) appointing or removing trustees; (ii) giving or refusing consent to the exercise of trustees' powers (eg, capital distributions, changing governing law or adding/excluding beneficiaries); (iii) deciding whether circumstances (specified in the trust deed) have triggered an automatic change of trustee.

There is a need to identify appointers and protectors and verify their identity at the point that they seek to exercise the powers conferred upon them by the trust instrument or they instruct an adviser to provide advice in their capacity as appointers or protectors.

6.   What is 'ongoing due diligence'?

'Ongoing due diligence' can involve checks on the following circumstances:

1.   Changes of trustees and appointers and protectors

2.   Revision of trusts

3.   Addition of funds

4.   Investing trust funds

5.   Distribution of trust assets and provision of benefits out of trust assets

Examples of ongoing due diligence in these circumstances can include the following:

1. Changes of trustees

It must not be forgotten that a trust does not have separate legal personality. When new trustees are appointed, appropriate identity and verification checks will need to be undertaken in respect of the new appointees. In complex arrangements, it will be necessary to identify and verify new appointers and protectors.

2. Revision of trusts

It is possible that trusts will be subject to ongoing revision if trustees or appointers exercise their powers. In particular, powers may exercised so that the beneficiaries entitled to trust assets are altered, either by new beneficiaries being added or the rights of existing beneficiaries being modified. It is therefore good practice to ask to be kept informed of such revisions.

3. Addition of funds

The simplest situation to deal with, will be when an individual, whose identity can be readily verified, adds funds to a trust. In certain circumstances it may not be readily apparent who has provided the additional funds. Examples may include cases where:

1.   Funds come from another trust; or

2.   Monies come from a corporate vehicle.

— *Funds coming from another trust*

The two most common situations which will arise are:

(a)   The trustees of an existing trust appoint funds to be held under the trusts of a new settlement.

(b)   A remainderman settles his reversionary interest in an existing trust on the trusts of a new settlement. On the termination of a life interest in the older trust the assets of that trust are added to the new trust.

In both instances it will be necessary for the trustees of the new trust to carry out appropriate client identification and verification checks on the source of the additional funds. In most instances it should be acceptable to identify only the trustees of the original trust on the basis that they, in turn, should have carried out appropriate checks as to the source of funds they received. However, it may also be necessary to confirm the identity of the beneficiary whose interest is being resettled and the settlor who initially provided the funds where there is any cause for regarding the transfer as being of high risk, although it must be appreciated that the tracing exercise which could be required to be undertaken in such circumstances could be onerous.

— *Funds provided by corporate structures*

It will be necessary to identify and verify both the company or structure, which is the immediate source of funds and the person with an economic interest in that structure who has given instructions for funds to be added to the trust.

4. Investing Trust Funds

In most instances, trust funds will be invested in conventional investments and property acquired at arms' length. Further investigation is required where assets are acquired at under- or over -value in transactions other than at arms' length. Payments to third parties who are not retained as advisers to the trust will also require further investigation.

ANNEXE 1

FATF 40 Recommendations: Key Sections for reference

FATF Recommendation 5 is outlined in full below.

—Customer due diligence and record-keeping

5.* Financial institutions should not keep anonymous accounts or accounts in obviously fictitious names. Financial institutions should undertake customer due diligence measures, including identifying and verifying the identity of their customers, when:

- establishing business relations;

- carrying out occasional transactions: (i) above the applicable designated threshold; or (ii)

that are wire transfers in the circumstances covered by the Interpretative Note to Special Recommendation VII;

- there is a suspicion of money laundering or terrorist financing; or

- the financial institution has doubts about the veracity or adequacy of previously obtained;

- customer identification data.

The customer due diligence (CDD) measures to be taken are as follows:

a) Identifying the customer and verifying that customer's identity using reliable, independent source documents, data or information.

b) Identifying the beneficial owner, and taking reasonable measures to verify the identity of the beneficial owner such that the financial institution is satisfied that it knows who the beneficial owner is. For legal persons and arrangements this should include financial institutions taking reasonable measures to understand the ownership and control structure of the customer.

c) Obtaining information on the purpose and intended nature of the business relationship.

d) Conducting ongoing due diligence on the business relationship and scrutiny of transactions undertaken throughout the course of that relationship to ensure that the transactions being conducted are consistent with the institution's knowledge of the customer, their business and risk profile, including, where necessary, the source of funds.

Financial institutions should apply each of the CDD measures under (a) to (d) above, but may determine the extent of such measures on a risk sensitive basis depending on the type of customer, business relationship or transaction. The measures that are taken should be consistent with any guidelines issued by competent authorities. For higher risk categories, financial institutions should perform enhanced due diligence. In certain circumstances, where there are low risks, countries may decide that financial institutions can apply reduced or simplified measures.

Financial institutions should verify the identity of the customer and beneficial owner before or during the course of establishing a business relationship or conducting transactions for occasional customers. Countries may permit financial institutions to complete the verification as soon as reasonably practicable following the establishment of the relationship, where the money laundering risks are effectively managed and where this is essential not to interrupt the normal conduct of business.

Where the financial institution is unable to comply with paragraphs (a) to (c) above, it should not open the account, commence business relations or perform the transaction; or should terminate the business relationship; and should consider making a suspicious transactions report in relation to the customer.

These requirements should apply to all new customers, though financial institutions should also apply this Recommendation to existing customers on the basis of materiality and risk, and should conduct due diligence on such existing relationships at appropriate times.

FATF Recommendation 34

Countries should take measures to prevent the unlawful use of legal arrangements by money launderers. In particular, countries should ensure that there is adequate, accurate and timely information on express trusts, including information on the settlor, trustee and beneficiaries, that can be obtained or accessed in a timely fashion by competent authorities. Countries could consider measures to facilitate access to beneficial ownership and control information to financial institutions undertaking the requirements set out in Recommendation 5.

Practitioners' Guide to Money Laundering Compliance Index

U.W.E.L. LEARNING RESOURCES

U.W.E.L. LEARNING RESOURCES